Jennifer's Justice

A Memoir of Murder

by
Dierdre Luchsinger-Golberg

Bloomington, IN   Milton Keynes, UK

AuthorHouse™
1663 Liberty Drive, Suite 200
Bloomington, IN 47403
www.authorhouse.com
Phone: 1-800-839-8640

AuthorHouse™ *UK Ltd.*
500 Avebury Boulevard
Central Milton Keynes, MK9 2BE
www.authorhouse.co.uk
Phone: 08001974150

This book is a work of non-fiction. Unless otherwise noted, the author and the publisher make no explicit guarantees as to the accuracy of the information contained in this book and in some cases, names of people and places have been altered to protect their privacy.

© 2006 Dierdre Luchsinger-Golberg. All rights reserved.

No part of this book may be reproduced, stored in a retrieval system, or transmitted by any means without the written permission of the author.

First published by AuthorHouse 5/2/2006

ISBN: 1-4259-2382-8 (sc)
ISBN: 1-4259-2383-6 (dj)

Library of Congress Control Number: 2006902301

Printed in the United States of America
Bloomington, Indiana

This book is printed on acid-free paper.

Dedications

To Jennifer L. Judge

Jennifer, I hope you think this book adequately tells your story. I miss you. Until we meet again, may God hold you in the hollow of his hand.

A gleeful Jennifer enjoys a pony ride while doting big sister Cathy supervises

To Jennifer's family

Throughout this ordeal you have been referred to time and again as strong. But you are also loving; of Jennifer's memory, and of the other members of your family. I am privileged to be a part of your extended family.

The entire Judge clan at Christmas in happier times.

Appreciation

To Jeff and Josh.
You gave me the everyday support I needed to write this book. I couldn't have done it without your encouragement and physical help around the farm so I had time and energy to write.

To my dad and mom.
Your moral and financial help were invaluable.

To Alison, Carol, Carrie, Cheryl B, Cheryl H., Joan, Greg and Tom
As my friends and co-workers you supported me throughout this ordeal and encouraged me in the writing of this book.

To Norma and Daryl.
You were my muses when I needed them, your home a welcome retreat.

To Bob.
You were a great editor and literary consultant.

To Jeannie, my dear "sister".
For all your support and the many respites at your home while I was writing.

To Anne and Dan.
For welcoming me to your home in Colorado, where I was able to have another focus for the first time after the tragedy.

To the Janesville Police Department including Chief Brunner; officers Hageman, Rau, Neighbor and Larson; detectives Davis, Goth, and Martin.
From relaying the terrible news to my brother, to working the scene, to gathering evidence, to testifying at trial, you made sure it was a nearly spotless investigation and handled attacks on your professionalism with dignity.

<u>To District Attorneys David O'Leary and Perry Folts.</u>
You put together and presented a strong case that nearly assured a conviction. You were also a source of strength for the family. You treated Jennifer and the entire family with great dignity.

<u>To Shelly of the Rock County
Victim Witness Program.</u>
You were supportive, efficient, caring and kind.

<u>To the Appleton Police Department,
especially Captain Helein.</u>
You, too, ran a solid investigation that led to a conviction.

<u>To the Oneida County Sheriff's Department,
especially Detective Schaepe.</u>
You had the initial contact with the perpetrator after the murder. You set the tone for an outstanding investigation.

<u>To the staff at the Clerk of Courts
office, especially Deb and Lynn.</u>
Your help with my research was tremendous. You made my workdays at the courthouse enjoyable.

<u>To the staff at The Janesville Gazette.</u>
You covered the case thoroughly and with professionalism. You also were of great assistance in the completion of this book, your photos tell a good deal of the story.

<u>To the family of Bill Mereness.</u>
You have suffered mightily, but had the strength to do what was right. Without you justice might not have been served. I will always admire your integrity.

Author's Notes

The idea to write this book occurred to me almost immediately after Jennifer Judge was brutally murdered. The reasons I have for writing it are many.

I believe this book will allow the memory of Jennifer Judge to live on. She was a remarkable woman and a wonderful teacher. She deserved to live a long, productive, happy life. Memorializing her story in print is a form of tribute to her life

Many people, like me, would never expect such a horrible event to occur in their family. We are middle class, mainly professional people. We live in a conservative mid-western community of 60,000 souls. We do our jobs, pay our taxes, love and care for our family and friends, and behave like proper citizens. Our close associates are sensible people. All of that gives one a security that certain tragedies will not befall you. Upsetting things might happen, but murder by one of our own was never within the realm of possibility. Telling Jennifer's story may open people's minds to the possibility of such a circumstance. That may change perceptions and actions, and could someday prevent a similar tragedy from occurring.

I believe there is a lesson in Jennifer's story. There were many red flags regarding Jennifer's relationship with Bill Mereness. If one other woman can read this book and take action to end a similar relationship, it will have been a worthwhile endeavor. I know the teacher in Jennifer. She would want to have this tragedy teach a lesson and help women make better choices in their relationships.

I hope to somehow ease the burden of Jennifer's death for the Judge family. They are a true American family; hard working, faithful, close and loving, but not perfect. I have always appreciated how kind and welcoming the Judges have been to me and my immediate family. They have suffered mightily and may find some comfort in knowing Jennifer's story is being told by someone who knew her and cared about her.

I believe telling this story may help other grieving families by reading about the difficulties experienced by Jennifer's loved ones. While I don't believe "misery loves company", there may be comfort in knowing others have been through a similar experience and survived. There are no guidelines for how to behave in these circumstances. People suffer tremendously. I fear some people feel they might not have behaved appropriately. Nothing could be further from the truth. Perhaps others may find comfort in knowing they are not alone in how, or how strongly, they have reacted to their grief.

Finally, and perhaps selfishly, writing Jennifer's story may help me to come to terms with this tragedy. It has been a shock from which we will all never truly recover. The best we can hope for is some acceptance, a sense of closure and the ability to go on with our lives.

Introduction

This is the true story of a brutal murder and its effects upon two families. These are my recollections and my feelings as I remember them, for better or worse.

The Luchsingers
Bobby, Cathy, DeeDee, Eunice, Bob, Sr.

The Judges
Tom, Jr., Tom, Sr., Jennifer,
Mavis, Cathy, Michael, Patti

The Judges of Wisconsin Rapids, Wisconsin, and the Luchsingers of Janesville, Wisconsin, are two families joined by marriage for more than a quarter of a century. The families together now number 28.

My family of origin, the Luchsingers, includes my parents Robert, Sr. and Eunice, my brother, Robert, Jr. (Bobby) and myself. In 1978 I married Jeff Golberg. We have one son, Josh. Bobby married Catherine (Cathy) Judge in 1976. Their children are: Nicole, Erin and Michael.

Tom Sr. and Mavis Judge had five children. The eldest, Michael, is married to Pat. Cathy, my sister-in-law, was next in line. The third child, Patti, is married to Mike Barker. Next came Tom, Jr. who is married to Marsha. Some eight years later, Tom, Sr. and Mavis had a daughter, Jennifer, the woman this story is about.

Mike and Pat Judge have four children: Jonathan, Jeannie, Megan and Molly. Patti and Mike Barker have two children: Brianna and Ryan. Tom and Marsha also have two children: Stephanie and James.

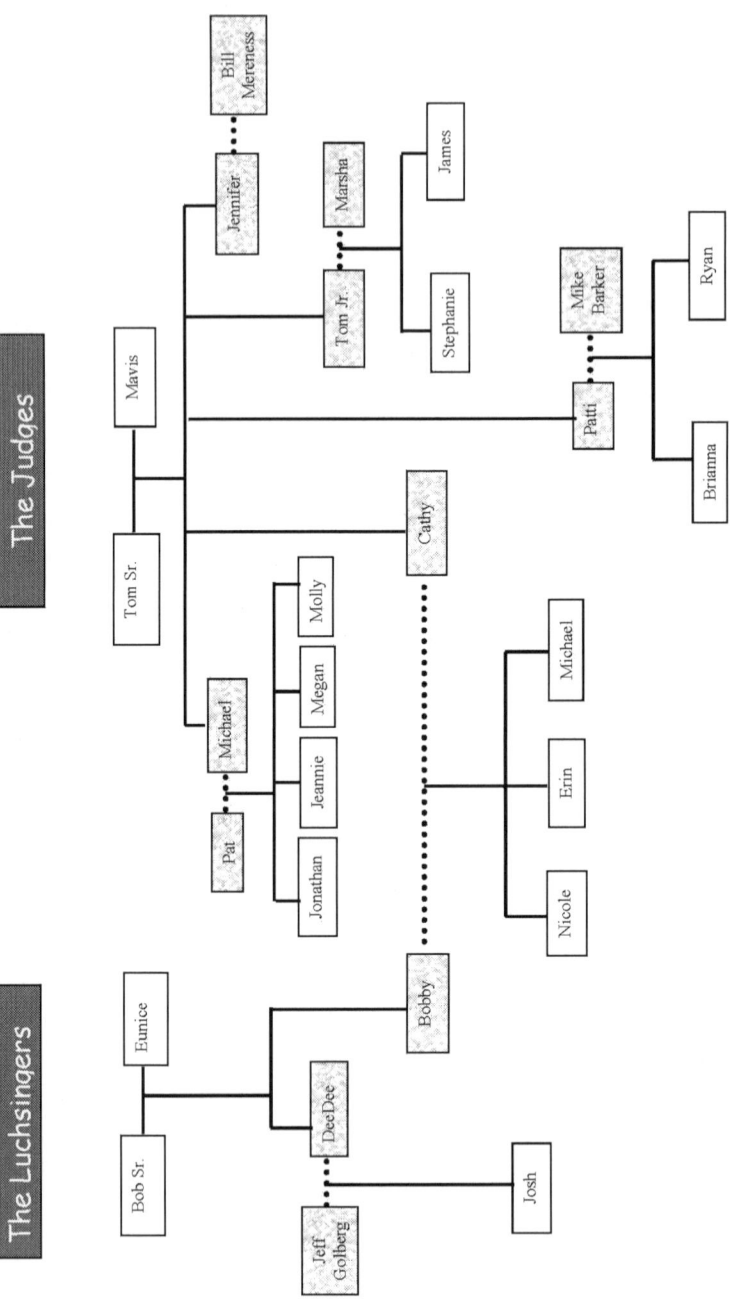

1

My brother's incomprehensible words reverberated in my head; "Cathy's sister Jennifer is dead. She's been murdered."

This cannot be true; I must be having a nightmare. I'm entombed in an airless space, ears buzzing, eyes glazing over. I close my eyes and shake my head to clear it. Lifting my lids, I know it's true; my brother, Bobby, is still standing before me. *He suddenly looks ten years older than he did when I saw him last week. He looks completely weary, as if he could simply crumple to the floor and fall asleep.* His brown eyes are focused on me, softly, as if giving me time to process.

Saturday, November 23, 2002, was to be an ordinary Saturday before Thanksgiving. My husband, Jeff, was planning to get up early to feed the dogs and horses. I hoped to sleep in until 8:00 a.m. then go to the grocery store for the items I'd need to make the pies for Thanksgiving dinner. I was pretty tired out because we'd been having problems with a contract settlement for our teacher's union. As past president, I was at the heart of the controversy. The membership meeting and vote was scheduled for Monday. I was looking forward to having that behind me.

Thanksgiving was to be hosted by my brother Bobby and his wife Cathy at their request. Bobby had called two weeks before and asked if we'd mind coming to his house for the family meal. That had come as a bit of a surprise since it had become more common for us to host Thanksgiving the past few years. While I loved to have people at our home, being able to skip the extra housecleaning required for entertaining sounded pretty appealing. "That'd be fine. Is there some special reason?"

"Well, you know, Cathy's sister Jennifer is going through a divorce, and we thought she might be most comfortable coming here. We know she'd feel welcome at your house, but this might be better for her right now."

"'Course, whatever you think would be best for Jennifer." And it was set. Or so we thought.

I had awakened about 7:45 a.m. and was just resting until my alarm went off when one of our dogs Abby started barking furiously. Since she only barks when "strangers" drive up the driveway, I knew something was going on. The door from the garage opened and then Jeff came into our bedroom. He had a very sober look on his face. "DeeDee, your brother's here, you'd better get up. He's got something to tell you." I was immediately concerned about our 81 year old parents. I jumped up, took note that my flannel pajamas weren't going to embarrass anyone, grabbed my glasses and walked out to the hallway where Bobby was standing. He looked haggard and thin, gaunt really. I could feel the stress and tension. *This was something very big.*

"I don't know any other way to do this, so I'll just tell you. Cathy's sister Jennifer is dead. She's been murdered."

I felt as if I'd been socked in the stomach. My mouth dropped open in a gape. Things went kind of fuzzy, like they show them in the movies when people get bad news. I stammered out all the questions at once. "Wh.. where? H..h..how? Wh, wh why? Who?"

Somehow we were walking slowly down the hall toward the dining area. I pulled out a chair and motioned for Bobby to sit down. He had deep dark circles under his eyes.

"She was found last night about 7:00. It appeared she'd been dead for several hours. She'd been hit in the head with a hatchet."

Nausea swept over me. My head felt as if it might float away. "Oh, my God. Who on earth could do such a thing?"

"The police are looking for Bill."

Bill? Her estranged husband? No one had even hinted that the divorce was acrimonious. I couldn't have felt more shocked and confused.

"Is he capable of that sort of thing?"

"Jennifer believed he tried to kill her two weeks ago."

"What?" My head snapped back in disbelief.

His voice low and tired, Bobby explained, "Someone stuffed the furnace vent at her new house. She noticed the furnace wasn't working and called a repairman. He found putty and stones plugging the outside vent. Luckily, since it was a new model, it automatically shut off when it wasn't able to vent the carbon monoxide. Jennifer had reported the incident to the police and they were investigating."

"Good God, why didn't she have someone stay with her or go somewhere else to stay? She certainly could've come and stayed with us." I was struggling to process this information. It seemed so unbelievable.

Bobby hung his head and shook it very slowly back and forth. "Her mother, brother Michael, Cathy and I tried to convince her of that. With our kids out of the house, we have three empty bedrooms. Jennifer insisted that she didn't feel her safety was threatened. I talked with her several times, but she was adamant about staying put. I wish I would have made her stay with us." He shook his head again, this time more forcefully, as if his regret was even greater than a moment ago.

"Don't. You couldn't possibly have known. Jennifer was very strong-willed; you couldn't have made her. Besides, who knows what could have happened? If Bill was determined to kill her, you and Cathy might have been victims too, and where would that leave *your* kids?"

Please don't let him be overcome with guilt, like I was when Josh was in his car accident. I had played over and over again the multitude of ways I could have prevented that tragedy.

"I hadn't thought of that. I just wish we could have done something."

"Of course, who wouldn't? Please don't blame yourself; people make their own choices. Hey, I wish *I* could have done something. I didn't even know about the furnace event." I paused, again trying to make sense of this. It was very quiet; the three of us lost in our own thoughts.

Finally, I asked, "When did you find out?"

"The police came to our house about 2:30 this morning. George Brunner was with a uniformed officer. I was really worried about it being one of the girls. I knew Michael was safe in bed upstairs. He brought a friend home from UW-Milwaukee for the weekend."

"I can't imagine what that must have been like."

"Unbelievable, really."

"I guess." *How does one accurately share the feelings you have when you receive earth-shattering news? The moment becomes so isolated in time and burns into your brain. Four years after Josh's accident I could still recall the moment as if it had just occurred. The gut-wrenching feelings always returned with the memory of that midnight phone call from the University of Wisconsin Hospital.*

"I thought it was nice of George to come."

"That was considerate."

My mind whirled back to our childhood. George Brunner and his young wife had lived next door to us. We liked them a lot and I even babysat for their first three children. They had eventually moved to a bigger place and George rose through the ranks to become Chief of Police. In our small city our paths had crossed often over the years, always remaining friendly.

I gave out a deep extended sigh. "Life is so strange. Who'd ever imagine that George would come to your house to tell you such a thing?"

My brother closed his eyes, dropped his head down, shrugged and shook his head in disbelief.

He began anew, "They took me down to the morgue to identify the body. But I couldn't."

Both Jeff and I drew in our breath. We looked at each other, waiting to hear why.

Bobby continued, his voice very mechanical, "There was so much blood congealed on her face, I couldn't make a positive I.D."

Jeff and I gasped and reached out to hold each other's hands. I put my other hand on Bobby's upper arm. I didn't know what to say or do.

My brother finished his report, "After being struck in the head, Jennifer had fallen forward and the blood had pooled around her face. In the hours after her death, it had dried and congealed on her."

Sort of like a tomato aspic. God, where did that come from? This is horrible beyond imagination and I'm thinking of cooking. Maybe it's a defense mechanism of some sort.

My brother's voice brought me back to the moment, "I told the police that it looked like Jennifer's figure, hair, and the kind of clothes she would wear; but I could not recognize the face. They can't clean her up at all until she has been examined at the state crime lab in Madison."

Jeff's and my faces must have been mirror images of each other; I felt my expression must have been as shocked as his. It was such an unbelievably disturbing thing to imagine going through. I was trying to visualize the scene at the morgue. I'd seen plenty of them on *CSI* and *Law and Order*. I'd also read a lot about forensics in novels by Patricia Cornwell. *Is it really like that? I will never ask.* It would have been an awful situation if you didn't know the person; but when it was a beloved family member, it became unimaginable.

I went to my brother and rubbed his shoulder and arm. He was bent forward in the dining chair in the corner, his head in his hands. "God, Bobby, I'm sorry."

Just then, our cat Skinny came over and began rubbing furiously against Bobby and, standing on her hind legs, meowing persistently to get his attention. Bobby was surprised since she was generally a shy cat and had resisted his overtures in the past. He smiled a bit at the irony. "Oh, hi Skinny, not now sweetie," he said to her. He stroked her head a few times, then gently pushed her away. It broke the tension a little.

"Be sure not to tell anyone about this," Bobby warned. "Until there is a positive identification, we have to be very quiet. You can imagine what a shock this will be to the community with Jennifer being a teacher."

It was just about a year ago that Jennifer had called me for advice about applying for an opening in the Spanish Department at Janesville Craig High School. She had been teaching in Verona and the drive was long. She loved her job, but it would be much nicer for her to work just minutes from home. Since I had been teaching for 12 years in the district, I was able to give her some insight into the teachers, department, school and district. *I had advised her not to mention being related to Bobby or me, as there were those in the administration who might not be interested in hiring a possible ally of ours. We tended to be completely frank and challenged issues of concern, and there were those who did not appreciate that. I knew Jennifer was a wonderful teacher, and she would probably be hired anyway, but why take a chance? Politics could be a powerful factor.*

I asked, "Do you know who found Jennifer?"

"Uh huh. A man named John who she'd been dating. He found her when he went to her house last night. He'd used the garage code to get in. She'd gone home from school sick at lunch. The police think she was killed shortly after that."

I frowned deeply. "That's odd. I wonder what she got sick from?" *It's so rare for a teacher to go home at midday; it's so much easier to just push through the day than to develop a plan for a substitute, especially for a foreign language. What could have happened? Would we ever know the story?*

Bobby shrugged exhaustedly; he had no idea.

My brother suddenly shifted topics, "I'm hoping you two can help us out today."

"Anything," Jeff and I said nearly simultaneously.

"Cathy and I were going to the Badger game today with Michael and his friend Adam. Then we were going to meet Erin after the game for dinner. Since it's her last Badger game as a student, we wanted to have a small celebration. Then Nicole is going to meet up with Michael, Adam and Erin for the men's basketball game tonight. They play UW-Milwaukee. Michael and Adam were to join up with some other friends there and ride back to Janesville with them tonight."

Where is he going with this? I found myself nodding to indicate I was following him.

"I have to be here this afternoon. The police will call when they bring Jennifer back from the state crime lab. They need me to try to make a positive I.D."

"Oh, yes, of course."

"Could you guys go to the game in our place? We hate to ruin Erin's last game, and it wouldn't be fair to Michael and his friend to miss out."

Oh my God. He's serious. He expects us to just carry on as usual after this has happened. He doesn't want to "ruin" Erin's last game as a student at UW-Madison? Isn't it about as ruined as anyone could possibly imagine? I just want to gather together as a family, support one another and wait for more information. But there is no way we can deny his request.

I tried some subtle reasoning, "Of course we will. But do you think the kids will really want to go ahead with the plans?"

"I'm not sure. Michael isn't awake yet, and we haven't told Erin or Nicole either. We'd like to offer this as an option, if you're willing."

"Absolutely. Just let us know after you talk with them. We'll be ready in any event."

Bobby stood up. He was ready to leave. *One step in this awful process was over. He'll have so many more before it's "over", I hope he can endure.*

Just then our son Josh came out of his room upstairs. He, too, was home for the weekend from college. He called good morning over the loft railing. I looked up at him and said, "Uncle Bob is here".

"Okay?" was his puzzled response. It was an unusual time for my brother to be visiting.

I just blurted it out, "Aunt Jennifer has been found murdered."

"Oh my God!" He pounded downstairs so fast I feared he'd trip and fall. He embraced his uncle in a bear hug. *It's wrong to see the younger comfort the older.* Josh told Bobby how sorry he was.

Jeff and I expressed our sympathy again, and said we'd wait to hear from him. Bobby was going over to our parents' house to tell them the news before going home. He'd call us after he'd talked to Erin and Michael.

After he left Josh stated, "I wish I knew what other fucked-up stuff was going to happen to this family. First my accident, then Grandma's attempted suicides and Grandpa's cancer. Now this."

I could not think of a response.

The shrill ring of the phone cut into the awkward silence. I answered. It was Cathy. S*teel yourself. Be sympathetic, yet strong and supportive. No crying!*

"Hi Cath, I'm so sorry. How are you?"

Her voice was a little weak, but she was not weeping, "I'm doing okay, thanks. Is Bob there?"

"No, he left a couple minutes ago. He was headed to mom and dad's to tell them. I'm sure he'll be there any minute. Is there something you need?"

"No, I just wondered when he'd be home. Michael is up."

She hasn't told him. She's waiting for my brother to handle it. What news to tell your 19 year old son.

"Do you want me to call Bobby at mom and dad's and tell him to hurry home?"

"No thanks, I guess I'll just wait for him." *She's so forlorn! Even her training and experience as a hospital administrator would be of little help in this personal crisis.*

Feelings of helplessness rushed over me again. "If there is anything we can do, please promise me you will call."

"I will."

2

Jeff, Josh and I talked about the incredible circumstances. When Josh heard about Uncle Bob's request of us, he, too, thought it would be quite bizarre to go to the game given the circumstances. I tried to convince myself as I explained, "Well, since people handle grief differently, it's important for us to do what they need us to." He nodded; I wasn't feeling very confident in my ability to do that. Josh had to work at WCLO, our local A.M. radio station, during the Badger game broadcast. We explained the need for secrecy, especially with the media. He completely understood.

The phone rang about 9:45 a.m. Bobby said Michael and Erin did want to go ahead with the plan for the day.

How can they? They must be handling this a whole lot differently than I am. This could be the greatest acting role of my life. Lying in bed in a fetal position would be a better choice for me.

"How did the kids handle the news?" I asked.

"Michael seems okay, but Erin is pretty upset. Nicole has practice this morning, so we won't contact her until after that is over."

With the game starting at 11:15 a.m., I said we'd come right over to pick up Michael and Adam. Because of the 45 minute drive to Madison, we needed to hurry if we wanted to be there for kickoff. Jeff and I quickly donned our "Badger red" sweatshirts and took off.

We arrived at Bobby and Cathy's and went into the kitchen. Cathy was standing by the sink. I hugged her for a long time. She gave into my arms; this was no polite holiday hug. Again I told her how sorry I was. Jeff did too. She looked pale and drawn, like she was in shock. I asked gently, "How are your parents holding up?"

"My brother Michael is trying to get ahold of our aunt who is visiting out in Arizona. He'd like her to go over and tell them in person rather than him telling them on the phone."

"That's a good idea. I can't imagine how awful this will be for them. I'm sure they'll be devastated." *Why does everything I say and do feel so horribly trite? What else can I say and do that could help?*

Michael and Adam came downstairs and Jeff and I quizzed them about their clothing for the game. Did they have hats, gloves, etc? Michael went searching in the coat closet. Adam followed him. We talked quietly with Bobby and Cathy. I wasn't sure how much they wanted Michael and Adam to know.

I inquired, "Have the police found Bill?"

Bobby and Cathy responded together, "No".

"How would he have gotten into Jennifer's house? He never lived in the new place, did he?" I asked.

Bobby responded, "The basement window had been broken. There was a hole in it and glass inside the basement. The police found a large rock that was probably thrown through the window to gain access."

Cathy seemed kind of numb. She said, almost to herself, "Do you know he asked her for a divorce in front of the banker and realtor at the house closing?"

I knew that they had decided to divorce in September, but I did not know any details at all. "God, that was really strange! Almost unbelievably cruel and hurtful," I reacted.

Cathy continued. "Yes, when they were finished closing on the house in Columbus Circle and were going to move on to the closing for the new house, the banker gave them some papers and told them to take them to the other closing. At that point Bill said, 'I don't need them. I'm not going to the new house. I want a divorce.' "

I was astounded, "That seems inconceivable. Did she have any idea he was unhappy with the marriage?"

Cathy lowered her voice even more so Michael and Adam wouldn't overhear. "No, as a matter of fact, they had sex that morning before the closings." I drew my head back in disbelief. I could feel my eyebrows shoot up. She nodded, then we both shook our heads.

What in the hell had happened to Bill? Why would he do such a thing? This is so surreal. I was casting around in my mind for something to say when suddenly I remembered Jennifer's two beloved Bichon Frise dogs. "What has happened to Jennifer's dogs?"

It was Bobby who replied, "The police let John take them to his house when they released him about 1:00 a.m."

"What will happen to them?" Jennifer and I had often talked of our mutual love of animals. I knew she would want them to be well cared for.

"I don't know at this point, I suppose a home will have to be found for them."

Jennifer's Justice

"In the meantime, we'll take care of them if you need us to". I was always taking in homeless animals as well as ones I found that were neglected or abused. My family had always thought I was a little too tenderhearted where animals were concerned. Even I realized it was an expensive and time-consuming endeavor. It was just something I couldn't help. I was very tempted to offer to adopt Jennifer's two, but knew a life on the farm would not be a real good match for two small, white, fluffy dogs. I wasn't ruling it out, but wanted to see if a more suitable home could be found.

"Thanks, we'll find out more about that today," Bobby advised.

Cathy spoke, again as if to herself, "Did you know he had it in the prenuptial agreement that the dog couldn't sleep on the bed?"

This is becoming more incredulous by the minute! Cathy's last comment tugged at my memory. *Jennifer had asked me to take her chocolate lab before she married Bill; he hadn't wanted her. I'd given her a bit of a hard time about that. At the time I'd wondered what kind of guy would make someone give up an animal they loved. I had asked if he was allergic. He wasn't. It surprised me that Jennifer was willing to overlook what appeared to be a real effort at control. I wasn't in a position to take the dog, since we had three of our own, but her parents ended up taking Mozart. They still had her.*

Cathy continued, "Yes, it was in the prenup that she had to get rid of the lab, but could keep the Bichon; but the Bichon was not to sleep on the bed."

I shook my head. "That surprises me. I always thought Jennifer was pretty strong-willed."

"Apparently not where Bill was concerned," Cathy concluded, somewhat bitterly.

Michael and Adam were waiting.

We told Bobby and Cathy we'd have our cell phones on and to call for any reason.

During the drive we talked about the murder. I asked Michael if he thought Bill was capable of such a brutal act. He didn't know. Then I asked about Bill's son, Christopher. He'd come to live with Jennifer and Bill when he was about 13. Jennifer had told me it was because he had been difficult for his mother to handle. Jennifer had worked very hard with Christopher, but they had recently clashed on several occasions. "Do you think Christopher could be responsible?"

Michael replied, "He has had some problems, but I don't think he would do that."

I knew that Christopher was now attending Craig High School. I'd heard a rumor he was in a special at-risk program and that he'd taken up smoking. He must have changed quite a bit from the polite young man I remembered from last Thanksgiving. *Please don't let him have a role in this tragedy.*

We made small talk with Adam and let him know that we felt badly that he was involved in this horrible circumstance. He was pretty mature about it, but didn't try to deny it was awful.

It's unlikely that Adam would stay friends with Michael for very long. An event like this would be enough to ruin just about any relationship, let alone a budding college friendship. The tendrils of tragedy reached out everywhere.

With Bobby and Cathy's parking pass, we found a spot in Lot 19 and walked the five blocks to Camp Randall Stadium. We arrived just in time for the kickoff.

It was a beautiful, sunny day, especially nice for late November. The sky was a lovely azure blue. I marveled at how the world just kept on turning when personal tragedy befell you.

Just like the fall of 1998. While driving home from Madison the night of Friday, October 16, about 10:00 p.m., Josh had been hit head-on by another vehicle. He was trapped in our truck. After he was cut out he was med-flighted to the University of Wisconsin Hospital, complaining of back pain. His back was broken and the doctors were surprised he hadn't been paralyzed. He had required a ten-hour surgery to repair the break with cadaver bone, screws and a plate. He was hospitalized for several weeks. The people who hit Josh were killed at the scene. Josh's two friends received relatively minor physical injuries and were out of the hospital that same night. Meanwhile, Jeff and I lived in Josh's room at the hospital and watched the world go by from his window. It appeared to be a spectacular fall. Visitors often commented on the loveliness of the fall weather and the fabulous colors of the trees. We missed it all.

We were in the sun for most of the game, and we were able to sit comfortably in our sweatshirts without gloves or hats. *All the games we've been to in the past had been so carefree. The outcome of the game had been the only thing that mattered. How trivial that was! It would never be the same. Badger games would be forever linked to this terrible event. God, am I being selfish thinking about how football games would never be the same again? Or is this another defense mechanism to protect me from the horrid reality?*

I tried to join in the moment; I couldn't. It felt dreamlike. *I'm inside a fishbowl and the world is going on around me. Jennifer is gone. Did any*

Jennifer's Justice

of these other seemingly happy 72,000 fans ever have such a thing happen to their family? Hopefully not. If so, how have they restored their lives?

Partway through the game I called Erin on her cell phone. She was over in the student section with her friends, "How are you doing?"

Football Saturday at Camp Randall Stadium on the campus of the University of Wisconsin-Madison

"Better now. It's good to have this distraction."

Hopefully she's a lot more distracted than I am! We made plans; she would come over and join us at her parents' seats after the game. We'd watch the "Fifth Quarter" together from there.

At half time I called Bobby. He was still waiting to hear from the Janesville police that Jennifer's body was back from the state crime lab. *Oh my God, she's here in Madison too! How strange. All the forensic scenes I've experienced through books, TV and movies, how true are they to what is happening to Jennifer? We sit helplessly at this sporting event and my brother waits, equally helpless, at home.*

Bobby also shared that he had reached Nicole, and she was quite devastated. He said, "Those girls loved their Aunt Jenny." We agreed I'd call when we got home, but that he would contact us if there was anything urgent.

The Badgers played well and were beating Minnesota, our rival for "Paul Bunyan's Axe". *How sickeningly ironic. Jennifer had likely been killed with a hatchet and we were at a game where an axe was the trophy.*

It seemed odd to be so disinterested in the outcome. Traditionally, we would have been cheering and yelling instructions to the players. Now we watched as detached bystanders. We've all been pretty enthusiastic Badger fans, with Bobby, Cathy and I being alumni. Bobby, Cathy, Tom, Sr., Mavis, Michael and Pat had all had

My ticket for the Minnesota game

13

season tickets for decades. *All those years tailgating with the Judges near Nielson Tennis Stadium had been such happy family times. With Tom, Sr. and Mavis wintering in Arizona now, would we ever see them in that venue again? Even if we did, it would be bittersweet at best.*

The Badgers won, and everyone was cheering and looked so happy. *Oh, to be so carefree!* A Wisconsin player grabbed "Paul Bunyan's Axe" and ran joyfully around the stadium. He was surrounded and cheered on by his enthusiastic teammates. *How strange life is that what was previously simply a trophy is now a murder weapon.*

Erin didn't appear immediately, but she called Jeff's cell phone. The security people would not let her come to our section. Students had to exit the stadium directly.

The world has changed in so many ways since 9-11, a tragedy for the entire nation that now impacts our personal tragedy. We were going to miss the "Fifth Quarter", a Badger tradition we'd always participated in. Memories flashed through my mind. Erin, Nicole and I hooking elbows and dancing on the stadium seats while the band played "Beer Barrel Polka". We laughed through the "Chicken Dance" and got really silly during the playing of "Tequila". *Will we ever be that joyous again? Does it really matter that we'll miss that tradition today? Maybe it was best this way.*

We decided to meet just outside the stadium on Breese Terrace.

We hugged. No one's eyes were dry. We walked, without talking much, back to Lot 19 and packed into our Avalanche. We decided to eat at Chili's, out near West Town Mall. Bobby had said it was one of Erin's favorite restaurants.

Since it was going to be a twenty minute wait for a table, I went outside and called Nicole. She started crying as soon as she heard my voice. "I'm so sorry, Nicole. Are you going to be okay to drive here for the basketball game?"

"I'm coming with some friends," she managed between sobs, "Someone else is driving."

"That's good. We don't need another accident right now."

We talked a bit about some of the facts we knew about the case. Her dad hadn't told her many details and she had been too stunned to ask. She was shocked as I revealed what I knew. She kept asking, "Why would he do that?" I admitted that I wasn't sure anyone could answer that except Bill. She was able to regain her composure; we exchanged endearments and said goodbye.

When it came time to order, I realized that I hadn't eaten anything but a cookie since my toast at breakfast. I still wasn't hungry. I ordered a side salad.

At dinner we again found ourselves talking about Jennifer. We speculated on the case and shared some stories about our experiences with her. We also talked about the possible funeral arrangements. We assumed the Judge's hometown of Wisconsin Rapids would be the site. With both Michael and Erin living away from home, I offered to pick them up and take them to the funeral or bring them home, whatever was needed. It was a somber evening.

We drove the kids back to Erin's apartment on Dayton Street, told them to have a good time, to be careful and to stay in touch.

As Jeff and I drove home, we talked about how quickly life could change, as we had found out four years before. Somehow it seemed that having an occurrence like that in your family should pretty well insure that nothing else really bad would happen; but, of course, we knew that wasn't so. There seemed to be no limit to the unfortunate incidents that could affect some families.

Shortly after we returned home, I received a call from another member of our union's executive board. Colleen expressed her condolences about Jennifer and went on to say that she was calling on behalf of the union president. The superintendent had informed him of the situation. She quickly added that all involved understood the need for secrecy until a positive identification was made. Meanwhile, an emergency meeting of the board had been called for the next day. Due to the violent death of Jennifer, one of our members, we needed to decid if the meeting and vote scheduled for Monday should be held or postponed. I thanked Colleen for the call, but told her I didn't really know if I'd make it to the meeting or not.

I phoned Bobby after that. He had a lot of news. He had been able to positively identify Jennifer when she'd come back from the state crime lab. Her head had been wrapped in gauze, so he couldn't see any injuries. But there was no doubt it was Jennifer. A rush of emotion cascaded over me. That small part of me that had been holding onto the hope that it would turn out to be someone else was crushed. *Why does it have it be our lives that have been turned upside down, our Jennifer who is gone? Upon whom would I wish it? No one deserved such heartbreak.*

Cathy's parents had been told; and they were devastated, as we certainly expected. They were making plans to fly back to Wisconsin Rapids. The funeral would be held on Monday or Tuesday. They wanted to get it over with as quickly as possible and go back to their home in Arizona.

Jennifer's two dogs did need a place to stay temporarily. So, if we were still willing, Bobby would go to John's house, pick them up and deliver them to us yet tonight.

"Yes, certainly, bring them out. We'll be waiting."

I'd already met Jennifer's dog B.C. several times, but I hadn't met the new pup she'd gotten in the summer. I knew Erin had dog-sat for them, so I called her to find out any tips she could give me on the youngster. She told me that Luna was very shy, and that she'd had a difficult time getting her leash on her so she could take her out for a walk. After Erin had cared for them after a day or so, Luna did warm up to her. I thanked Erin for the information; it would help in how I approached the pair.

About an hour later Bobby arrived with B.C. and Luna in their crate in the back of his Trail Blazer. They peered out at me in the darkness. Their coal-black eyes were soft and questioning. Emotion overwhelmed me again. *These poor little dogs have lost their beloved mistress. Will they ever understand that she didn't abandon them?* I fought the strong urge to insist on adopting them on the spot; we were going to try to find the best home for the dogs.

Luckily, John had had the presence of mind to take their dog food with him from Jennifer's. At least their diet would not be disturbed.

We settled them in their crate in the living room. Bobby reported that John had been held by the police until 1:00 or 2:00 in the morning. He had been, of course, thoroughly questioned. John told Bobby that since he hadn't met Jennifer's parents yet he would not attend the funeral. John thought that might be too hard on them. Bobby had thanked him for his thoughtfulness and for caring for the dogs. My brother had gotten the impression that John was a very decent man. *What would the future have been like if Jennifer had married again? If they'd have adopted children our family would have grown and we'd have had little ones to love and spoil. How wonderful.*

Meanwhile, Jennifer's parents had decided the visitation and funeral would both be Tuesday. The visitation would start at 9:00 a.m. at the funeral home. The funeral mass would be at Saints Peter and Paul Church at noon.

I was transported back a quarter of a century. *Saints Peter and Paul. The lovely church Bobby and Cathy had been married in. Proudly I'd served in their wedding party. Jennifer was a maid of honor too, just thirteen at the time. She'd done her best to keep up with us college kids. She'd tagged along when we partied, but we hadn't paid too much attention to her. We should have been kinder.*

Jennifer's Justice

Young Jennifer with her parents at her first communion

O gosh, it was also the church where Jennifer and Pepe had been married. She'd most likely been baptized and received first communion there as well. Quite possibly all the sacraments of her life will have been celebrated at that church. How sad it was to be holding a funeral mass for one so young. Waves of intense sadness swept over me.

Bobby was speaking; I snapped out of my reverie. "Mavis isn't taking this too well. We're really worried about her. She suggested the two dogs be put to sleep and buried with Jennifer." He was hanging his head and shaking it back and forth.

I tried to be helpful. "She's not thinking straight. She's so overcome with grief."

"I know, but that's pretty scary. I hope she'll be okay."

I shrugged. "What's okay in these circumstances? I don't think there's a guidebook to follow. It will just take time for her to heal. To what degree is hard to say. I can't imagine."

He agreed.

"Besides," I reminded him, "Jennifer wanted to be cremated."

"That doesn't necessarily mean her parents will agree to that. They are somewhat opposed to cremation. We'll just have to see what they decide."

Whew. This is exhausting. There are so many decisions to make. And these decisions are irrevocable. Hopefully, Tom and Mavis will be able to make ones they will be able to live with. It just isn't something parents should have to go through.

We moved on to a discussion of plans. Bobby and Cathy would leave for Wisconsin Rapids around noon on Sunday. The police would not let Cathy into Jennifer's house to get clothing for her to wear in the casket. Something would have to be purchased.

There's that punch in the stomach again! I hadn't anticipated the clothing situation. I had tried hard to stay ahead of everything to avoid being surprised. It provided some measure of control to have an idea of what might come next. I must increase my vigilance!

How would it feel to go shopping for your sister who had been killed due to violence? It's inconceivable. Who would carry out that task? Just one more awful piece of the whole dreadful situation.

I told Bobby I would have to find out what days I could take off for the funeral; but, at the very least, I would drive up Tuesday morning. Jeff would stay here to take care of our animals and Jennifer's dogs. We decided to talk again in the morning about transportation north for Erin, Michael and Nicole.

Then I told my brother of the special union executive board meeting. He felt that the teachers at Craig High School should decide what is best. They were the ones who had worked with Jennifer and would be most affected. I promised I would relay his feelings to the rest of the board.

After Bobby left, I took B.C. and Luna out for a walk. Luna was shy, but I did convince her to let me put on her collar and leash. B.C. "did her duties", but Luna just sniffed around. When we came back in, B.C. ate her food eagerly; but I had to hand feed Luna. She was only willing to eat about a fourth of her food. Fortunately, they both drank plenty of water. I left them out of their crate and soon they were playing with each other. It was good to see, as I'm sure they were aware of their mistresses' death. They had been in their crate in another room, but they would have been able to hear all that transpired. *I wonder what they could tell us?*

Later, B.C. was cuddling with Jeff on the couch. While Luna did let us pet her, she didn't want to snuggle.

I called my friend Cheryl. She would already have known what had happened, since she was also on the union's executive board and would have received a call as I did. Cheryl offered sympathy, of course. She said that if we couldn't find a home for the dogs, her family might be willing to take them. I was touched by her generosity. I thanked her and told her I would tell Bobby and Cathy that their home would be a wonderful placement for the pair. Cheryl's son and daughter were students at Craig High School, and they too had been horrified by the news. Although they hadn't had Jennifer as a teacher, they were well aware of who she was and that she was popular with the students.

After discussion, we decided to go to the executive board meeting on Sunday together. I would be happy to have her company on the way there and back.

Suddenly, I remembered what I had originally planned to do on Sunday. I was going to take a drive to the Elegant Farmer in Mukwonago. It's a very unique bakery and gourmet food store. I'd gotten into the habit of buying their pre-made piecrusts. They were made with lard and were old-fashioned good. It saved me the time and trouble of making my own crusts. With six pies to bake, that dough preparation and rolling could be very tedious. And, truthfully, their crusts were better than my own.

I mentioned my intention to Cheryl and wondered if she'd like to go too. It would be a couple of hours of diversion. Since she'd never been to the store, she agreed it would be a worthwhile outing. We were set.

Then I called our union president. I told him of the discussion I'd had with my brother. Also, unless there was some change, I would be at the meeting Sunday. However, if I didn't make it, I requested he relay my brother's wishes to the rest of the executive board. He willingly agreed and offered condolences.

B.C. jumped up on the couch next to me. My memory was jogged. *Her name stood for Before Children. How wretched. At the time it had been such an optimistic name.*

BC and Luna, Jennifer's beloved dogs

I looked at B.C.'s bone-shaped, somewhat worn, blue identification tag. It had three lines of information: B.C., Jennifer Mereness and a phone number. My eyes filled with tears. I removed B.C.'s collar and took off the tag. I held it tightly in my closed fist and fought back the tears. I returned the collar to B.C.'s little neck. I noted that it was probably a notch too loose, but I didn't tighten it. I stroked her fur, left her on the couch and went into my bedroom to put the tag in my jewelry box. I would keep it until I knew what was going to happen to the dogs. Then I would decide what should happen to that cherished item. Next I checked Luna, but she did not have a tag. *It was something Jennifer was going to take care of.*

Around 11:00 p.m. I settled the dogs into their crate and we went to bed. Sleep was elusive.

3

I lay in bed, thinking back to when I'd first met Jennifer, 11 year old Jenny then. It was back in 1975 when Bobby and Cathy were dating. Bobby, Cathy and I were all students at UW-Madison. Jenny was a bright, somewhat pudgy preteen who struggled to be taken seriously by her significantly older brothers and sisters. The closest sibling, brother Tom, was seven or eight years older.

Young Jennifer Judge, when we first met

Dierdre Luchsinger-Golberg

After Bobby and Cathy were married, we often had joint family gatherings. I always made a point to talk with Jenny, but I could tell being "the kid sister" in her family frustrated her. I felt for her, being a kid sister myself. I wondered how much that influenced her life choices. She had been an excellent student at Wisconsin Rapids Assumption Catholic High School. I admired her independence when she became a foreign exchange student in Bolivia. Having studied and taught Spanish myself, it sounded wonderful. I'd never taken advantage of any of those programs when I was a student.

While in Bolivia, she fell in love with a young man, Pepe. It was very dramatic. The Judge family was concerned that she was acting impulsively. There was some relief when the year was over and Jenny came home.

However, once Jenny got home, she was determined to get back to Bolivia and Pepe. Her family was supportive, but I did get the feeling they assumed that time and distance would bring an end to the relationship. Not so.

Jennifer in Bolivia

During college, Jenny returned to Bolivia. Soon, Jenny and Pepe were to be married. It was a very romantic story and certainly was the center of the family's attention. Jenny was going to have all her preteen nieces in the wedding. Nicole, Erin, Jeannie, Megan, Molly, Stephanie and Brianna were incredibly excited about Aunt Jenny's wedding. Even Josh got caught up in the anticipation, as she was his "Aunt Jenny" too.

It was a beautiful summer event. The weather was sunny and perfect. All the young girls were dressed in rose-colored bridesmaid's dresses; a mature, slimmed-down Jenny looked stunningly beautiful and happy in a gorgeous dress and headpiece with a veil. I couldn't have been happier for her.

Aunt Jenny with her nieces as her young attendants

It would have been idyllic except for one issue. Pepe had left Bolivia without serving his required term in the military. Because of that, should he return to Bolivia, he would be arrested and imprisoned. We all felt bad that it would probably be a long time before he was able to see his family, since they were not wealthy enough to travel here. However, even that added to the overall romance of the story. It was finally Jenny's moment to shine. It was just like a fairy tale!

All seemed to go well for some time. The couple lived near Wisconsin Rapids. Jenny earned her teaching degree and Pepe went to college for a degree in paper science. We saw them occasionally and kept up with their lives through Bobby and Cathy.

We'd heard that Jenny might be pregnant. Everyone was excited, since she had always been eager to have her own children. She was so good to the nieces and nephews. In fact, before her marriage, she always insisted on sitting at the "kid's table" at holidays. She claimed it was "more fun". I didn't disagree, since I enjoyed being with the kids too. *She is going to be a great mom!*

But there was no pregnancy after all. It was a sad time. Eventually, we heard she and Pepe were undergoing expensive and extensive fertility tests. We ultimately learned that Jenny was unable to have children. It seemed an incredibly cruel twist of fate for someone so child-oriented. But Jenny and Pepe seemed to take it in stride.

One year, when Josh was in high school, probably 1993 or 1994, Pepe's parents were scheduled to be here for Thanksgiving. Bobby and Cathy were going to host. Jeff, Josh and I, along with my parents were to celebrate with them. We were informed that Pepe's parents spoke no English, so I would be expected to try and converse with them in Spanish. *Oh boy, having taught nothing more than first year Spanish for ten years, will I be able to fulfill my duty? I hadn't practiced much of the past tense or subjunctive in a long, long time. My vocabulary is pretty limited, too. I don't imagine we'll talk about classroom items or going swimming or getting a tan as we did in class. But I was ready if they needed to know where the bathroom was!*

I needn't have been anxious. It was a holiday experience of a lifetime, welcoming people to our country for the first time and celebrating the many things we had to be thankful for. Pepe's parents were charming. They were very appreciative of my attempts to converse. My conversational skills were somewhat marginal, but at least I was another person to talk to, limited as it was. When I got stuck, Jenny or Pepe would help me out with translation. I said a lot of "Como se dice….", but we muddled through.

I tried to goad Josh, Nicole, Erin and Michael into speaking a bit of Spanish since they'd all studied the language. They acted silly and embarrassed and retreated into the family room to use the computer. Pepe's parents were very understanding of the young peoples' reluctance to venture into a foreign language outside of the classroom. They didn't press at all. We all liked them very much and were sad to see the day end.

Before we left for home, Jenny reminded me of her standing invitation for me to chaperone her summer school trips to Spain. I thanked her for the offer and assured her that once Josh was "grown and gone" I would definitely join her.

Shockingly, about a year later Cathy told us Pepe and Jenny were getting a divorce! She said Jenny was really upset about it and would only tell her parents and her brother Michael the reason. After a phone call from Jenny, Michael had gone to pick Jenny up at her home and that was the end of the marriage. The only comment Jenny would make was that she wanted us to remember Pepe as we had known him. Of course that just made everyone wonder all the more, but we never did hear anything further. Speculation was that it might have had something to do with her inability to have children clashing with his traditional Hispanic values. But we never really knew.

We did know that Grandpa Judge was not happy about the divorce. Being a staunch Catholic, it was not acceptable. There was considerable tension in the family at that time. Eventually, though, things smoothed out.

Time passed. We then heard that Jenny had met someone new. I was happy that she had been able to move on with her life. Bill Mereness was older by nine years and was divorced with three children. His job status with Wal-Mart was very secure. It was just the stability Jenny seemed to need at that time.

When we saw Jenny at Nicole's high school graduation party; Bill was unable to attend. I talked with Jenny, and it was apparent that she was serious about Bill. Bill was financially secure; he loved the property she had purchased near Minocqua and she found his maturity comforting. Jenny said she had a good relationship with Bill's children, which wasn't hard for me to imagine. She reported that Bill's first wife had practically driven him away with her erratic behavior. She'd even accused him of trying to kill her.

That had touched a nerve. I'd heard lots of stories of bitter divorce behavior, but never anything remotely concerning murder. I'd also lived long enough to learn that these situations were rarely totally one-sided. Red flags had popped up in my mind.

I remember hoping Jenny was not "on the rebound". She had always been such a free spirit and independent woman; this relationship seemed rather out of character.

I was also wary about the story concerning the ex-wife. I wanted to warn Jenny about keeping an open mind, but I knew it wasn't my place. Nor would my unsolicited advice have been likely appreciated or heeded. So, it seemed, all I could do was hope for the best for this enjoyable relative and friend.

Bill and Jenny's wedding ceremony in 1999 was for "immediate family only", so Jeff, Josh and I were not invited. That was completely understandable, it being a second wedding for both of them. Bobby and Cathy reported it was very "low-key". Nicole hadn't even attended.

Not too long after the wedding, Bill and Jenny were going to relocate to southern Wisconsin. Jenny had gotten a teaching job in Verona, about an hour's drive northwest of Janesville. Since Bill's territory covered the southeastern part of the state, they decided to buy a home in Janesville and split the traveling difference.

I was excited that Jenny, now going by Jennifer, was going to be close. I hoped we'd see more of her; but the opposite occurred. I knew she was very busy with her two-hour daily drive and the place up north, but I felt that perhaps Bill was discouraging her from spending time with us. Maybe it was being newlyweds, but I was suspicious it was controlling behavior, especially considering the incident with the Labrador.

Before too long, Bill's son came to live with Jennifer and Bill. Christopher was early in his high school career and was having some problems living with his mom. Having seen similar situations many times with students I'd taught, it was not surprising. The young man was growing up and "needed a father's influence". I had no doubt that *Jennifer* would be just what Christopher needed, whether he knew it or not.

I was surprised, though, when Christopher was enrolled in school at Verona, rather than here in Janesville. He was going to drive back and forth with Jennifer. When basketball season started, Jennifer waited after school until practice was over, then drove home with him. I thought that was really above and beyond the duty of a stepmother, but that was Jennifer. She would do whatever it took to do a great job with kids. I admired her effort and hoped Bill and Christopher appreciated it as much as they should.

That November, Bobby and Cathy invited us to spend Thanksgiving with them. My mom and dad were also invited, as were Bill, Jennifer and Christopher. I was eager to get to know Bill better and hoped Christopher would fit in well with our kids. My contribution to the dinner was to be pumpkin and apple pies, three of each.

When we were introduced to Bill, he was aloof. I thought he might be a little overwhelmed being with so many new people. Not everyone appreciates an outgoing, rather boisterous family like ours. It had taken Jeff a while to understand our occasional silliness. He'd never really embraced it, but he tolerated it well.

Throughout the meal, it became apparent that Bill did not want to become a part of us. He wasn't shy, or rude, but he held himself apart. Despite many attempts to draw him into conversation, it appeared he wanted to keep to himself. His answers were brief and often monosyllabic. He never initiated a topic of conversation. Bill smiled when it was appropriate, but the smile never quite reached his eyes.

I'd always been a quick judge of character and thought Bill's behavior was not so much anti-social as asocial. It was clear that he did not wish to enjoy our company. It puzzled me as to what in the world Jennifer saw in him. He had to be totally different when they were alone. Amid our company he didn't seem appealing in the least. I didn't like him, and it sure didn't seem as if he was remotely interested in any of us.

Christopher, on the other hand, answered pleasantly when questioned and seemed shy, but at ease. He seemed a likable young man and appeared to want to fit in with the family.

After the dishes were cleared we announced our intention, as was custom, to play a game. On Thanksgiving, Christmas Eve and Christmas Day our family always played "Scattergories", "Pictionary", "Taboo", or "Outburst". The teams are generally guys vs. girls. However, with two additional guys, and my mom opting not to play, we were debating if we should choose teams in another way. Bill announced that he was not going to play. Jennifer turned to him in surprise. She seemed a little piqued. "Why not?" She inquired.

"I don't want to," was the bland reply.

Jennifer was mildly insistent, "Well I do".

The rest of the family tried to busy themselves organizing chairs, pencils, paper, etc. so Bill and Jennifer could debate without an obvious audience. It was an awkward moment. They walked into the dining room. After a few minutes, they came back into the kitchen. Jennifer's body language indicated defeat. She was round-shouldered, her eyes downcast and devoid of their usual sparkle. "I guess we're going home after all," Jennifer announced.

We all groaned and begged them to stay, but there was no changing their minds. They thanked Bobby and Cathy for hosting dinner, said goodbye to all and left.

Nothing was said of the matter; we played our game and had fun, as always. After a couple of hours of laughing, teasing and real competitiveness we were all exhausted. The holiday had reached its end.

On the ride home Jeff, Josh and I couldn't help comparing this Thanksgiving to the one we had spent with Jennifer, Pepe and his parents. What a contrast. Jeff and Josh felt pretty much the same way I did about Bill. In Bill's defense, Jeff did point out that he had opted out of games in the past. "Your family does get really goofy sometimes, you know."

I agreed. "But he wouldn't have known that yet. Besides, you would never expect that we would all go home so Josh and I couldn't play."

Jeff acknowledged that was absolutely so, "I would never do that, I'd just watch TV or take a snooze in the recliner."

None of us could understand what had attracted Jennifer to Bill. It seemed a classic mismatch. To be fair, we did conclude that it wasn't our place to determine what made people happy in a relationship. As long as it worked for them, that was what mattered. We did predict that we would not be spending many more holidays with Bill and Jennifer, though. The future would prove that correct.

We only saw them together again one more time. That same year Jennifer, Bill and Christopher came over for our Christmas Eve celebration. It, too, was being held at Bobby and Cathy's, as we were hosting Christmas Day. We'd again played one of our silly games. Surprisingly, Bill did agree to join in. I wondered if there had been some serious discussion of his unwillingness to participate at Thanksgiving. While Christopher was really enthusiastic and appeared to be having fun, Bill remained quiet and detached. As the evening progressed, he made it clear that he was not enjoying himself. Jennifer laughed a lot and seemed to have fun. I couldn't help but think she must have been a bit disappointed in Bill's lack of enthusiasm. He did his best to be unlikable. It was another uncomfortable situation.

Since we never saw them together again, I often wondered if there had been an additional debate after Christmas Eve, with Bill prevailing in his desire to avoid us.

Since Jennifer was teaching in Janesville, we did see each other at some district and union functions. We always had a pleasant conversation. In January, I got a big kick out of seeing her in her classroom when we took our eighth graders on a tour of the high school. I popped my head into her classroom and we exchanged a few words in Spanish, amazing all of my students who thought of me as "just a science teacher". It was a pleasant encounter, leaving her to happily explain to her students what had just transpired.

Jennifer had kept in touch by phone. Shortly after the 2002 – 03 school year had started; she'd called to find out if there was anything in our teachers' contract regarding leave of absence for adoption. She told me that she and Bill were planning to adopt a child from Guatemala. After I expressed my delight, we got down to business. I didn't have my contract at home, but I was concerned that since she'd only just started in the district there might not be much to offer her. I thought the only option might be an unpaid leave. She explained that she'd been working another job at Kohl's Department Store to help finance the adoption. She did have money put aside. I encouraged her to contact our teacher rights' chairperson to see what might be done. I wished her luck and much happiness in adding to her family.

More recently, in mid-September Jennifer had called me at school to offer Jeff and I some Badger Football tickets for the West Virginia game. They were her parents' season tickets which she had taken and planned to use, but something had come up. I immediately said yes and thanked her. We worked out the details of how we'd get the tickets and said goodbye.

That evening, I found out that the ticket situation had caused some friction in the family with Bobby and Cathy. I apologized for my role in the mess; but Bobby assured me it would all work out, that we were to go ahead and use the tickets. I never found out the details, but did drop Jennifer a note in inner-school mail thanking her and apologizing for any problem we'd been a part of.

That was our last communication. Suddenly the heavy weight of guilt was crushing my chest. *Why can't I just sob like a baby and get it all out? Because I can't allow that self- indulgence; I have to be strong for Bobby and his family. Why hadn't I called her when I'd heard about the pending divorce? Being busy with school and my horses seemed such shallow excuses. I also hadn't wanted to be intrusive, so I'd been looking forward to catching up with her at Thanksgiving. Oh dear God!*

4

I must have dozed off at some time in the wee hours. I remember last looking at the clock around 2:30 a.m. At a few minutes after 5:00, I was awakened by the whine of one of Jennifer's Bichons. I took them outside and B.C. made it obvious why she'd been whining. Luna still wouldn't go. I was getting a little nervous about her. I crated them and went outside to do the chores.

After I finished feeding the horses and ponies I fed our three dogs. Then I took them on our usual walk down the long driveway to pick up the morning paper. The bold, inch-tall headline of *The Janesville Gazette* screamed at me: "Teacher is Slaying Victim". A photo accompanied the story. I felt nauseous and weak at the knees. I folded the paper in half and tucked it under my arm for the walk back to the house. My vision was a bit blurry, as if I'd forgotten to put my glasses on. *How in the world does something like this happen? How will we get through it? How will Cathy accept losing her sister like this? How will Bobby ever get over having to identify Jennifer's body? How will Tom and Mavis survive the violent death of their youngest daughter? What would I do if it were my child? Who could provide the answers to these questions?*

Once inside I made some toast and tea. I glanced at the article. It was quite long. There was a photo of Jennifer; it was obvious it was the one from her school I.D. I had always referred to those as our "mug shots", since the photographic process for getting one was a bit like being processed for a crime. With the low-quality photographs taken in a back room at school, teachers always ended up looking like suspects or actual criminals. Having the badges was somehow supposed to make our schools safer. Since Columbine, we needed to be aware of who belonged in school and who didn't. Oddly, the students were not required to wear I.D. badges, only staff. It was another conundrum in our modern world.

There was also a photo of Jennifer's home on Sandstone Drive. Sitting there at my dining room table, it was surreal. It seemed like some sort of a sick dream from which I would, hopefully, soon awaken.

The article said the police were investigating "What they're calling a homicide". It told how much admired Jennifer was by Craig teachers, students and administrators.

Preliminary autopsy results had indicated the cause of death was blunt trauma to the head. *How many times had I seen the same sort of thing on the television crime shows? This was certainly a different feeling, knowing who received the "blunt trauma".* While the grief was intense, it had a certain "out of body" feeling to it. It was like I was in the scene, yet watching it too.

The article also indicated the police would not discuss the whereabouts of Jennifer's stepson or whether her estranged husband had been interviewed. No one was in custody.

In addition, it was written that fellow teachers had been aware of difficulties in Jennifer's personal life.

I closed the paper and shut my eyes. *Will I ever understand this? How in the world will those closer to Jennifer ever cope?* I saw my brother's face, the way it had looked the day before. How much older he had looked, as if instantly fast-forwarded ten years. *Will that fade, and he'll look more like he had again? Or is the change permanent and he'll continue to age from this new point? How will he ever get over seeing Jennifer's dead body, particularly when he'd found her unidentifiable?*

I got up and retrieved my teaching contract from the kitchen cupboard. I discovered that I could have two funeral leave days per school year, for someone "not of immediate family". I felt a bitter taste in my mouth. *What would happen if someone else died?* I remembered a recent speaker at a district inservice. He'd advocated that teachers should be allowed to take the time they needed to grieve. In districts that had such policies, there was no incidence of abuse of the system. Apparently, just knowing that time was available often made people feel better. He was appalled that districts felt it necessary to put a timeline on matters of grief. He'd jokingly said, "Immediate family, two days. Anyone else, grieve from afar".

Unfortunately, our district did not feel inclined to change our policy after our guest speaker. My brother was entitled to four days.

I came up with two plans. One was to go to school Monday morning then leave at noon for Rapids. That way, I'd have to be back for school on Wednesday at noon. Since Wednesday was a teacher workday with no students, that would be manageable. Otherwise, I could teach all day Monday, then leave after school for up north. That idea appealed less, as I would be on the road after dark. I decided to wait to hear from Bobby, as to their needs with the kids.

When my brother called, he had a good deal of news. The police had been in contact with them and brought them up to speed on the case. Christopher's alibi had checked out, but Bill was still under suspicion.

There had been a construction crew working on the house next door to Jennifer's and police had talked with them. Two of the workers had observed a man, not unlike Bill, leaving from the back of Jennifer's house around the time of death. The workers described a middle-aged man, average height and weight, with dark hair and glasses. He was wearing sweatpants, a two-toned Columbia-style coat and white gloves. He was carrying two bags. A lump formed in my throat. *That sure did not eliminate Bill as the murderer. Was I subconsciously hoping it had been some random act of violence by a disturbed stranger; not someone I knew, someone I'd shared holiday meals with, and one of the Judge family members? Emotionally, the crazed stranger scenario would be better for everyone.*

Additionally, one of the construction workers had heard a woman scream shortly after Jennifer arrived home. *If only they'd stormed the house after hearing the scream. Of course, no one would do such a thing. I'd often heard random yells in our neighborhoods in town and never investigated. But in hindsight, it could possibly have saved Jennifer, or at least, caught the perpetrator. Where was life's "rewind" button I'd often wished for? Are the "what-ifs" normal in these circumstances?*

The police had located Bill at the home near Minocqua. They had questioned him and were "keeping an eye on him". Before I had a chance to complain that Bill hadn't been arrested, Bobby explained that the police wanted to be sure they had all the evidence they would require for a solid case before making an arrest. I understood the logic; I didn't like it.

I told my brother of my friend Cheryl's offer to adopt Jennifer's dogs. He told me to thank her sincerely, but there had been another offer from a friend of Patti's. The family would discuss the options over the next few days.

He and Cathy were heading to Rapids that afternoon. Nicole and Michael would come from Milwaukee Monday afternoon and pick Erin up in Madison. There was to be a family dinner Monday at 5:00 p.m. at the Mead Hotel.

I apprised Bobby of my choices, and decided that since he didn't need me to transport kids, I'd be up there early Monday evening. If there was anything he needed me to bring up, I said he should call me at school Monday morning.

I inquired as to flowers. Bobby said the family preferred memorials to Jennifer's high school, Wisconsin Rapids Assumption. They would set up a scholarship fund there in her name. I told him I'd relay the news to dad and mom. I'd also inform the union executive board members at the meeting in the afternoon.

Finally, I told Bobby to tell Cathy not to worry about Thanksgiving. We'd just wait on the plans. We could continue as planned, I could host, we could go out to a restaurant to eat, or simply not celebrate. The decision would be entirely theirs. My brother wanted me to talk directly to Cathy, so he handed the phone to her. I repeated what I'd told my brother. "That's really generous of you. I really appreciate it. Hopefully we'll be able to make a decision soon. Thanks for everything you've done so far."

How do I respond to her words when I've felt so inadequate? "Well, I just hope it can help in some way."

When we discussed my plans for the funeral, she insisted that I attend the family dinner on Monday night. While I was deeply touched, I told Cathy I did not think it was my place to be there. She remained insistent, "Our girls would really appreciate their Aunt DeeDee being there."

Dear God this is so hard! It's just like when they asked us to go to the Badger game. "Cathy, I'll do whatever you think is best for all."

Then my sister-in-law asked me for a favor, "Could you possibly scan a photo I have of Jennifer and e-mail it to *The Janesville Gazette* and the *Wisconsin State Journal*? They've asked for one the family would like them to use."

"No problem, can you bring it by on your way out of town?"

"We sure will. Thanks so much."

After I hung up the phone, I told Jeff how awkward I would feel at that dinner. I appreciated Cathy's kind inclusion, but just didn't feel entirely comfortable being there. We agreed that for Cathy, I'd just have to manage it.

Needing a room for Monday night, I called the Mead Inn and made a reservation. *How strange. I haven't stayed at the Mead since Bobby and Cathy's wedding back in 1976. How life does go in circles.*

I stood in front of my closet, thinking about what I would wear to the funeral. *Whatever I choose will be marked forever. Like the shuttle disaster in the 1980's or September 11. I never again wore the clothes I'd had on at school those days. Those tragedies were just too severe to be reminded of in that way. This too.*

I walked Jennifer's dogs again, and Luna finally "did her duties". I was remarkably thrilled by the biological. I knew I couldn't bear it if the sweet little thing became ill or, worse yet, died while in my care. It was a bigger responsibility than I'd originally realized. Since it was quite cold out, with temperatures only in the teens, I hustled them back into the house. *Did Jennifer have little sweaters for them? Quite probably, but I wouldn't be allowed to have them from the house. We'll just have to make due without.* I made a mental note to check with Erin about it, and be sure the new owners knew the situation. Given the trauma they'd already been through, the more consistency B.C. and Luna could have the better.

About 1:30 I left the house. I picked Cheryl up and we drove to the meeting. Many of the executive board members did not realize Jennifer's relationship to Bobby or me. With all of us having different last names, it wasn't surprising. They all offered sincere condolences.

When I explained Bobby's sentiment about deferring to Craig High School staff about Monday's meeting, the group concurred. A meeting of Craig staff was being held at 4:00 p.m. Our president would have them make a determination.

Even after I explained the family's wishes regarding flowers, the group felt strongly that some floral remembrance should be sent to the funeral home. It was decided that a living plant be sent, with directions for it to be given to Jennifer's high school after the services. It was a compromise of sorts. I left the meeting just long enough to call my dad to find out the name of the funeral home in Rapids. The treasurer would be responsible for having the plant sent to the Richay Funeral Home.

It was also determined that, should the contract ratification meeting be held on Monday, a free-will donation would be held. All monies collected would be put into the scholarship fund in Jennifer's name at Assumption High.

The president also said that it looked as if a memorial service would be held in Janesville for Jennifer on Monday or Tuesday after school. The district wanted an opportunity for students and staff to pay their respects if they were unable to travel to Wisconsin Rapids. He wondered if my brother would have any objection to that. I stated, with confidence, that I didn't believe he would, but said I would contact him later after I'd spoken to Bobby.

The meeting ended and, after receiving many individual condolences, Cheryl and I left.

How silly to be going shopping; though it does feel good doing something ordinary and normal. The original movie, *O God!* with George Burns and John Denver popped into my head. When "God" first appeared to Denver it was in the bathroom. Denver's character was completely freaked out. "God" recommended that in crisis, people should do something normal. It seemed like good advice, but the funny twist was that "God" suggested that Denver go ahead and shave! *Besides, if we did celebrate Thanksgiving, the piecrusts would be needed.*

On the drive we talked about the murder, Jennifer's life and funeral plans. Since Cheryl also knew my brother fairly well, she felt deeply saddened for him too.

As we entered Walworth County, it began to snow. I assumed it was just a few flurries and would pass quickly. It continued. By the time we reached Mukwonago, an inch had already accumulated. I was glad we were in my big four-wheel drive Avalanche.

We made our purchases and headed home. The snow was still coming down and the roads were quite slippery. I could feel the tension building in my shoulder muscles. *If I'd known it was going to snow, I sure wouldn't have planned this trip. Sometimes meteorologists really miss the boat. I know it's a difficult science, but I sure don't need this right now!*

At one point on County Highway A, we saw an approaching car crest the hill we were ascending. As it came over the top, it spun a few circles and ended up on the shoulder on our side of the road. We weren't fifty yards from being hit as the car spun out of control! Luckily for the occupants, there was no ditch on that part of the road, but they narrowly missed crashing through a farmer's fenced-in horse pasture.

I drove past the car, pulled into the farmer's driveway and got out of the car. I went to the other vehicle and asked the two occupants if they were all right. They indicated they were fine and would just pull back out on the road and continue east. I urged them to take it a bit more slowly.

Now Cheryl and I had something other than the murder to talk about. We became concerned for our own welfare.

We were relieved when we entered Janesville city limits; but, amazingly, the snow abruptly ended. While my vehicle was covered with snow, the streets of Janesville were bare. It was most bizarre.

I dropped Cheryl off and headed for home. Once there, Jeff said I had a message to call Frank Schultz, a reporter for *The Janesville Gazette*. I'd worked with Frank many times during my union presidency. I liked him a lot and always thought he did a fair job by me. I assumed he was doing a story on Jennifer's murder.

I called Frank back, and he explained that he had been able to reach my brother on his cell phone. Bobby had talked to Frank en route to Wisconsin Rapids. *Good! I don't want to end up being the family spokesperson!*

I told Frank I didn't know how much I would have been able to share with him, as a good deal of what the police had said was highly confidential. Frank said the story was more about Jennifer's life, and that my brother had been able to give him what he needed. Frank said, "Your brother seems like a nice guy".

I chided him, "Would you think otherwise?" He laughed. He had once described me in an article as "fiery", and I had gotten on him a little about that. He'd explained that he knew me as one who would "fight mightily for what you believed in". I took that as a compliment, but knew he didn't think of me as a sweet gal.

I finished packing, then called my principal to inform him of my plans. Mike expressed his condolences and asked me to relay them to my brother. Many years before, Mike had been the principal at one of Bobby's schools, and the two remained friendly. Mike said he would make sure a substitute teacher was hired for Monday afternoon and Tuesday. After offering to help in any way he could, we planned to talk at school in the morning.

Next I called my parents to let them know about the no-flower request for the visitation and funeral. Dad said he would write a check for the scholarship fund if I could fill in the exact name when I got up north. I promised that I would do that, and that I would pick up the check from him tomorrow after I left school at noon.

About 9:00 p.m. Bobby called. The family had discussed Jennifer's dogs and it had been decided they were to go to Patti's friends in Des Moines. They had raised Bichons for years and had recently had to euthanize two of their older females. It seemed like the perfect match. He asked me to thank Cheryl and her family again for their offer. The whole Judge family appreciated their generosity. They were also hopeful that I would bring the dogs up to Wisconsin Rapids with me tomorrow.

I agreed that was possible, but was concerned as to where the dogs would stay overnight and during the services on Tuesday. Bobby explained that Tom and Mavis wanted to have the dogs at their home after the dinner Monday night. I commented, "Mavis must have had a change of heart".

"Yes, she's come out of the deep shock she was in at first. They'd both like to spend some time with Jennifer's dogs before they go to their new home. Patti will take them to Iowa with her when she returns home on Wednesday."

"That all sounds fine, except for where will the dogs be when everyone is at the dinner Monday?"

"Oh, that's another thing," my brother's voice had changed. He was feeling very awkward. "Would you mind if you didn't come to the dinner? Cathy feels bad since she'd already invited you, but there's some concern about immediate family."

"Not a problem. I was feeling strange about it anyway. I'll just dog sit at the Mead until the dinner is finished. That'll work out perfectly."

He was relieved. It was a delicate issue. I wasn't sure where the concern had come from and didn't really care. I'd always felt it was a matter exclusively for immediate family.

Bobby continued with the updated information. "Tom and Mavis have also agreed to have Jennifer cremated. There will be a closed casket at the visitation. They do not want to see her. They want to remember her in life."

Thank goodness Jennifer's parents chose to honor her wishes about cremation. Hopefully, though, they might reconsider their decision about viewing her body. They could miss out on the kind of closure they may need in the future. It's distressing to look at people who have passed on; it does however, provide a feeling of finality. The spirit is truly gone; the body is a "shell" that has become an empty vessel.

We next discussed the proposed memorial service for Craig High School students and staff on Monday. Bobby agreed that it was a fine idea. He just hoped those concerned would understand that there would be no family representative present. I promised I would relay the information.

We planned that I would contact him at the Mead when I arrived. *Hopefully the hotel will allow me to have the dogs in the room with me. It's way too cold to leave them in the car or even to stay in the car with them for several hours.* Bobby had reported that the temperature up there was in the single digits. *I might have some fast-talking to do when I arrived.*

When I called him, our current president was happy to hear that the family had approved of the memorial service. He said the staff at Craig had determined that it would be best to postpone the contract ratification vote, out of respect for Jennifer's memory. It would be announced on WCLO in the morning and by each principal in the buildings as well. *Oh, Lord! That's an appropriate decision, but now my struggles with that issue are going to drag on. I just really want it to be over; my energy to fight an unfair settlement is gone. Besides, bargaining for a contract seems relatively less important now. I'll just have to deal with that when the time comes.*

As tired as I was, I wasn't able to sleep. My thoughts pitched around in my brain like a small boat in an ocean storm. I tried to avoid looking at the clock. I envied Jeff's even, sleep-induced breathing. Every time I tried to think of something pleasant, thoughts of the murder crowded in. I tensed then relaxed all the muscles in my body. Nothing worked. The sky had begun to lighten and I'd just about given up on sleep for the night. Then the 6:00 a.m. radio news broadcast woke me with a start. I was glad to have gotten a bit of sleep.

5

My shower Monday morning refreshed me somewhat. My brain started whirling. *I should have something to give the family members as a token of understanding for their loss. Maybe jewelry or some sort of quotation. Why hadn't this idea occurred to me sooner? Now my timeline is so tight, I don't have time to think properly. Maybe I'll stop at the mall before leaving for Rapids and see if something strikes me.*

Jeff did the chores so I could get to school a little early. I spoke with Mike, my principal, and filled him in on the situation and my plans. He was very supportive.

Our police liaison officer came into the lobby as I talked with Mike. I beckoned him, "Hey Kevin, do you have any inside information you can share with me about the murder?"

"I wish I could, but it's very hush-hush right now. We've got to be really careful until an arrest is made."

"Completely understandable. I'd like to be able to offer the family something positive when I arrive today."

"Sorry, no. On the other hand, I can tell you the officers who worked on the scene said it was the worst they'd ever seen. But that's not something the family wants to hear." He shook his head.

"You're right. I think I'll keep that to myself. Maybe something will have been done before I get back on Wednesday."

"Let's hope so. Good luck."

I saw a colleague getting ready for hall duty at the top of the stairs. She was a quick thinker and had good ideas. I went up and mentioned my quandary as to a token of sympathy for the family. She thought a moment and then said, "What about those Guardian Angel pins?"

"That's exactly what I need! Thanks so much! Any idea where I'd find them? I know they were everywhere a few years ago, but haven't really noticed them lately."

"Maybe a drugstore or the jewelry boutique at the mall? I haven't seen them lately either."

I thanked her again and went to my team area. My team members were there and offered their sympathies. I told them what I knew and about my plans. They would support me however they could.

I spent my first hour preparation time getting things ready for the substitute teacher. I didn't want the days to be lost to instruction, but knew not every substitute teacher is prepared to handle the content of grade eight biology and U.S. history. I came up with something instructional, yet manageable for a non-specialist. I was fairly well satisfied.

When the students arrived for my second hour science class, I was surprised at how emotional I became when I told them. I'd been on "autopilot" for some time and didn't expect to get teary-eyed. The students were wonderful. They were quiet and sympathetic. They promised they'd be good for the substitute teacher. We moved on to the day's lesson.

My third and fourth hour classes responded similarly. They were remarkably poised for young teenagers. I was very grateful for their mature behavior. I would not forget their kindness.

As soon as lunchtime arrived, I said goodbye to my team members and left school. I went to my parents' to pick up dad's check. Both he and mom directed me to drive carefully and give their best to the Judge family. I knew my dad would liked to have gone, he'd mentioned it on the phone. But since mom had been housebound for months, he couldn't really get away for an overnight trip.

I headed for a drugstore to look for the Guardian Angel pins. No luck. I went on to the mall. Boston Store had some little cartoonish ones I didn't think were appropriate. I was getting a little discouraged and thought maybe I'd have to think of something else, or forget the idea all together. I needed to get going if I was to arrive in Rapids before dark.

I went to the jewelry boutique and a card store with no results. I tried a second card shop and hit paydirt. They had the perfect gift. They were affixed to a small card with a rose-colored angel cherub and a sympathetic statement. It explained the pin of "Guardian Angel Wings" was to comfort them in their time of sorrow. They had six left. I'd wanted to get one for each immediate family member, but could at least have one for Jennifer's parents and siblings. It would have to do. I made my purchase and went home to collect the dogs and my things.

After putting my luggage in the back seat I put the dog crate on the front seat, so they could be next to me on the trip. Since John hadn't brought their leashes, I selected two of mine to take along. *Why hadn't I thought about that sooner? I could have stopped at the pet shop and purchased two nice new ones. My timing sure is off; my usual quick assessment and proactivity were sluggish. Stress must be muddling my thought processes.*

I chastised myself for missing this detail. I'd just have to give the Judge's my leashes and purchase new ones for my dogs when I got back home. It was a small concern, given the scope of things. I'd try not to be too hard on myself about it.

B.C. and Luna seemed concerned at first, then settled down in their crate. I kept talking to them and reassuring them that things would be okay.

The day was sunny and cold, driving conditions were excellent. As I took the route we'd traveled so many times for happier occasions, I couldn't help but think again how tragic this all was. I turned on the radio to try to drown out my thoughts and help me focus on the road. The trip went fairly quickly. The temperature readout on the rearview mirror told me I was headed north, the number kept dropping as the miles passed.

I pulled up to the Mead under the portico and went inside. Just as I was nearing the front desk, Bobby and Cathy came in from a door on the opposite side of the lobby. They were dressed in sweat suits, and had obviously just finished a run. Cathy's cheeks were quite red from the cold, but she sounded and looked better than she had on Saturday. *It's good she and Bobby have kept on with their running program. It will help them stay healthier through this time.* It reminded me I'd been neglecting my walking the past few days. I decided that as soon as I got checked in and settled, I'd take the dogs out for a long walk.

When Cathy gave me a hug and kiss on the cheek I felt her cold skin against my face. "Thanks for coming. How was your drive?"

"Fine. How are you doing?"

"All right. It's good to have the family together. We've been at the funeral home, met with Father Karoblis about the mass and Patti and I went shopping at the mall. We picked out something for Jennifer to wear."

"I'll bet that was hard. I'm sorry."

"Yes, but at least we had each other." She straightened as if she was dismissing the negative. "Now, I suppose you'd like to get checked in and relax a bit. Were you able to bring Jennifer's dogs?"

"Uh huh, they're in the car. I'll get checked in and take them for a walk."

Bobby entered the conversation. "Our dinner starts at five, so we've got to get going. Sorry to leave you alone. Tom and Mavis would like us to bring the dogs over after dinner. Do you want to go along?"

"Absolutely. I can fill them in on the things I've figured out about B.C. and Luna so far. What time do you think you'll be back?"

"Probably between 7:30 and 8:00."

"Okay. I'll be in my room, just give me a call or come up when you get back."

Cathy interjected, "If you're still willing we would like to come to your house for Thanksgiving."

"Of course, I'm glad you'll be coming over."

My brother got back to the unfortunate business at hand, "By the way, it's been decided that there will be a viewing of Jennifer for any family members who'd like to. It will be before the visitation tomorrow morning. Are you interested?"

I answered without hesitation, "Yes, I am."

Bobby said he would not be viewing the body, as he already had. *Oh yes, at the morgue. The way very few people ever see loved ones.*

Cathy and I agreed to meet in the lobby 8:00 a.m. in order to arrive at the funeral home in time.

I went to check in. The clerk was somewhat friendly, but not as nice as I would have thought given the circumstances. The entire Judge family was staying there for this sad event. I'd expected a bit more empathy. I explained the situation with the dogs, and requested they be allowed to stay with me in my room for a couple of hours since it was so cold out in the car. She was very uncertain and hedged about. Before she could tell me no, I quickly said, "Of course I'll keep them in their crate the whole time."

She countered, "Will you be staying in the room with them the entire time as well?"

"Absolutely."

"Well, I guess it would be okay. I hope they won't bark."

"I'll see that they don't. Thank you." I quickly hustled off before she could change her mind or ask a superior who might say no.

As I rounded the corner, I nearly ran into Erin and Nicole who had come down the elevator to go to the dinner. We hugged. *What to say? How can we have a normal conversation about anything but the weather, which we agreed, was cold?* I asked how their room was. They said they needed to work out the sleeping arrangements, since they had two rooms and there were five of them. I offered the spare bed in my room if they needed it. They appreciated that and would keep it in mind.

Taking the luggage cart, I went out to the Avalanche. The dogs were very happy to see me. I put their crate on the cart, added my luggage and went into the Mead.

By that time, a few of the Judge cousins had arrived in the lobby and were greeting one another and hugging. Everyone had moist eyes when they looked at Jennifer's little dogs in the crate. They all put their fingers through the crate's bars to pet B.C. and Luna. *Amazing how these little creatures tug at everyone's heartstrings.*

Of course, I had lied to the clerk at the desk. As soon as I got into the room I let B.C. and Luna out of their crate. Poor things had been through enough. If they did any damage in the room, which I couldn't imagine, I'd pay for it myself. They curiously sniffed around this third "home" in as many days.

I unpacked a bit, then bundled back up and took the dogs out for that long walk. As I left the Mead I saw the Judge clan heading out of the parking lot in their various vehicles. They waved. *This memory will stick with me. They all look so forlorn.*

After walking for thirty minutes, the dogs were obviously tired. My face was quite cold, and it was getting dark. I headed back to the hotel. We'd been down by the river and the two Bichons were sure they wanted to chase the Canadian geese who were significantly larger than they were! I laughed when they strained on their collars and yapped furiously at the huge birds. *When was the last time I'd laughed?*

I took the dogs up the back stairs, hoping no other lodgers would see me and complain to the management. On the way out I'd gotten a few sideways glances. *I sure don't need a hassle at this point. I might lose it if someone complains; at the very least they'd get an earful.*

Once in the room, I turned on the TV and settled on the bed. Both dogs jumped up to snuggle with me. I realized I was hungry. I looked around for the room-service menu. There wasn't anything on it that appealed to me. I really just wanted a salad and maybe a roll.

I called the in-hotel restaurant. They said I was welcome to order a salad from their menu and come pick it up. That meant I'd have to leave the dogs alone for a few minutes, but I'd have to risk it. I ordered. It would be ready in twenty minutes.

I put the dogs in their crate, dashed down the stairs to the restaurant, paid my bill and took the stairs two at a time on the way back up. I was gone less than five minutes. I didn't detect any barking or whining while I was coming down the hall. *Whew!*

While I ate my salad, the dogs begged for tidbits. I shared just a little of my roll. I didn't know how delicate their digestive systems were and didn't want there to be problems in that department at Tom and Mavis' overnight.

There wasn't much on TV. I surfed the channels, then settled on an old movie. I called Jeff to let him know I'd arrived safely and to see how our animals at home were faring. All was well. The only news he had from Janesville was that a co-worker had told him he'd heard Bill's son had not been at school last Friday. *The rumors have already started. Dear God, don't let Christopher have been involved in this!*

Eight o'clock came and went. I was really tired. I didn't want to fall asleep, though, and have Bobby come to the door. I tried to focus on the movie. B.C. had taken up residence on the other bed and Luna had laid down with her whole body stretched out against my left thigh. I stroked her incredibly silky fur. When I stopped she lifted her head to look at me. I petted her some more. I was most worried about Luna. B.C. was more outgoing and self-assured. Luna's dark eyes were so expressive. *She seems both sad and confused. Their new home sounds perfect, but I'll miss them so much. It will be hard to turn them over.* Tears filled my eyes.

It wasn't until 9:20 p.m. that the knock came at the door. The dogs started barking immediately. I shushed them up, scooted them into their crate and answered the door. It was Bobby and Mike Barker.

Since I had kept the luggage cart in the room, we wheeled the dogs down in the elevator. It didn't really matter now if other guests became upset since the dogs were leaving.

In the car Bobby said the dinner had been very nice, with much happy reminiscing about Jennifer's life. He thought everyone was as prepared for the visitation and the funeral as they could be. *How in the world does one do that?*

During dinner, Michael Judge had shared that on Sunday evening Bill's parents had called him. Bill's mother had said, "We know our son has done a terrible thing, but we loved Jennifer and would like to come to the funeral if it is all right with the family."

Michael had welcomed them.

So here was another tragic part of all of this. Bill's parents had to somehow deal with the possibility that their son had committed murder. As a parent, that might be even worse than having your child be the victim. Would they blame themselves, wondering what they might have done wrong with him as a child? The pain of this terrible event was spreading into a wider and wider circle.

We arrived at Tom and Mavis'. I gave them both a huge hug and offered my sympathy. Mavis was ready for bed. She looked tired but elegant in her long robe with the satin lapels. She was always impeccably groomed, right down to the fingernails. When she looked at the dogs, she put her hands to her face and wept softly for a minute. As soon as the dogs were out of the crate, Tom sat in a chair and B.C. jumped in his lap and started licking his face. Tom actually giggled as he pet her. *This was definitely the right thing to do.*

Tom and Mavis invited us to sit down. I filled them in on what I had learned of B.C. and Luna. They were familiar with Bichons since they had one of B.C.'s pups at their home in Arizona, along with Jennifer's lab Mozart. They obviously missed their dogs and were enjoying this diversion. The dogs checked out their surroundings and stopped to be petted by all. I expressed concern for the dogs' care the next day. With the visitation, funeral and luncheon, they would be in their crate for a long time. I said I would be happy to come back here at some point and walk them. Tom and Mavis appreciated that.

I offered to take the dogs for their last walk of the night and Mike accompanied me. We walked in the cold, quiet darkness of the neighborhood and agreed on how bright the stars were. *With such a loss they should be a little dimmer.*

After I tearfully parted with B.C. and Luna, we bid goodnight to Tom and Mavis and drove back to the Mead. Bobby and Mike said the family had been headed to the bar, so we went in to join them.

Bobby's family had already turned in for the night, but Michael Judge was there along with his daughter, Jeannie, and son Jonathan. Michael hugged me enthusiastically and claimed that I was a "hero" for bringing those dogs along. He said it really would make his parents' night better. I had "saved the day". It felt good to be helpful and I appreciated Michael's warmth.

I ordered a ginger ale and talked mostly with Jeannie, who introduced me to her fiancée. Jeannie was so grown up, and her young man seemed a very kind and supportive fellow.

After about thirty minutes, I realized I was very tired. I said goodnight to all and went off to bed.

It seemed lonely in my room without Jennifer's dogs. I turned on the TV for company and fell asleep without too much trouble.

6

I met Cathy and Patti in the lobby of The Mead at 8:00 a.m. on Tuesday, November 26. They insisted I ride with them to the funeral home in Patti's car. Cathy explained that Bobby and Mike would come over later in their vehicle, so we'd have plenty of transportation. I felt I might be intruding at some point in the day, and really wanted to take my own vehicle. However, I wasn't inclined to argue with them on this day. We rode over to the Richay Funeral Home in relative silence except for some talk about how cold it was.

The three of us went in and I was introduced to the directors. The senior Mr. Richay had been a friend of Tom and Mavis' for over thirty years. He seemed more personally aggrieved than any other funeral home director I have ever seen.

I gave Cathy and Patti their Guardian Angel Wings. They both thanked me and pinned them on immediately. We proceeded to the visitation room.

I followed Cathy and Patti to the casket. Both sisters gasped simultaneously. Their hands went to their hearts. It was a very intimate moment. I felt like a complete intruder. To give them some privacy without making a scene, I tried to stay a few feet behind them.

I looked down at Jennifer. *Thank goodness, she looks peaceful.* I'd been afraid that her violent death would be reflected in her expression. *It's odd though, that she isn't smiling. The bubbly, talkative, friendly Jennifer is not here.* I realized I hadn't often seen her in repose, and certainly never in sleep. *She is truly gone.*

She was wearing a sweater-set in royal blue and black. A lovely turquoise rosary was in her hands. *Did Mavis and Tom bring it from Arizona?* Jennifer's hair was nicely styled, but I thought I did detect a small area on her scalp that appeared to have quite a bit of makeup on it. *Hopefully, that's not one of her injuries, and Cathy and Patti noticed it too.* Just the thought conjured up horrible images.

Patti looked at Cathy, then at me. She spoke through tears, "That's probably more dressed up than she would want to be. Maybe we should have had her in a Badger sweatshirt." Cathy smiled wistfully, and I shrugged, fighting back tears. Patti continued to look at her sister's body. She was crying a bit more when she said, "You know, she never did have her nails done."

Jennifer and I really were the tomboys. Who will I have now to reassure me that it's okay to prefer blue jeans and yard work to manicures and shopping at the mall? I should have tried harder to spend more time with her. I should've taken the time to go on one of her trips to Spain. It's too late now.

I left Cathy and Patti at the casket with their sister.

I looked around the room, there were quite a few floral arrangements, despite the Judges' request. I took some time to look at them all, and to see who had sent them. I recognized many of the names on the cards. I found the plant from our teachers' association, and would be able to report back that it was a lovely tropical plant. *I'm glad there are some flowers. It just wouldn't be right for the room to be completely barren. I guess sending floral arrangements to a funeral home isn't such a waste of flowers and money.*

As Cathy and Patti moved away from the casket I fell in behind them. We moved toward the back of the long room filled with rows of folding chairs. There were two easels with posters filled with photos of Jennifer. One photo was of a very young Jennifer sitting in the saddle on a pony that looked remarkably like my pony Buckshot. Her elder sister Cathy was at her side watching out for her sibling's welfare. Jennifer's expression was pure delight. Another item had been clipped from a newspaper and was yellowed with age. In the photo, Jennifer was 13 years old and was sitting on a big branch up a tree with her dog Tara. *That sweet little tomboy is gone. Hopefully she and Tara are together again.*

The casket was closed.

Other family members were arriving at the funeral home and I gave Tom Jr. and Michael Judge their Guardian Angel Wings. They seemed appreciative.

The somber silence was disturbed by the echoing sound of someone vomiting in the men's restroom. I looked around to see who was missing. It was Mike Barker. No one said a word. Everyone tried to act as if they hadn't heard it.

Mike came out of the restroom and Bobby discreetly offered him a mint. The funeral directors told us that there were refreshments downstairs.

Mike Barker went downstairs: a little later I followed. "Are you feeling okay, Mike?"

"Oh, yes, better now, thanks. I just don't handle these things well. I couldn't even discipline my own kids."

"Hey, everybody handles these things differently. It's not like there are any guidelines to follow. Don't be so hard on yourself. If your stomach is still upset, I do have plenty of Mylanta back at the Mead. I never travel without it. Would you like me to go get you some?"

"No thanks, I think I'll be all right now. I couldn't eat any breakfast, but now maybe I'll nibble on one of these bagels."

"Okay, but let me know if you need me to go. That's what I'm here for, whatever is needed." I patted him on the back and went upstairs.

Soon Tom and Mavis arrived. Tom stepped inside the door about the middle of the visitation room. I made an attempt to give him his Guardian Angel Wings. I don't believe he heard me or even saw me. Cathy was very sensitive. She took the pin from me and said she'd give it to him later. I was able to give Mavis her pin, and she thanked me.

Tom turned his head to the left and saw the casket. He moved as quickly as his aging body would allow. He hurtled toward the casket. Everyone stood motionless. He was, as best I can describe, wailing in grief. When he got to the casket, he draped his body over it and pounded on it with the palm of his open right hand. He begged over and over, "Dear God, please take care of my Jenny!"

It was more sorrowful than anything I could ever possibly have imagined.

His wife and children hurried to his side to comfort him. Nicole rushed out into the vestibule crying. I stifled my tears the best I could and followed her. She was sobbing uncontrollably. I hugged her and rubbed her back. She spoke between sobs, "I can't breathe, I just can't breathe!" I kept trying to comfort her and told her to try to think of something else just now. After a few minutes, she was able to control her crying and breathing. *It is so wrong for her to have to feel so much anguish at her young age! Curse you Bill Mereness!*

The rest of the family came out into the vestibule. Tom and Mavis had decided they did want to view Jennifer after all. It was a small comfort to me, as I was afraid if they hadn't, they would always regret it.

The middle doors to the visitation room were closed, but those up in the front were left open. We could hear Mavis' cries of grief as she viewed her daughter's body. The sound was incredible in its intensity. It brought to memory the sounds the mothers make at the Wailing Wall. *This is unbearably sad. Where is Tom and Mavis' God now?*

After a few minutes the crying subsided and the middle doors were reopened. We all went inside. Up in front, to the right of the now closed casket, the siblings formed their receiving line with Tom and Mavis. I saw Cathy pin the Guardian Angel Wings on Tom's lapel. I went to sit on one of the settees in the back of the room. The mourners were arriving.

There was a steady stream of people who had come to pay their respects to Jennifer. Many were strangers to me, but it was obvious from their facial expressions and gestures toward the family that they cared deeply for Jennifer and were horrified at what had happened.

Much of the time I sat at the back of the room visiting quietly with Mike Barker and Jennifer's nieces and nephews. Our presence was not required in the receiving line, but I considered myself to be an ambassador of sorts. When other mourners sat near me, I would introduce myself and we'd talk about their connections with Jennifer. The vast majority were former students, many now well into their twenties. Some younger people were with parents. All of them had heartwarming stories to tell about how Jennifer had impacted their lives.

One particular young lady had been a student of Jennifer's in Verona. She was sobbing and filled with emotion, but managed to collect herself to tell me what an inspirational teacher Jennifer had been. She'd previously had problems in Spanish; but Jennifer had made class so fun, she'd gotten caught up in the enthusiasm and become a proficient student.

I inquired, "How did Jennifer make class fun?"

"Oh gosh, she told silly stories about her life and her travels and her dogs. When her dog had puppies she brought the whole litter in and kept them in a confined area in the back of the room. If we did well in class, we'd get to play with the puppies."

I smiled at the young lady. "I'll bet that was a real motivator for you students."

"It sure was, everyone loved those puppies."

"And no one objected to her having the dogs in the classroom?"

"No, not at all. In fact, our principal would come in and visit the puppies too. It was so cool."

"I can imagine. You were lucky to have such a great experience."

I was momentarily lost in thought. In our district we had a new "Live Animal Policy". I too had brought many animals into the classroom, but the new policy was so onerous, it was becoming almost impossible. As union president I had fought hard for a colleague who trained service dogs. Administrators denied access to her new pup because they claimed it would have been a distraction to her students. *How I wish they could hear this young lady tell her story.*

I refocused my attention on Jennifer's former student, who had started speaking again. "I'm going to miss her so much. We'd been e-mailing since she left Verona. Mom took me to Janesville to visit her a couple of times. We even met in Madison for lunch some times." She began to cry anew. Her mother rubbed her back and continued the conversation, while her daughter tried to regain her composure.

"Jennifer was more than my daughter's teacher, she was my friend. Despite our age difference, we just hit it off when we first met and have been good friends ever since. This is especially hard because we just lost my mother a few weeks ago."

I was overwhelmed with empathy. I offered my condolences and then steered the conversation to happier memories.

Later, one young man caught my eye because he spent a very long time looking over the collages on the easels. He even lightly touched some of the photos in an endearing way. After he touched a photo he would look around the room as if he feared he might be scolded for his actions. He was nice looking, and well dressed, with dark hair and a slim build. He appeared to be in his early twenties. I walked up to him and introduced myself.

Again, this mourner had been one of Jennifer's students. His words poured out as if he were at confession. "She made all the difference in my life. I'd been making some bad choices, but she would always talk with me and help me after school and show how much she cared. I turned my life around. I can't believe this has happened to her. Who would do such a thing?"

"The police aren't sure yet, but they are looking for her estranged husband."

The young man hung his head, shoulders slumping. He looked again at one of the photos. He spoke. His voice was so quiet I had to lean closer to make out the words. His manner was extremely shy, as if it took all his strength to utter the words, "Do you think I could have one of these photos?"

I wasn't sure but he seemed to be asking to take a photo from the collage, which wouldn't be appropriate. I didn't want to add to his anguish by assuming, so I measured my response carefully, "Would you like me to send you a copy of one of them?"

He brightened considerably, straightened up and looked me right in the eyes, "Could you?"

"I will do my very best, but it might take a while."

He pointed to a photo of Jennifer with Cathy. Both sisters were wearing red sweaters and were toasting the camera with glasses of white wine. Both women had wide smiles and sparkling eyes. "I'd like that one," he said. His very deep brown eyes misted over.

"Let me write down your name and address," I responded as I dug frantically in my purse for paper and a pen or pencil. Out of the corner of my eye I could see him watching me expectantly. My search was only partially successful. Thoughts flew around in my mind. "Please excuse me for a minute while I find some paper. I will be right back."

Sisters Cathy and Jennifer at their parents' 50th wedding anniversary celebration

The young mourner shifted back and forth nervously from foot to foot. He glanced around, almost in a frightened manner.

Putting my hand on his forearm, I gently insisted, "Wait right here, I'll be back in no time." He nodded.

I moved as quickly as decorum would allow. The director's office door was open and I could see the elder Mr. Richay at his desk. I knocked on the opened door. The director looked up, startled, "May I help you?"

"I hope so. Would you happen to have any note paper I could use?"

Mr. Richay rummaged in his desk and then held out a small pad of multi-colored paper.

"Thank you very much, but I only need one sheet."

"Take it, you may need more later."

"Thank you so much." I hurried back to rejoin the young man.

He hastily wrote his name and address on the top sheet, handed the pad back to me, bowed his head, thanked me, turned quickly and walked away.

Wherever you are, Jennifer, you must be really proud. You helped him find the courage to care about himself. He's straightened out his life, thanks to you.

Soon a contingency of staff and students from Janesville Craig entered the room.

After they passed the casket, had a few words with the family, and looked at the photo display many of them walked in my direction. I stood up and greeted them. We shook hands or hugged. Everyone expressed his or her shock and horror about what had happened. We talked about their relationships with Jennifer and her gift for teaching. Most had an amusing story to share. It was comforting to hear the happy tales and to know so many shared in our grief.

Nicole and I began to visit. I was bemoaning the fact that I hadn't driven by myself, as I didn't want to intrude on anyone and ask for a ride to church.

"You can ride with Stephanie and me, but we have to go over early to practice our readings."

"That'd be great. When are you leaving?"

"In about fifteen minutes."

I checked my watch. It was 11:00. "Okay, I'll just have to tell your dad so he doesn't wonder where I've gone."

I circled behind the family members in line and tapped Bobby on the shoulder. I whispered as discreetly as I could; he nodded in understanding.

7

Stephanie, Nicole and I walked out into the cold, clear air. It was a silent trip across town to Saints Peter and Paul church. I was transported back to Bobby and Cathy's wedding. It had been a gorgeous early August day. It was warm, but not humid. The sun was bright. As two of Cathy's bridesmaids, thirteen year old Jennifer and I had worn very feminine peach dresses with outer layers of white eyelet. I'd been a little embarrassed because the dress was rather low cut and had two layers of deep ruffles at the bust line. I never liked to wear anything so revealing, but I'd survived the day. *Funny the things you remember.*

Bookend bridesmaids

It had also been a picture-perfect summer day when Pepe and Jennifer had been married. *What a happy occasion that had been. Our kids had been so excited, they were at such an impressionable age, being awed by the whole experience.*

My reverie was broken when the car came to a stop and Stephanie turned off the engine.

Stepping inside the massive wooden entrance door and into the church vestibule, it took a moment for my eyes to adjust to the relatively dark interior. I was taken aback to see our school Superintendent Tom Evert and School Board member Tom Wolfe standing in the entryway. The latter had been a friend of Bobby's since we were in our junior high days. He'd even been an usher for Bobby and Cathy's wedding. He looked at his watch and spoke, "We didn't think we had enough time to make it to the visitation so we came directly here."

I responded, "You probably would have been okay. There was still quite a long line when we left; the visitation will probably run past noon. But I'm sure the family will be touched that you are here. Thanks for coming."

Both men spoke at the same time, "Of course."

Bobby's friend was emotional, "How is Bob doing?"

"I guess as well as can be expected. It's been so unbelievable. Everyone's still feeling so much shock. I do know that identifying Jennifer's body was extremely hard on him."

"I can't imagine what that was like. I hope he's doing okay."

"He's strong, but I'm not sure how someone gets over something like this. Hopefully time will help."

The superintendent was also showing signs of grief, which was not surprising. Even though we'd clashed during our contract negotiations, I generally found him to be a sensitive man. "Please let me know if there is anything I can do to be of help to the family."

"Thank you, and thanks again for coming."

Passing through the second set of heavy doors, I entered the church where Jennifer would receive her final sacrament.

It was just as I had remembered it, deep and narrow. The long central aisle was flanked by many rows of dark-stained wood. The walls were painted white; the stained-glass windows were tall and narrow. It was a simple but beautiful church. The sanctuary with its altar was small and intimate. It suited Jennifer.

I picked up a program from the stand just inside the door. *Dear God, Father Karoblis is presiding! Hadn't he been quite elderly when Bobby and Cathy were married twenty-five years ago? Or had I just been a callused youth who thought anyone over thirty was ancient? He'd been rather long-winded on that occasion. I hope he realizes that people are already emotionally exhausted and don't need to sit for a great length of time.*

None of us were sure exactly where we should sit, since we hadn't discussed such logistics. We sat several rows back on the right side of the main aisle.

"I'm really nervous about my reading," Nicole confessed.

"Why? You're an excellent reader."

"I'm afraid I'll break down and cry through it."

"Well, if that's what happens it's all right. People would certainly expect you to have very strong emotions right now. If that's how you feel, then that's what will happen. Don't worry about that, just be yourself."

She sighed deeply, "Okay, but will you listen while I practice and give me pointers?"

"Sure."

Stephanie and Nicole practiced their parts. I complimented both young ladies; they'd read beautifully. My only reminder was to concentrate on reading slowly because they would be nervous and have a tendency to speed through the reading.

The girls sat down and we chatted. Nicole explained how each of the nieces and nephews had a role in the funeral. Michael and Erin would serve as pallbearers and cousin Molly would be singing.

"Wow," I commented, "That could be really difficult, singing when you are so upset."

Nicole was confident. "Molly has such a beautiful voice, and she's performed a lot so she'll be fine.

The altar boys in their long robes were gliding silently about the sanctuary, preparing for the mass. They lit candles, set out The Bible the priest would use and placed the chalice where it would be needed for the communion rite.

According to my watch, it was 12:45. I thought aloud, "The visitation must have run late, there were still so many people in line."

Both girls nodded in concurrence.

Almost on cue, the huge doors opened and people began to file into the church. It was quickly filled to capacity, but astonishingly quiet.

Funerals are so sad, especially for one so young and taken so violently.

Father Karoblis appeared and stood in front of the altar. He looked frail, aged and almost broken.

The organist began to play; the assembled stood. Once more the massive double doors opened. The casket, now draped in white cloth and on a tall, wheeled conveyance, was guided by a dark-suited gentleman from the funeral home. Behind him were the parents, siblings, in-laws, nieces and nephews of the woman in the casket. They were in a tight knot, holding each other's arms for support. It was the single most sorrowful sight of my life. The anguish on the faces of Tom and Mavis was immeasurable. The siblings, followed by their spouses, were in obvious pain, their faces ashen. Bobby had deep, dark circles under his eyes, but his posture was tall and stalwart. I felt a swell of pride in my chest. *This image will stay with me forever; the box with Jennifer followed by her grief-stricken family.*

The group proceeded up the aisle to the altar. Cathy and Bobby were on the right of the casket; and as they approached me, Cathy's eyes met mine. She leaned forward and grasped my forearms. I didn't know what to do, so I leaned toward her. She released me as the procession passed by. Then my brother motioned for Nicole, Stephanie and me to come out from the pew and follow him. I was embarrassed, but did as directed. The family filed into the front rows on the left; I was flanked by Michael and Bobby.

The mass began. Father Karoblis was clearly stricken. He spoke of his special relationship with Jennifer, how she'd been active in the church in her youth and been very special to him. It was obvious that he was not exaggerating. He talked of her zest for life and how much he would miss her. It was touching.

Stephanie and Nicole did an excellent job with their readings. Nicole was composed, but tearful.

But then, as I had feared, the priest launched into a lengthy speech. He began by saying it was not a sad day, but a happy day, because Jennifer was now with God. I looked around. It didn't look like there were any others in the church who agreed with this man of the cloth. We wanted Jennifer back among us.

I tuned out after that, lost in my own thoughts but I could hear others shifting in their seats. When I checked my watch, twenty-seven minutes had passed and Father Karoblis was still speaking. I looked in the missal for relief. It read that at this point in the funeral mass, the priest would give "a few brief words". I nearly laughed out loud. *I'm definitely getting dangerously close to the limit of my ability to sit still.* I caught Nicole's and Michael's attention. I pointed to the phrase in the missal. We gave each other small smiles of understanding. I scolded myself: *that was a bit irreverent.*

When the priest finished and sat down the relief was palpable.

Michael Judge began his eulogy of his littlest sister. He spoke briefly but poignantly. Most of the assembled began to weep. He shared the real Jennifer with us. Michael explained how it had always been so hard to stay mad at Jennifer for long, even when she had done some things that exasperated the family. *That was another bond we shared. We were the "trouble makers" in our families. I'll miss my comrade.*

It was time for the closing hymns. Up in the choir loft Molly began to sing. Her voice was strong, clear and absolutely angelic. First she sang "The Rose". I was surprised, because it isn't a real popular song, but was truly one of my favorites. I'd usually listen to it when I was feeling insecure or anxious. I'd often thought I would like to have had that sung at my funeral. *Another connection.* The phrase in the song, "and those afraid of dying who never learn to live" was so appropriate for Jennifer's life. Even though she exasperated her family at times, as I know I do, she had lived life in a big way.

People who had managed to keep their tears at bay could do so no longer. While I did not weep openly, tears did slide down my face.

After Molly sang "On Eagle's Wings" so artfully, the mass was over; we were to go in peace.

The casket was wheeled out of the church with the family following. As a part of that contingent I felt honored but extraordinarily sad. The church doors opened into the bright blue sunlight and cold air of late November in Wisconsin.

Pallbearers Michael and Erin helped other cousins place the casket into the hearse. *This is not something a young man or woman should ever be called upon to do. Curse you again, Bill Mereness!*

The hearse door was closed. It would drive Jennifer's body to its last destination, the crematorium. I watched until it went out of view. *Goodbye Jennifer, I hope to see you again one day.*

At that point Mike Barker and I got together because we'd promised to go to Tom Sr. and Mavis' house to walk B.C. and Luna. Everyone else would go directly to the Mead for the funeral dinner. It was a cold, quiet walk through the neighborhood. Though we spoke little, I was comfortable with Mike. I appreciated having the time to collect my thoughts and emotions.

The air was crisp and the dogs bounded along, sniffing here and there as if they didn't have a care in the world. *I hope they're as happy as they seem.* I gave them each a final hug, wished them a happy life and tucked them back in their crate. We headed for the hotel.

On the drive, I asked Mike if he'd seen Mr. and Mrs. Mereness at the visitation. He had. They had come through the receiving line toward the end. They both seemed extremely sad, with Mrs. Mereness being obviously ill. She was on oxygen. I knew she had suffered from emphysema for some time. *This stress can only complicate that condition.*

How terrible this must be for them. They know their son is a murderer and they have lost a beloved daughter-in-law. Are they questioning themselves as parents? Do they blame themselves for their son's violent behavior? Will they be forthcoming with the police investigation? That will take extraordinary courage. Jennifer's parents are the obvious grievants; but Bill's parents have experienced a tremendous loss as well, and might even be held at fault by some. They are in a difficult place. Hopefully, they will be able to weather this horrible storm.

The buffet table at the Mead was laden with food, but I wasn't hungry. I walked into the ballroom to find it packed with people. *Another fine testament to Jennifer.*

I mingled among the guests, thanking those I knew for coming. I visited a while with the contingent from Craig High School. They reported that the memorial service on Monday in Janesville had been very well attended.

Aggrieved students and staff leave the memorial service for their teacher and colleague (*Courtesy of The Janesville Gazette*)

Rejoining the family, I complimented Molly on her lovely voice and asked if she had plans to pursue a career in music. Vocal music would indeed be a part of her course of study when she began at Wagner University the next fall.

Cathy entered the conversation, "Say DeeDee, who was that young man you talked to for a long time near the photos?"

"He was one of Jennifer's former students. He told me she was instrumental in turning his life around. It was really touching."

"All day that's what we kept hearing as people passed through the line. It was pretty overwhelming, but meant a lot. But I don't remember him coming through the line."

"I wouldn't be surprised if he skipped it; he seemed pretty anxious. He told me he was hoping to get a copy of one of the photos, the one with you and Jennifer making a toast."

My sister-in-law smiled ruefully. "That was at my mom and dad's fiftieth anniversary party."

"It was a good photo of you two. I told him I'd try to get him a copy, but we don't need to worry about that today."

"Stephanie put those collages together. Can you try to work it out with her?"

"Yes, I will."

I could feel my energy level dropping rapidly. I was worried about being able to make the long trip home and toyed with the idea of staying another night in Rapids. I'd have to get up very early and drive straight to work in the morning. It would be an added expense, but perhaps worth it. I decided to have something to eat and drink a caffeinated beverage then see how I felt.

As I was sharing my dilemma with Erin and Michael, they indicated an interest in going home instead of staying the night as was originally planned. They were growing very weary of the whole situation and were anxious to have some time to themselves. My decision was made. I offered to leave within the hour and drop Erin in Madison and then take Michael to his parents' house in Janesville. If I was to go today, I wanted to get started so I could be home before it was too dark. However, I was concerned that Bobby or Cathy might be upset about Erin and Michael's desire to bolt. I warned them to approach their parents cautiously and not make things worse for them.

In a few minutes, my niece and nephew returned to report that they would be going with me. They headed upstairs to pack while I said my good-byes to the family. Everyone thanked me for my assistance, but

Michael Judge was particularly effusive. "I don't know what we'd have done without you!"

His comment made me laugh. "It wasn't that much, but I'm glad I could help out."

Michael smiled, shook his head and hugged me warmly. "You were wonderful."

My throat felt thick and my eyes prickled.

We parted and I went to wait for the kids in the lobby.

The trip was subdued; we listened to music CD's and talked very little. Mainly we wondered if the police were making progress in the case. I asked before I played my Bette Midler rendition of "The Rose".

I dropped Erin off at her apartment in Madison and was glad to see that some of her roommates were home. Then I took Michael to his home in Janesville. I made him promise to lock the house up securely and maybe even leave some lights on all night long. I was afraid. We didn't know Bill's whereabouts. He was certainly acting guilty. He'd never placed a phone call to Jennifer's family. *Even if you were estranged from your spouse; if she or he was brutally murdered, wouldn't you call the family? If this was "the perfect crime" as Bill planned it, you'd think he'd be smart enough to play the role of the innocent, the bereaved spouse.*

It was good to be home. I shared much of what had happened with Jeff and Josh, then called my parents and updated them. I went to bed early and slept fairly well until 8:00 a.m. I did the chores and got ready for school.

It was quite surreal. The world had kept turning in my absence. It looked exactly the same. *Yet my world is so different.*

Many staff members offered condolences throughout the afternoon, which I appreciated. I didn't talk too much about the visitation and funeral because I didn't want to break down. I muddled through the afternoon and went home.

I had four days before I had to be back at school and teach. I'd try to work through some of this. Otherwise, I'd just have to settle for going through the motions.

There is so much unknown. Where is Bill? Will there be an arrest soon? How long will it be until a trial? How will Jennifer's family hold up through this?

We've laid Jennifer to rest; tomorrow is Thanksgiving. How do we go on with life as usual?

8

I was sufficiently busy all morning, stuffing and roasting the turkey, baking pies, making mashed potatoes, sweet potatoes, salad and vegetables. Also, I finished a project I had started for Jennifer's parents and siblings as well as my nieces and nephew. I'd found an Innuit legend that I thought was appropriate and used my card program to center it on a starry night background. Then, I put the finished products in dark blue frames. They read:

*Perhaps they are not stars in the sky,
but rather openings,
where our loved ones shine down
to let us know they are happy.*

It reminded me so much of the night Bobby, Mike Barker and I had delivered Jennifer's dogs to Tom and Mavis.

I had precious little time to think, which was a relief. I was happy to have my mind occupied with something other than the murder and funeral.

Bobby, Cathy, Erin, Michael and my dad arrived for Thanksgiving dinner. Sadly, Nicole would not be with us. The UW-Milwaukee team had a holiday tournament in Arizona. Not only would we miss her, it would be difficult for her to be away from the family at this time.

Fortunately, she would be near enough to Tom and Mavis' home and would be able to have dinner with them. Her presence would brighten an undoubtedly very dark day.

Mom would not be taking part in our celebration either. She hadn't attended family gatherings recently; she'd just not "been up to it". Despite years of professional consultation, no one seemed to know if it was depression, anxiety or agoraphobia, but she hadn't left the house in months. Mom wasn't even getting dressed these days, simply spending her time on the couch in her pink nightgown and robe, reading books my dad checked out for her at the library. *Silly, but I'll really miss hearing her compliment my cooking.* Her praise had always meant the most to me because she was such a superb cook and had taught me most of what I know. *Another sadness.*

I gave the framed sayings to Cathy, Bobby, Erin and Michael. "I wanted to give you something for Thanksgiving that had a comforting message."

Everyone thanked me. Cathy pressed hers to her chest. "Thank you so much, where did you find this?"

"Well, I found the saying in one of the catalogs I get, so I worked it up on my card program."

"It's lovely."

"I'm glad you like it. I have one for your mom and dad and your brothers and sister too."

"That's really kind of you. I'm sure they'll like them."

I felt a little warmer for having made the gesture.

Cathy reported that the police had informed her that Bill was at his parents' home in Appleton. *At least we don't have to worry about him lurking around Janesville today.*

The meal itself was pretty somber, although everyone ate pretty well. My brother surprised me by having a good appetite. I'd imagined he'd been off his feed for awhile, that usually happened to him during times of stress. Since he was already so lean, I was concerned that he might get himself so thin he'd have no reserve in case of illness. Seeing him take second helpings eased my anxiety on that account a bit.

Since the dining table is in our great room, we had the television on so we could keep track of the NFL game. As the meal wound down everyone was paying less attention to food and conversation and more to the game. Somehow, a player's helmet came off and his face was injured; it looked for certain that at least his nose was broken. There was a close up of the bloody face, and Bobby immediately turned away from the scene, his own face stricken. *It must have reminded him of seeing Jennifer in the morgue.*

I looked at my dad, and could see that he'd picked up on Bobby's reaction too. It was a disturbing sight for anyone, but my brother had been so profoundly affected. *How would he ever, ever get over that? When would we be rid of these sudden unexpected intrusions into our lives? I hate that this happened to us. On this day I am grateful for the good fortune in our lives, but this tragedy is very nearly too much to bear.*

After the meal no one even brought up the idea of the traditional holiday board game. We all sat on couches and chairs and watched the football game or dozed off. It was good to see both Bobby and Cathy close their eyes for a while. After an hour or so, we decided to end our "festivities".

Before leaving, Cathy mentioned that she had been delegated by the family to make a thank you card. It would be sent to all those who had sent flowers to the funeral home or made a donation to Jennifer's scholarship fund. The family wanted something uniquely special. My sister-in-law seemed somewhat overwhelmed with the task, so I volunteered to help her. I'd been making greeting cards, business cards, posters and other projects on my computer for years and was comfortable with the software. She was grateful for my offer and we planned for her to come over the next day about 4:00 p.m.

At the appointed time Cathy arrived and we first rehashed what we knew of the police investigation. There had been search warrants issued and carried out for Bill's apartment, the home in Minocqua, Bill's car and even Bill's person. His car had been impounded and he'd rented one for his transportation requirements. The authorities in Janesville, Minocqua, and Appleton, where Bill's parents lived, were in communication and keeping track of Bill's movements. Lieutenant Danny Davis of the Janesville police had kept in touch with Bobby and Cathy and assured them that the case was progressing, but evidence was still being processed by the state crime lab.

As we went upstairs, Cathy put her cell phone on the banister. "I want to be available if the police call again."

"Of course." We made ourselves comfortable around the computer desk. "Is there anything you have in mind for the card?"

"I'd like to use Jennifer's real-estate photo you scanned for the press. Then I was thinking about some shamrocks and an Irish saying of some kind."

"That sounds excellent. What about that Irish Blessing that talks about the sun on your face and the wind at your back?"

"Do you think that is overused?"

"I think it's used a bit frivolously, but this is exactly the situation for which it should be used. Let me try to find it on the Internet and we'll see."

After a bit of a search I found it. It read:

May the road rise up to meet you,

May the wind be always at your back,

The sun shine warm upon your face,

The rain fall soft upon your fields,

And until we meet again may God

Hold you in the hollow of His hand.

We looked at each other with our eyebrows raised. I offered, "I can't imagine anything more suitable."

Cathy agreed.

I searched for shamrocks on my card program and found some. They were small and rather pale; they would make an excellent background for the blessing.

Jeff had come upstairs to help me with some technical issues with our photo program. As usual, he solved the problem. He remained with us in case I had another problem.

As I was constructing the card, with Jennifer's photo on the front and the shamrocks and blessing inside, Cathy's cell phone rang. She stood up to retrieve it from the banister.

There was silence on her end for a minute or so. I watched her face as she stood by the footstool she had been sitting on. Her forehead was puckered and her eyes darted back and forth as she listened intently. Suddenly she let out an anguished cry and collapsed on her knees. It was almost a faint. She was leaning on the footstool for support while still holding the phone to her ear. I jumped up from the chair and knelt beside her. Jeff stood close by.

She had still not said a word. My mind raced. *My God, what has happened now? Has her father had a heart attack?* The possibility had worried me throughout the visitation and funeral, since Tom had already undergone by-pass surgery. Certainly both he and Mavis had to be stressed beyond normal human limits.

She finally spoke into the phone. Her voice was almost breathless. "We're almost done. I should be home soon."

Cathy hung up the phone and turned to us. Her words came out slowly, one at a time, as if she couldn't believe she was saying them, "Bill admitted to his parents that he killed Jennifer. Then he took some drugs and ran his car into a wall. He's at the Appleton hospital in a coma. He's not expected to survive."

Thank you God.

Cathy was clearly in tremendous anguish. I tried to be of comfort. "I'm not so sure this is bad news. If he does die, it could save the family a lot of grief. There's no guarantee of how a trial would go. This really finalizes things."

She sobbed gently, "I wanted him to be brought to justice for this."

"Maybe this is justice. He'll be answering to the highest court."

Cathy calmed visibly, "I see what you're saying, but I just don't know." We sat silently for a few moments, each lost in thought.

Then we forced our focus back to the card. Within a short while it was complete.

"Thank you so much, it's perfect."

"It was good to be able to help. You know, at least now you know Bill did it for sure. You can stop worrying about that part."

"That's true." She processed for a moment. "I'd better get home and wait for more news with Bobby."

I prayed Bill would die. After having seen how our justice system worked in the O.J. Simpson trial, and regarding a settlement in Josh's accident, I did not have a great deal of faith in it. A successful suicide would provide finality. *Please God let him die.*

On Saturday Bill was still comatose but his vital signs were all fine. There didn't seem to be a compelling physical reason for him to be unresponsive.

By Sunday Bill had regained consciousness and was asking for a private meeting with his family. We were hopeful that he was going to confess to his family and then to the authorities.

But it was not to be. It seemed the old Bill was back. He'd called his mother, father, sister Sallie and brother Jim, Jr. to his beside to plead with them for unconditional support. Of course, that would mean his parents would remain silent about his confession. Bill reminded them of all the things he'd done for them throughout his life. He then insisted that they owed it to him to be there for him now.

According to the police, this further devastated Bill's parents, which was understandable. They'd already told the police of his confession on

Friday after the suicide attempt. If they did as their son requested, they would have to recant their story. Bill's brother and sister were primarily angry that Bill refused to take responsibility for his actions.

What a tortuous position for Bill's parents! First their son commits murder and now he's trying to use guilt to coerce them into lying to the police.

Meanwhile, we all wondered why Bill hadn't yet been arrested. The police advised that there were two reasons for the delay. First, they were still waiting for evidence from the state crime lab and they were making sure all of their evidence was rock solid, including witnesses, phone records, teacher and student interviews and the crime lab results. Second, since Bill was physically unable to leave the hospital, they had time to solidify the case before making the arrest. It made sense.

The arrest was made in the hospital on Tuesday, December 2. The charge was first-degree intentional homicide. Bill was to make his initial court appearance in Rock County on Thursday, December 5. That date would be less than a week since he'd tried to kill himself. *He's made a miraculous recovery.*

Shockingly, we found out that Bill was to be represented by local attorney Tod Daniel. Tod had been our attorney when Josh had his accident. We'd always thought that Tod was an advocate for the unjustly treated. Although, we had been disappointed that he had been unable to secure a settlement for Josh. It hadn't seemed to us as if Tod had been very aggressive in Josh's case, but we had resigned ourselves to the outcome. Still, this seemed beyond our view of Tod's ethical standards.

While I didn't want to see Bill, I felt compelled to watch the evening news to see the arraignment at the Rock County Jail. It seemed so unreal right in my living room. With the jail less than two miles from my house, I had a decidedly sick feeling. Bill had shuffled in, head down, making eye contact with no one. He was wearing an orange jail jumpsuit, with his legs shackled and wrists in handcuffs. It looked as if his hair was thinner than when I'd seem him last. He looked older and rather weak. *Was this an act?* Oddly, he was wearing a pair of rather oversized, outdated aviator style glasses. *He had more modern glasses the last time I saw him. Perhaps they'd been smashed in the suicide attempt or like in Josh's accident, the glasses he'd been wearing simply disappeared.*

The reporter stated that, according to the forensic pathologist, the cause of Jennifer's death was head trauma. One of at least six blows to Jennifer's head created a wound that exposed her brain. *Dear God, I can*

Jennifer's Justice

only hope it was over quickly, but why so many strikes to her head? It sure has the signature of a personal attack.

The story continued. Court Commissioner James VanDeBogart had set a cash bond of $150,000. *That seems shockingly low considering the charges.* District Attorney David O'Leary did not object to that amount, but he did ask that Bill be forbidden from making contact with his family, since they were witnesses in the case. The request was granted. While Tod Daniel was not at the hearing, a substitute attorney had argued for a lower cash bond saying the charge against Bill was an "unsubstantiated allegation based on hearsay." His plea was denied. The date for the preliminary hearing was set for Monday, December 30. The reporter finished his story by explaining that the purpose of the preliminary hearing was to make sure there was enough evidence to bind Bill over for trial. It was a critical step in the quest for justice.

Bill Mereness, accused murderer at his first court appearance (*Courtesy of The Janesville Gazette*)

I was as pleased as I could be given the circumstances. The timing of the preliminary hearing was fortunate for Bobby and me. School would be out for winter break. We would be able to attend without any problems from the district. There were no contingencies for trial attendance in our contract, unless you were the subject of the court proceedings. I had determined that my attendance in court was critical for me to get through this, get over it, and possibly make some sense out of it. I had worried that the district would not allow Bobby and me time off. For now, that crisis was averted.

My brother and I had both worried about the timing of the trial and how in the world we'd be able to attend should it begin before school was out for the summer. While Cathy's employer had already granted her as much leave as she needed, we doubted that would be the case for us.

After the arrest, Bobby and Cathy told us that the family had filed a wrongful death suit against Bill. While it was a civil rather than a criminal charge, such a suit could allow them certain advantages where the properties were concerned. *How fortunate that Michael, as an attorney, knows these things!*

Before the preliminary hearing *The Janesville Gazette* printed a chronology of Bill's life. No one in the Judge family had been aware of some of the incidents included in the article. They were certain that Jennifer had had no knowledge of such facts or she would certainly have broken off her relationship with Bill.

According to police reports, interviews, probation and parole records, Bill had a significant legal history. In January of 1996, Bill committed false swearing by testifying in his divorce hearing that his father had loaned him $15,000. In February 1998, Bill was charged with false imprisonment and battery to a child. He'd dragged his 13-year old son to his car and ripped an earring from Christopher's ear. In April of that same year, Bill jumped bail by not being photographed and fingerprinted as a condition of his bond for the incident regarding Christopher. A few months later, in July, Bill was convicted in Outagamie County Court after pleading guilty to bail jumping, battery and false swearing. He was sentenced to three years probation, 60 days in jail with work-release privileges, $10,458 restitution and 80 hours of community service. *If only she'd known! How well does one person really know another? Should everyone have a background check done on prospective partners? Were we remiss in not looking into Bill's past given the comment Jennifer had made about his ex-wife accusing him of trying to kill her?* I knew I was just trying to find a way to explain all of this, a way tragedy could have been avoided.

I tried to shake these thoughts from my mind and focus on Christmas. There were gifts to buy and wrap, cookies to bake, a house to decorate, cards to be sent. *All this without the tiniest bit of joy. Yet somehow we must go on. I wonder how?*

Though we celebrated in the usual way, the holiday had a hollow feel. Everyone went through all the motions, but we'd been changed. *Will we ever recapture the way we were?* I feared not.

9

December 30th finally arrived. I'd never been in a courtroom in my life. I didn't know what to expect. I'd watched a lot of *Perry Mason*, *Murder She Wrote* and *Matlock* so I had some idea what courtrooms were like, but that was the extent of my experience. Fortunately, Josh was going to attend since he was still on winter break from UW- Whitewater, but Jeff had declined. Even though I would have liked for him to be there for support, I had learned that it's important to let each person cope with tragedy in his or her own way. After Josh's accident Jeff had been anxious to get back to work, while I couldn't imagine it. It's hard to compromise in such instances, but we muddled through the best we could. Hopefully, we'd do the same this time.

Jennifer's immediate family was to have a meeting before the hearing with the victim-witness liaison, so Josh and I went up the elevator to find Courtroom D. In the large hallway, District Attorney David O'Leary was talking in a tightly knotted group of professionally dressed men. Then I noticed a young man about Josh's age sitting on a bench against the wall. He looked out of place because he was wearing a plaid flannel shirt and blue jeans. His face was scrubbed shiny and his hair was still wet from being forced into place. *He probably usually wears a ball cap.* He looked rather uncomfortable, a frown across his brow, eyes darting about. Quick judgement had it that he was polished up for a court appearance. Since he struck me as a rather upstanding young person, I hoped he was not in too much trouble.

The courtroom was modern looking, with light woodwork and off-white walls. The public was divided from the court officials by a low wood-spindled railing, which Michael told me was called "the bar". There was a gate in the bar through which reporters and official-looking people passed.

The reporters were setting up still cameras and video cameras on tri-pods in the jury box, which was on the left. They chatted amongst themselves as if they were comfortable in their own society. In front of the bar were two separate tables, which would accommodate the prosecution and the defense. On the far wall the high judge's bench was flanked on one side by the witness stand, and on the other by a low desk area. I imagined that was where the court reporter would sit. On our side of the rail the public could sit in any of ten wooden pews, five on each side of the aisle leading to the entry door. I knew it was important that we not be seated on the side for the defense, so I asked someone which table was which. We then settled ourselves in the second row behind the prosecution's table, which was on the left. I felt that Jennifer's immediate family should have the front row for themselves, and when they arrived they were ushered there by the victim-witness liaison, Shelly. We chatted desultorily while waiting for the proceedings to begin.

The pivotal players began to enter the courtroom. Tod Daniel and the DA entered through the gate in the bar and took up their positions. Bill, in an orange jumpsuit with handcuffs and leg shackles entered from a side door. He was accompanied by a Rock County deputy. We members of the family collectively drew in our breath. His eyes were first focused on the floor while he shuffled in. After he was seated and spoke with his attorney his eyes focused straight ahead. He never looked around the courtroom. For that I was grateful. I absolutely did not wish to have eye contact with him! I'm sure the rest of the family felt exactly the same way.

Finally, Judge James Daley entered the courtroom. His presence was announced by the bailiff and we rose upon command. We sat down again after the judge took his chair behind the bench. Judge Daley was a middle-aged, average-sized man with brown hair. His face was smooth and a bit flushed. His manner gave the impression of short-temperedness, that he would truck no nonsense in his court.

The judge directed the district attorney to call his first witness. Our DA was approaching middle age, gray hair fighting out the blond at his temples. The tall, lanky man rose, buttoned one button on his suit coat and called for Officer Glen Hageman.

Officer Hageman, a very young man of average build, took the stand. He stated that on the night of November 22, 2002, he had been directed to 4219 Sandstone Drive. When he arrived at Jennifer's house there was a man standing in the doorway of the garage. The officer reported that he had been at that residence before. *Yes, when Jennifer reported the furnace incident and told this man she suspected Bill.*

When Hageman entered the home, he found a female lying on the floor in the foyer. He was unable to identify her because she was facedown in a large pool of blood. Again, I could feel I was part of a collective breath draw. The officer did not call for help because he knew the fire department would already be en route as was standard in our community after a 911 call.

Two weapons were found near Jennifer's head: a wooden-handled hatchet and a yellow-handled sledgehammer. Another intake of air. *Why was all this having such a shocking effect upon us? We'd heard it all before. Somehow hearing it related by the police officer himself was like hearing it again for the first time.*

At that point Officer Hageman believed he would need assistance, so he stepped out of the house and waited for another officer to arrive.

Soon Officer Rau arrived on the scene. The two swept the residence. In the basement they found a broken window screen and glass on the floor from the egress window. There was also a large rock on the floor.

The district attorney thanked Officer Hageman for his testimony and turned him over to the defense attorney.

Tod Daniel was aggressive in his cross-examination. He seemed to belittle the witness by making him admit he'd been with the Janesville Police Department for less than three years. Daniel was disbelieving when Hageman said he had not prepared for his testimony today in any way. He'd not reread his report of November 22 nor had he met with the DA. The police officer explained that it was not standard procedure to prepare for a preliminary hearing.

The defense attorney next addressed the call from dispatch on the night of November 22. Hageman testified that the call had come on his lap top not on the radio. Both he and Rau responded to the report of a "pulseless non-breather" bleeding from the head who had been struck by a hatchet. *So that's how our Jennifer was described. Dear Lord.*

Daniel was concerned about emergency equipment and vehicles on the premises. The witness calmly explained that there was a Ford Taurus in the garage and an SUV of some kind in the driveway. He had not determined to whom the SUV belonged. *Another implication that this officer was inept. Is this the strategy the defense will employ?*

Officer Hageman then explained that there was a male subject in the doorway of the garage who was on the phone to 911. The police officer instructed the man to stay on the phone.

The witness could not recall if the lights in the house were on. He thought that perhaps the kitchen lights were on. The foyer, sized approximately six by eight feet, housed a table with a lamp and some pottery. The table seemed to be askew but nothing had been tipped over or broken. The floor of the foyer was of tile and he did not believe the foyer had a closet. *Whew, this witness' memory is being severely tested. Hopefully he'll be able to maintain his composure.*

According to Hageman, Officer Rau arrived within three to five minutes. The body was facedown with the feet toward the exterior door and the head toward the living room. It was laid out flat and full-length.

The witness reported that the exterior door was closed; but then he admitted he had not checked to see if it was locked. *Another misstep ferreted out. Daniel had done his homework.*

The unidentified male had told the officer that he'd gotten into the house through the garage; but he had to agree with Daniel, that if the front door hadn't been locked, it was possible he could have entered in that way.

Hageman reiterated that he and Rau secured the interior to see if anyone was in there.

The defense attorney wanted to know if the firemen had contact with the body. They had not. *It had been obvious that she was beyond assistance.*

The witness then explained that there was blood on the east foyer wall some six feet off the floor, some less than a foot above the floor. The blood was close toward the door and the victim's feet. More blood was found on the outside of the front door about six feet up and on the exterior siding of the front porch. *This is what our school police officer had been talking about. God, it must have been a horrific scene.*

Officer Hageman next reported that he had not touched the wooden-handled hatchet that was propped up on its blade against the victim's head. There was blood on the entire blade and the handle. The maul had blood on the handle and it was sitting in the pool of blood surrounding the victim.

The witness testified that he had exited the house the same way he'd gone in, through the garage.

The officer's response to Daniel's next question showed he was growing perturbed with these attempts to make him look unreliable. When Daniel queried as to which part of the house the officer secured, Hageman shot back testily, "All of it".

Daniel pressed on, just how had the search been conducted? Officer Rau had been with Hageman and they had separated for part of the search. *So Hageman, himself, did not search the entire house as he'd said. He'd fallen into the web spun by the defense attorney.*

Daniel next inquired as to whether the house had been in disarray, ransacked or burgled. The witness said there was no evidence of such in the kitchen, laundry room, east bedroom or bathroom. The west bedroom was either ransacked or "made to look like that".

Mr. Daniel wished for more detail. The bed was messed up, dresser drawers had been pulled out and there were clothes on the floor. *Oh,* now he's going for the angle that it was a robbery! All stops were being pulled out to create doubt that Bill had been the perpetrator of this heinous crime.

The officer hadn't checked the bedroom closet, but the attached bath appeared normal. He did not believe anyone checked the crawl space above the ransacked bedroom. *No doubt the burglar/murderer was hiding there the whole time and the bumbling cops had missed him.*

The basement was next described in full. It was accessible from the foyer and was unfinished. Therefore, the entire room was visible from the bottom of the stairs. The egress window had a pit outside of it. A rock the size of a basketball was seen. More broken glass was inside the basement than outside. *That would indicate the rock was thrown into the house allowing the perpetrator access.*

Finally, Officer Hageman completed his testimony by explaining that after they'd swept the house he'd canvassed the neighborhood and brought in the crime lab technicians.

Overall this witness was an asset for the prosecution. He'd been quite thorough in his work and despite not reviewing his report his memory was excellent. Although nothing he'd said directed suspicion at Bill, except perhaps the personal nature of the attack.

Next, District Attorney David O'Leary introduced evidence from The Wisconsin State Crime Lab. It had been documented that shards of glass found on the floor of the driver's side of Bill's car were consistent with the glass from the broken window in Jennifer's house. Mr. Daniel had no comments or questions about the report.

The DA called for Nicholas Demrow. I nearly dropped my teeth when in walked the young man I'd seen on the bench outside the courtroom. It hadn't occurred to me that he had been called to court for this case. He looked so young and clean-cut. *What could he possibly know about this murder? Poor kid.*

Nick testified that he was a construction worker, a rough framer. His date of birth indicated he was twenty years old. On November 22 he'd been working on Sandstone Drive, which is a dead-end street. *What an appropriate, yet grizzly term.*

The street had two completed houses and one under construction. All three were on the same side of the street. Nick had been working on that particular house, next door to Jennifer's, for about a week and a half and he'd become familiar with a lady who came and went from the house. *A lady. Hmm. I guess to such a young man, Jennifer, at 39, was just that.*

On the 22nd of November the witness had arrived for work at 7:00 a.m. He did not observe anyone leave the house. He did observe "the lady" returning home. While he couldn't describe this woman, he was sure it was the same lady. It had been around 11:20 a.m. to 11:40 a.m. Nick was eating lunch in his truck, which was facing Jennifer's house. He'd had his truck running to provide heat. The lady drove into the garage in her four-door green car. He did not see her get out of her car because she closed the garage door behind her.

Next, according to Nick Demrow, his co-worker Jeff appeared at Nick's truck window. Jeff wanted to know if Nick had heard that lady scream. He hadn't. The witness then clarified that about one minute had passed from the time the woman entered her garage until Jeff appeared at his truck.

A short while later the witness saw a man leave the back of the house. Nick said he could not describe the individual, but then reported that he was wearing a dark, Columbia-style coat and gray sweatpants. He was carrying two bags, one a portfolio type and the other plastic. The man wore glasses, had dark hair, was a white man between the ages of 35 and 55, and wore white gloves.

The man then walked across the street and turned left. The witness, driving his truck, started to follow the man. Nick drove around the block then returned to the construction site. Then he and Jeff went to look for the man but they could not find him.

Nick Demrow worked until 4:00 p.m. but did not see anyone else come or go from Jennifer's house.

Under cross-examination, the defense attorney wanted to know if and when Demrow had spoken to the police. He had once, the night of the murder.

Again Daniel wanted to know if the witness had reviewed his statement before his testimony. Demrow indicated he had revisited the police a few weeks after the murder. *Aha! Here was a witness who had been coached by the police!*

At that point the district attorney interrupted. He clarified that the second visit with the police was to sign his original statement. *Not to attend a coaching session.*

Next, Mr. Daniel asked a series of statements and questions I thought were designed to discredit Nick Demrow. He put forth that the witness hadn't actually seen the woman in her car when she approached the house. He couldn't see the back of the house from his truck at lunch, and therefore, couldn't honestly say the man came from inside the house. Further, he didn't hear the woman scream. The construction worker could not deny any of it. Nick tried to control the damage by explaining that his truck was loud when running, so he wouldn't have been able to hear much.

The witness was dismissed.

This testimony certainly clarifies the time of the murder. The description of the mystery man did not rule Bill out, but was far from a positive ID.

David O'Leary explained to the judge that he had only one more witness to call because his fourth witness was unable to make it to court due to illness.

The district attorney called James H. Mereness to the stand. Bill's father hobbled, shoulders hunched, ever so slowly to the witness chair. It was as if he were going to his own execution. With his minute amounts of white hair and extremely pale skin he looked about ninety years old. *What has Bill done to his poor father? He looks to be a completely broken man.*

The first thing Mr. Mereness did was apologize to Judge Daley because he wasn't feeling well, he'd been ill. He also explained that his wife was critically ill and that he didn't think she was going to make it. *How sad for this poor man. He looks like he's on death's doorstep himself.*

When asked to identify his son, the senior Mereness pointed at Bill. It was an emotional moment for all in attendance.

Before answering the DA's next question, Bill's father asked O'Leary if he could please speak up, as he was having trouble hearing due to his illness. The district attorney cleared his throat and then asked the question again. Mr. Mereness explained that he'd found out about Jennifer's death on Sunday, November 25. His other son, Jim, had called him with the news in the morning. *And Bill's dad had called Michael Judge that evening, inquiring if he and LaBelle could attend Jennifer's services. He'd also said at that time that Bill had done something terrible. He must already have known that Bill was guilty since Bill hadn't even informed his own parents of his wife's brutal murder.*

The witness then explained that Bill was at his house on Friday, November 29. He had found him in the bathroom at 8:00 a.m. with a knife and plastic wrap. He was sitting in the bathtub and LaBelle was speaking with him. After he heard Bill utter, "I did it"; his father interrupted him and said he didn't want to hear anymore because he didn't want to have to testify against him. The elder Mereness went to the kitchen. Bill joined him there later. The father and son discussed possible ways that the situation could be handled. The father suggested three options: give himself up, go to trial, take his life.

After that conversation Bill went to his room to lie down. About 9:30 a.m. Bill told his parents he was taking his rental car back to Janesville.

The DA had one more question for Mr. Mereness. Had his son mentioned anything about not wanting to go to prison? He had.

On cross-examination, it appeared that the defense attorney tried to make Mr. Mereness look old and doddering. The questions were asked quietly and the witness had to keep asking for them to be restated. Did he really remember the scene in the bathroom? Bill hadn't really said those words to him, had he? He'd said them to his wife. Who had asked the question about guilt? Not him, but his wife. Bill hadn't really been talking to his father, he was merely a bystander.

Next, Daniel reviewed the encounter in the kitchen, when Mr. Mereness had mentioned the options to Bill. Then, the defense put forth, Bill left the house and crashed his car into a wall. Daniel drew more information from the witness. Bill had not been acting like himself during the Thanksgiving Holiday. He didn't eat much, though he did come to the table. Bill had arrived at his parents' house later on the Sunday they'd found out about Jennifer's death. The Janesville Police had come to their home to interview Bill about Jennifer. The family had read the articles in *The Janesville Gazette*, though they did not accept all of what they read as the truth. While his father couldn't say that Bill expressed being upset about Jennifer's death, he had come and gone from the house several times, he hadn't eaten much and he'd kept to himself. *Where was Tod going with all of this? The old man was doddering and old, therefore unreliable? The admission of guilt to his mother was hearsay? Bill's father had actually driven him to attempt suicide because no one believed in his innocence?*

Finally, the DA explained his last witness was unable to testify because she'd suffered from blood poisoning. He then asked for a continuance so that the witness could recover and testify. There was also some discussion about traveling to Appleton to videotape Mrs. Mereness' testimony. The parties would discuss the matter further.

Tod Daniel then requested that his client be allowed to wear civilian clothes at his next court appearance.

Judge Daley granted a continuance until Monday, January 13th at 1:00 p.m. at which time Bill could wear his own clothing.

Oh, no, that's a school day! The district might not allow us to have time off to attend court. I need to be here!

The defendant's father testifies at the preliminary hearing
(*Courtesy of The Janesville Gazette*)

I knew my contract well since I'd been on the last two bargaining teams. Bobby and I had two possibilities. We had one personal day granted per semester. I had not yet used mine, nor had my brother. However, there was a caveat to the use of those days. At the middle and high school level only two teachers per building could be granted a personal day during the last few weeks of the semester. There had been problems with too many teachers taking off at he end of the semesters and substitutes had been hard to find. Consequently, the teacher group had agreed to these end-of-semester limitations. However, I did know that there was also a contingency for "Emergency Use of Personal Days" in our contract. I was hopeful that both of us would be able to attend the hearing given these possibilities.

To that end, I immediately called my principal, Mike Kuehne, at home. Mike said we should meet early on Wednesday, our first day back, to look things over.

Jeff and I rang in the New Year unceremoniously, no toasts, no celebration. The continuation of the preliminary hearing hung over my head like a scepter. *What if Bobby or I were not given permission to attend? What if Bill wasn't bound over for trial? What would Jennifer's family do? It would be very hard not to take matters into their own hands. Remember John Grisham's 'A Time to Kill'?* We watched a movie and went to bed before Dick Clark presided over the dropping of the ball in Times Square.

On the day school resumed, I went in before the students arrived so I could meet with my principal. According to his records, two people had already requested the day for personal leave. Mike went beyond the call of duty and asked each of the individuals if they could change their plans. Neither could. Mike was going to call "downtown" and inquire about the emergency use of my personal leave day. Meanwhile, during my preparation period, I called Bobby and found out he was fine. There was a day available at his school, so he could attend without problem. *Thank goodness. At least he would not have to wait and wonder.*

It was afternoon when Mike came up and apologetically informed me that our Human Resources Director, Steve Johnson, had denied my request for emergency personal leave. He related that Johnson had said broken water pipes were more in the realm of a reason for emergency personal leave. He also did not wish to set a precedent. *Dear God, broken pipes versus a murder in the family? How is that even comparable? How can anyone be so cruel and cold-hearted? This could set a precedent? Hordes of teachers would be requesting emergency leave for preliminary hearings for those accused of murdering their family members? If there were a sudden plethora of murders, I would hope our district would honor such requests! Or, is this a way to get back at me for my past role as union president and negotiator? This feels personal.*

I got through the rest of the day teaching, but was determined that I would attend the preliminary hearing even if it meant calling in sick and risking disciplinary action. If I was docked pay I would go to the newspaper and bring to light how inhumane our district could be to those teachers in crisis.

I called Jeff at work to warn him of my plan. He couldn't believe the decision either and was supportive of whatever I felt I had to do. I was grateful for his understanding.

Then something popped into my head. I remembered Superintendent Tom Evert's words before the funeral; "Just let me know if there is anything I can do to be of help to the family." *Okay, I'll take him up on that offer.*

I called Evert's office, but he was not available. I left a voice mail about the situation and said that it was urgent that I speak with him as soon as possible. I left him my home and cell phone numbers.

I took my cell out to the barn with me as I did my chores. *Am I more angry or hurt? It sure is dehumanizing.* As usual, it affected me in the gut. I had a nasty stomachache. Fortunately, just being with my animals and providing them with food eased my stress a little.

The ring of the cell phone cut into the quiet atmosphere in the barn. It was the superintendent. He had spoken with Steve Johnson and determined that the three of us should meet in his office the following morning at 7:00. At that meeting, he believed, we would clear the matter up. His manner was business like but not unkind. I held out some hope that this would be resolved without drastic action on my account.

At the early morning meeting I did get a little teary. I explained that after all we'd just been through, to be treated in this manner was really inhumane. Even if I was allowed the day, more damage had been done to an already delicate emotional situation. I said I had hoped that my employer would be a lot more supportive than I'd just experienced. I was concerned for the future and for my brother. We would have no control over what the courts did, and I wanted to think that the district would work with us, rather than against us on this.

In his bland monotone Steve Johnson stated that he was simply "going by the contract" and there was nothing he could do about it. *Bullshit. If this were happening to your wife or a teacher friend of yours this would have been a done deal.*

Finally, Tom Evert suggested that I contact my union president or teachers' rights chairperson. Steve Johnson insisted that that was what had been done in the past in such cases. I was mad enough to argue. My union leadership went back a decade and I had never heard of such a thing. Johnson said, nevertheless, the protocol was that if the president or teachers' rights chair would ask for the emergency day on my behalf, then it might be granted. *I get it. He is just trying to save face. Evert had given him a chance to get out of this gracefully and he was counting on me being so grateful that I wouldn't even question the process. Well, someone once told me that I would clutch my principles to the grave, and I had concurred.*

I agreed that I would follow this "protocol" even though I was registering a protest as to how this situation had been handled. Evert reassured me that he was confident that this would work out. I countered that while that would be good; it would not erase the additional grief caused to my family and me.

I went to school and talked with Colleen, our teachers' rights chair, and she was also dumbfounded by the claim that this was the protocol. However, she played along, made the call and within an hour brought me an e-mail that assured me the day was mine. *Relief and resentment. What kind of people am I working for? How long will it take me to get over this insult? They threw the drowning man a brick, then when he was about half dead, tossed out the lifesaver. Then they expected him to be eternally grateful.*

My goal for the present was to try to push aside these immediate negative feelings and get on with the business at hand. I would attend the preliminary hearing, support my brother and his family, discharge my duties as a teacher, care for my animals and endeavor to be a good wife, mother and daughter. All that would be a sufficient drain on my energy; I could not afford to waste any on bitterness, though I was nearly choking on it.

10

On the evening of Thursday, January 3, 2003, we received news that Bill's mother, LaBelle, had died. I was overrun with emotion. I was sure that Bill's actions had caused her death just as if he had hit her with the axe and sledgehammer too. It was so sad that the poor woman had died and the Mereness family had lost their matriarch. But we had lost a key witness in the case against Bill! I was terrified he would get away with this heinous crime. While LaBelle had spoken to the police about Bill's actions, she had never given sworn statements nor testified under oath. *How would this affect the prosecution? Since Daniel had tried to imply at the preliminary hearing that Bill's father was merely a bystander during the conversation between Bill and his mother, would he now try to prove that his testimony was only hearsay? That's all it might be with the police as well. Dear God what will happen?*

District Attorney David O'Leary indicated that he would continue ahead with the prosecution at the resumption of the preliminary hearing on January 13. *But will he be successful?*

The prosecutor also said that in normal cases, suspects in custody had been allowed to attend relatives' funerals. Possible arrangements for Bill would be discussed with the defense attorney and the Rock County Sheriff. O'Leary made it clear that should Bill attend the funeral he would be in custody with security.

Bill declined to attend his own mother's funeral. I wondered about his rationale. It was doubtful that he was trying to save his family from additional pain. Was he angry with them because they hadn't helped him? Was he worried about being seen in public while in custody? It would seem to his advantage to be seen as a grieving son. Yet, perhaps none of that mattered, as it would have no bearing upon the trial.

For a brief time I wondered if it would be appropriate that someone in the Judge family attend LaBelle's funeral. I didn't think it was my place to ask, so I tried to let it go. *More sadness and pain.*

The ensuing days passed by in a surreal fashion. I went through the motions of teaching, chores, and life in general, but nothing seemed to have meaning. I felt like I had after Josh's accident, as if my heart had been turned to stone.

Of particular difficulty was my students' annual tour of Craig High School. It brought back specific memories of happier times when I'd visited with Jennifer briefly in her classroom. We went by her room, but I did not know the teacher in it. There would be no friendly repartee.

As my group rounded a corner near the auditorium, I came face to face with a bulletin board with Jennifer's picture prominently displayed in the center. The entire board was dedicated to Jennifer and was full of papers on which students had written eulogies for their popular teacher. There were also silk flowers attached to the board, making it a lovely shrine to her memory.

It is so sad that these young people have had to go through this. I'd had a favorite high school teacher die after a freak accident and that was sad enough. To know Jennifer was murdered had to be especially hard on the students.

On January 13 we were directed to Courtroom B. This time Bill appeared to be healthier. He was wearing street clothes, so he looked less the prisoner except for the leg shackles. He had on black pants and a white shirt with thin green stripes. He looked like a million other men going to work dressed in "business casual".

This time the proceedings were governed by Court Commissioner Murray. I didn't know why there was no judge present, but assumed someone knew what he or she was doing.

The District Attorney wanted to enter Bill's photo at intake into the court record. Mr. Daniel objected. The photo was allowed after O'Leary argued that it showed Bill's clothing and that he was wearing a Columbia-style coat.

Next the DA announced that since his final witness, LaBelle Mereness, had passed away, he would call no further witnesses.

Defense attorney Daniel argued that The State had not established probable cause.

Court Commissioner Murray stated that he believed Mr. Mereness had probably committed this felony and that he would be bound over for trial. *Thank God.* Relief washed over me.

It was brief. District Attorney O'Leary spoke, "I believe Mr. Daniel has a motion." *What now?*

The defense asked for a motion hearing in front of the judge. One was scheduled for Friday, January 17 at 11:30 a.m. It was likely that at that time Daniel would ask for a dismissal of the charges against his client.

While I was quite anxious about that, the Judge family was not. Michael seemed confident that it was just part of Tod's job as a defense attorney.

At least the date was fortunate because our district had an end of semester break day scheduled. My brother and I would be free to attend court. *Thank God I won't have another go-round with the administration over this!*

The motion hearing on Friday had begun prior to 11:30. When I arrived, District Attorney O'Leary was reading from the transcript of Bill's father's testimony. Judge John. P. Daly was presiding. I glanced quickly at the defendant. He wore the same outfit he'd had on Monday; his legs were still shackled.

Judge Daley asked Mr. O'Leary if he had any other evidence. He had. The state crime lab had determined the glass in Jennifer's egress window was consistent with the shards found in Bill's car. The DA reminded the judge that the police had determined the murderer had entered Jennifer's house through that window.

It was the defense's turn. Daniel told the court that the evidentiary rules for a preliminary hearing relied upon probable cause, which was based upon facts. Reasonable inference equaled reasonable probability that was supported by admissible evidence; and, hearsay was not admissible. The senior Mereness' testimony was hearsay.

The defense attorney continued with his supposition. Since the testimony of Bill's father was not admissible there was no credible connection of Bill to the crime. There was no probability that it was Bill who committed the crime. There was nothing in the testimony of Officer Hageman to connect Bill to the crime.

Judge Daley interrupted. Officer Hageman's statements established death.

Daniel disagreed. Hageman described where the body was found, in a six by eight foyer. It also proved that the body was found face down with the feet to the door. The officer also explained that the injuries were on the back of the victim's head.

The judge halted the defense attorney again. Hageman had not testified to the injuries.

Mr. Daniel checked his records, agreed with Judge Daley, but continued with his theory. The door opened onto the east wall of the foyer and the body was going away from the front door. There was no disarray; the only object in the foyer was a table.

One more interruption from the judge. *This was becoming an argument between these two men.* Judge Daley reminded Daniel that the table was "kitty-wampus".

The ball bounced back to the defense. There was blood outside of the house and Mr. Demrow could see the front door during his lunch break. *Is he implying that Demrow would have seen the perpetrator if the murder had occurred during that time?*

Demrow had been roughing in the interior of the house to the east. Sitting in front of the Mereness home, he saw a car come down the street and turn into the home, but he did not see the driver. A scream directed his attention to the house. He gave a description of a man that did not fit Mr. Mereness. Mr. Mereness was not six feet tall, nor did he weigh 180 pounds. When Mr. Demrow was asked if he could identify Mr. Bill Mereness in court he could not.

Judge Daley's face had flushed. His voice held just a hint of irritation. Mr. Demrow didn't identify *anyone*.

Daniel continued unabated. The police didn't have the time of death. There was blood outside the house, as if the homicide took place inside with the front door open. There was no blood trail. The senior Mereness' testimony was hearsay. He heard an answer without asking a question. Bill's mom had asked the question and so that was hearsay as well. The crime lab report did not connect the defendant to the crime. The microscopic shard of glass from the driver's seat and from the driver's floor could have come from this house. It could have come from anywhere. The crime lab report did not even say that the glass shards were "consistent with" the window glass. The glass did not connect Bill with the crime.

The DA finally hindered Daniel's discourse. O'Leary claimed that the defense attorney was trying to argue as if this were a trial. He was trying to discredit the witnesses. At a preliminary hearing reasonable inference was allowed. Further, the statements of Bill's father were admissible and would be at trial. So would the question asked by Mrs. Mereness, according to State Statute 90801. The DA then cited another case that explained there were exceptions to the hearsay rule and these statements would be allowed.

Daniel interjected that he was not pushing for a ruling on the hearsay evidence.

Daley's face flushed deeply. He cut in. Mr. Daniel would get a ruling since the judge had read the transcript.

The District Attorney reclaimed the floor. The evidence given in the preliminary hearing had given a plausible description of how the murder could have taken place. It was only his responsibility to show probable cause, not go beyond reasonable doubt. The description of the suspect included that he was a white male, middle-aged and had dark hair. That was consistent with Bill.

The defense attorney interrupted. That description would fit three-fourths of the people in the courtroom. There had been no statement of guilt by his client. There was merely an inference. Without the question there was nothing in the record to support it. The conversation at the kitchen table was about three options Bill had in any case. He had been followed around by authorities and read about police suspicions in the newspaper for a week. His fear of prison was not unusual.

Judge Daley had had enough. He was ready to make a ruling. He'd reviewed the transcript and agreed with Daniel that the connection to Bill was very thin.

I nearly fell out of the pew. *Thin? His own father testified that Bill admitted he'd killed Jennifer. It didn't get much 'thicker' than that!*

The judge continued. The State had intended to call another witness. The evidence from the crime lab indicated the glass could have been from Jennifer's window. It did not provide probable cause.

Dear God, he's going to let him go!

However, Daley added, when he connected in the statements of the senior Mereness about conversations while Bill was in the bathtub and in the kitchen…the judge interrupted himself. The question was the predicate to the answer. This was not the intent of the hearsay rule. There were guarantees of trustworthiness because it was a mother and father talking with their son.

The judge had to admit the connection was thin. The glass could have been a match and with the statement of the accused to his parents he was going to deny the motion to dismiss the charges.

Thank God! I wanted to stand up and cheer. But we weren't done yet.

Daniel wanted his client's bond to be reduced. He did not have $150,000 in assets. At the time of his arrest Bill was a resident of Janesville, his son was living with him, he had a job with Wal-Mart and owned real estate. The strength of The State's case made it highly "tryable". His client had been on probation before for an incident with his son and for falsifying documents. He was released from probation and had no other record. He'd been under incredible surveillance and pressure from the police yet had not bolted. *No he tried to avoid prosecution by killing himself!* Bill had assets, a joint property in Minocqua. Even his guilt would not prevent his getting one half the property. The wrongful death suit should not affect this. The defense attorney wanted the judge to amend the bond so that Bill could put up his amount of property as collateral. With his client in jail it was harder to get things done for the defense. It hobbled his attempts to prepare.

The DA opposed a reduction in bond. The State wanted $250,000 because the defendant had real estate, a work history and assets. O'Leary also requested there be no contact with the defendant's family. They were concerned about contact with Bill and feared retribution.

The defense attorney felt that a look at the preliminary hearing didn't support bond.

Judge Daley thought that since the defendant was facing significant punishment there was a risk of flight. As to the amount of bond, he was modifying it to $125,000 cash or property if the county believed that was appropriate. His aim was to be sure the defendant made it to trial. Further, there was to be no contact with the family of the deceased, directly or indirectly.

District Attorney O'Leary requested Bill also have no contact with his father, brother or sister.

The Judge agreed. The bond and its conditions were set. Court was recessed at 12:15 p.m.

Once outside the courtroom Jennifer's family caucused. We turned to Michael Judge, the attorney, for his interpretation. It had been a victory. Bill would be bound over for trial and the bond was significant enough to keep Bill in jail until that time.

Since it was so cold out, as soon as we reached the parking lot we hugged one another, said our good byes and hurried to our vehicles.

It had been a victory, so why did it feel so hollow? I had anticipated this decision would make me feel better, but it didn't really. I had been quite taken aback by the lack of decorum in the courtroom. My experience was based on television, movies and books, but I'd never imagined the defense would be allowed to argue back and forth with the judge. It made me very nervous about upcoming proceedings. Also, the fact that Judge Daley had found the prosecution's case to be thin was utterly shocking. Given that, I desperately hoped The State would have a lot more evidence to bring to the trial. *Bill simply must be found guilty. That's the only outcome that could possibly provide closure for this family. They need that and deserve it.*

11

Life went on. The cold of winter had settled in and it was the long stretch of the school year between winter and spring break. It was hard to be motivating for my students when I felt so low myself. But it wasn't their fault this had happened. I owed them my best teaching, so I plowed on.

Every day when I went to and from school on Highway 14, I drove past the Rock County Jail where Bill was in residence. I thought of him each time I went by. Frequently I was tempted to stop and visit him. I fantasized that I would sit down across the table from him, look him in the eye and ask him why he did it. Then he would break down, apologize and tell me why. But I never stopped.

I did wonder how he spent his days of incarceration. It certainly wouldn't be easy for a person with Bill's controlling nature to have his every minute scheduled and supervised. The thought made me feel a small measure of justice had already occurred.

The trial was tentatively set to begin on Monday, August 11, 2003. It seemed a long time to wait. It would be eight months of waiting and wondering, we'd be in some kind of purgatory. I supposed the prosecution needed the time to build a solid case, and the defense would attempt to do likewise. The idea of a "speedy trial" did not seem like it should drag on for so long.

On Thursday January 23, Bill's attorney filed a pre-trial appeal with the Fourth District Court of Appeals. The appeal requested the bind-over for trial be dismissed. The appellate court had discretion on whether or not to even take the appeal. In *The Janesville Gazette*, DA David O'Leary was quoted, "Usually the court likes to look at when the trial has been concluded." It didn't seem as if he was worried.

A related article in the *Wisconsin State Journal* stated that Daniel had also filed a motion asking that the wrongful death civil suit be dismissed. He was also challenging the probate case in which Michael and Cathy had been appointed as administrators of Jennifer's estate. Since Jennifer did not have a will, state statutes require that, unless there are extraordinary circumstances, it would be customary for her husband to handle the estate. *Of all the unmitigated gall! I guess being arrested for murder isn't enough of an 'extraordinary circumstance' for Bill or his attorney. I hope all of this is just Tod going through these steps so it looks like he's earning his money. Oh well, they're just a few more things to be anxious about.*

Late in January, Bobby and Cathy went up to Jennifer's home in Minocqua. Cathy had never been there before. *Another example of how Bill tried to estrange Jennifer from her family.* Cathy loved the place. She talked about how the family was going to keep it in Jennifer's memory and name it for her. It was obvious to Cathy that her sister had worked very hard to decorate the cabin and make it look just right. After viewing the photos Cathy'd taken I couldn't have agreed more. It was beautiful. It looked just like the homes I'd seen in the pages of log home magazines. The expression "to die for" came to my mind. I'd never liked using terms about dying in a casual way, now I was extra sensitive.

Lake view of the cabin on Pier Lake Road in Minocqua, Wisconsin

One evening when we met for dinner, Cathy asked Jeff and me if we would be willing to go up to the cabin with her and my brother. They were thinking about the weekend in late February when our schools had a break day.

Bobby entered the conversation, "There are some trees and other brush that need to be cleared. Jeff, I'm hoping you can bring your chainsaw and be the lead on this."

What could we say? We'd already talked about our roles as supporters throughout this nightmare, so we looked at each other briefly, then agreed to help.

When we were alone at home, I confided to Jeff that I was not looking forward to staying in a place Bill had lived. Particularly, the place he'd gone after he'd killed Jennifer. The idea didn't bother Jeff, but it really gave me the creeps. I would, of course, go through with it for Bobby and Cathy and the entire Judge family. Since it was one of the few things I could do to be of help, I'd have to deal with my emotions somehow.

As the time grew nearer, and I was becoming quite anxious about the trip, news came about the civil suit and the disposition of Jennifer's estate. Judge Welker, who was handling that case, had made it clear that the Judge family was not to go into the properties, nor do anything to them until the situation was more settled.

So our trip to the cabin was cancelled. I felt a great relief, but then guilt for feeling so selfish.

The days dragged along. I continued to go through the motions of living. I fulfilled my duties at home and at school, but felt no real joy. I'd always been a person who tried to find joy in every day, but this was too much. Sometimes, in an effort to be supportive people would say to me, "God never gives you more than you can handle."

I wanted to scream and challenge them, "Just how much have you had to handle? Has your son been in a horrific car accident? Has your mother suffered a lifetime of depression and attempted suicide twice? Does your dad have cancer? Has someone you've known and loved for thirty years been murdered by someone you've shared holidays with? Why does God think I can handle all of this." Instead I would say, "I hope God's looking because I'm waving a big white flag."

In late February, Judge James Daley granted the prosecution's request for a videotaped deposition of James Mereness, Sr. Bill's father had recently suffered from convulsions while in the hospital visiting his son, James, Jr. The younger James had been badly injured in a car accident. *This is Bill's fault too. His brother is under so much stress and tension he's probably distracted all the time. However the accident came about, I'm sure James didn't react as he would have if Bill hadn't committed this heinous crime.*

Judge Daley was quoted in *The Janesville Gazette*, "We know what happened to Mrs. Mereness, and I'm concerned that we'll lose this witness also, based on age and, from what I recall from his testimony at the preliminary hearing, his mental outlook."

At the same time defense attorney Daniel told the judge he planned to again request that his client's bond be reviewed. *Not that again. He is just trying so hard to get Bill out on bail. How can this be happening?* I tried to remember that Michael Judge had explained to me that the court had to see that the bond was reasonable, but Michael was confident they would always keep it out of reach. *So why on "Law and Order" did they always get a million dollars bond for a capital murder case? This is not something the victim's family should have to worry about. Bill was a dangerous man, and he could very well harm someone else or disappear in order to avoid prosecution.*

An order for an appraisal of the Minocqua property had yet to be carried out. After that Bill would have an amount of equity available to offer as bond. Rock County Corporate Counsel Tom Schroeder said that the county would not accept the real estate as property for the bond unless Bill could get title insurance. Schroeder said he would "be surprised" if a title insurance company would issue such a policy because the estate was tied up in probate court due to the Judge family filing the wrongful death lawsuit against Bill.

It brought a little order to the chaos because Michael Judge had been so proactive in this situation. It wasn't surprising due to his intelligence and law degree. But, given the stress he had to be under, it was remarkable that he was able to think so clearly. *How fortunate it is to have an attorney in the family.* Most victims' families were not so blessed.

The senior Mereness' videotaped testimony took place on Saturday, March 8, 2003. It was the same information as he had given at the January preliminary hearing. He was required to retell the whole story from Bill's suicide threat in the bathroom, to his confession and then to his suicide attempt in the car. While Mr. Mereness looked a bit healthier than he had two months before, the pain and anguish had still obviously taken a toll.

On Sunday, March 9, the lead story for *The Janesville Gazette* was titled "Family Wants Suspect to Cut Deal". Two photos flanked the story. One showed Bill leaning toward his attorney, a question in his expression. The other showed Bill's father speaking into the microphone from the witness stand. Reporter Sid Schwartz did an excellent job of conveying the feelings of Bill's family. It was heart wrenching to read of their travails.

Bill's sister, Sallie Drier did most of the speaking for the family. She blamed her brother Bill for the deaths of Jennifer and their own mother. Sallie had actually told Bill that the stress of testifying would be too much for their parents. She was quoted, "When he took his stand to fight this after he confessed, I said, 'We'll lose Mom and Dad', and we've lost my mother as a result." Her mother had not wished to testify against her son.

Neither had her father. James, Sr. queried the *Gazette* reporter, "It can't get any worse than that, can it?"

Sallie also explained that her first time to talk with Bill after Jennifer's murder had been in the Appleton hospital, after he awakened from his coma. Again, Bill's sister was quoted, "He started talking about how he had always been there for us. I stopped him and said that my instinct was, 'Yes, you did it,' but I didn't completely know until you confessed." According to Sallie, Bill had responded, "'I have the rest of my life to be thinking about.' He said he felt he'd suffered enough those days trying to commit suicide."

The article stated that Sallie thought Bill should plead guilty and get the case over; the stress on the family was "Indescribable". She was also cited on her own feelings, "I want no contact with him whatsoever."

Bill's sister also told the *Gazette* reporter that Bill had sent flowers to their father after the death of their mother. Sallie recalled, "He tried to call Dad, but Dad didn't return his call. His words were, 'I don't want any flowers from him.'" Sallie took the flowers to a local nursing home.

As far as testifying, the elder Mereness thought, "It gets a little easier, that was the second time, now."

Before leaving the courtroom the senior Mereness stopped at the defense table and shook his son's hand. The father told the reporter, "You've got some feelings for him."

The reporter asked how he balanced his oath to tell the truth against his love for his son? The father responded, "I've asked myself that question quite a few times. I still don't know. I'll never figure it out, I guess."

The newspaper article next explained that Mr. James Mereness, Sr. was scheduled to be deposed again on Thursday, March 13. At that time he was to testify as part of the wrongful death lawsuit filed by Jennifer's family. His thoughts about a third court appearance were compellingly sorrowful. "You're trying to get over it, and then you have to testify again."

The final information in the article was about Bill's bond. Judge James Daley had lowered it to $100,000, cash or property. Rock County Corporation Counsel Tom Schroeder indicated he was going to review Bill and Jennifer's prenuptial agreement as well as a mortgage insurance policy to determine if Bill had enough finances to satisfy the bond.

Dear God, no! Bit by bit the bond was being whittled down. I couldn't imagine it was necessary for the court to look that reasonable. Things seemed to be coming dangerously close to the critical point.

12

I had been looking forward to the week of March 25. It would be one full week of spring break. I'd planned to do very little but go to Milwaukee for a visit with Nicole and practice my natural horsemanship with a friend and our horses.

Bobby and Cathy were off on a cruise with Patti and Mike Barker. I was happy for them and hoped it would be just what they needed. At Bobby's fiftieth birthday party on March 19th, I'd hugged Cathy and given her instructions, "You have a good time, away from everything. You deserve it." I'd never before told anyone that they deserved anything. In fact Jeff and I often joked about people who said that. We both felt that you took what came your way and did the best with it. Life owed you nothing. However, since Jennifer's death I'd been feeling a little differently.

The trip had initially been planned a year ago. Then, with the murder everything was on hold until the trial date was finally set. We'd all been assured that nothing would happen until August. So, with much urging from all the family, they decided to go ahead and take the trip. It certainly had a different feel than was originally intended, but everyone realized that not going couldn't bring Jennifer back. I knew in my heart that Jennifer, the traveler, would want them to go.

Since Josh was also off, we planned a Tuesday shopping trip to Madison. He was in need of spring clothes. For lunch, we'd stopped at Broux Nellie's Diner in Oregon. As we waited for our food we read the *Wisconsin State Journal.* Josh put the paper down and said, "This is today's paper, right?"

He had such a stunned look on his face. I couldn't imagine what was in the paper. I responded, "Yes."

Josh folded the paper in half and turned it toward me. I was confronted with a photo of Bill Mereness. The headline read "Suspect allowed dead wife's property".

I had the exact same feeling I'd had when Bobby told me of Jennifer's murder. Socked in the gut. Stunned. Josh just stared at me as I read the article.

A hearing had been scheduled for 9:00 this very morning to go over the terms of William Mereness' bond upon his release. *It was already over. I hadn't even known about it.* With Bobby and Cathy out of the country, I'd lost my liaison. There had been no advanced notification of the hearing on WCLO or in *The Janesville Gazette*. I couldn't imagine when the hearing had been scheduled and why the local media hadn't picked up on it! This was a first-degree murder charge!

The article then explained that last week Judge James Welker had ruled against Michael and Cathy's probate case, thereby making all property of Bill and Jennifer's available to him to do with what he wished. He could put a lien on either property or sell them to make bond and/or pay his lawyer.

This is unbelievable! Isn't the purpose of the law to make sure a murderer does not profit financially from his spouse's demise? I had always known that should Bill be found guilty, half the property would belong to Jennifer's estate. Should he be found innocent, all the property would be his. The problem I saw with this situation was that Bill had control of the property now, before the trial. If he sold it before he was found guilty, it would be too late! I couldn't believe the property wasn't held, awaiting the outcome of the trial.

As I finished reading, I realized I wasn't alone in my assessment of the situation. Hank Starkey, co-leader of the Wisconsin Chapter of Parents of Murdered Children had been interviewed. He commented that the judge's decision victimized Jennifer's parents all over again. *Exactly!* He said, "I think this decision shows the whole system isn't working correctly. Wisconsin is one of the more progressive states regarding victim's rights, but it's got a lot of holes."

I hope Tom and Mavis have sought support from this group.

Meanwhile, this was the final piece Bill needed to earn his freedom. Judge Daley had already reduced Bill's bond to $100,000 cash or equity. Now it was possible.

How could this happen? The perfect scenario had played out. Bill's bail had been reduced twice and changed from cash only to property. Then with Judge Welker's decision Bill was given full control over the marital property.

The article even said Bill could live in Jennifer's house on Sandstone Drive if he wished. *The home he refused to move to. The home they were closing on when he announced he was divorcing her. The home in which he beat her to death.*

Our food arrived. Neither of us had an appetite. We picked at what was on our plates while discussing the situation. I wished I could cry. I was afraid for him to be out of jail. Who knew what he might do to my family members? *Oh God.*

We decided to go on to Madison, there wasn't much we could do regarding Bill. It was done. But I wanted more information. On my cell phone I tried to reach the editor and two reporters I knew from *The Janesville Gazette*. My efforts were unsuccessful.

I suddenly realized my dad would not know of this either and would be shocked when he read it in tonight's *Gazette*. I quickly called him and warned him. He, too, was incredulous. "How can they let this guy out?"

"I sure don't know Dad. But I will try to find out. I'm not sure if Bobby and Cathy know. I'll call Michael Judge tonight and see if he's told them. If not, I'll call their ship tomorrow and tell them."

"Do you think you should do that? Maybe you should just let them enjoy their vacation. Besides, Bobby said those calls to the ship are really expensive."

"I don't care what it costs. I do not want them coming back here Saturday not knowing he's out of jail. What if he's somehow sabotaged their house? I think they need to know."

"Well, let me know what you find out from Michael. Hopefully he will already have told them."

After that I called Jeff to tell him the news. He was going to look on the *Gazette* web site to see if they were carrying the story and call me back.

A few minutes later Jeff reported that there was a story in the *Gazette* and it was similar to the one in the *State Journal*, except that it said Bill would probably be released Thursday or Friday. His attorney had stated that he would probably live in the Minocqua residence. Also, Judge Welker had ordered Michael or Cathy to sign the mortgage from Sandstone so Bill could use it.

I wondered aloud, "What would happen if neither of them would sign it?"

Jeff said, "They'd probably be put in jail".

"So, they'd have to go to jail to keep their sister's murderer in jail?"

"I guess."

"It's an interesting thought. Thanks for the info. See you tonight."

I also realized there was a good chance that Bobby's kids knew nothing of Bill's impending release. *I need to call them tonight too.*

We arrived at the Big and Tall store and half-heartedly looked at the clothes. Both Josh and I agreed we'd lost interest in shopping. I purchased two short-sleeve shirts for him and we headed home.

Once there, I tried my contacts at the newspaper again with no luck. I realized I'd have to wait until evening to call Michael, so I'd might as well get the chores done.

Meanwhile, Josh looked up Michael's work and home numbers on the Internet. We'd exchanged Christmas cards, but never spoken on the phone. Normally, I'd have gotten his number from Cathy, but couldn't do that now.

After dinner I began trying Michael. I had no luck for over an hour. I looked for Tom, Jr.'s number on several Internet sites, but he was unlisted. I decided to call my nieces and nephew.

I reached Nicole first. She said she had seen the article when she'd checked the *Gazette* on line. She started to cry. "I just don't understand how this could happen. How can they let him out?"

"I'm trying to find some answers. Meanwhile, I just wanted you to be aware."

"I'm scared. Have you talked to Erin yet?"

"Not yet."

"She's planning to come to Janesville Thursday and stay over at mom and dad's. Please tell her not to do that, will you?" She was still crying.

"I will forbid her from staying there. She can stay at our house if she needs to be in Janesville. "

"You know our back garage door lock doesn't work. He could get right in."

"I will go over there and check it out. If it's still not working I'll figure something out. Uncle Jeff might need to put in a new lock."

She sighed and regained her composure. "Okay. Do you want me to call Michael and tell him?"

"That would be great if you would. Tell your brother to call me if he has any questions. I'll call you if I have any more news. We'll get through this. I love you."

"I love you too. Thanks for calling me, Aunt DeeDee."

Erin didn't answer her cell phone so I left a message for her to call me as soon as possible. She did within ten minutes. She hadn't heard about the bond.

Her voice was very high and tight. She asked the same questions Nicole had. I did my best to reassure her about the back door at her mom and dad's. She promised not to stay over on Thursday, just to stop in to pick up a few things.

"Listen, I'm trying to get ahold of your Uncle Michael without luck. Do you have Uncle Tom's phone number? I can't find it on the Internet."

"No, but I'm sure it's at the house. Do you know the garage code?"

"I think so. Is it still lucky 5?"

"Yup."

"Thanks a lot Erin. I'll get it tomorrow if I can't get a hold of Uncle Michael tonight. Please let me know what time you'll be in town Thursday; I'll meet you at the house. I don't want you to be there alone."

"Okay. I'd appreciate that. It's pretty scary."

"I know. I'm going to recommend to your mom and dad that they have a home security system installed. It's a long time between now and August 11. I want them to be safe too. Meanwhile, I'll call you if I hear anything else."

After exchanging endearments, we hung up.

I decided to give Michael one more try as it was after nine. He answered on the second ring.

He did know about the circumstances. He was furious. Michael had always been very soft-spoken and calm. I believe he'd reached his limit. He talked very candidly.

"I don't know what is going on down there in Rock County. It seems they have made a concerted effort to get this man out of jail. They also have behaved in such a casual manner. 'Hey, wanna have a hearing?' 'Sure, how about tomorrow?' 'Okay.' It's ridiculous."

I inquired, "Were you at the hearing this morning?"

"No, I wasn't able to make it on such short notice."

"How can they get away with this?"

"That is a good question for the citizens of Rock County. Here is a guy who beat his wife in the head eight times with a hatchet. Then he drives his car into a wall. Why would those judges make any effort to get him out of jail?"

"I sure don't know Michael, but I will do my damnedest to find out. I've already tried my newspaper contacts. I will continue to pursue that, as well as the radio. Also, is it appropriate for me to call the DA?"

"You bet. He's your employee. Where has he been during all of this? How is he protecting the citizens? You know, I've been quiet through all of this, assuming the system would take care of things. But it hasn't. Do you know that the Judge family has spent over $28,000 for Jennifer's funeral, as well as house payments and car payments so that the estate would remain intact? Now it's all his! Well, I've had it. Today I talked to a reporter from the *Wisconsin State Journal*. The article should be in the paper tomorrow. You might want to pick one up."

"I sure will. I'm so sorry about how your efforts to keep the estate intact ended up helping Bill. Something is seriously wrong with the law or these judges. What can I do?"

"Ask questions. Those judges do come up for re-election every once in a while. Maybe the voters should know how they've treated a man who has committed the worst of crimes."

"I will stir things up here as best as I can. By the way, do Bobby and Cathy know about this?"

"Yes. Cathy called me tonight to see if anything was happening. She must have had a feeling. I didn't want to tell her, but she could tell by my voice that I was hiding something. I told her, but I also insisted she try to enjoy her vacation as much as possible. There's nothing she can do about this now."

"I'm glad you told them. I've contacted Nicole and Erin. Nicole was going to tell Michael."

"DeeDee, I continue to appreciate your help. I'll be spending a few days with my parents in Arizona, trying to put some of this aside."

"You should. It has been really hard on all of you. Can you leave me their number if I should need to get a hold of you?"

"Sure."

Michael gave me the number and thanked me again.

I immediately called Nicole and Erin to let them know their Uncle Michael had told their parents. The girls were both relieved to know that they wouldn't be coming home unaware.

Next I called Josh at WCLO. I asked him if anyone was in the newsroom.

"Kyle is, do you want to talk with him?"

"Yes, please." He transferred my call.

I explained what was happening to Kyle. He was very supportive. He said he'd leave a message for the news director, Stan Stricker. Stan should receive the message in the morning and would call me if he had questions.

It was nearly midnight, but I was still too full of adrenaline to sleep. I sat on the couch and flipped through channels for a while until Josh got home. I updated him, then finally felt tired enough to go to bed. I tried to crawl in without disturbing Jeff. It didn't work.

"I'm so sorry about this."

"Thanks, honey. We'll just try to survive it."

In the morning I drove to the corner gas station to buy a copy of the *Wisconsin State Journal*. As Michael Judge had promised, there was, indeed, a story about Bill's imminent release.

Many of the facts were restated from the dropping of Bill's bond to Judge Welker's decision about the property belonging to Bill.

It also told of Judge James Daley reiterating conditions of Bill's bond. He was to have no contact with any members of Jennifer's family or with his own family. He was not allowed to leave the state.

Oh, then no problem. A guy who would attempt to kill his wife twice would be absolutely certain to follow these restrictions to the letter. We had nothing to fear. My mind flooded with a litany of stories I'd read about men who'd violated restraining orders, conditions of probation and bond. *What a farce!*

Michael Judge was quoted in the article. He said the family was "dismayed" by the decisions of judges Welker and Daley. He also stated that he thought the bond should have been higher. Next, Michael explained how the family had paid Jennifer's funeral expenses and had been paying the mortgage, utilities and other bills for both homes. He explained, "We've tried to keep our nose out of this. We paid the bills to preserve the estate. We trusted the justice system to do the right thing and now the system seems to have taken a left turn here." *Good for you, Michael.* Someone needed to speak not only for their situation but, also, for other potential victims and their families. Michael was perfect for the role.

A final comment was from Sallie Drier. "He confessed. I don't understand this. This has been extremely hard on all of us and from day one we have tried to do what is right. This is terribly stressful."

I was in a daze. I started to do the chores. As I opened the dog kennel, instead of stepping back, I stood right in front of the gate. The dogs jumped on it and blasted it open. The latch hit me right in the middle of my forehead. I saw stars. I reached up to feel my forehead; it was moist. My fingers were covered with blood. I staggered into the house, sat down and yelled for Josh. He came dashing down the stairs and nearly fainted from the sight. Blood was streaming between the fingers I had pressed against my forehead. I instructed him to first get a towel and then an ice pack. He reacted quickly. I did not want to spend the day in the emergency room if it wasn't necessary, so I asked him to call our neighbor who is a nurse. She came right over. After examining my wound she advised me that if I didn't want a scar, I should probably go in for some stitches. Otherwise, it was not too serious but, as was typical of head wounds, it had bled a lot. That I knew. She also feared a concussion. I thanked her for her help and decided to tough it out. I took some aspirin for the pain and iced it throughout the day. I had other work to do.

13

I needed to get to Bobby's house and check the back garage door as I'd promised Nicole. It was broken. There was no way to secure the garage as it was and a new lock wasn't the answer. The frame was cracked and needed to be replaced. I was not capable of that kind of work and didn't want to burden Jeff to do such a project after work. Also, since it was a somewhat significant problem, I didn't want to presume to fix it without consulting my brother. What to do? My head still throbbed from being hit by the kennel door. I wasn't in the best shape to problem solve. Since Bill wasn't due to be released until "later in the week" I figured I had one more day to fulfill my promise. I could give myself 24 hours to think this through.

Once home I had an overwhelming desire to take a nap. I hadn't been sleeping well, but I could have a concussion. I hoped it was the former. I called Jeff to let him know I was taking a nap and if I hadn't called him in two hours he should probably come home.

I set the microwave timer for one hour and forty-five minutes. I slept well and felt much better upon awakening.

The phone rang. It was my friend Carrie. She'd heard the news about Bill's release and wanted to know how I was doing. We chatted a while and she expressed her shock and disapproval at the combined decisions of the judges. I concurred.

Putting my mind to the problem of Bobby's door, I brainstormed all the possible ways I could prevent someone from entering through it. I settled on a two by four brace. I'd need to go back to my brother's in the morning to measure the door. Then I'd go to the hardware store for metal braces and screws. I'd need to get the wood at the lumber company. I didn't know what Bobby had for tools, so I'd take along Jeff's electric drill and use that. I made a list so I didn't forget anything essential.

I was still worried about the Luchsinger family's welfare. I called the police. I spoke to an officer about the impeding release of the accused murderer and my concerns. First, he expressed his own displeasure at the recent turn of events. The officer explained that it was very frustrating for the police when they would "catch the bad guys" and the judicial system let them go. I appreciated his empathy and kind manner. Second, he assured me that the department would be keeping an eye out for Bill. While he couldn't promise any increased patrols in Bobby's neighborhood he said, "I'll see what I can do". I was satisfied that the local authorities were as concerned about this problem as I was.

When Jeff came home from work he looked at my forehead with concern. The wound was starting to scab over and I had a good-sized bump. I tried to assure him that I was feeling much better, even if I did look like hell.

I bounced my idea for Bobby's door off of him. He thought it was a viable plan and offered to help if I had trouble. I hoped I wouldn't.

My project worked out well. The way that door was braced someone would have had to smash it with a battering ram! I was proud of myself. There were, of course, still ways for Bill to harm the family, but at least this possibility could be taken off the list.

Sid Schwartz of *The Janesville Gazette* called me to get my reaction to this latest twist in the case. I offered my opinion and thanked him for the job he had done thus far in reporting the case. "You've handled it in a very professional matter, and I do appreciate that. I know the story could be sensationalized and cheapened. Thank you for not going there."

"You're welcome, but I'm just reporting the facts."

"I think we both know that you are taking the high road on this. It hasn't gone unnoticed or unappreciated."

Bill was released from jail on Friday. It was too late to make the evening paper, but it was awful to know he was "out there" somewhere. The *Gazette* did have the article by Sid in it.

It started out similarly to the one in Tuesday's *Wisconsin State Journal*. The headline was a quote from Michael Judge and read: "'We thought we were doing the right thing'".

Michael explained how the mortgage payments by Jennifer's family had kept the property out of foreclosure and allowed Bill to post bond and be released. Michael was cited in the article, "'The last thing we thought…was that it would come back like this.'"

Further, Judge Welker was credited for ruling against the Judge family and for ordering Michael to sign the mortgage to the Minocqua property.

Later in the article, Michael's words were angry, "'It just seems like every effort was made to get this guy out of jail. We thought that it wouldn't be right to allow these properties to go back to the bank when that is why he killed my sister. If we had let them go into foreclosure, if we had let the estate be insolvent and let the equity go to hell…then what equity would we have?'"

Schwartz's story delved deeper into the case. It explained that Jennifer had signed a prenuptial agreement because it was the only way Bill would agree to adopt a child. According to the agreement, should Jennifer and Bill divorce, he would not have to pay child support for the adopted child. *How could she marry such a man? How could she even love someone who wouldn't want to pay support to his child? She must have been so desperate for the child that she would not worry what the future might bring.*

The circumstances surrounding the house closings and Bill's request for a divorce were written about:

> 'My mother had to advance the $18,000 for the Sandstone house for the deal to close,' Michael said. 'What happened is that Bill thought the marital agreement would still stand,' Michael said. 'It became evident to him afterwards that even though there was nothing in the prenup about the adoption….people knew it was a quid pro quo—the prenup for adoption.
>
> 'That would make the prenuptial agreement null and void," Michael said, 'because Jennifer signed it under duress.
>
> 'When he realizes things aren't going according to Hoyle, he wants to get back with her,' Michael said.
>
> Court documents indicate Mereness had gone to Jennifer's home asking to reconcile, but she refused.
>
> 'It was two or three weeks prior to her being killed that she went to school and she was ill. That's why teachers in the teachers' lounge said, 'That's a new house. You better check your furnace.'
>
> Jennifer called police October 29 after finding that the vent pipe for her furnace had been plugged with dirt,

rocks and putty. Jennifer told police she believed William was trying to kill her.

Twenty-five days later, Jennifer's boyfriend found her beaten to death in her home.

Michael Judge said he can't understand why Rock County Judge James Daley lowered Mereness' bond from $150,000 cash to $125,000 cash or surety and finally to $100,000 cash or surety.

'It just doesn't make sense to me at all,' Judge said.

He's disappointed in the rulings by Welker and Daley.

'I don't know what to think. I've never heard where people are working in concert—two judges—for a person charged with first degree murder to get out.

'My parents have eight granddaughters and they're all afraid. This isn't a death that occurred in the heat of passion because of a boyfriend or a gun that accidentally went off. This was a planned, disguised invasion of the home in which an ax was used.

'From talking to all the girls in the family, they are all worried.'

The rest of the article included my responses to Sid's interview.

'I talked to both of my nieces last night and they were crying. They're afraid,' Golberg said.

'If he disappears, it's never over,' Golberg said. 'If he harms himself, there will be no chance for him to be brought to justice, either.

'You like to think that the system is going to more or less ensure that he's going to be held responsible for the crime,' Golberg said, 'but now that he's getting out, it puts all that into question.'

I was very satisfied with the article. It certainly clarified a number of areas and allowed the public to see some of what had been going on.

Our phone began to ring. Many friends and neighbors called to say that they'd read the article and were thinking of us and keeping us in their prayers. I appreciated the kind gestures. It was good to feel supported during this difficult time.

Saturday morning's *Janesville Gazette* had a color photo of Bill upon his release from jail. He was facing his attorney and looked as if he was talking when the photo was taken. His brow was slightly creased in a frown. Bill was wearing the same outfit he'd worn in court and it was obvious he'd gotten some up to date glasses. The freed man was holding a paper bag reported to contain his belongings. While it was possible to see only the side of Bill's attorney's face, it appeared he was smiling rather broadly. The lawyer was dressed very casually in a red, half-zip jacket and ball cap.

The accused is released from jail (*Courtesy of The Janesville Gazette*)

It looks like two friends having a casual conversation. How can that be?

The accompanying article, again by Sid Schwartz, explained that Bill hadn't had a ride when he walked out of jail at 3:17 p.m. Friday. He'd used a pay phone to call his attorney who arrived 26 minutes later. *That explains Tod's casual dress. He quite possibly was at home when he received the call.*

Mereness, 49, declined to comment as he waited for his ride. When asked if he has any plans now that he's out from behind bars for the first time since Dec. 3, he said: "I haven't had a chance to make any, yet."

Janesville police Lt. Danny Davis said Friday that police in Minocqua have been notified that Mereness probably will be living there until his trial, scheduled to start in August.

Davis said his department also contacted law enforcement in the Appleton area, where Mereness has family, to let police know Mereness was being released.

As a condition of his bond, Mereness is not allowed to have contact with his family.

Oh yeah, I'm sure that will take care of everything. Ha! Ha!

Several hours later, I got a call from Bobby. They had disembarked from their ship in Florida and all was well. They would be home soon. I told him about fixing his door, and he chuckled. "We don't have anything to fear from Bill. He probably doesn't even give us a thought."

"Well, I disagree. I'm scared for all of you. Besides, your girls were really upset and concerned about that door."

"Then it's good that you took care of it. Thanks."

We agreed that he'd call again when they got home.

The day dragged along. I didn't know what to do. My spring break was just about over and it had been consumed with Bill's release. I was more exhausted than I'd been before the time off. I knew I had to do something to interrupt the intense spiral of negative emotion. What would be significantly engrossing enough to distract me from all of this that is beyond my control? I thought about it all day, then slept on it.

On Sunday I knew the answer. I would try to get in to a weeklong clinic at the Mecca of my natural horsemanship: The Parelli International Study Center in Pagosa Springs, Colorado. I'd always wanted to participate in the "extreme experience", but couldn't justify the time away or the expense. Jeff agreed that the circumstances warranted a plan of this type. It would give me something to look forward to and would occupy me in the interim, getting my horse and me in shape for the clinic.

I e-mailed Mary, the manager of the sales department, whom I had met before. I explained briefly what was going on and wondered if I could still get into the clinic beginning at the end of June. I was also hoping, given the dire circumstances, that I could be granted the "early bird discount", even though the deadline for it had long passed.

Mary, e-mailed me back within hours. She was so sorry to hear of our troubles, and had enrolled me in the June course at the discounted rate.

I was happier than I had been since the murder. At last I had a focus that would be pleasant and absorbing. It had been a great idea. I was grateful to Jeff for his encouragement and for Mary for making it happen.

Thank you, God, for opening this window.

14

During the months of Bill's freedom I rode a roller coaster of emotions. After the initial shock, anger and disbelief that a person accused of such a heinous crime could possibly be out on bail wore off, there was still the fear that he was "out there".

Although intellectually I knew Bill would have no interest in me, I was still full of anxiety. I had problems sleeping. Getting to sleep wasn't too difficult, but I often awoke with a start and found myself listening for sounds on the porch outside our bedroom window. If I was walking the dogs late, I felt differently about the darkness; it could hide someone. I reminded myself that Bill had attacked Jennifer in broad daylight, so darkness really wasn't a factor in her killing. Try as I might, reason with myself as much as I could, the fear and anxiety persisted.

Some students at school had questions about how Bill could be out of jail. I explained that I did not understand that myself.

The April 2 edition of *The Janesville Gazette* had an interesting item in it's anonymous call-in column. "It's unfortunate that the *Gazette's* staff decided to put an article on the front page Friday about Judge James Daley and his opinions of the war in Iraq when a question that more people would like to ask him is why he would show disrespect to the family of Jennifer Judge by twice lowering the bond for a suspected killer."

At least someone else in the community was concerned about the situation. I had wondered if we were just hypersensitive because this had happened to a family member. Seeing those words in the paper reassured me a little.

In mid-April, we found out the details of Bill's wife's claim that he had tried to kill her. There was an article in the *Gazette* because his first wife, LyAnn Beatty, had asked for a court order to keep him away from her while he was out on bond. It was a compelling story and only too believable.

> LyAnn Beatty, who divorced Mereness in 1996, told *The Janesville Gazette* that she believed Bill tried to poison her by putting something into her soda in 1994. "I

had to spit it out it had such a horrible taste," Beatty said. "It was sort of like a polishing taste. It was some sort of cleaner or something."

The poisoning attempt, she said, happened after one of the three times she filed for divorce.

"Shortly after that, my oldest daughter came to me and said she was the one who put that in there," Beatty said. "I truly didn't believe that. I said to Bill, 'Maybe we should report this.' He said, 'No, it's a family matter.'"

Beatty said she called police anyway, and detectives questioned her daughter.

"My daughter told police that Bill had told her to say she put it in there," Beatty said. "He asked her to take the blame, thinking that I wouldn't divorce him.

"They questioned Bill. I know he was going to take a lie detector test and then he cancelled it."

The case was referred to the Outagamie County District Attorney's Office, she said, but no charges were filed.

"They didn't feel there was enough evidence to charge him with putting something in my drink," Beatty said.

Beatty and the son she had with Mereness—Christopher, 18—both said they want to be on the no-contact list of Mereness' bond, too.

"I've been told by Janesville police that we are potential witnesses, and based on past behavior and his criminal history toward me, I didn't think it was too much to be included in the no-contact," Beatty said.

She said Rock County District Attorney David O'Leary has declined to help.

"I talked to Mr. O'Leary one time," Beatty said. "He said, 'No, you would need a restraining order,' but I can't get a restraining order because Bill has made no threats to me at this point."

O'Leary said that "the reality is" that Beatty and her son already are covered by the bond conditions, which prohibit Mereness from committing any new crimes.

"If he creates a disturbance or harasses her, he's committing a new crime," O'Leary said.

"Only victims directly involved in a case can be placed on the bond conditions," O'Leary said.

"I just can't put anybody in the community who had a dislike for the defendant on bond conditions," he said. "It has to be approved by the courts."

O'Leary said he doesn't have a basis to ask the court to add Beatty and her son to the bond conditions.

"They have to have a direct involvement in the case," he said.

Christopher, who was living with his father in Janesville at the time of Judge's murder, doesn't want to see his father, either.

"We're dealing with a violent man, here," Christopher said.

"The history he's had with my family…I think that alone would speak volumes about why me and my mom should be put on the no-contact order," Christopher said. "That's the dissatisfactions we have."

Christopher, who now is living in Appleton with his mother, said he is afraid of his father "just because of what's happened in the past.

"He was violent to my mom. He was violent to me. Now, he's probably cocky and arrogant. He could go after that side of the family or our side of the family," Christopher said.

"When we woke up three months ago, we knew where he was. Now we don't. What's he doing? He doesn't have a job," Christopher said.

Beatty said her daughters—Lisa, 23, and Ashley, 19—are afraid, too.

"I have two daughters who are terrified, just because they know Bill's personality," Beatty said. "They're afraid he will come around and bother them.

"It's hard to explain unless you've lived with him and know how he does things," Beatty said. "It probably doesn't make a lot of sense to people on the outside. Usually what he does is sneaky, not blatant where he'll come out and do something."

Beatty said Mereness called her the day after Judge was killed.

"His words were: 'Whatever happened, I didn't have anything to do with it, but now I'm going to inherit her debt.' I thought that was a very strange thing to say after being questioned by police and finding out that your wife is dead," Beatty said.

Christopher believes his father is guilty of murder.

"My dad is extremely money hungry. That is all he was afraid of. He was afraid he was going to lose his money," Christopher said. "It was a ruthless invasion of the house, and it's really despicable that he's out on bond and driving around. I heard reports that he spent a couple nights at her house. That's sick. That's really sick. That irritates me.

"He's my dad, and I'm not going to turn my back on him like his family did," Christopher said. "I love my dad, but I don't have the respect and look at him in the light that I once did."

I couldn't disagree with their feelings because I was afraid, too.

If Jennifer had contacted Bill's first wife to find out the details of her "crazy" accusation, would all of this been prevented? I admonished myself for not suggesting she do so way back when we'd talked at Nicole's graduation party. I knew it was unlikely she would have followed my advice and I had been hesitant to say anything because it was "none of my business". I vowed that should such a situation ever present itself to me in the future, I would not hesitate to speak my mind. In an effort to keep Jennifer as my friend we ended up losing her altogether.

Meanwhile, we heard very little about Bill. The Janesville police had been in communication with those in Minocqua. It appeared that Bill was living in the log home on Pier Lake. His car had been spotted in the driveway at various times of the day and night. He wasn't under surveillance, but it felt good to know someone was "keeping an eye on him".

The home in Janesville, where Jennifer was murdered, was largely ignored. Bobby and Cathy had heard from the neighbors that Bill hadn't been seen around at all. They had been watching for him. The grass was growing out of control. Since my nephew Michael was home from college and waiting for his summer job to start, he was assigned the task of mowing the lawn at Jennifer's. I told Michael I hoped he would keep his eyes open. He looked surprised.

"Well, I just wouldn't want you to be caught off guard if Bill simply drives up to the house. There's nothing to stop him. I don't know what would happen with the restraining order if you were on the property, which, according to Judge Welker, is his."

"I see what you mean, but I don't think he's likely to show up here, do you?"

"I have no idea. I hope not, but keep on your toes just in case."

"Okay."

Try as we might, it was sometimes while doing the most mundane things that brought the murder right back into the forefront of my consciousness. One Saturday Jeff and I drove up to Madison to Sam's Club to shop for a few bargains. Just going to Sam's triggered unpleasant memories, since that was the company Bill had worked for.

On that particular day we had some specific items to purchase, but we cruised all the aisles to check for unanticipated money-saving opportunities. The next thing I knew, we were in front of a large display of hatchets. My stomach flopped and I could feel the blood pounding in my ears.

What did the hatchet he'd struck Jennifer look like? I would see it at the trial, but was it large or small? *Was the handle of wood or plastic?* The ones with the bright yellow handles caught my eye. *The blood would look particularly vivid on that type.* All of these thoughts occurred in an instant. The situation wasn't anything I could have predicted or prepared for. I was both angry and sad that I couldn't seem to get away from this. The feelings could be ignited anywhere, anytime. It wasn't as if I would allow it to ruin the entire day, but it was my new reality. The unexpected intrusions would, hopefully, fade in time.

On a Friday in May, one of my colleagues at school stopped in to see me during my seventh hour class. He had come to warn me. "There's more news about your murderer in tonight's paper. Just thought you'd want a head's up."

I thanked him for his thoughtfulness and decided to delay reading the article until I got home. I didn't want to get my brain all "fogged up" before my drive home.

The court had declared Bill partially indigent. Due to his employment status, he was unable to pay his attorney's fees. The county of Rock would now pay Tod Daniel $75 an hour and Tod's intern $25 an hour to defend Bill.

Michael Judge had been interviewed about this latest decision. He'd said that if a person had a $100,000 bond based upon his ownership of property and it appeared those properties were going to go back to the bank, shouldn't that individual be put back in jail?

I agreed with Michael, it seemed like the law was protecting Bill more than the victim's family. I also wondered about Bill being declared partially indigent, and his being able to have the attorney of his choice. I thought if a person couldn't afford an attorney one would be provided for him or her. That was what public defenders were for.

It was all so confusing. Things even seemed to vary from county to county. There had been a recent case in Walworth County where a man had been charged with the kidnapping of an elderly woman. The woman had been found physically unharmed, but he suspect was being held on a bond of one million dollars. And just one county to the west, our murder suspect had been given a bond of one-tenth that amount. Now, even that was in jeopardy. From all appearances it seemed far more beneficial to commit a crime in Rock County.

Will I ever truly understand or accept these things?

Additionally, Bill's attorney had petitioned for a change of venue. The claim was that the barrage of news coverage at the time of the murder would make it impossible for his client to have a fair trial in Rock County. Daniel was quoted in *The Janesville Gazette*; "'It influences the public opinion against William Mereness to a point that there is reasonable likelihood that a fair trial cannot be had.'"

Judge Daley would rule on the venue request sometime in the future.

More trouble. For certain it would be a real hardship for the family if the trial were held elsewhere. Having Bobby and Cathy's house as well as our house within minutes of the Rock County Court House, we could provide places for other family members to stay throughout the trial. If the venue were changed, we'd all have the added expense and inconvenience of motel living. I knew there was nothing that could be done about this new wrinkle and tried to leave it in the hands of fate, but it did add one more spoonful to an already brimming cup.

The article also explained that Bill was living in the house in Minocqua and earning some money doing lawn work for people in that area. *Who on earth would hire him to work on their property? It was probably absentee Illinois owners who quite possibly knew nothing of his being accused of murder.*

I kept trying to remind myself that according to the American justice system, a person was innocent until proven guilty. That was not the case here, for me.

Some weekends I took my horse to a friend's indoor arena and we would practice our horsemanship. It was one of the few things I could do that completely took my mind off of the depressing circumstances. I was anxious to perform well at the course in Colorado, so I concentrated at perfecting some of the tasks we'd undoubtedly be asked to do.

Bobby and Cathy invited us to their house for Memorial Day. I was surprised when I got there and found that Dad wasn't coming. He'd called

Bobby to explain that he'd been ill with diarrhea all morning. *He must be really sick! He never misses a family gathering.* I made a mental note to call him as soon as I got home.

During our visit, Cathy revealed that both of Bill and Jennifer's homes were going to be foreclosed upon. She had received notifications from both banks. Bill had not been making the payments, so the banks would take the homes back. It was just a question of time.

"Won't Bill have to go back to jail then?" I asked.

"We'd assume so, but we'll have to wait and see. Michael said he *should* be incarcerated if there is a foreclosure."

"Well, that would put me at ease," I offered. "With the trial coming up I'm still afraid he's going to bolt."

Cathy summed it up, "I think that's how everyone feels. It would be a relief to know he's in custody."

We didn't discuss the case for the rest of the day and were able to have a pretty decent, if subdued, celebration.

It turned out my dad was having a bout of colitis. I was sure the stress of the situation didn't help an already delicate condition. It would be hard to prove a direct cause, but it certainly was likely a contributing factor. I knew he was concerned about the effects the murder had already had on his son and his family. And with the trial looming ahead, more stress would be forthcoming.

As school was coming to a close I began to seriously plan my trip out to Colorado. I planned to leave on June 21 and spend a week with my friends Dan and Anne before the course started. Extra planning time was necessary because I was taking my horse, Rose, with me. That entailed finding lodgings for her as well as for me on the trip west. I was hoping the decision about the change of venue would be made before I left and that Bill would be safely back in jail due to the foreclosures. Unfortunately, there had been no word on either front.

On the 17th of June my mother collapsed on the bathroom floor. Dad called to tell me the ambulance was at their house and would be transporting her to the hospital.

"I'll meet you there."

"Oh, thanks, Deed, I was hoping you could come."

After a battery of tests, the doctors determined my mom had a bleeding ulcer and she'd lost several units of blood. The bleed was blamed on an anti-stroke medication, but I felt that the stress of the murder played a role also. Mom tended to keep her emotions in and that played havoc with her health.

The next day a successful cauterization was performed on the bleeding blood vessel in my mother's stomach. With time, she was expected to make a full recovery. Unfortunately, she had to be taken off the anti-stroke medication so that worry moved to the forefront.

While Mom had been stabilized, I debated canceling my trip. I could help Dad by sharing visits to the hospital and could undoubtedly be useful when she was discharged. I called my acquaintance, Mary, at the International Study Center in Colorado to find out my options. She was sympathetic to this latest dilemma and said that, while not refundable, my fee could be carried over for a course the following summer.

I sought advice from my brother. He was very firm with me. "You need to go. You need the time away; it'll really be good for you. I'll handle anything that comes up here."

"You've already got your hands full with Bill's case. It isn't fair that you should also have to handle Mom's health crisis alone. Besides, who knows if dad will have another bout of colitis and then you'll be caring for both of them."

He was insistent. "I'm sure it'll be alright. You go and don't give it another thought."

"Easier said than done."

"I know, but you'll be more valuable to everyone if you can get away for a positive experience."

That did it. If it was going to benefit others, I could give myself permission to go. I'd still feel guilty, but I could justify it that way. "Thank you, Bobby. I can't tell you how much I appreciate this."

"You've done a lot for us these past months, now go do something for yourself."

He was right. I did need some time away. I hoped things at home would be okay in my absence. It wasn't as if I could just fly home in an emergency. I'd have my horse with me, and it would take me three days to get home with the truck and trailer. I also was hopeful that I would be able to make the clinic a valuable learning experience with everything that was going on in our lives. I wasn't very good at compartmentalizing, but I'd need to try. However, I did decide to delay my departure for two days to get everything, including my emotions, in better order for the long journey.

15

As I prepared for my adventure I realized that it was the first time I'd left home since Jennifer's funeral. It brought the memories close again. Just taking out my travel bag triggered feelings I hadn't had in a while. It had been long enough that it was beginning to feel like the whole thing hadn't even happened. From Josh's accident I'd learned that that was part of the healing process.

The three-day drive alone out to Southwest Colorado provided me with a chance to sort through some of the feelings I'd been too busy to address. I took a micro recorder and talked about events and my feelings. It was a catharsis of sorts; but I realized there were already so many details that had been blurred by time. I could well imagine how having a trial so many months after a crime could be a problem for witnesses. The part of the brain that wanted us to forget and heal was in competition with the part that wanted to remember so we could be good witnesses and help bring about justice. I thought particularly of the construction worker and how Tod Daniel had tried to tarnish his credibility at the preliminary hearing. I could only imagine how brutal the defense attorney would be at trial.

I also wondered if anyone from the District Attorney's Office could help a witness review his or her testimony before a trial, or was that some sort of tampering? It was obvious to me that I knew woefully little about our legal system. I was happier when I didn't know what I didn't know.

Previously, whenever I'd passed Des Moines in my travels west I had thought of Patti and Mike Barker. Now the feelings were bittersweet, since we had the bond of tragedy between us. I also wondered how B.C. and Luna were doing with their new family. *How do they grieve? Will they ever forget or will they be haunted forever by their memories of murder?*

Then I thought about Bill and wondered what he was doing on this lovely summer day. Was he enjoying his freedom? Was he planning a future? I had absolutely no confidence that he would show up at his trial. He might even be plotting to harm witnesses, including his own father.

I completely enjoyed my two days staying with Anne and Dan in their cozy mountain cabin. It was so peaceful, surrounded entirely by trees and the Rocky Mountains. We dined on the porch overlooking Rose and their four horses in the corrals. When darkness fell, mule deer came out of hiding to graze and the coyotes started to howl. It was the best medicine I could have had. I almost forgot our troubles. When the time came for me to move to the study center for the week, they insisted I continue to stay with them and drive the half-hour back and forth daily. I nearly cried.

Anne and Dan's cabin in the mountains near Pagosa Springs, Colorado

The peaceful view from Anne and Dan's porch

During my travels and throughout the clinic, I called home daily to check on everything from my parents' health to my animals' care to the murder case. Fortunately, my parents and my animals were all doing well; but on the night of Wednesday, July 2, Josh told me there had been some developments in the case. He'd been at work and the news staff at WCLO told him they were working on the story along with *Gazette* staff.

"You could check the *Gazettextra* website tomorrow to see what's up, but I think Judge Daley denied the change of venue."

"That's great!"

"Well, there's more."

"What now?"

"Apparently, Daley's in the National Guard. He's been called to active duty. He's got to report in August."

"Holy shit! What's gonna happen?"

"Daley's turned the case over to Judge Werner."

"But he's a juvenile court judge!"

"I don't know everything that's involved. They're still working on the story. The article will be posted on the web site tomorrow. I think something's going on with the bail too."

After I hung up, I shared the latest news with Anne and Dan. They, too, wondered about a "juvie" judge handling the trial. Though the more I thought about it, the better I felt.

"Actually, I think this might be a good thing. We haven't been too happy with Judge Daley's handling of the bail situation, and it sure seemed as if Daniel pushed his buttons during the proceedings so far."

Anne inquired, "But does this new judge have the experience for such a high profile case?"

"You know, I've known Rich Werner for about 20 years. One of his three sons was in Josh's class, and all of them were students at the Catholic school where I used to teach. He's certainly intelligent and seems really even-tempered."

"That sounds promising."

"I'm afraid to think it, but maybe things are finally starting to go the right way in this case."

"I hope so."

When I got to bed I couldn't sleep. That was no surprise. I tossed and turned, thinking about the latest developments.

Next day, tired and distracted as I was, I attempted to focus on my lessons with Rose. I envied the others in the class for not having a divided focus. While I was sure everyone had things going on in their lives, this was so weighty. I'd also decided not to tell the instructors or students about my situation because I didn't want to draw attention to myself or act as if I was making excuses. It was hard for me to keep it all in. I was thankful for Dan and Anne's company each evening.

That night, however, I was resentful that this ugly business intruded upon my life. I was 1,700 miles away, but it's tendrils reached out to wind around me and pull me in. I looked up the article on the Internet and printed it out.

It echoed what Josh had said. I shared it with my friends.

Judge Daley was quoted several times. First he explained his decision about the change of venue. Daniel had claimed that due to the sensational nature of the publicity about the murder, the pool of potential jurors in our county would be tainted.

" All things considered, I do believe that, in fact, on a whole, it was factual reporting and is not objectionable." Daley said.

"I do believe that Rock County has the right to try this case and the defendant has a right to be tried in Rock County by a jury of his peers," Daley said before denying the change of venue motion from defense attorney Tod Daniel.

Jeepers. I'm not sure I agree with that, but I'm sure glad Daley's ruled this way!

Next, Daley took himself off the case. The article explained that he was a brigadier general in the Wisconsin Army National Guard. His active duty would begin on August 19 and last for about six months. The trial was expected to last three weeks, so even though he could be in court for the beginning of the case, he wouldn't be able to finish it. Apparently, Daley had first suggested that the trial begin on August 4 and be limited to two weeks, with 12 trial days. That way he could still preside over the case. That suggestion was not accepted.

"Counsel has said there is no way they could try it in 12 days," Daley said Wednesday. "The Court is satisfied that all counsel are experienced trial counsel. Therefore, there's no way I can try this case."

Also, the article stated, the defense had the right to refuse Werner's appointment. They had 10 days to file a request to substitute another judge.

Oh for heaven's sake. We just get one concern settled and another pops up.

The final issue the article addressed was the bond situation. Deputy District Attorney Perry Folts had asked Judge Daley to revoke the bond due to the imminent foreclosure on both properties.

"There is no bond anymore," Folts said. "They're going to foreclose on that property. What's going to be there to secure his appearance in court?"

Rock County Corporate Counsel Tom Schroeder also was interviewed regarding the bond issue.

"My concern is that the county have sufficient protection to make sure it recoups whatever money it pays Mr. Daniel," Schroeder said.

Judge Daley put off making a ruling until the foreclosures occurred.

"If it goes into foreclosure, we're in a different position than when we were when I ordered the bond," Daley said. "Then, in fact, the county is no longer assured of $100,000 and, in fact, the court will then have to either order the cash or custody."

Well, at least that could be good news. I'd love to see him behind bars, the sooner the better.

I returned home from Colorado somewhat refreshed, but filled with trepidation. The only thing that I could see before me was the trial.

On July 9, the night I arrived home, the *Gazette* had a story about foreclosure proceedings on the Janesville property. It would soon be sold on the courthouse steps. The DA declined to do anything about the situation, as there was little equity in that home. Should the Minocqua property follow suit, he would look at requesting Bill be returned to custody.

If he could be found.

That Friday, Patti and Mike Barker with their daughter Brianna were going to be visiting in Janesville. We gathered at Bobby and Cathy's on a lovely, cool summer evening. We visited out on the deck while enjoying a crackling fire in the fire kettle.

"How are the Bichon's doing in their new home?" I asked.

"Actually, we've had them at our place quite a bit," Patti responded.

"Really? Why is that?"

"My friend's mom has been ill and they've been going to stay with her some. We're the primary dog sitters."

"I'm sorry to hear about their trouble, but are they happy with the dogs?"

"Oh yes, they just love them and the dogs seem to be well-adjusted and happy."

"I'm so glad. I've often thought I should have kept them, but I just couldn't imagine those two little white fluffy dogs on a farm. They'd either be constantly dirty or I'd be spending a lot of time giving baths."

"Don't give it another thought, they have a fantastic home."

"That's good to hear." At least this was something I could be pleased with.

Cathy spoke, "You know, I was deposed by Tod Daniel last week."
Oh, maybe I shouldn't have brought up the subject of Jennifer at all. "No, I didn't, how did that go?"

"Not well. Our attorney in the civil case, David Finegold went with me. After Tod kept being so rude to me, David told me we were leaving."

"Oh, that's awful, but that's how Tod can be."

Cathy continued, "I thought he was going to question me about the civil suit but he kept asking me questions about the statement I gave to police on the night they came here to tell me about Jennifer. I honestly don't remember a lot of what the police report said. I'd never seen it, and it's been so long since then."

I interjected, "A person's memory during times of such stress isn't really great. I'd had the same concern after Josh's accident, but the therapist I went to told me not to expect too much from myself, it was totally normal."

"Well, he kept saying, 'She hasn't seen this report? I can't believe she hasn't seen this report. Why hasn't she seen this report?' Then he persisted in asking me about statements I had made. I didn't really remember and told him that. After a while, it was obvious I was getting upset, so David ended the session."

Then Cathy did something I'd never heard her do in the 30 years we'd known each other. She swore. "Tod Daniel's an asshole."

Jeff and I laughed and said almost simultaneously, "That's why people hire him."

Mike and Patti were curious.

"Well, that's why Jeff hired him for his divorce back in the early '70's and why we hired him for Josh's accident," I explained. "However, we really regret that we didn't hire one of the big personal injury law firms from Madison or Milwaukee. Many had sent us information at the time of the accident. I guess they were 'ambulance chasers' to some degree. But we thought it would be better to hire someone we knew, someone local and someone with a reputation as a real 'tiger'."

Then Jeff gave an account of Tod's representation during his divorce. "I basically got everything in the agreement. That was in the days before marital property law, so it was me versus her. I'm not sure if I should give all the credit to Tod, since my ex-wife didn't really care what she got; but her attorney should have fought for something."

"Well," said Mike, "I sure have a better idea of what this guy is like now."

We moved on to a discussion of the possible change to Judge Werner. Cathy explained that while Tod did have the right to refuse him, another judge would be assigned. "So he may decide to stick with the known rather than take a chance on the unknown."

I sent up a silent plea for Judge Werner. The more I'd thought about him, the more I was convinced that he was the man for us.

Accommodations for the upcoming trial was the next topic. Cathy had gotten their finished basement all set up and felt they would have beds for all. Jeff and I offered our place for anyone else who might need overnight lodgings.

All of this planning for the expected three week trial reminded me of *The Godfather*. When the two Mafia families were warring, they each set up mattresses in secret locations for their henchmen to stay. It was like that in a way. Our family was going to war against Bill and his defense team in an effort to obtain justice.

The defense did not move to block Judge Richard Werner as the new judge. This small "victory" had me feeling guardedly optimistic.

On Monday, July 28, Tod Daniel renewed his request for a change of venue. Since Werner was now the judge in the case, the defense attorney was going to see how the request would rate with him.

According to *The Janesville Gazette,* Daniel had written, "The inflammatory nature of the publicity is clear." He cited 20 articles in the *Gazette* as well as five in the *Wisconsin State Journal.*

Daniel also filed requests that the jurors be allowed to view the murder scene before hearing testimony.

In a final motion, Daniel asked that the jury be sequestered throughout the trail.

Not to be outdone, the prosecution had also filed a motion. They wanted Werner to allow testimony from Appleton police detectives about statements made to them by Bill's mother. Since LaBelle had died, there was still a possibility her statement could get in, if Werner found the circumstances to be an exception of the hearsay rules.

The change of venue motion was of major concern. We needed the trial to stay here. Although I had recently found out that change of venue might mean just having a jury brought in from another part of the state. That didn't seem to be a problem, any group of people from anywhere should be able to see Bill's guilt.

The motion to view the murder scene was not a concern for me. I knew the house had been cleaned up, but didn't think there would be any harm in them seeing the house. It would give them a better understanding of the floor plan as well as the position of the body, point of entry and other details. I knew Daniel had a purpose for this request, but I couldn't think of how it would harm the prosecution's case.

As for the jury being sequestered, I thought it was a good idea. While it would cost the taxpayers of Rock County a significant amount of money, I didn't want it to be an issue for possible appeal should Bill be found guilty. The trial needed to be as "clean" as possible so appeals would be fruitless.

There was no doubt in my mind that we needed the powerful testimony of the Appleton police officers. LaBelle's words should not be allowed to die with her. The jury needed to hear that the son had confessed to his mother.

I waited with bated breath until the rulings would be handed down on Thursday.

Judge Werner was quickly living up to my optimistic expectations. Most importantly, the hearsay testimony of the Appleton police officers was in!

Then Werner ruled that the trial would stay in Rock County. *Thank God.* He reaffirmed Judge Daley's earlier decision that the newspaper's reporting had been "objective, factual and not inflammatory".

Finally, the jury was to be sequestered, but they would not tour the home in which the murder took place.

All in all, it was a very positive outcome for us. Considering all the circumstances that had conspired against us until this point, we now had reason to be hopeful that the final verdict would be ours. That was the ultimate goal.

The next day, *The Janesville Gazette* published an editorial that brought tears to my eyes and caused a swell to rise in my chest. Affirmation was a wonderful thing.

> The murder of Jennifer Judge has captured the attention of this community as few other crimes in recent history.
>
> That's why the trial of the man accused of killing her belongs in Janesville, despite his attorney's claims that a change of venue is warranted.
>
> William Mereness is charged with first-degree murder in the death of Judge, his estranged wife. He is accused of using a hatchet to kill her in her northeast side home Nov. 22.
>
> Judge was a teacher at Craig High School, and the brutality of her murder sent shockwaves throughout the city. Since the killing, the events leading up to Mereness' arrest and subsequent developments have added drama and intrigue to an already stunning case. Mereness allegedly

confessed to his parents in the Appleton home a few days after Judge's death, but his mother has since died, and his statement was vague enough to leave questions.

Despite executing search warrants in Janesville and at Mereness' second home up north, police found little or no physical evidence tying the suspect to the murder. The trial is certain to be compelling, and the outcome is not a sure thing.

Tod Daniel, Mereness' attorney, made a motion this week to move the trial out of Rock County because of pre-trial publicity. He cited 20 articles in *The Janesville Gazette* and five in the *Wisconsin State Journal*.

'The inflammatory nature of the publicity is clear,' Daniel said.

It was Daniel's second attempt to have the trial moved, and judges rightly rejected his requests both times. Judge James Daley turned Daniel down in July, and Judge Richard Werner rejected the change of venue Thursday.

In fact, the coverage of the case has been fair and factual. Beyond that, it's a sad fact that many people don't read newspapers these days, evidenced by the continuing circulation challenges of papers across the country. That widespread ignorance makes it relatively easy to find objective jurors who have no opinion on or even no knowledge of the latest news.

Local residents might want to attend this important trial to see how justice is served. Or they may just want to monitor the trial through news coverage. Holding the trial here gives them that option.

Jennifer Judge lived and died in this city. The people in her community have a right to have the man accused of killing her tried in their midst.

And that is just what we would do in just nine more days.

But it was to be any exceptionally difficult wait.

At the end of July my mother collapsed again, and was taken to the hospital by ambulance. When she regained consciousness she was extremely disoriented and her speech was halting and slurred. A battery of tests revealed nothing specific, but doctors clinically diagnosed a stroke.

The next day Mom was still confused, and was pronounced to be incompetent to make her own decisions. Even though her health had been deteriorating for years, this was a startling step. However, since there was nothing further the hospital could do for her medically, she was to be released. Bobby, Dad and I were all set to make the decision to have her discharged to a nursing home. We worked all day with the hospital social worker to find an available and acceptable placement.

Almost miraculously on the subsequent morning, my mom had regained her faculties. While we were extremely pleased at this amazing turn of events, we were also in a complete panic. The decision as to her discharge plans was now in her hands. She had always abhorred being in the hospital and was dead-set against the idea of a nursing home or assisted living facility. If she insisted upon going home, there was nothing we could do about it. Dad would somehow have to find a way to have in house care. She was still physically weak and likely to fall down. Her mind was not sharp; she could easily leave a lit cigarette that could start a fire. The couch and carpet already had small burn holes in them. Fortunately none of those incidents had caused a major blaze. Someone would have to monitor her 24 hours a day and physically help her with locomotion, eating, bathing and dressing.

Bobby, Dad and I met and decided we would need to use all of our powers of persuasion to get her to agree to at least a short rehabilitative stay at the skilled nursing facility.

We steeled ourselves for a knock down drag out fight. We had one, complete with many refusals, tears and irrational accusations.

Finally, she acquiesced to a "temporary stay until she regained her strength".

The 20 mile trip to Evansville to install Mom in the Manor was another emotionally taxing event. I was sure my reserve was just about gone.

I went to visit Mom every day until the trial began. She was unhappy and angry. She only participated in physical and occupational therapy so she could "get out of here". She was a difficult resident. I tied my best to comfort her, but failed miserably, though she did not want me to leave her company.

It was hard to tell her that I would probably not be able to visit her for the duration of the proceedings, since I would have chores to do each night. I told her I would check on her progress with dad, and call if I was able. We both admitted that phone conversations would be difficult due to her hearing loss.

I felt so badly for her, but there was nothing I could do to make things right.

16

Monday, August 11, 2003. I could scarcely believe it. The day had finally arrived. It had seemed an eternity since November 22, 2002. We'd all been so focused toward this day. I could honestly say that I had made no plans beyond the trial. I knew school was starting in late August, but was prepared to use my sick time to attend the trial if need be. I knew I had to be there for every minute.

I was filled with anticipation and dread. This would be "the end" to Jennifer's story. If Bill were found guilty he would probably spend life in prison. If he were found innocent he would be free. I did not want to think about the ramifications of that second possibility.

I had no idea how many people would be in attendance and was worried about everyone in the family having a seat. To save time, Jeff took care of the dogs before work and I managed the horses. I quickly showered, dressed and redressed twice. I couldn't decide what to wear. I wanted to be comfortable but not casual. I felt it was important that the jury see the victim's family in a good light. I wanted to represent Jennifer well. She was a professional woman. On the other hand, if the day in court were to be over nine hours, comfort would be important too. I wished I'd decided on an outfit before. *I can't believe I'm waffling around about what clothes to wear! How ridiculous. With all that's at stake, I need to get focused and get going!* I decided on some ribbon-trimmed capri jeans and a coordinating blouse.

At the last minute I remembered I'd wanted to take seat cushions. Those wooden pews would be incredibly rough on the backside after an entire day of sitting. I looked around quickly and grabbed Josh's two collectors Brewers baseball stadium cushions. I'd explain it to him later.

I arrived at the courthouse at 8:15 a.m. and proceeded up the main staircase and through the metal detectors on the second floor. As had occurred each time I'd attended court in this matter, the two security guards seriously and silently studied my bag on their x-ray machine. Thankfully, I did not set off the alarm.

I took the interior stairway up two floors. It was so quiet on those stairs. I was the only one in there and my footfalls echoed eerily.

Alighting on the fourth floor, I observed Cathy, Mavis, Michael and Pat Judge and their daughter Molly standing in the hall with the district attorneys and Shelly, the victim-witness liaison. Michael motioned me over as the DA's were heading into the courtroom.

Michael began, "Bill was arrested yesterday by the Sate Patrol. He made contact with his dad trying to get him to not testify. Dad called Sallie Drier, who called the police."

I was aghast, "Thank God for Sallie."

"Bill had written a letter to his father saying even though he had admitted killing Jennifer, he really hadn't."

"Naturally. But that was really foolish of Bill. He must have been desperate. At least now he'll be locked up for the duration of the trial."

"He sure will. And you'll never guess, Bill had a girlfriend who didn't know anything about the murder."

"You've got to be kidding? How could anyone not know?"

"I've no idea. But when the police told her she freaked out."

"I can only imagine."

"The girlfriend said Bill had told her he was going to Canada fishing this week."

"Ever the liar."

"She is going to cooperate with the police in any way."

"That can only help."

Michael checked his watch; "We'd better get inside."

As we walked I turned to Mavis; "Did Tom, Sr. decide to stay at home?"

"No, his doctors won't let him attend. They found some scar tissue on his heart that indicates he's had a heart attack. They think it's from the time we were told the news about Jennifer."

"I'm so sorry! Is he feeling okay now?"

"He has bursitis in his hips and is using a walker, but is otherwise all right. I just hope he listens to his doctors and doesn't come driving down here before the trial is over."

"I hope so too." I put my hand on Mavis' back in a gesture of support as we entered Rock County Courtroom A.

Shelly indicated we should sit in the back three rows on the left, behind the District Attorneys' table. She explained that the potential jurors would have to sit in the first rows as well as on the entire right side, behind the defense table. We filed into the first two of the available pews. The pew behind us was empty. I was glad because I knew my dad was coming later so he would have a place to sit. I wasn't sure if any others in the Judge family were set to arrive that day, but there certainly should be seating for them if they did.

Momentarily, Judge Werner entered the courtroom. Since I'd known him for years, I took little note of his appearance except for the robe he was wearing. It did make him look very judicial. I tried to see him through the eyes of a potential jury. Seated behind the bench, he looked as I'd always known him. His blond hair, which was thinning, appeared to have a bit of gray blended in. He had a handsome face, oval and sharp-featured. Richard Werner's countenance was that of an intelligent, serious man. I was again pleased that the case had been handed over to him due to Judge Daley's call to active duty.

Judge Werner announced that it was "The State of Wisconsin versus William Mereness." He stated the case number: 02CF3911. The judge then announced that counsel was present. Next he asked the attorneys if there were any additional witnesses whose names needed to be read to the jury panel. Both attorneys replied in the negative. Werner then said the first 30 panelists were to be seated in the box and the rest behind the bar.

District Attorney David O'Leary spoke up. " There is a matter to take up first. The defendant was arrested yesterday. We will file bail-jumping charges today. Mr. Mereness attempted both by phone and letter to contact Mr. Mereness, Sr. James saw his son drop off the letter, which began 'Please destroy this after reading it or I will have to go back to jail'. We would like to modify bond and revoke the part that allows for property. If he's out he'll try to influence witnesses in this trial."

Werner responded. We would cross that bridge when we came to it. Meanwhile, the bail-jumping charge was not to be brought to the attention of the jury now or ever. It had nothing to do with the trial itself.

DA O'Leary wondered about the jury seeing the defendant in shackles.

The Judge said he could arrange that the jury not see him coming and going. Daniel interjected that that would not be a problem, as his client was not in shackles or restrained in any way.

With that problem solved, the judge instructed the bailiff, Mr. Bliss, to give the list of the first 30 potential jurors to the attorneys. After Mr. Bliss did so, Daniel was complaining quite vociferously that the names on the list were not "in order". Judge Werner explained that these were the first 30 randomly selected from the pool; therefore, they would not be in any particular order.

Daniel requested and received time to get organized for the first 30 panelists.

During the lull, the first thing I did was turn to Michael, "Why is he trying to seat 30 when a jury consists of 'twelve of your peers'"?

"With a trial this long he'll probably want four alternates instead of two, so that'll require sixteen jurors. Each side will have seven strikes to remove individuals from the panel. That'll trim the 30 down to16."

Gosh, the things I am learning at this trial. I thought briefly that this would sure provide me with first hand examples to give my U.S. History students about the judicial branch.

Next, Shelly showed us the list of witnesses for the prosecution. I noted there were several names of people who were employed at Hormel. Those individuals would likely testify that John Furgason was at work on Friday, November 22. No doubt, one of Daniel's tactics would be to point the finger at John as a possible suspect. Having already talked with my friend, who worked at Hormel, I knew John had been at work that day. It was just important that the jury hear the same information I had.

There were a few teachers on the prosecution's witness list as well as Nick Demrow, the construction worker, who'd testified at the preliminary hearing. My brother's name was on the list as were the names of Bill's father, brother and son.

While I had known James Mereness, Sr. was due to testify, I did not know James, Jr. and Christopher were scheduled to offer testimony against Bill. Of course, had his mother lived, she too would have been on the list. *How sad for that family. As much as Jennifer's family has been devastated by her murder, Bill's family must be nearly destroyed.* I felt a great deal of empathy for them.

Also on the prosecution's witness list were the names of quite a few detectives and other law enforcement personnel. No surprise there; I'd expected to hear from the Janesville and Appleton Police Departments as well as the Oneida County Sheriff's Department.

The remaining names on the list were unfamiliar to me. I would just have to wait and see who those individuals were when they were called. I could have quizzed Shelly about them during a break, but she had enough to do. I would find out in due time.

After about 20 minutes Daniel finally indicated he was ready. Werner instructed the bailiff to bring in the first 30 panelists.

They filed in, entering through the same door we had. One of them looked particularly young, which made me realize I did not know what the age requirement was for jury duty. *How pathetic.* I'd lived in this country for 49 years, and even taught U.S. History, but I did not know this basic fact about our judicial system. I vowed to find out.

None of the panelists looked particularly elderly and I wondered if there was an upper age limit for jurors. Again, I would endeavor to find out.

Many had books in their hands, having prepared for a long morning idly waiting at the courthouse. The bailiff told one young man, and none too gently, to remove his ball cap.

Those 30 individuals went through the small door in the bar and were directed to sit in the jury box. Those in the remaining jury pool were guided to the pews across the aisle and then to the pews in front of us. I was a bit annoyed, as my view was no longer unobstructed. Then I realized, since there was not going to be any testimony, this was just jury selection, I wouldn't really need to observe a great deal.

To begin, Judge Werner apologized for the time it had already taken. He explained that he didn't usually have juries of this size. I turned to Shelly with a questioning look. She explained that there was another jury trial beginning that day also. That one was for medical malpractice. So, two juries needed to be empanelled.

My gosh! That trial was for our neighbor, an orthopedic surgeon. He was accused of being negligent in the death of one of his patients. I'd been so wrapped up in our situation, I hadn't even realized he was due to go on trial at the same time. I felt remiss.

Our neighbor had operated on Josh's leg twice during his recovery from his auto accident. He'd done an excellent job with him. We'd also grown friendly as neighbors; he'd attended all three of the barn parties we'd held. He'd brought his kids down to visit the horses on occasion. I saw him nearly every morning; him on his jog, me doing chores. I should have called him or written him a note of encouragement. I'd have to do something when these trials were over.

Werner then announced the case again and said it was important that everyone was able to hear him and the attorneys. He instructed the panelists to raise their hand if they couldn't hear. One older man raised his hand. *Hmm, If he couldn't hear him, how did he know to raise his hand?*

The judge spoke louder. He introduced DA David O'Leary, ADA Perry Folts, defense attorney Tod Daniel, Daniel's intern and the defendant, William Mereness.

Judge Werner explained that the charge in this case was that William J. Mereness, sometime on the day of Friday, November 22, 2002, killed Jennifer L. Mereness. I felt a stab in my gut. Just hearing the charges in this way was like hearing them once again for the first time.

Werner indicated that Bill had pleaded not guilty.

The judge advised the potential jurors that the District Attorney had to prove the charge without a reasonable doubt.

At that point, the judge had the 30 panelists stand and raise their right hands for a joint swearing. I never knew such a thing took place. I knew witnesses took an oath, but I didn't know jurors did too.

After calling the roll, Werner explained that his goal was to seat a fair and impartial jury. He reiterated that it was important to hear. He stated that he was aware that jury service could be a burden, but that it was also "a privilege and a responsibility". We were "fortunate to have it".

Finally, the judge explained that he expected the trial to last ten to fifteen days, and that the jury would be sequestered. He wanted the panelists to tell him if that would pose a problem for them.

Ten hands shot into the air. I was floored. One third were already attempting to avoid their duty. I listened as they told the judge their problems: a boss with a high risk-pregnancy, a wife and two sons at home who needed care, a vacation in Canada already paid for, no babysitter, a financial burden to be off work, another babysitter problem, an employer who didn't pay employees serving on jury duty, two children leaving for college, a dog, a wife who didn't drive so she couldn't get to work coupled with a case of tonsillitis possibly requiring surgery, a handicapped daughter who needed help, a case of rheumatoid arthritis and a husband who handled all medications, two children--one of whom had an upcoming doctor's appointment.

After listening to these concerns, Werner excused eight of the ten. I wasn't sure which two of the excuses he didn't buy; hopefully the dog was one. I owned five dogs and would never use them to avoid jury duty. Such a disregard of responsibility to our system was shocking.

Names were read aloud to fill in the empty seats from potential jurors on our side of the bar.

After three names were called Daniel called out, "I'm behind" and asked for the second and third names to be repeated. This was the second time he had slowed down the selection process. I wondered if it was purposeful. I couldn't imagine he was really that inefficient. Finally, the eight "replacement" panelists were seated.

The judge again asked if there were problems with the length of the trial and sequestration. Luckily, only one hand was raised. The man's problem was that he'd been laid off since January and, presently, he had a possible job opportunity. Werner excused him.

This man was replaced, and fortunately that individual did not have a problem with being sequestered.

The next question for the panelists was "Are you related by blood or marriage to William Mereness, Tod Daniel, David O'Leary, Perry Folts or Jennifer Mereness who was sometimes known as Jennifer Judge?" Werner directed the potential jurors to raise their hand if they were related to any of those individuals. No hands were raised.

The subsequent question was whether any of the 30 knew any of the aforementioned individuals. Two knew Daniel as an attorney; one knew O'Leary as a basketball coach. Werner asked of those individuals, "Would this preclude your being impartial?" All replied in the negative. They stayed.

Werner then queried, "Has anyone heard or read anything about this case?" A rash of hands went into the air. I slumped in my seat.

The judge explained that he would adjourn to a side conference room with the attorneys to ask questions of each of these individuals.

That process took about an hour, which we filled with desultory conversation.

When the questioning was finished, eight of the panelists were excused.

More names were called. The entire process began again with these eight. Two had problems with being sequestered. One individual was "invaluable" at work, while the other had an eight-year-old son and worked in a business with only two employees. They were excused.

Their replacements had problems too: childcare and needing to work to earn money for college tuition due in the fall. They were excused.

Gratefully, the replacements were okay with being sequestered.

Next Werner went on to the relationship question with these eight new individuals. No problems.

The next question for the new eight was about knowing any of the major individuals in the case. I was holding my breath. *Please!*

What will happen if thirty people could not be gathered from this pool? I had no idea.

One knew Perry Folts, but was confident their professional relationship would not cause a bias. *Whew.*

Werner wanted to know if these eight had heard or read anything about the case. Seven hands went in the air. *Good God! We we'll never get a jury. Maybe Daniel was right about a change of venue.*

Another half-hour passed while the judge and the attorneys questioned the seven panelists individually in the conference room. When they were finished Werner excused four.

The same set of questions was posed to the next four replacements. One had a work issue.

The next replacement had a babysitting problem. *Oh, wow, he'd been one of my students years ago! Hopefully he'll be excused.* He'd had so little interest in learning that I have no confidence in his ability to be an effective juror. Gone. *Good.*

The next replacement had a ten-week-old child, was laid off and due to start school on August 25. Excused.

The subsequent replacement had to start school and was released by Judge Werner.

Finally, the next replacement was okay with being sequestered.

These four survived the relationship question and the familiarity question. I was crossing my fingers. *We're almost there!*

Three of the four had heard or read about the case. They were taken into the conference room. 10 minutes passed. One was cut from the field.

The next replacement passed on all accounts.

Hallelujah! At 12: 30 p.m. we finally had a full thirty in the jury box!

Mercifully, Judge Werner called for a lunch break until 1:30 p.m. I believe it had been the longest morning of my life. The only things that even compared were when I had to sit for interminably long hours with my son, mom or dad in an emergency room.

17

The family traveled the twelve or so blocks to Bobby and Cathy's house for lunch. Patti and Cathy set out bread, deli meat, cheese, vegetables with dip and some chips. It was quite a feast. I was not hungry, but I did eat a half a sandwich. I chose a Coke to drink since caffeine seemed like a good idea with a long afternoon ahead. Most of us sat outside in the shade on the deck. It was hot, but it was nice to be outside for a little while. From the two patio tables we conversed back and forth while we ate.

Most of the discussion was about the jury selection, with Bobby and I comparing notes about which individuals we had known as students. We talked about Bill's financial situation and how the county was paying for Bill's defense. Michael and Cathy informed us that they'd been sent papers to sign, which would allow for the sale of the Minocqua property. That was shocking indeed. Perhaps Bill did imagine he would be found guilty, since he was suddenly willing to part with a piece of property he had killed for. Michael and Cathy, of course, had no intention of signing the papers. They fully intended that the property be kept and used by the family in memory of Jennifer.

When I arrived back at the fourth floor of the courthouse, I saw Christopher in the hallway. I said hello to him. He looked a bit puzzled, so I reminded him of who I was. I'd told him I remembered him from the Thanksgiving and Christmas Eve we'd spent together.

He nodded in polite but nervous understanding.

I tried to ease his tension a bit, "This must be very difficult for you, I'm sorry you have to go through it."

"It's pretty bad, but thanks."

I extended my hand, he took it and gave a light shake; I went into the courtroom.

It was exactly 1:30 p.m.

Michael indicated we could move up to the front of the prosecution's side since many of the jury panelists had been eliminated in the morning session. We were claiming new seats when I observed a middle aged, dark-haired woman with two, twenty-something, dark-haired young ladies in the row behind me. I was feeling protective of space for the family. I turned to the women and said, as kindly as I could, "Excuse me, but we're trying to save this row for Jennifer's family."

The woman responded, "I know, I'm Ann Beatty, Bill's first wife. She gestured to the younger women, "These are my daughters."

I almost fell out of my seat! I'd never expected them to attend the trial, but the more I thought of it, the more it made sense. Christopher was testifying. They would want to be supportive of him. While they certainly were not Jennifer's family, I wasn't about to ask them to move! It was completely understandable that they would not want to sit on the side of the courtroom behind Bill. We'd all just have to squeeze in together.

I introduced myself and welcomed the three women. Ann explained that they hadn't let Christopher come in because they weren't sure if he was allowed since he'd been subpoenaed to testify. I relayed that Cathy had been subpoenaed and there was no problem with her being in the courtroom during jury selection. Ann thanked me for the information and one of Christopher's sisters went out to get him.

At 1:35 p.m. roll call of the jury was taken. Two of the thirty were missing and one of the remaining pool was AWOL.

I quickly asked Michael what would happen if those missing didn't appear. He surprised me with his answer, "A warrant will be issued for their arrest. Judges don't take this behavior lightly."

Obviously not! I hoped those missing would appear shortly. Then, one by one, between 1:40 and 1:42 p.m. the errant jurors reappeared. I was surprised they weren't admonished immediately and harshly for being tardy.

The bailiff announced once again that this was "Circuit Court Branch 6, the Honorable Richard Werner presiding."

Judge Werner noted that we were once again, "Back on the record in the State versus William Mereness."

Then Werner advised that during the lunch break something had come to his attention. Apparently one juror had to take medication that made him drowsy. He had reported to the bailiff that he had nodded off during the morning. While initially he had thought he could make it through the trial, he had become doubtful. Judge Werner excused the gentleman.

I can't believe it. Just when we're ready to move forward, we have to take a step back. Hopefully a replacement won't be difficult to seat.

My desires couldn't have been further from reality.

The first three from the jury pool had problems with sequestration, the fourth was okay with being sequestered, but had worked with Jennifer at

Kohl's. The woman told the judge she believed she could still be fair and impartial. Then when Werner asked her if she'd heard or read anything about the case she responded affirmatively. Off went judge, attorneys, defendant and potential juror to the conference room.

I sighed deeply in disappointment.

In fact, after that particular candidate was rejected, Judge Werner decided they would simply call the potential jurors into the conference room, one at a time until one was found to replace the man with the medication problem.

From our vantage point in the courtroom we observed the parade of potential jurors come and go from the conference room. During the long pause, we discussed Bill's bail jumping. It had been determined that there were to be two charges, each carrying a $10,000 fine and ten years in prison. The charges were a Class D felony, which, according to Michael, was "bad". The fortunate part of this for the Judge family was that should Bill be found innocent of killing Jennifer, the state could press for the maximum prison term on the bail jumping, netting him a twenty-year sentence.

My spirits were buoyed. It was a great back up. Should Bill somehow beat this murder charge, twenty years in prison would mean Bill would be 70 years old at the time of his release. I think most of us could be somewhat satisfied with that. In all likelihood, Jennifer's parents would not be alive to see that terrible day.

The details on Bill's illegal activities included him calling his father to try to get him to meet with him at the high school in Appleton. When that didn't work, Bill drove by his father's house and put a letter in his mailbox. James, Sr. called Sallie and she went over to her father's house. At that time Bill drove by again and Sallie asked him what he was doing. Bill drove off. Sallie retrieved the letter from the mailbox and read it, then turned it over to the police.

Apparently, the letter was full of denials as well as a statement that he would always love his brother, sister, dad and deceased mother.

This time when the conference room door opened everyone filed out into the courtroom. *Finally!*

The thirtieth juror was found and seated in the jury box. It was time for the judge to continue his questions of the panel. After that, each attorney would have a turn to question the jurors.

Judge Werner's fourth question involved a reading of the lengthy witness lists for both sides. He then asked the jurors if they knew any of the witnesses. Many jurors admitted knowing witnesses.

Horrors! Here we go again.

The judge then asked each of the jurors if their particular relationship with a witness would affect his or her impartiality. Unbelievably, all the jurors responded in the negative so no one had to be replaced.

Whew.

However, it was apparent the attorneys were taking notes. I realized that many of the jurors who said they knew my brother, or a police officer or teacher on the witness list would likely be stricken by the defense. But since there were ten jurors who knew individual witnesses in those categories, Daniel would not be able to strike them all.

Werner next wanted to know if any of the jurors had a preconceived outcome for this trial. None had.

The next question from the court was if any panelists had served on a jury in the past. Three had. A man had served on a trial in 1991, which resulted in acquittal. One woman served on a civil case in the 1980's, while another was a juror on a criminal case in which the defendant was found guilty. *Daniel would probably strike her.*

The judge's seventh question regarded law enforcement. Panelists were supposed to reveal if their parents, spouse or children were employed in law enforcement. Four indicated so. All four were first asked if that situation would affect their impartiality. "No," the four responded in turn. The potential jurors also were certain they would not place any extra weight on the testimony of a police officer.

Judge Werner then asked the rest of the panel if any of them would give more weight to the testimony of law enforcement personnel. None would.

It seemed as if the process was humming along efficiently now. I pleaded to the moon and the stars for the selection to continue in this vein.

The judge's next inquiry was whether or not any of the panelists had been convicted of a crime. Two men had been. Werner then wanted to know if they felt they had been treated fairly in their court cases. One had, one had not.

Question ten was about potential jurors being victims of crime. Again, two answered affirmatively. Both reported that they felt they had been treated fairly by the legal system. I assumed the woman who had been a victim of sexual assault would be on the defense's list to strike.

Then the judge asked his eleventh and final question, "Would anyone be unable to try the case on the evidence presented and to be fair and impartial?" None of the jurors felt they would have that problem.

Judge Werner turned the jury panel over to the District Attorney's Office.

Assistant DA Perry Folts asked questions about biases and prejudices. He reiterated that the defendant deserved a fair trial and so did the State.

Folts showed the thirty a framed eight by ten photograph of Jennifer. He asked if anyone recognized her face. None did.

Eight of the thirty had previously been witnesses in court, but only five had testified in a jury trial. Of those five, only three knew if it had been a criminal case. Folts asked them to explain what type of case they were involved in. One was a paramedic testifying about an accident he'd responded to. The second was the woman who had been sexually assaulted. The third had involved bartending.

Again, I was certain the defense would strike the assault victim. It seemed a shame. She appeared to be a very bright young lady and would likely have made a good juror.

Next, Folts told the prospective jurors that Jennifer Judge had been bludgeoned in her home by a hatchet and maul.

I detected no reactions of horror from the panelists. That surprised me. They seemed to have good control over their emotions; but then, if I hadn't been involved in the case, I could probably have been objective too. However, in the future I was sure I would be one who was stricken from a jury panel.

The accused was her estranged husband. At the closing for their new house he dropped the news about the divorce. Folts wanted to know if any of the panelists were divorced. Several hands went up. Were any of their divorces unfriendly? Just one woman raised her hand. When called upon, she explained that her divorce had occurred back in 1974. The woman was sure that it would not affect her impartiality.

This panelist seemed like an articulate and independent woman. The unfriendly divorce wouldn't win her any points with the defense, however.

I was trying not to become too attached to any of these individuals. Since fourteen were going to be culled, I didn't want to be left feeling too disappointed. Unfortunately, I was already forming opinions and hoping certain people would be chosen.

The fourth question from the district attorney was about the burden of proof. He reminded the jury panel that the State only had to prove beyond a reasonable doubt, not beyond all doubt. Folts asked, "Is that burden too high?" None of the jurors stirred. The prosecutor said, "I see no hands."

"Is that burden too low?" Again, there was no response from the panel. The ADA repeated, "I see no hands."

"No hands" was Folts' observation to the next question. He wanted to know if any of the 30 thought the State should have to prove more than the fact that Bill caused Jennifer's death and that he acted with intent to kill.

None of the panel felt motive should have to be established or disagreed with the concept of "innocent until proven guilty".

There were no religious or philosophical reasons to preclude anyone from voting guilty.

An older man admitted that he could not read or write, but he thought he could function fine if certain documents were read to him.

None of the thirty were dyslexic or had any physical limitations about sitting through the trial.

Folts noted, "no hands" to questions about judging the facts not the law as well as difficulties with applying the law to the facts in the case.

No one was worried about sentencing, nor would they have a problem looking at graphic photographs. The ADA informed them that the victim was hit with a hatchet, which damaged her head and caused death.

I thought about some of the facts of the case that Folts was weaving into his questions. Earlier, he'd indirectly told the possible jurors that the divorce had been "unfriendly". Twice he'd mentioned the weapons and cause of death. I was a bit surprised the defense attorney didn't object to this tactic. It must have been permissible. Daniel would never have stood for it otherwise. I admired the assistant DA for being clever enough to use this opportunity to lay some foundation for those who would ultimately be chosen.

Actually, as I had begun to fully understand the system, it would be for those who weren't stricken by either side. In effect those left would comprise the jury. So, were they really *chosen*? Clearly, I'd never thought about it before. *Who had?*

Folts saw, "No hands," for his last concern, that panelists might have problems with graphic descriptions of scenes or injuries to the victim.

The group was turned over to the defense.

Daniel continued to have a helter-skelter delivery. He told the 30 that each side "got to pick whom they don't want for whatever reason." Then he said that the questions might seem intrusive, but he was just getting a sense. Then he talked about the trial being fifteen days in duration, but not on Sunday. The defense attorney explained that the State would go first and the defendant had no control over the length of the trial. Further, he added, the judge controlled the pacing of the trial. He requested that they "take estimates of time with a grain of salt" and "cut us some slack". Daniel finally had a question; "Did anyone have a problem with that?"

Jennifer's Justice

One woman said she had to begin college on the 30th of August. Werner interjected that that would "probably be okay".

It was obvious from Daniel's start that he too was going to embellish his questions with influential statements. It appeared that it was acceptable.

Four of the 30 were or had been employed in health care. There was an EMT, an ER nurse, a labor and delivery nurse and a plasma center employee. I assumed the defense would have reason to strike any or all of those individuals.

Three had family members in health care. And while none worked in the mental health field, one had a relative involved in that field.

None of the panelists were related to an attorney, nor had friends who were attorneys.

There was not a teacher in the group, but seven had friends or family who were teachers.

As Daniel questioned them all individually, I realized one woman had grown up down the block from me and that I had taught with her brother. Her last name had not been familiar because she had married and taken her husband's name. I hadn't recognized her face because I hadn't seen her in over thirty-five years. *It is truly a small world.*

No one was involved in the heating or air conditioning business but six had friends or relatives who were.

Why would the defense be concerned about that? I was certain that the vent-stuffing incident was not going to be allowed in this trial. Perhaps there was some other issue I was unaware of, or Daniel was just making sure in case the furnace tampering was somehow brought in.

There were no members of domestic violence advocacy groups, but one woman had been a victim of domestic violence. I couldn't imagine she would make the cut.

None of the 30 had been accused of domestic violence, which surely would have caused concern for the prosecution.

Seven had had their residence or car burgled.

Two had close family members prosecuted, one for assault and battery in a bar fight. I imagined the prosecution'd remove him. He might be able to identify with a violent act.

Daniel's next question concerned whether any of the jurors' children had been divorced. Five panelists admitted to that.

One woman said she had entered into a marital property agreement, but none of the potential jurists saw anything "unromantic, wrong or sinister" about that.

Three in the group owned property up north, while an additional panelist had an uncle with a place in the Tomahawk-Minocqua area.

I was growing weary. Daniel had already outstripped the prosecution in the number of questions he'd asked, and there was no sign he was about to slow down. I stretched my neck and shifted in my seat. *I could use a break. Hopefully, one of the jurors will request a "biological break".*

The twenty-third question from the defense was regarding visits to Minocqua or Tomahawk. Four volunteered that they frequented the area.

The defense attorney saw "no hands" when he asked if anyone thought the believability of police was judged by a different standard.

There was some discussion about the next question. Daniel asked if anyone did not understand that a police officer could legally tell untruths to someone. One man said, "I didn't know that." Several other hands went up.

The defense attorney asked, "Does anyone have a problem with that?"

One man piped up, "I do." Though after further questioning he didn't think that it would influence him as to credibility. *The prosecution will take a hard look at that fellow.*

Daniel wanted to know if anyone didn't understand character witnesses, and that character evidence only went to the credibility of the witness. The potential jurors didn't flinch, but I didn't even understand what he was talking about. Maybe I was just getting tired from concentrating so hard. It didn't seem like a major concern anyway, since I couldn't imagine Bill finding anyone who would be a character witness for him.

Next the defense attorney launched into what I would consider an opening statement. He talked about the fact that "the crime is not on trial", but never really did ask a question. I was curious as to why the DA's didn't object. Daniel also wanted the jurors to understand that whatever they thought of him, they couldn't take it out on Mr. Mereness. He babbled some about reasonable doubt, but tacked on a "is there a problem with that" so as to make a question.

That strategy was used again about the high burden of proof and the equally high stakes. Then the defense attorney said, "You can't prove you didn't do something."

Egad, he's really grasping here. Hopefully, the 30 souls in the jury box are getting as annoyed as I am, and they would hold it against his client.

Daniel pressed on, this time about the inequity of resources and the power of the government.

The DA said, "There doesn't seem to be a question here."

Finally!

Before Werner could react Daniel added, "Mr. Mereness had no burden here."

"Objection, there are no questions here."
Folts is going to rescue us from Daniel's diatribe!
The judge sustained the objection.

It was as if the ADA had stuck a pin in a balloon. Daniel wound down in a dramatic fashion.

He stated that the decision must be unanimous and wondered if any had a problem with the responsibility of making that decision. No one did.

The final "question" from the defense was if any of the 30 had philosophical problems with the case. None did, or they were too numb to speak.

At long last he's done! Relief from the family was palpable.

Judge Werner had further instructions for the jury. He explained that counsel would have the opportunity to exercise the right to strike testimony.

The judge added that there would be times the jury might be excused from the courtroom because he needed to decide if they could hear certain things.

Werner assured the jurors that they would, in future, have more breaks than they had today.

Yes, this is brutal.

Hopefully, according to Werner, things would move along quickly and we would "get to the truth here".

The panel heard that there would be a jury of twelve with four alternates. The reason, the judge explained, was that it would be a long trial and emergencies could happen. No one would know who the alternates were until the end of the trial. At that point, the names of the alternates would be "pulled out of a drum after a fair trial for all concerned."

At about that point, I was distracted by a number of people entering the courtroom. They appeared to be "spectators" of some sort. As they entered, the bailiff directed them to sit in the pews behind us, well away from the potential jurors.

The judge moved on to more immediate concerns. They'd talk about motel reservations.

"The bailiff, Mr. Bliss, will take care of you." If the jurors had questions, they were to write them down for the bailiff to give to the judge, or simply ask the bailiff.

The panelists were told they were not to discuss among themselves during the trial. They were to wait until the end when he would give them instructions for deliberations. Werner's final words were, "I will be quiet now and let the lawyers do their work."

It was 3:40 p.m. The bailiff stood out in front of the counsels' tables, mid-way between the two. He took a paper, which I presumed to be the list of panelists, to one table, then, the other. Each time they received the paper, the district attorneys would discuss for a while, and then O'Leary would cross off a name. Daniel did likewise with his intern and Bill's input.

I recalled reading one of John Grisham's novels. In it, the defense had hired people who were experts at jury selection. They investigated the backgrounds of all the panelists to make a more informed decision about their "strikes". I didn't imagine Bill had the resources to be able to do that.

About twenty-five minutes later the list was taken to Judge Werner by Bailiff Bliss.

The judge spoke, "Ladies and gentlemen, if your name is mentioned please stand." He proceeded to read sixteen names. Werner told them they had been selected for this jury. He thanked the other fourteen and told them they were free to go. They rose and walked past us on their way out the back door of the courtroom. Some of them looked at us, I think they must have figured out we were Jennifer's family.

I had a mixed reaction to those stricken and selected. It was no surprise that the EMT was gone, nor the non-reader. On the other hand, I was shocked that two nurses remained on the panel, including the one who had been sexually assaulted. It was a pleasant turn of events.

As the jury for the case of The State of Wisconsin versus William Mereness was seated in the jury box, I noted that there were ten women and six men. I believed that would be to our advantage.

Judge Werner told the sixteen to go home and be back to the courthouse by 6:15 p.m. At that point they would be taken to their motel. In the two hours they had, they were to get something to eat and pack. They were not to talk about or listen to anything about the trial.

The trial, the judge informed them, would run Mondays through Saturdays from 8:30 a.m. until "6:00 p.m. or so".

The jurors were instructed to stand. They were given an oath, and led out of the courtroom by Mr. Bliss.

Judge Werner addressed the District Attorney, "You have a matter to take up, Mr. O'Leary?"

"Yes."

"We'll take a break until 4:20."

During the break we all discussed the jury as selected. Everyone in the family felt it looked good for us. The ratio of female to male was a welcomed surprise to all. We had similar feelings about the EMT and the nurses. *Dare we be optimistic?*

Court was not reconvened until 4:35 p.m. I was beginning to think that times were not going to be strictly adhered to in this case. When I asked Michael about that, he chuckled, "You catch on quickly."

The judge talked about the motion. He believed it to be for bail jumping, and it was a criminal complaint. He checked to see if Daniel had a copy. He did, and claimed the two complaints were the same, meaning Bill had only broken one condition of his bond. The defense would likely argue that point to make a potential sentence less lengthy.

Werner said he would take that under advisement.

That's our safety net, he can't allow Daniel to sabotage it!

The district attorney made his argument. He had two concerns. The property bond that was adjusted by Judge Daley had a payment due in August. Also, this was a case of felony bail jumping. Bill's father was a key witness in this case and the defendant attempted to dissuade him from testifying on the eve of the homicide trial. O'Leary was certain that if Bill were out on bond, he would continue to violate it.

Daniel disagreed. He claimed that the assurity on the Minocqua property was up to date. There was other property being controlled by the State in foreclosure. The charges in this situation, that a letter was allegedly left, was in no way threatening, nor was personal contact made. Further, the defense attorney argued, the purpose of bail was to ensure the defendant's presence in court, and he had been at every proceeding. He had even been in Janesville when arrested. There were no allegations to support a flight risk.

The judge explained that there were two cases of bail jumping. The conditions of the bond were very clear. There was to be no contact with his father, brother or sister. The defendant had signed it, whether it was cash or otherwise. He was told in open court what the conditions were. Further, Mr. Mereness, Sr., was a witness in this case.

Werner agreed with Daniel that bond did assure appearance in court and he acknowledged the defendant had done so; but bond also set forth conditions and those had to be followed. Due to the seriousness of the allegations, the judge ruled a $5,000 cash bond on each charge.

Family members were pleased. We knew Bill could not come up with that kind of money at this point. He would be going back to jail.

O'Leary then asked to modify the bond on the homicide charge given the new criminal activity by the defendant.

Naturally, Daniel disagreed.

Werner was clear and decisive. He reiterated that the conditions on the bond have been clear on this homicide for no contact. The defendant had signed four bonds with those conditions. Since these were serious allegations he was going to reinstate the cash bond of $100,000. "With that then, court is in recess."

We were ecstatic! Everyone felt the judge handled the bond situation and Daniel perfectly. All felt confident they would sleep better tonight just knowing Bill was, once again, "a guest of the county".

As I drove home I thought about Bill having jumped bail. While I had feared that he might try to avoid prosecution by fleeing, or that he might possibly try to kill himself again, it hadn't occurred to me that he would try to contact his father. It showed a certain vulnerability I hadn't credited Bill with.

It also showed that the two judges had been remiss to modify the bail as they had, which of course we claimed at that time.

I was very grateful that Bill had made it to trial, and that no witnesses had been harmed or intimidated.

By ignoring the conditions of his bond, Bill proved that he had no respect for the law. And, as I'd wondered previously, what good would it have done if Jennifer had obtained a restraining order against Bill? Quite likely, none.

18

I awakened with a great sense of anticipation. It was another big day, the first day of testimony. It was also the day Jeff would leave for his Air Force reunion out west.

Before we heard from any witnesses, we'd hear jury instructions from Judge Werner and opening statements from both sides. Michael had thought the instructions would be fairly brief, but opening arguments would likely last through the morning hours. That seemed like a long time for jurors to sit and listen to lawyers talking about their version of the truth in the case. I hoped it wouldn't be too long and drawn out; especially from Daniel, who seemed to have a propensity to enjoy the sound of his own voice.

Jeff's Air Force reunion had been planned for over a year. It was to be held in Cheyenne, Wyoming, his home base during the Vietnam War era. We'd initially planned for the two of us to take the trip. I had been looking forward to meeting his Air Force comrades and to extended trips we were going to take to the Tetons and Yellowstone Park.

I was resentful that Bill's actions had interfered with our lives in this way too.

At 8:00 a.m. we said our good-byes and I left for the courthouse. My eyes were a bit misty. It was going to be so hard for me to be without him during this trial. I'd miss being able to talk with him about the events of the day. I'd miss his emotional support and the physical help around the farm. I'd miss the shoulder rub he could give to ease my stress.

Jeff had offered to stay home, but I had insisted that he go. This was the first reunion his unit had ever planned. He'd worked hard at contacting his service buddies and was sincerely looking forward to the experience. He simply should not have to miss it.

I had steeled myself to handle the trial alone; but when faced with his departure, I felt weak and needy. Not wanting to wallow in self-pity, I straightened myself in the seat, swallowed down the lump in my throat and gave myself a "stiff upper lip" pep talk.

At least parking was not going to be the problem it had been on day one. With both juries chosen, far fewer people would be at the courthouse. The weather forecast was for sunny skies and temperatures in the 90's again, so I was happy to find a parking spot in the shade a few blocks away. The short walk would be good before sitting for the entire day.

The family gathered outside the courtroom. I noticed my brother was limping badly.

"What's wrong with your leg?" I inquired.

"I think I might have shin splints from running."

"Ouch, I had those once. It was really painful and took a long time to heal," I commiserated. "Did you wrap your leg?"

"No, I'm just taking off a few days to see what happens."

When it rains it pours! At just the time when he needs stress relief, he can't run.

"That stinks. Is Cathy running alone then?"

"No, she and Michael are running together."

"Well, it's good those two can keep up their programs. Sorry you're laid up."

"I'll manage."

Always the stalwart one.

Since I'd had a difficult time keeping up with handwriting notes the day before, I opted to bring a borrowed laptop to use for the day. I searched everywhere in the gallery for an outlet but found none. I decided to go on battery power. I checked the level; I had three hours. I'd keep my eye on my watch and take the laptop to the victim-witness room for recharging at least 15 minutes before I'd run out of battery. Stephanie agreed to take notes for me while I was gone on that mission.

At 8:32 a.m. Judge Richard Werner convened the court. He again stated, "This is the matter of Wisconsin versus William Mereness". The judge wished the record to note that the attorneys were present, as was the defendant. Werner then noted that the jury was not in the box and inquired of the attorneys, "Is there anything we need to do before we bring them in?"

O'Leary responded first, "No."

Daniel was more formal, "No, Your Honor."

The bailiff, Mr. Bliss, went to the door on the far right side of the room, beyond the defense table. After the door was opened, I could hear voices coming from within the jury room. The voices were raised, as if questions were being asked. Mr. Bliss quieted them, led the 16 out into the courtroom and directed them to the jury box.

Theirs was an awesome responsibility. They held the fate of one man in their hands. To a lesser degree, they also held our futures. Our lives had already been irrevocably changed, but a guilty verdict would provide justice for Jennifer and some closure for the family.

The faces of the jurors reflected their charge. It was obvious that each of the 16 was taking the responsibility seriously.

I wanted to somehow notate the jurors for myself, without using names. I remembered there was a number system used by courts, and scolded myself for not having thought to ask Michael what it was.

Well, I'd better make something up in a hurry.

I made a table and included a brief description of each individual in his or her cell. I'd wished I were a more capable artist, so I could draw each juror's face.

I'm thinking of these things too late! I should have tried to find someone who could help me in this!

Judge Werner greeted the jury, "Good morning ladies and gentlemen."

The jury responded in unison and with proper solemnity, "Good morning."

Werner began his instructions. He informed the jurors that their charge was to decide guilt or innocence in this case. No personal feelings about age, origin, etc., should enter into it. Further, the judge advised, they were not to begin deliberation or talk about the case until instructed to do so. During the recesses when they were dismissed, they were not to listen to conversations, use dictionaries, computers or other reference materials.

I knew most of what the judge was talking about, but I wondered why they couldn't use reference materials.

Then Judge Werner supplied an answer for my question. He explained that the case was to be tried only on the sworn testimony on direct and cross-examinations, the exhibits and any facts to which the lawyers have agreed.

Not on research!

Further, the judge continued, the attorneys had the right to object, so the jurors were not to draw conclusions due to objections.

Then the jurors were told they would not be allowed to take notes.

Hmm. With this long of a trial with mainly circumstantial evidence, wouldn't note taking help the jurors put the pieces together?

The educator in me would want to have the advantage of hard data. I would hate to argue with a fellow juror about what she or he thought they'd heard. It would also frustrate me if others didn't remember bits of testimony or evidence I thought were important. *I must ask Michael about this.*

The judge told the panel that they "are the sole judge of the witnesses' weight and credibility." Those two criteria were to be surmised by the witness' interest or lack of interest, conduct, appearance, the clearness of their recollection, their reasonableness and apparent intelligence. The jurors were to use their common sense and experience to guide them.

Wow. This is really subjective.

Next the 16 were advised about the meaning of first-degree intentional homicide. "It is committed by a person who intentionally causes the death of another person. Intent means that the mental purpose of the individual was to cause the death of another human being. There need not be any appreciable time between the intent and the act that caused death."

The jurors were not to confuse intent with motive. The State was not required to prove motive, and motive alone did not "establish guilt".

The defendant was not required to prove his innocence. "The evidence must satisfy you beyond a reasonable doubt. That is not all doubt, but doubt based on reason and common sense."

Lastly, the judge cautioned the jurors that the opening statements they were about to hear were not evidence.

"Good morning. I'm David O'Leary, District Attorney. I and my assistant, Perry Folts, will try this case."

The DA held up an eight by ten framed photograph of Jennifer. I recognized it as the one we'd used on the thank you notes Cathy and I had made the day Bill tried to kill himself.

It seemed to be a good tactic for the prosecution to use. It could make the jury see the victim as a real person. That photo would be especially effective, in it Jennifer looked so lovely and serene.

O'Leary said that the person in the photo was Jennifer Lynn Judge. "This is a day she's waited a long time for."

The lump returned to my throat. *How true for us as well.*

The prosecutor then summarized Jennifer's life. She'd been born on October 13, 1963. "She was a teacher, a lot braver than me. She taught high school Spanish."

Jennifer moved down here with William to a home on Columbus Circle. She was hired at Craig High School in December of 2002. The marriage appeared to be happy, and while Jennifer couldn't have children, she was excited about an adoption that was soon to occur. "But that all ended when he asked for a divorce." The adoption was cancelled. Then Bill changed his mind, but Jennifer said "no", she moved on with her life.

Then the DA summarized the prosecution's case.

They would present telephone records from the day before the murder. Then, since Bill hadn't told his parents about the divorce, Jennifer had to call them. There would be testimony from teachers who saw her crying after that phone call. Attendance records would show Jennifer had then gone to the office and taken four hours of sick time. On Thursday, a fellow teacher heard an angry voice mail at school.

The jury would hear from John Furgason who stayed with Jennifer that Thursday night and went to work on Friday morning.

The court would also hear from the construction workers from the house right next door. They'd explain how they saw Jennifer come home and drive into her garage while they were sitting in their vehicles with their radios on eating lunch at 11:30. One of these workers would say he'd heard a woman scream, turned off his radio, approached another worker's vehicle and inquired whether he'd also heard the scream. At that time, both men saw a man leave the back of her house. They would describe the man as a middle aged white male with glasses and dark hair. He was carrying two bags in his white-gloved hands.

I looked at the jury. My juror number eight was looking directly at Bill. I hoped she was thinking that the description fitted Bill perfectly.

The district attorney continued. One of the construction workers would explain how he followed the man, but didn't know what to do. He waited for his boss, but the boss never appeared. So he went back to work.

Then John Furgason would tell the jury how he'd had dinner plans with Jennifer. He left work at 4:30 p.m. from Hormel and went home. When he couldn't reach Jennifer on the phone he checked for her at her second job at Kohl's. John then went to Jennifer's house, entered and found her dead. He called 911.

The police went through the house and found no one, but it was obvious that Jennifer had been dead for some time. Police would testify that they found the entry point, a rock had knocked in a screen, there were muddy footprints.

O'Leary then explained that there were "certain things given". For example, how she was killed. He picked up the murder weapons, the axe and sledgehammer.

I noticed the jurors straighten in their chairs.

The DA then pulled the weapons out of their plastic covers, held them up and said, "This was an intentional homicide. She was struck six times."

There were audible gasps from the gallery, but not the family. This was the first time the rest of the on-lookers were hearing the brutal detail.

Their reaction transported me back to the first time I'd heard that news. *From Bobby. He was sitting in the corner chair in my dining room.* I felt my visceral response again.

The DA paused. I believe he wanted to give the jurors time to process the horrific truth. The panelists were wide-eyed; some had flared nostrils. A few gave deep sighs. They had been seriously affected by the district attorney's words.

O'Leary began again. He explained how the police looked into Jennifer's murder. Bill told them he couldn't have done it because he had taken his son to school then driven to Minocqua. That drive took five hours. The police drove it in three hours and 30 minutes. The Department of Transportation considered it a three hour and 20 minute drive.

As soon as Bill got to Minocqua, he went directly to Wal-Mart, because they employed him and he wanted to congratulate a friend who'd gotten a promotion. A security camera filmed Bill arriving at 3:33 p.m. He then went to a dumpster and put his hand into it. Next he bought a candy bar and asked for a receipt. He talked to a supposed friend at 3:39 p.m. and left the store at 3:44 p.m.

Bill's boss would tell the jury that he didn't work for Wal-Mart, but for Sam's Club optical. Then Bill's story to the police changed. He said there was going to be a new optical department at the Minocqua Wal-Mart and he went to check on that. His boss would tell you that was not true.

A store clerk remembered Bill because of an unusual situation. He bought a brand new blue and black Columbia jacket with a combination of cash and check. The defendant called the clerk at the store later to say he needed his check back and would bring in that amount in cash. Another call to the store after that was Bill requesting to have a new receipt, one that reflected the purchase as simply cash. The clerk found the whole episode to be odd.

O'Leary asked aloud, "Why did Bill do that? Evidence."

Bill's own brother was going to meet him at the cabin in Minocqua. He got an unusual phone call from his brother. The defendant asked him to arrive at a certain time and go to a certain store for groceries. He was to be sure to get a receipt for the groceries.

The defendant showed up at the cabin and locked himself away downstairs doing laundry. Later, he scrubbed his glasses under water multiple times.

When the police came to the cabin to tell Bill of Jennifer's death, he ran to the wastebasket and took out a red object. When his brother inquired as to what he was doing, Bill replied, "Never mind".

The police began a search. Bill's son will testify that they found no Columbia jacket. Some shoes were found of the same size and style as the muddy prints, but they were a newer pair. Glass fragments were found, the crime lab determined the fragments were consistent with the glass in the window in Jennifer's house.

The police checked phone records. Bill had a cell phone for work. The records show that the story that he left Janesville at 10:00 a.m. was not true. The records showed him making calls in Janesville up to 10:50 a.m. At that time there were two calls from the Craig High School tower. Then the phone was silent until 12:10 p.m. when a call was placed from the Edgerton tower. After that the phone records followed Bill up the interstate.

The crime scene was searched for DNA; there was none on the hammer or hatchet. But construction workers would say the man they saw leave the home wore white leather gloves.

Bill's own father would testify that on Friday, November 29, in the morning the defendant was at his house. Bill went to the kitchen and got a knife and Saran wrap. He went to lie down in the bathtub. His parents followed. Bill's mother, LaBelle, asked, "Did you kill Jennifer?"

Bill responded, "Yes, I did and I'm sorry."

During that time, my jurors number one and eight were looking at Bill frequently. The remaining jurors were riveted on the district attorney.

Bill's father would also tell the jury that he did not want to testify against his son, so he covered his ears because he didn't want to hear any more.

The defendant then went to the kitchen. His father talked to him about his options. There were three. He could admit the murder and take responsibility. To that Bill responded, "I'm not going to jail." The other choices were to deny the murder and go to trial or kill himself.

To that, Bill said, "Good bye", took another knife and left the house. Several hours later Bill's parents received a call from the Appleton police informing them of Bill's attempted suicide by crashing his car into a brick wall.

Again, I was swept back in time. *Cathy and I were in the loft working on the thank-you card. She stood up to answer her phone. It was Bobby telling her about the suicide attempt. Cathy collapsed. I'd prayed Bill would die. We wouldn't be here today if he had.*

O'Leary's voice brought me back. Bill's family had rushed to the hospital. The police asked them if he had any reason to try to kill himself. Mrs. Mereness told the story of what had happened earlier in the day.

The district attorney explained that the charges were first degree murder. The State did not need to prove why one human being would hit another in the head six times with a hatchet.

Shock value again. It had been effective earlier.

DA O'Leary then told the jury that they would call many witnesses, each one holding a piece of the puzzle. He asked the panel to listen and be patient, "We've waited a long time for this day, and so has Jennifer. I thank you."

The presentation had been pretty moving. My juror number one was looking at the family. It appeared juror number three was crying. The district attorney had done an outstanding job. He'd summarized the case effectively and dramatically. He'd kept the jury's interest throughout his thirty-minute presentation.

It was Daniel's turn. My stomach churned mightily. I felt part curiosity, part dread. I wanted to know how he would spin the truth, but didn't want to become upset by it.

The defense attorney explained that he believed there was a different interpretation of the facts. He surprised me by hemming and hawing a bit in this portion of his opening argument.

He did concede the horror of the crime.

The jury needed to concern itself with who did it. They needed to keep their focus, "Did Bill do this?"

Daniel asserted that the record would show that each of the Merenesses were married before, each had jobs, etc. Mr. Mereness had three children; he was older than his wife and further into his career. As a result they entered into a marital property agreement with economic issues and adopting a child. That agreement basically resulted in Jennifer ending up living in the new home in which she was killed, while Bill had the cabin up north.

According to the defense, "Ms. Mereness" was already in another relationship on the day she was killed. Bill was in Janesville; the day before he was in Appleton on business. He was a single parent who came home and his evening was uneventful.

Mavis was shaking her head. *Now she knows Daniel will drag Jennifer's character into the mud. He'll try to show she had 'loose morals' and had put herself in a position to be vulnerable to murder. As a mother, I understand the outrage she must be feeling. She'd probably not realized that the defense would try to sully her daughter's reputation.*

The defense attorney continued his story. Jennifer's Thursday evening was also uneventful. Mr. Furgason spent the night; she taught her a.m. classes Friday and left at 11:25 a.m.

Another reference to Jennifer's life-style. How far would he go to convince the jury that Jennifer was like the main character in "Looking for Mr. Goodbar"? Please let Mavis endure whatever he dishes up.

According to the defense, Jennifer made a cell phone call to John Furgason at 11:26 a.m. and the earliest she would have arrived home was 11:35 or 11:40 a.m. She pulled into the driveway and into the garage.

I noticed my juror number 13 was yawning a lot. Some of the other jurors had a glazed-over look in their eyes, which indicated they were attempting to appear alert, but had ceased listening.

The construction workers were working on the interior of the house to the east. They were on lunch in their cars. Two were facing Jennifer's house. One heard a woman's voice; he didn't hear her words. So he asked the man closer to Jennifer's house. He did not hear anything.

Someone came around the house; the person was not hurried, excited or nervous. He waked down the street, turned, walked and turned. There was no vehicle, no fleeing. Demrow followed the man then turned and came back, "Probably closer than we are and Demrow said, 'I've never seen that man before.'"

That's an outright lie! That was not the testimony Demrow gave! Obviously the opening statements aren't evidence, since they could contain lies. I hope the jury listens to the testimony of Nick Demrow and compares it to Daniel's story. That should go against his, and then his client's credibility.

Daniel continued with his perception of the facts. Someone in the neighborhood was seen matching the description of the defendant.

The defense attorney paused for several minutes. The lapse was inexplicable. Maybe he had misspoken, not meant to speak to the accuracy of the eyewitness. It was very curious. The jury looked puzzled. Gallery members began to look at one another to see if anyone might know what was going on.

Finally, Daniel lurched on. At 4:30 Furgason was off work. There was nothing to prove exact time of death. When the officers arrived, Furgason was on the phone. The police checked the scene and no one was there. They didn't check the closet. There was forced entry in the lower level, but the rock was outside. There was evidence of a burglary to the master bedroom; the drawers were ransacked. Jennifer's sister looked at what was missing: Jennifer's jewelry and a statue.

Cathy had told Daniel about the jewelry and statue in her deposition. She'd figured Bill had taken them as a way to recoup money. But Bill's lawyer's going to purport a burglary theory.

The defense attorney admitted that they had no issue "as to cause of death." He claimed the jury needed to focus on whether or not the State could prove beyond a reasonable doubt.

Then Daniel seemed to contradict himself. He went on about how Jennifer was found, as if it was of some consequence in the case. *I'm sure not following his thought pattern. I can't imagine the jurors are either.*

The body, the defense explained, was found in the entryway facing north, face down. Her head was into the building. The blows that caused death weren't the first blows, but two to the base of the brain. There were injuries to the forehead and sides of the head. There were blood spatters in the entryway four feet up and across the wall. There was also blood on the outside of the door and out onto the outside wall of the entryway. The front door was open. There were defensive wounds to her hands. There was not much of a struggle. The table was moved but not knocked over. The vase was okay. There was blood on the laundry room door and stains going to the basement.

What in the hell is he doing? If there was no question as to cause of death, why is he going into this elaborate crime scene information?

Daniel switched topics to the police investigation. There was a thorough examination that turned up a number of sets of footprints from the window up the steps and from the entry back down, like a break-in and burglary.

Now this I understand. We're back to the burglar theory.

What was critical, the defense attorney contended, was what the crime lab didn't find. They found fingerprints that matched John Furgason, Jennifer and the construction workers. There were some fingerprints for which there were no matches. There were people in that house that weren't accounted for. There were none of Mr. Mereness'.

The basement window had the screen removed. There were "identifiable but unidentified" fingerprints on it. There were also "identifiable but unidentified" fingerprints on the service door to the garage. The master bedroom had evidence of a burglary. There were unidentified prints found there. There were no prints on the hatchet or hammer, but the blood pool would have prevented that.

Mercifully, Judge Werner interrupted the litany. He indicated one of the jurors needed a biological break. We were in recess for five minutes. The jury fled out the side door into their room.

We stood up to stretch. I asked Michael just what was meant by fingerprints that were "identifiable but unidentified."

He explained that the prints were good, and could have been used for evidence, but they did not match any of the people for whom the police had taken prints.

I got it. "So that would support the unknown burglar theory?"
"Presumably."

"And can you tell me why the judge isn't going to allow the jurors to take notes?"

He nodded. "It's because he wants them to rely upon their collective memories. With note taking, people have different skills and then there can be arguments about who wrote what down. More weight might be placed on someone's notes than on another person's memory."

"Gee, I never would have thought of that, but it makes sense. Thanks."

Thank goodness for Michael's expertise. Without it I'd be even more confused and frustrated.

Just then two men whom I'd noticed in the back row approached and gave a bouquet of flowers to Mavis. They introduced themselves and said they'd been in a foster parent class with Jennifer. They both hugged Mavis.

One offered words of condolence, "We miss her."

"We do too." Mavis' eyes brimmed with tears as she thanked them.

The rest of the family introduced themselves to the kind strangers and offered appreciation for the kind gesture.

We disbanded when we heard the bailiff call out, "All rise."

When the judge and jury were in their places Daniel continued as if there had been no interruption. His delivery was fragmented as if his mind was hopping from one thought to the next with no concern for transitions.

The sweatpants at the house in Minocqua had Bill and Jennifer's DNA on them, but that could have been from Jennifer wearing them previously. There was no DNA and no fingerprints at the scene.

Huh? I thought he just was telling us about all the fingerprints? Was he now referring to the fact that Bill's fingerprints weren't found at the scene?

The police did find shards of glass "consistent with" but there was no way to say with confidence that it came from that window because of all the possible sources.

The footprints. Police recovered shoes. They did electrostatic impressions and checked them against the workers and known persons. There were identifiable but unidentified footprints in that basement. They were of the type of shoes Mr. Mereness had. They had been excluded.

Other evidence at the cabin. Towels in the field where septic tanks were pumped, they pumped his septic, searched and found no matching towels.

Police did a thorough search of Jennifer's, Bill's apartment, house in Minocqua and car, person, rental car, other Taurus, septic tank and house. There was no evidence, whatsoever, to connect Mr. Mereness to this terrible thing.

Really? He'd just said there was evidence: glass shards, footprints and towels were possible links.

The cell phone evidence. We'd hear how a call was routed and the number of calls on that morning would corroborate Mr. Mereness' story.

Well, he's right about that. It is a story...as in fairytale.

Someone regurgitated into the toilet. No one cleaned themselves at the scene.

Just then my laptop began to beep and a message popped up about the battery being low. *What? It hasn't been anywhere near the three hours it had promised!*

I looked up. Bailiff Bliss was glaring at me. He thrust his whole arm out and pointed toward the door to the courtroom.

I was embarrassed beyond belief. I leapt up and tried to leave as surreptitiously as possible, but my damn laptop beeped again. I closed my eyes in humiliation and dashed for the door clutching the thing to my chest in an effort to muffle the sound.

My heart was pounding and I could feel my face was flushed. I hurried down to the victim-witness room to recharge the technological monster. *I will never trust it again! I'll need to continuously check the battery level, so that I'll never be admonished again. How will I live down the embarrassment I'd brought upon myself and the family? It isn't possible to apologize sufficiently.*

I slunk back into the courtroom. Stephanie handed me my notebook and pen, which she must have quickly taken from my backpack so she could continue with the notes. *She's a lifesaver!*

The defense attorney was still talking. The distances were within ordinary acceptable drive time. When the police officer made the trip it was Sunday morning. Mr. Mereness had gone on the Friday before deer hunting when here would have been two to three times the traffic. The comparisons were not going to be valid.

Mr. Mereness was located at Minocqua Saturday morning, stopped by Oneida County on his way to Duluth. He was interviewed a couple of times by police in different and varying ways. He consistently maintained his innocence. It's legal for police officers to lie to suspects. He'd just received the news he was the top of the suspect list. He was lied to and despite "psychological warfare" he has maintained his innocence. The police had the mindset that Bill was the perpetrator. The newspaper bought into it. The family bought into it. It's an acceptable technique but it was used prior to other evidence. Bill finally cracked, broke down. His brother threatened him, "Look what it's doing to our family." Mom had a history of bi-polar affective disorder, which used to be manic-depressive. Bill figured, "Everybody says I did it, no one will believe me, why don't I just admit it." He knew realistically that he could get convicted for this. Illinois just freed thirteen people who had been on death row and had confessed to the police.

Daniel said something about "keeping the chronology", but it didn't make sense to me. I could only guess it was the beginning of his summary.

Then the jury was told that Mr. Mereness was not there, not involved. Under tremendous pressure, he cracked.

The defense attorney thanked the jury for their patience and asked them to keep an open mind until they heard the whole story. He sat down.

I thought I detected a collective sigh from the jury.

I was certainly relieved. After an hour, Daniel was finally done rambling all over the place. It appeared that he had grasped at everything and anything that might cast doubt. But to me, it seemed very frantic and desperate.

Judge Werner thanked Mr. Daniel and turned to face the DA. "Mr. O'Leary, are you ready to call your first witness?"

"Could we have a break?" the district attorney inquired.

"Yes, let's break for ten minutes." It was 10:29 a.m. It felt like a lifetime had passed since the court session began.

19

Everyone was grateful to get up and stretch. We went into the large hall. Bobby, who was to be the first witness for the prosecution, was talking with O'Leary and Folts.

I apologized profusely to the rest of the family about my battery debacle. I explained about the supposed three hours of battery power that turned out to be less than two! They were gracious and told me not to worry about it. I was not relieved in the least.

Then we discussed Daniel's opening statement. We were in agreement that it seemed disjointed and confusing. Others had also observed the jurors looking bored or sleepy.

I called Jeff on his cell phone. He was making good progress through Iowa and hoped to be at our friends' house in Sibley by 4:00 p.m. He would have a nice evening visit with them before setting out for Cheyenne in the morning. I wished him safe travel; he wished me good luck with the rest of the day's worth of trial.

Then a young man who had been tending to the television camera for Channel 27 out of Madison approached me. He introduced himself as Joe Mason, and we chatted a bit about the case and Jennifer's family. He seemed intelligent and interested in a fair judgement. Joe wondered whether I'd be willing for him to interview me in the future. I was. When I was the teachers' union president I'd given plenty of television and radio interviews, so I was comfortable with it. It would make me feel useful to have the chance to make a positive statement for the family.

By that time, Bobby had finished talking with the DAs.

"Good luck with your testimony."

He was matter of fact, "There's no luck about it. I just tell the truth."

"I know, but Daniel could get nasty during his cross-examination."

"I'm not worried about that. If he does, it'll only make him look bad. I know the truth and I'll tell it."

What a great attitude. He won't allow the defense attorney to intimidate him.

As I returned to my seat I reflected on my brother's words. I guess if I'd have been in his position I would have said something similar. During my presidency members of our state and federal legislature had questioned me and I'd been able to maintain a calm and collected appearance. As a professional tennis umpire, I'd outwardly retained my cool under the stress of tantrums by spoiled athletes. In the classroom I'd maintained my composure with the most difficult of students. However, in all cases my gut had been churning and my adrenal glands had been running at full throttle.

Is Bobby having those feelings now?

At 10:45 a.m. Judge Werner made his announcement, "We are back on the record." He noted that counsel were present and asked if they were ready to bring in the jury. Heads nodded at both tables. The judge directed Mr. Bliss, "Bring in the jury."

After the jury was seated, Werner addressed the DA, "Mr. O'Leary, are you ready to call your first witness?"

Here we go. I drew in my breath in anticipation.

"The State will call Robert Luchsinger."

As my brother walked to the witness stand, Daniel asked the judge a question. He wanted to know if the witnesses were being sequestered. Judge Werner directed that they should be.

O'Leary asked for an exception for members of Jennifer's family. Werner agreed.

That meant Christopher, Sallie and Jim, Jr. along with others on the witness list would have to leave the courtroom. Bill's son, sister and brother did so, as did some uniformed police officers and other people dressed in street clothes. I would find out who they were in due time. Meanwhile, they would be left out in the hallway waiting for their turn.

As I observed my brother approaching the stand I felt a tremendous surge of pride well up in my chest. I'd always been proud of my older brother. He'd been a basketball and baseball star in high school. He'd earned a basketball scholarship to UW-Madison, where I'd loved watching him play for "Bucky". I'd also enjoyed watching him during the many years he was a high school basketball coach. He had always behaved with dignity, just like an ideal role model should.

His bearing today was dignified, almost regal. He was tall and slim with posture worthy of the military. I detected the slightest hint of a limp. He must really be concentrating on not showing he's injured. That might indicate a weakness.

Bobby was neatly dressed in a crisply pressed white dress shirt, dark pants and conservative tie. His salt and pepper hair was cut short and his tanned face was very handsome and distinguished looking. Again, my heart swelled with pride, but it was mingled with sadness that this cruel task had fallen upon him.

If the jury weighed his testimony as Werner had directed; by his conduct, appearance, reasonableness and apparent intelligence, he would be a valuable witness for the prosecution.

My brother raised his right hand and swore, "To tell the truth, the whole truth and nothing but the truth, so help me God."

District Attorney O'Leary had Bobby establish that Jennifer had been his sister-in-law and that he'd known her since 1973 when he began dating his future wife. In a dramatic touch, the DA again held up the framed photograph of Jennifer.

The witness then testified that Jennifer had been a teacher, had taught Spanish in Eau Claire, Neenah, Verona and at Janesville Craig. It was established that Jennifer had enjoyed taking groups of students to Spanish-speaking countries during the summer.

The ones I never took the time to go on with her.

O'Leary had Bobby provide a chronology of Jennifer's life. He told the jury that she'd been born on October 13th in 1963. *He'd known her since she was just ten years old.* Some years ago Jennifer had moved to Janesville because it was near the Madison area and more affordable.

It should be obvious to the jury that Bobby had been actively involved with Jennifer's life, not just an obscure brother-in-law.

The DA wanted to know about Jennifer's life with Bill. My brother recalled that they were married in the summer some years ago. He said he was "just guessing" it was about six years. That was when Bobby met Bill.

O'Leary asked my brother to identify Bill and Bobby looked steadily at and pointed to the defendant.

The prosecutor asked if Jennifer was able to have children. Bobby said no, but she wanted to adopt because she loved children and wanted a family. She had been planning to adopt in the winter of 2002.

"And why didn't the adoption take place?" O'Leary quizzed.

It was because of the divorce, which was initiated by Bill.

Bobby advised the court that he had known Jennifer had been upset about the divorce.

The DA asked how my brother had learned of Jennifer's murder. He explained that at 2:30 or 3:00 on the morning of November 23, 2002, an Officer Fritz and Police Chief Brunner had come to his house. They told Cathy and him that there'd been a death and they believed it to be Jennifer. The officers further explained that they needed to have someone make an identification of the body. My brother then testified that he had tried to do so but could not.

"Why not?" O'Leary questioned.

"Because of blood and swelling."

O'Leary wisely waited a moment for the jury to process those words. Their faces looked stricken. They weren't gasping aloud, but I could tell the words had had the desired impact.

"Were you able to identify her at a later date?"

"Yes, at about 2:00 p.m. at the Schneider Funeral Home."

The DA picked up the thread of the chronology. Bobby explained how Jennifer and Bill had originally lived on Columbus Circle, but that Jennifer had moved to the house on Sandstone after the divorce was filed. He did not believe that Bill had gone to live with her there.

"Had you been to the house on Sandstone?"

"Yes, my son and I went there to move a dresser for Jennifer."

The DA began to piece his puzzle together. "Did you touch anything in the house?"

"Yes, I'm sure I did."

"Were you fingerprinted?"

"No."

Ah ha! He's speared a hole in that argument. All those identifiable but unidentified fingerprints could belong to Bobby and his son, Michael.

There were no additional questions for the witness.

Surprisingly, Daniel had no questions. My brother was free to leave the witness stand.

As he strode from the stand to his seat in front of me, I was more than pleased with his testimony. *It's one piece of the puzzle, one step in the right direction.*

The State called Glen Hageman.

Mr. Hageman was one of the young, uniformed police officers who had been directed to leave the courtroom moments earlier.

The fresh-faced, handsome officer took the oath and sat down. I recognized him from the preliminary hearing back in the winter.

Officer Hageman began by offering information on his professional background.

Then he explained that on the night of November 22, 2002, he received a call from dispatch for a pulseless, non-breather at 4219 Sandstone Drive.

When he arrived at the scene the officer found a man in the garage talking on a cell phone. The man identified himself as John Furgason. Hageman had a brief meeting with Furgason and directed him to move out of the doorway. It had been established that Furgason was on the phone with 911.

The police officer then told the court that there was a Ford Taurus in the garage and a red SUV in the driveway of the residence.

Assistant District Attorney Perry Folts asked Officer Hageman if he was familiar with the property. The witness responded in the affirmative.

Clever. While the fact that Jennifer thought Bill stuffed her furnace vent could not be brought up, the simple fact that the police had been familiar with her address should at least pique the jury's curiosity. They should be able to make a deduction.

The officer then entered the home and went to the foyer where Furgason had told him the body was located. He'd gone through the laundry area with its washer, dryer and a crate with two dogs in it.

Folts asked, "Did you find any weapons?"

"Yes, a hatchet and a yellow-handled sledgehammer."

The patrolman had then stepped from the house believing it to be the scene of a homicide. He would wait for another officer.

The ADA then handed the defense attorney a rather tall stack of photographs. Daniel began to look at the photos. Bill stared straight ahead for a long time, then looked at some of the photos.

The photographs were returned to Folts. He presented them to his witness one at a time for identification and clarification.

Exhibit Number Three was of the residence. It looked the same as it had on the night of November 22, 2002, except in the photo the front door had been replaced with plywood. It was hard for Hageman to positively determine if the photo showed the same vehicle in the driveway, but he thought it did.

The exterior of the house was shown from a different angle in Exhibit Four.

Exhibit Six was of the kitchen showing the doorway to the hall and laundry room.

The kitchen and dining room were the subjects of Exhibit Seven. Hageman explained that the dining room led to the west bedroom. He identified an object on the counter as being soap.

Exhibit Eight showed the west bedroom. It was unusual because the room appeared disturbed, with items thrown around and dresser drawers open.

The west bedroom was again pictured in Number Nine, but from a different angle.

Exhibit Five showed the door to the garage and laundry area.

The tenth exhibit depicted the west bedroom again and the bathroom accessible from it. Hageman had gone into the bathroom on the night of the 22nd, but had noted nothing unusual.

The dining room and kitchen behind a three-quarter wall were shown in the next photo, Exhibit Number 11.

Twelve was of the living room. It showed "the body" lying in the foyer. It also depicted the body on the floor with the hatchet and hammer visible.

I shuddered. *I do not want to see that photo.*

When will the jury view the photographs? It will be difficult for them emotionally. Even though they didn't know Jennifer, looking at photos like that could certainly lead to post traumatic stress disorder.

I realized that these jurors' lives would also be changed forever by Bill's vicious act.

Next, the ADA picked up the two weapons in their plastic bags. Officer Hageman identified Exhibits 39 and 40 as "the hatchet that was lying near the body" and "the maul lying against the body."

Folts stressed that Exhibit 40 was "a four pound roughneck sledgehammer." He hefted it in his hand to demonstrate its weight.

I drew in a deep breath and closed my eyes. *How could anyone strike another human being with either of those weapons? Maybe if someone was attacking my loved ones or me I could do so in defense; but to use them in an unprovoked, depraved assault?*

The ADA returned to the photographs. Hageman identified Exhibit 13 as a photo of the body and the two weapons, while 14 was a closer view of the same scene.

A different angle of the body, the weapons and the victim's shoes were the subjects of Exhibit 30.

The body was again depicted in Exhibit 16; with 17 showing the body and the weapons as the murderer left them.

Exhibit 18 showed the body with stains of blood on the foyer floor. 19 showed the body again but with blood spatters on the foyer wall.

The next two exhibits featured blood spatters on an interior wall and on the door to the laundry room.

Hageman's identification of Exhibits 23 through 27 caused a stir among the jurors. They added a new dimension to this murder. Those photos showed blood spatters on the outside of the front door and on the exterior wall of the house. This information meant, of course, that the victim had gotten to the front door and opened it at some point during the attack.

How that information had upset me when I first heard it! To imagine that Jennifer had been inches from getting away from Bill and living was almost unbearable. Hopefully the jury is feeling the same thing I did.

Folts had Hageman emphasize that he had seen the blood spatters on the outside of the home on the night of November 22nd.

The subject of the next series of photos was the basement area. The stairs from the basement were shown, the broken basement window, broken glass, the window well with a large, basketball-sized rock were evident in Exhibits 29 through 32.

The officer testified that he had gone into the basement to secure the residence.

Exhibits 33 through 36 were photos of the window, screen and broken glass that was found both inside and outside the window.

The final photograph, Exhibit Number 37, was of Jennifer's vehicle in the garage.

The ADA had the witness reiterate that all the photos looked the same as the scene had on the night of the murder with the one exception: the plywood that had replaced the front door.

Folts then asked that the photos be admitted into evidence.

There was no objection from the defense.

The ADA made a second request, "I'd also ask that the jury see them at this time."

Daniel responded quickly, "Can I be heard on that?"

The judge dismissed the jury and asked that the record reflect that the jury was outside the courtroom.

The defense attorney went through the photos, saying he had no objection to some, but he wished to exclude Exhibits 13 though 17 because they were "cumulative and prejudicial".

I knew without reviewing to my notes that he was referring to the photos of Jennifer's body. The defense did not want the jury to see the brutality of the murder more than once. As I learned from watching *CSI*, that level of brutality almost always indicated a personal relationship between the killer and the victim, and that would point to Bill.

With the jury out of the room, Daniel behaved quite differently. He was casual in his stance; he leaned against the jury box and folded his arms in front of his body. He chewed his gum dramatically and his manner was far less solicitous to Judge Werner and the DA's. At one point Daniel was at the defense table and Bill was whispering a lengthy comment to him.

Folts argued that the photos under debate were more "prohibitive than prejudicial".

The two attorneys sparred back and forth.

Daniel claimed that since the first photo of the body showed the position wounds and shoes, the others would add nothing but would inflame and prejudice the jury. He reminded the judge that the cause of death was not under question.

While Judge Werner studied the photos in question, Folts argued that the cause of death hadn't yet been established. Further, the other photos showed the anger the killer must have had.

Daniel said that statement was "a stretch".

Werner announced he was ready to make his ruling.

I was on pins and needles. *Please. It's so important to show the anger in this case. Bill was the only one who was angry with Jennifer. Without sufficient detail, it might look like a random burglary and killing.*

The judge thought number 12 showed the torso on the carpet and the legs on the tile. The others were at different angles, had more detail, showed Ms. Mereness and her shoes, as well as blood on her hands and head, the carpet and the tile. He felt number 17 showed the spatters on the wall. The closer shot specifically showed Ms. Mereness' head and the volume of blood from that angle. Number 14 was more straight-on and showed the cross of the weapons and shoes.

That would certainly refute the random burglary theory! Taking the time, after a murder, to arrange weapons and shoes clearly showed a personal relationship.

Werner then said that while the objection had been that the photos were cumulative, he thought they showed the same individual closer, with enhanced surrounds and circumstances that provided details of wounds, blood flow and spatter. He was ruling that the photos of concern were not cumulative because they did add something to the case.

As for being prejudicial toward the defendant, the judge said bluntly, "They usually are."

He told Daniel that it was something he could have addressed in his opening remarks.

"I will allow them all. The jury will come back in."

Thank goodness for Judge Werner. He's decisive and firm with no ego involvement. He knows exactly how to put Daniel in his place. Maybe a higher power is at work here after all.

The judge informed the jury that the photos would be published to them at an appropriate time.

Folts resumed his examination of the witness, Officer Glen Hageman. It was explained that he searched the residence after his back up, Officer Brad Rau, arrived. The two officers split up the residence with Hageman taking the west side and basement, Rau the rest of the house.

Hageman testified that the lights had been on in the kitchen, living room and foyer. He had not checked the appliances, but he hadn't observed anything running. In the basement he saw the broken egress window, the screen and glass on the west side. The officer did not touch anything and he had worn gloves during his search. His job at that time had been to secure the residence as far as suspects were concerned. He did not find anyone.

Next the witness explained that the area in which Jennifer's body was found was approximately six feet by eight in size. The body's head was to the north, feet to the south. The blood spatters depicted in the photographs were accurate. The only furniture that had been out of place was a "coffee table" on the east wall of the foyer.

Actually, it was a library table: taller with a smaller surface area than a coffee table. The distinction is probably of no consequence.

Either Folts did not catch Hageman's error or simply decided to let it pass.

These attorneys have to be constantly listening, processing and reacting to the witness, the judge and the defense attorney. A lot like my classroom. Every single day I make thousands of observations and decisions. While my job doesn't involve life and death, it is similar. How exhausted these men must be after a day in court.

Hageman explained that the table had been a little "off kilter" but the lamp on it had not been broken.

Folts inquired if there had been any pets in the house.

The witness testified that there had been two dogs in the crate in the laundry room.

The ADA asked if the officer knew the breed of the dogs.

The officer shook his head and said apologetically, "Small, white, fluffy dogs".

It was a light moment in a very serious courtroom. The family, remaining gallery members, jurors and even Judge Werner were bemused by Hageman's description.

It was accurate! I had sometimes referred to them as "Fluffy and Fluffier". A small pang of guilt pierced my heart. *Should I have kept them?*

Hageman then reported that there had been another dog, of a type he couldn't recall, in another crate in the dining room by the patio door.

That would have been Furgason's Doberman puppy. He would have seen the attack from his cage. If only dogs could talk.

The assistant district attorney thanked the witness for his testimony.

The cross-examination began.

Daniel wanted to know where Hageman had been when he received the call from dispatch. He'd been about one-half mile away in the parking lot of Skatin' Place.

The witness restated that Rau had been the other officer dispatched to the scene. He indicated that there was no other information other than that of a "pulseless non-breather". Daniel wanted a clarification; had the dispatcher given any other information like there'd been an accident? Hageman indicated that dispatch had said something was coming by laptop.

What purpose does Daniel have in this line of questioning? Is he trying to establish that other people in the community could have heard of Jennifer's death on their police scanners? Of what significance could that be?

Officer Hageman explained that while he had responded with his lights and siren he did not approach the residence with lights and sirens because of the safety issues involved.

The defense attorney probed, "Did they tell you there was a man?"

"Yes."

The police officer then reported that he had not been given any information about whether the man had been armed or not.

Is Daniel trying to make Hageman look incompetent?

The police officer then reported that while the garage had been open he did not recall if the lights had been on. He stated that he saw Mr. Furgason and specifically answered that he had seen Furgason's hands. Jennifer's friend had been standing in the doorway to the house. The officer had had a brief conversation with him initially, but then had no further contact with him.

Next Daniel was interested in knowing which lights were on. Hageman retraced his steps and testified that the kitchen and living room lights were on and that he did know where the switches to those lights were located. Then the officer cut through the dining room. The laundry room light was not on.

The defense attorney asked if Hageman had taken the path Mr. Furgason would have.

"Speculation," objected the DA.

"Sustained," responded the judge.

Daniel wanted to know if the TV had been on. The officer indicated that it had, and that it was located in the northeast corner of the living room.

Hageman reported that Furgason had not indicated that he'd turned any lights on.

Meaning, Hageman was negligent in his duty by not asking about the lights? If the murder had occurred in the day, then no lights would have been on when Furgason arrived on the scene and he would have turned them on. It could have been significant information.

The defense attorney inquired as to whether either of the dog cages were "soiled".

They were not.

Daniel made what looked like three more attempts to reduce Hageman's efficiency and credibility. First, he wanted to know if Hageman had asked Furgason if he'd touched the body. He had not. Second, Hageman admitted that during his security sweep of the house he had not checked the closets. Third, Hageman could not recall if the light at the front door had been on or not.

I winced. *Had Hageman been neglectful? If a certain task had not been his responsibility in the sweep, would he have said so? Hopefully the jury will see that this witness had followed correct procedure, but might not have been perfect.*

The defense attorney switched to the topic of the foyer table. Hageman described it as being three feet high, one and one-half feet wide and four feet long. Daniel wanted to know if the center of gravity on the table would have been high.

"I can't say," the officer responded.

Is he now trying to establish that there hadn't been much of a struggle in the foyer if the table hadn't been knocked over?

The topic shifted again. The witness testified that there would have been a number of "normal ways" to gain access to Jennifer's house. On the main floor, entry was possible from the front door, through the garage and via the patio door. The officer then indicated that there had been no signs of the doors or windows being "jimmied".

In the basement, the egress window had no door handle, but there was a rock outside of it.

If the rock had been used to gain entry to the house by throwing it through the egress window, why was the rock outside? Had the perpetrator taken the time to throw the rock back outside after he'd gained entry? If he had, it made the murder sound even more like a pre-meditated act than a robbery gone bad.

Hageman explained that the master bedroom on the west side of the house, which was used by Mrs. Mereness, had been "ransacked". Daniel asked if it looked like a burglar had been there.

The prosecution objected. The question called for speculation by the witness.

The objection was sustained.

Daniel moved on. The officer did admit that he had not checked to see if the front door to the house was locked.

Ouch. Another implication of incompetence.

Officer Hageman had checked the outside in front of the house. He'd seen an earring on the porch but did not pick it up. Nor did he know if it matched the one Jennifer had been wearing.

Why doesn't he say that he'd left it for the crime lab team? It's highly likely the jury doesn't know of the varying roles in an investigation.

The defense attorney had no more questions for the witness.

The DA did not wish to re-direct.

Why not? They could do a little damage control by asking the witness to explain the different tasks specific to the various investigators. Maybe the prosecutors were pleased enough with the witness. He had appeared sincere and capable.

Officer Glen Hageman stepped down from the stand, walked between the lawyers' tables, through the bar and out the door.

At exactly 12:00 noon, Judge Werner declared that court was in lunch recess until 1:15 p.m.

20

"All rise," commanded Bailiff Bliss. It was 1:18 p.m. The jury was seated and the judge directed the prosecutor to call his next witness.

Assistant District Attorney Perry Folts informed the judge that he would like the jurors to see the photographs from the crime scene. Judge Werner directed the bailiff to give those exhibits to the panel.

As the stack of photos was being passed from juror to juror, I was able to observe their reactions.

My juror number one appeared to take a very scientific or detached look at the photos. The young woman sat bolt upright in her chair, head tilted back with the photos held at arm's length. If she had been older I would have deduced she was gazing through her bifocals. It looked as if she would have liked to have a magnifying glass to help with detail. Number two, a middle aged woman, was studious but seemed to be more personally involved. She bent over the photographs, examining them closely. In the third chair, the individual was very intense and had a furrowed brow throughout his examination of the exhibits. The woman, whom I had noted was a nurse, put a hand to her face and rested her head on her fingers. It appeared that she wiped a tear from the corner of one eye then took some deep breaths. Juror five took a very quick look at each photo before passing them on to the bailiff, who then took them around to the next row and my juror number six. After number seven looked at the photos, he peered over at those of us sitting in the family section. When he realized I was looking at him, he quickly looked away. Juror eight studied the family at length after she'd finished with the exhibits. Jurors 13, 15 and 16 looked at us as well, with sixteen swallowing hard a few times.

What are they thinking? I imagine they're feeling sorry for the family and they must be horrified by what they'd just seen. I'm glad I'm not in their position.

In due time, Mr. Bliss returned the photos to the evidence table in front of the bench. Judge Werner announced, "The photographs have been published to the jury."

DA O'Leary called for John Furgason. I recognized him immediately as one of the young gentlemen I'd seen sitting in the hallway.

Poor man. What had started as a promising romance had quickly become life altering in a horrible way. I hope he's getting some professional help with this.

John was somewhat casually dressed in a white polo shirt and khaki pants. He was rather handsome with dark, fairly short hair and a well-trimmed mustache and goatee. He was also wearing glasses and a brown necklace that appeared to be made of beads. It was one of the hallmarks of the younger generation, to wear those hemp-type necklaces. I was reminded that Jennifer was a full ten years younger than I.

John Furgason testifies about finding the lifeless body of Jennifer *(Courtesy of The Janesville Gazette)*

Jennifer's friend testified that he worked at the Hormel Company in Beloit. He was an equipment programmer and had been employed as such for eight years. He'd lived at the same address on Ruger Avenue in Janesville for several years.

After acknowledging that he had known Jennifer since early November of 2002, Mr. Furgason explained that he'd met her first online and then in person the week before she was killed.

The DA once again held up Jennifer's framed photograph and the witness identified it as Jennifer's likeness.

John knew a great deal about Jennifer. He knew her divorce was to have been final in January, since they'd had some discussion about it. He also knew about her plans to adopt a child and how those hopes had been dashed.

However, John did not know Bill, nor did he know exactly when the divorce had been initiated.

When prompted by the district attorney, John recalled an event that had occurred the Sunday prior to the murder. He and Jennifer were at her home watching a football game when someone came to the door. That someone was "him". The witness pointed toward Bill, who did not flinch. The DA needed a name. "Mereness," Furgason responded.

According to John, he had been unable to hear the actual words that were spoken between Jennifer and the visitor, but he could tell the tone of the conversation was emotional. After the short encounter, Jennifer came back into the house and she was "a little bit upset".

The pair saw each other several times later that same week. On Thursday they had gone to the Italian House for supper and then he went to her place and watched television while Jennifer graded papers.

So that's how Jennifer had spent her final night on this earth. What a dedicated teacher she'd been. Even while in the midst of a new relationship she took time at home to check student work.

John reported that he'd eventually fallen asleep on the couch. When he awakened at 4:30 a.m. he felt ill. He vomited in the bathroom toilet and then laid on the couch until he could call in sick around 6:00 a.m.

So they hadn't been intimate, as Daniel had suggested in his opening statement. John just put a hole in the "Looking for Mr. Goodbar" defense. I hope Mavis is feeling better that her daughter's character has been somewhat repaired by this testimony.

Furgason's testimony has also filled in the puzzle piece as to who had been sick in the bathroom. The implication in Daniel's opening statement was that it was some unknown burglar who'd become sick after killing Jennifer because she'd surprised him during the robbery.

The witness continued. Jennifer had arisen about 7:00 a.m. John waited for her to get ready for school and since he was feeling better he went off to work at the same time she had.

Mr. Furgason had arrived at work at Hormel about 8:00 a.m. He worked on a new machine and then had lunch with Gene Wright, an electrician. After lunch, John continued to work on the machine until he left at about 4:00 p.m.

John had then checked his cell phone for messages. There was one from Jennifer saying she was going home sick and that she would let the dogs out. She was referring, John clarified, to her Bichons and his Doberman. He'd taken his dog over the night before and all the dogs had been kept in their cages. When Jennifer got home, her dogs would have the run of the house.

Patti and I made eye contact and had to stifle our laughter. *Of course they "had the run of the house"! Those dogs were like her children, and they were pampered, perhaps even spoiled a bit. They'd been lucky little dogs.*

The jury could deduce from this testimony that Jennifer mustn't have been home for long before she'd been attacked or she would have let the dogs out. Perhaps she'd heard the television on in the living room and gone there straight away to investigate.

The witness then told the jury that he and Jennifer had originally planned to meet at the Janesville Mall, where she worked as a cashier at Kohl's Department Store. When John arrived at his house he called Jennifer' home and cell phones. Since she did not answer either call, he went to the mall. Jennifer wasn't there. He then presumed she must have been at home asleep, since she'd been feeling ill.

At that point, John explained, he went over to Jennifer's home and used the garage code to open the door and proceeded into the house.

O'Leary was looking through the photos that had already been taken into evidence and published to the jury. He selected one and showed it to the witness.

"This is Exhibit Number 37. Is this her car?"

"Yes."

"What type was it?"

"I'm not sure of the make."

John continued with his chronology of the fateful day. He had taken off his coat and put it on a barstool by the kitchen island. He'd put his duffel bag on the floor. It was dark outside, but he could see by the light from the television, which was on and had a normal volume.

He saw that Jennifer was not on the couch, so he went to her bedroom and turned on the light. He could see that the room had been "trashed".

O'Leary halted the witness to have him identify more photos. Exhibit Three was of Jennifer's house. Number seven had been taken from inside the garage door toward Jennifer's bedroom. The witness identified his coat and duffel bag as well as what looked like Jennifer's coat on the counter. Exhibits Eight, Nine and Ten showed Jennifer's bedroom with the dresser drawers pulled out and clothing strewn about. John testified that that was not the usual condition of her bedroom, and that what was depicted in the photo was what he had encountered as he entered the bedroom on the evening of November 22, 2002.

After leaving the bedroom, Mr. Furgason headed back to the living room and that was when he'd seen her "laying there" so he grabbed the phone and called 911. He could see something was wrong. He turned on the light to the entry, then went to check her for a pulse as the dispatcher had suggested. She had been cold when he touched her.

There was that visceral feeling again. It twisted my gut. I could not imagine what poor John Furgason had gone through. *And dear Jennifer, lying like that for so long, until her body was cold.* Her soul would have long departed, but it was torturous to think of her lying there, growing cold.

At that point, John said he'd wanted to move her, but he changed his mind.

District Attorney O'Leary wanted to know if it seemed like she'd been there a while.

The witness thought so. Her body was stiff. Blood was soaked into the carpet and already dried.

What a scene! My stomach continued to churn.

Exhibit 12, according to the witness, accurately depicted Jennifer's body in the entryway as he had found it. The next photo showed the same scene only closer up, and the hammer and hatchet next to Jennifer's head were visible. The weapons were in the position they had been in that night, as were her shoes.

At that point John recalled that the police dispatcher had told him to open the back door for the officers who would be arriving soon. There was a concern that there might still be someone in the house. John went into the garage and the police arrived within minutes.

Furgason finished his direct testimony by stating that he had not seen either of the weapons before that night and that he was unaware of whether Jennifer had tools of her own.

On cross-examination, Mr. Furgason gave his date of birth and age. He was a mere 34 years old. He reiterated that he resided in the County of Rock and that he'd met Jennifer online. Daniel asked John to explain what that meant.

For the jury, most of whom probably knew full well what meeting online meant, John explained that both he and Jennifer had profiles on Yahoo.

Daniel wished to know if that was a dating service. It was not. The witness explained that it was like a community that anyone could join.

Tod wanted this to be sleazy.

The defense attorney pressed on. Was John's Yahoo identification different that his real identity?

"Yes."

Ah, some potential dirt to heap on the victim and this witness, her lover.

Daniel delved deeper. He wanted to know how long it had been after meeting online that the two had met in person. It had been a month, even though they had known right away that they were from the same town.

The defense attorney wanted to know details of the first meeting. John had picked Jennifer up at her home and taken her to the Milwaukee Grill. It had been the week before the murder, on Friday the 15th of November.

John testified that they'd had a date pretty much every day after that except when Jennifer had to work at Kohl's.

Daniel referred to Exhibit Seven. The witness explained that it depicted articles on the kitchen counter, what were probably Jennifer's purse, her school bag and his duffel bag.

The defense attorney wanted to know what was in his duffel bag, and when John responded with the predictable answer, "Clothes," Daniel demanded to know how long he'd been staying over night at Jennifer's.

The touch of sleaze he'd been after.

John stayed very cool when he responded, "Since the middle of the week."

Poor Mavis. What mother would want to hear about her child's sex life in open court? I hope she'd been prepared for this, but it still has to be incredibly hurtful.

Now that the dirt had been dug, the defense attorney led the witness on some lengthy testimony about the dogs.

Jennifer's dogs were in a separate crate from his dog, a six-month old Doberman puppy. The dogs could not see each other from their crates. John had been going to be the one to let the dogs out until Jennifer had notified him in her earlier phone message to "not worry about letting the dogs out". While the dogs had not soiled their crates at the time John arrived at Jennifer's and discovered her body, they had soiled them by the time he was able to let them out about 1:00 a.m.

What is Daniel getting at? Is he trying to imply that the time of death was later than 11:45 a.m., because Jennifer must have had the time to let them out or they surely would have messed their crates by 6:00 p.m.?

I wanted to jump up and shout, "Those darn Bichons could hold it for hours!" I desperately wanted to inform the jury of the worry I'd had about Luna not going to the bathroom for over 24 hours when she was in my care. And that was with frequent walking and encouragement!

Somehow in the middle of the dog testimony the defense attorney asked John about his being sick in the early morning hours of Friday. John stated that he thought the food he'd eaten "hadn't agreed with him."

Furgason also testified that when he'd left Jennifer's home on Friday morning, the master bedroom had not been in disarray, nor had the east bedroom been disturbed.

Then Daniel wanted to know if John had moved Jennifer. He had tried; he'd touched her shoulder but was unable to move her due to the stiffness of her body.

So he'd touched the cold, rigid body of his recent love. Had he been having nightmares in which he relived that gruesome moment? I sure would have.

He's sure been able to maintain his composure during testimony, with just a few shaky moments. He seems like a good and decent man. Would he have been the right man for Jennifer? She certainly deserved to meet and spend a lifetime of happiness with someone who appreciated her. Would this have been the man?

The cross-examination returned to the subject of the dogs. John explained that he did usually leave his puppy in its crate all day while he was at work. The Doberman was usually able to make it through the day without soiling his crate.

More pooping dog evidence. Hopefully Daniel will soon explain just what the significance of this line of questioning is. It's really annoying.

Then the defense attorney wanted to know if it had been Jennifer's practice to go home at lunch. John didn't know for sure, but he assumed she did so whenever she could.

Why did Tod ask about that? The information was potentially harmful to the defendant. If Jennifer did habitually go home at lunchtime, which the family and some of her co-workers knew, it would explain why Bill could have known to be there at that time to surprise, attack and kill her.

Daniel's final question seemed to be posed to re-emphasize the sordid aspects of John and Jennifer's relationship. He wanted to know why the two of them had stayed at her place more than his.

John calmly explained that his brother, sister-in-law and their children were staying at his house while theirs was being renovated.

Well, a person of lesser morals would have no problem flaunting a sexual relationship in front of youngsters. Perhaps they weren't so tawdry after all.

On redirect, the DA simply wanted to know if Jennifer and John had had an original plan for him to let the dogs out after work. The answer was affirmative.

I'm still not getting this dog aspect. I hope it'll be revealed soon.

With that, John Furgason was excused. He walked past us without so much as a glance and out of the courtroom.

I'd likely never see him again, the man who might have been Jennifer's "knight in shining armor". Perhaps we'd have spent holidays together in the future. He seemed likeable, honest and forthright. It appeared he cared for animals. Quite the opposite of Bill. Would we have become friends? What a waste.

21

The prosecution's next witness was Steve Nording. As Mr. Nording spelled his name for the court reporter and took his oath with the Clerk of Courts, I made my observations. He was a middle-aged man with blond, thinning hair. He wore glasses and a dark striped shirt, open at the neck. His white T-shirt was visible.

Mr. Nording testified that he was employed as a plant engineer at Hormel. He knew John Furgason, who was an electronics technician who did programming and troubleshooting. John's regular hours were 6:00 a.m. to 4:00 or 4:30 p.m., Monday through Friday.

Exhibit Number 41 was John's time sheet for the work period of November 3 to December 1 of 2002. The time sheet was kept in the ordinary course of business as a payroll record. It indicated that John Furgason was working on November 22nd. He had been late, arriving a little before 8:00 a.m.

Nording explained that John had called in sick earlier, but the boss had called him back. He needed John to work on a new machine. John had worked on the new machine all day and left the plant at about 4:30 p.m. He'd had a lunch break with the guys he worked with. Nording himself had seen John about four times throughout the day in addition to the time he'd come into work.

The prosecution was finished with the witness. The defense had no questions.

Next, the DA called Gene Wright. Gene was a tall man, also of middle age. He was balding, but the dark hair he had was rather long and tucked back behind his ears. He had a dark, fairly well trimmed mustache. His face was tanned. His looks struck me as those of an aging hippie. However, his dark shirt was of a conservative style, as were his glasses.

After the swearing in, Wright told the jury he was a maintenance electrician at Hormel. He too, knew John Furgason. In fact he had worked with John on Friday the 22nd of November. He was not able to recall exactly when John had arrived at work that day, but the two did take their lunch break together. Mr. Wright was certain that John had not left the plant at any time during that day. He thought the two of them had left the plant about 5:00 p.m. As they'd left work, John was on his cell phone retrieving a message from his girlfriend. Wright recalled that he had teased John because he hadn't known about Jennifer until that day.

The defense had no questions for Mr. Wright.

So, one of the lines of defense, that John Furgason had killed Jennifer has been disproved. The DAs had done an excellent job of establishing John's alibi. With two co-workers to verify his whereabouts, he could not be considered by any reasonable person to be a suspect.

The next witness for the State was Robert "Cass" Wisco. Mr. Wisco was a handsome man, probably in his thirties. He had dark, short-cropped hair and was well tanned. His French blue dress shirt was complimented nicely by his multi-toned tie.

Mr. Wisco informed the jury that he was employed as the store manager for the Minocqua Wal-Mart. He had attained that position on November 1, 2002. He had worked for Wal-Mart since 2000. The witness understood the differences between Sam's Club and Wal-Mart; but since he worked for the Wal-Mart division, he wasn't exactly sure how Sam's Club was run.

Cass Wisco was also familiar with the defendant, William Mereness. The two had met in Dubuque, Iowa. At that time Bill had been running the food department of the Wal-Mart store and had been assigned to train Mr. Wisco. The witness recalled that Bill had left him mainly on his own and didn't seem to have time for him. Bill had left Wal-Mart midway through the training period. Wisco categorized their relationship as "neutral to cold". He would not describe them as being friends.

He's one of Bill's supposed alibi witnesses. Funny how he's testifying for the prosecution.

The DA wanted to know if Wal-Mart was trying to get a Super Store at the Minocqua location. The witness answered in the negative.

The prosecutor wished for more detail. If there had been such a plan, would Sam's Club have had any involvement?

"Not that I know of," Wisco replied in a sincere voice.

He went on to explain how, when he had worked at Wal-Mart in Eau Claire, there had been both a Wal-Mart and Sam's Club store on adjoining properties. He had to wear his Wal-Mart badge or show his own Sam's Club card to gain admittance to the Sam's store.

Mr. Wisco then told the court that he had last seen the defendant on November 22, 2002, at about 3:00 or 4:00 p.m. At that time, Wisco was working on control inventory reports in his office. A customer service representative came into his office to say there was a man who "insisted on seeing him". Wisco relented.

The visitor was Bill. When the defendant entered Wisco's office, he'd said that he'd heard his name announced on the intercom and wondered if he had become the store manager. Wisco informed Bill of his recent promotion. Bill congratulated him.

The witness then related that Bill had not told him of his purpose for being in Minocqua, nor did he say anything about a store remodel.

Next, Mr. Wisco explained that he had reviewed the store's three or four security tapes for the day and time in question. He had observed the defendant enter the vestibule then veer away and come in through the exit door. He saw Bill put his hand into a Rubbermaid garbage can then go into the store. On another tape, the defendant had been seen at a check out purchasing a candy bar. On a third tape Wisco had identified Bill at the service desk and then standing in the doorway to his office.

Throughout his testimony, Wisco wore a chagrined expression. His eyebrows were fixed in a diagonal position. At the center they were high and then they slanted steeply down toward the outside corners of his eyes. His mouth was often held in a grimace off to the left side of his face. He was so animated; I drew a small sketch of his face in my notebook. Cass Wisco was an interesting witness to watch. He wore his emotions much more openly than any other witness we'd had to this point.

The prosecutor wondered if the tapes would have indicated how long Bill had been in the store. Wisco hadn't reviewed the tapes for that, but imagined that it was less than fifteen minutes. The witness also explained that the times on the surveillance tapes were not accurate at first, but then they were adjusted for daylight savings time. That problem had kept Wisco from initially being able to locate Bill on the tapes. The witness could not recall how Bill had left the store.

This is excellent testimony for the prosecution. We know that Bill had told the police that he couldn't have murdered Jennifer because he was in Minocqua. He'd given two reasons for being in Minocqua; Wisco's statements had refuted both. There had been no remodel planned for the Minocqua store; and even if there had been, Bill would have had no role in it. Secondly, Bill had told the police he was in Minocqua to congratulate his great and good friend on his promotion. Cass Wisco made it clear that the two were not friends at all.

Daniel took over the witness. He wanted to know if Wal-Mart and Sam's Club were different divisions of the same company with the same stock. Wisco agreed.

The witness disagreed when the defense attorney purported that they were the same kind of store.

The Minocqua manager did agree that both companies were run out of Bentonville, Arkansas, and that there was some crossover between the two companies.

Daniel had the witness recount his history with Wal-Mart. He'd started in Dubuque with groceries, where he was supposed to have been trained by Bill. Then he had moved on to Eau Claire and finally Minocqua.

Hadn't we already heard this? Is the defense attorney trying to discredit the witness by catching him in a slip up of his own work history?

Next Daniel asked Wisco to explain what "Pipeline" was. It was a web page on the Internet where some Wal-Mart employees could see positions posted. Store managers did have access to the site, but he did not know if Bill would have had access or not.

Wisco testified that Bill had stopped in to the Minocqua store one time to use the fax machine.

As for the store's security cameras, Wisco explained that some of them were able to pan, but some were not. Also, the entrance and exit cameras, as well as those on the registers, were always on.

Daniel submitted Exhibit 42 for Wisco's examination. It was a register tape from his store on November 22, 2002, at 3:34:32 p.m. Since the register had not needed to be adjusted for daylight savings time, the time stamp was accurate. Wisco verified that Bill was shown on the tape making his purchase.

The tapes themselves were taken into possession by the Janesville Police Department on the 25th or 26th of November. It was at that time when the Minocqua manager viewed them with representative from the Janesville PD.

Wisco then reiterated that after the other tapes were adjusted for daylight savings time he and the police were able to see Bill coming into and leaving the store.

Daniel emphasized that "the thing" at the front of the store was just a big garbage can. Wisco agreed.

On redirect, O'Leary asked two questions. Did the receipt show the correct time and was the purchase made shortly after the defendant entered the store through the exit doors? To both questions Wisco replied a firm, "Yes".

Court was in recess until 3:05 p.m.

During the break, Patti asked, "Did you see the faces that guy was making?"

I laughed and showed her my little sketch, "Do you think I captured the essence of the man?"

She laughed and nodded.

"He'd make a lousy poker player," I added, "but he was a great witness."

"Yes he was, I wish they were all that good."

Most of the family members were busy stretching their legs and backs. We commiserated about how hard those wooden pews were. I mentioned that I had only been able to manage because I had Josh's Brewer cushions. The others vowed to bring some type of padding in the future. It had been two days and we were already becoming bone weary.

Court was back in session at 3:11 p.m. It was most the most punctual recess for the trial thus far.

The prosecution called Nick Demrow. I remembered Nick vividly from his testimony at the preliminary hearing in December. He looked as I recalled: young, fresh-faced and innocent. Nick had dark hair and today he reminded me quite a bit of my nephew Michael. I imagined the red-checked, long sleeve shirt was about the dressiest clothing Nick Demrow possessed.

Nick testified to his age and occupation. He was a mere 20 years old and a carpenter by trade.

On the fateful day Demrow had been working on Sandstone Drive, framing a house. The walls were up and they were rough-framing the interior. He had arrived at work at 7:00 that morning. His co-workers that day were Jeff Jones and Mike Armitage.

The three had taken their lunch break at 11:00 a.m. The witness sat in his truck, which was parked in front of the house they'd been building. Mike was in his vehicle across the street and Jeff was behind Nick in his own vehicle.

The witness described Sandstone as a dead end street. *Ah, that wonderful term.* The house they were working on was at the end; there was another house next door and then a duplex on the corner.

Mr. Folts showed Nick Exhibit Number Three. Nick identified it as a photo of the house they were building and the one next to it. Since it also showed part of the street, the ADA had the witness mark the photo with an "x" to indicate where his vehicle had been parked on November 22. Nick clarified that his vehicle was pointed toward Wuthering Hills Drive and the finished house which, we knew, was Jennifer's.

During lunch on that day, Nick was eating and listening to the radio. He saw someone pull into the garage of the finished house. Soon after, Jeff came up to his car and asked him if he'd heard the lady scream.

Folts stopped the testimony, "Who?"

"A lady."

Folts showed the witness the photograph of Jennifer. He did not recognize her from it, but assumed whoever pulled into that garage was the woman who lived in the house.

Well she was bound to look different than in a professional photograph. Besides, she'd had her hair cut short since that photo had been taken.

Nick continued. He'd thought Jeff was kidding. He'd had his car running and his heater on. Then Demrow saw someone come from behind the house.

The ADA again halted his witness, "What was it like behind the house?"

"It was a bean field."

By that, most mid-westerners would know exactly what that looked like. Soybeans grew to a height of not quite two feet and at that time of year they would have been dried and yellow. It would have been easy to see a person walking through such a field.

The carpenter then described the person he'd seen. It was a middle-aged, white male with dark hair and glasses. He was wearing a black and blue ski coat and gray sweatpants. He was carrying two bags in his right hand. One was a portfolio bag about the size of a briefcase. Demrow held up his hands to indicate the size. The other bag was a plastic grocery-type bag.

The man had walked north on Wuthering Hills Drive.

Folts needed more from the witness, "Was there anything else on his hands?"

Nick then recalled that the man had been wearing white leather gloves.

At that point in time, Nick drove his truck and followed the man. He passed him then went around the block and saw the man down the road "a ways". There were no sidewalks, so the man was walking in the street. He was on the opposite side of the street from Nick, so he didn't really see his face.

Demrow estimated that it had taken him about two minutes to get around the block and the man was on the next street walking west.

Again, Folts needed more, "Was there anything on his face, glasses, or anything else like a hood?"

The witness did not remember.

The ADA asked Nick why he had followed the man.

"It felt weird."

I could detect small gasps in the gallery.

So this young man had a sense that something untoward had occurred. Were those who gasped thinking the same thing I had when I first heard Demrow's testimony? If only he would have stayed with the man or called the police immediately. Though it was unlikely Jennifer could have lived, at least Bill would have been apprehended right away. That would have saved a great deal of grief for both families.

At that juncture, according to Nick, he went back to get Jeff and resume following the man. Unfortunately, they couldn't find him. They decided to wait until Fred, the general contractor who came to the site everyday, arrived. Then Nick and Jeff would suggest he knock on "the lady's door", but Fred did not arrive that day.

Demrow admitted that he had not called the police at that time.

The witness was able to identify Jennifer's car. He said it was a Ford, four-door, green car. It looked like the one in the photo, Exhibit 34, which Folts showed to him.

The prosecutor had Nick reiterate that the man he'd seen was carrying two bags in his right hand. However, the witness had not noticed anything in his left hand.

Demrow also testified that the man had been walking at a "normal pace".

On cross, Daniel went on the offensive. He demanded to know if Mr. Demrow recalled testifying at a previous hearing in this matter. Nick did. Daniel recalled the date of December 30. 2002, and reminded the witness that he'd taken the same oath on that day. Daniel suggested that matters had been, at that time, fresher in his mind and that he'd answered the questions the best he could have. Demrow agreed. Daniel re-emphasized that Demrow's memory was better back in December. Demrow agreed again, but his expression showed a mix of curiosity and annoyance.

I'm not picking up on any discrepancies in today's testimony. Where is Daniel off to with this? During the preliminary hearing Daniel had been alternately rude and patronizing to Nick. Would he dare treat the witness that way in front of the jury? He's not being as overt in his behavior, but he is implying Nick had committed perjury.

Daniel read from the transcript of the December 30 hearing. Demrow had said the house was closed in, there were no windows at that point and from inside he couldn't see everything. He'd also testified that between 11:20 and 11:40 the lady who lived next door came home. After a few minutes Jeff had come to his truck window. Nick had not seen who was in the car, but assumed it was the lady. He hadn't gotten a good look at her face. When Jeff came to the truck he'd said that he thought he heard that lady scream. Demrow agree to all this previous testimony. His expression had darkened with concern.

Then Daniel asked who was next to the truck at that time.

"Just Jeff."

Could Nick see the front door of the lady's house from his car?

"Yes"

What's the problem? About the only difference I could note was that in December, Nick had explained that he hadn't gotten a good look at the lady's face, but had assumed it was she. Under direct examination he'd once again assumed it was Jennifer. Daniel had every right to clarify that under cross, but he didn't need to make the witness out to be deliberately lying under oath.

Daniel approached the witness stand with a photograph. Nick recoiled in his seat a bit and looked suspiciously at the defense attorney.

I imagined he was feeling like I was; waiting for Daniel to yell, "Aha, gotcha you liar!"

The defense attorney showed Nick Exhibit Three. He twice demanded to know if from where his car was parked he could see "her" door. The witness answered affirmatively. Then Daniel asked if the door had been opened or closed.

"Closed," rejoined the witness tersely.

For emphasis the defense attorney inquired again if "the whole time you were observing the door was closed?"

"Yes."

Ah, I get it. If Nick Demrow had been sitting in his truck at the time of the murder, he would have seen someone come out the door. It had been established that there was blood on the outside of the house and on the outside of the front door. At some point the door had to have been opened and Nick would have seen something. Therefore, the murder could not have taken place at the time the police had proposed. So, if the murder had occurred later, Bill would have a legitimate alibi in being en route to Minocqua.

I thought it through. *But Demrow's attention would not have been drawn to the door until after the scream, when Jeff approached Nick's truck. More than likely, the door had been open when Jennifer screamed; and, by the time Nick focused his attention on the house, she'd already been pulled back inside. Hopefully the jurors will reason their way through this shallow attempt to discredit the witness.*

The young construction worker continued with his testimony. He explained that it had been "a few minutes" after Jeff came to his truck window before he saw the person come out from the side of the house.

Daniel tilted his head. Hadn't it been from the back of the house?

The witness stood firm, "No, between the houses."

The defense attorney and witness were having a small skirmish. Nick explained that the man had walked behind the house next door to Jennifer's. Daniel insisted he wouldn't have been able to see that and that the person must have walked right out to Sandstone. Nick shook his head to emphasize his answer, the man had gone behind the house and he had seen him.

Daniel reminded Demrow that he had testified that he had come within ten feet of the person and saw him well enough to see that he had glasses. Then the defense attorney read from page 58, line four of the December transcript. Demrow had stated that the police had never shown him a picture of Mr. Mereness and that he'd never seen his picture in the newspaper. It was established that the witness had never seen Mr. Mereness outside the courtroom.

Defense attorney Daniel was finished with the witness.

He'd been able to establish that Nick had not given a positive identification of Bill as the man who had left Jennifer's house.

Big deal. Nick never said it was Bill. He'd merely given a description and that had fit Bill.

On redirect, Mr. Folts had Demrow clarify that he'd driven behind the man, which didn't mean it hadn't been the defendant.

Daniel objected, there was no question.

"Sustained," said the judge.

Folts provided a question, "You couldn't identify the person's face, could you?"

"No," Demrow said emphatically.

Next the prosecutor showed the witness the photos of Exhibits Three and Four. He asked Nick if there were any trees in the scene.

"No."

"Was there a clear view?"

"Yes." He voice was strong and steady.

It was further clarified that the person had not come out onto Sandstone Drive but onto Wuthering Hills Drive. Also, Nick had not been watching the front door the entire time he was on lunch break. He had only looked at the door when the lady came home and then after Jeff had approached his truck and asked him about the scream.

Excellent! The prosecution did a fine job of sorting through the mess the cross-examination had caused. I felt confident the jury would understand.

22

Jeff Jones was the next witness for the prosecution. He was a tall blond with a tanned face and a goatee. He looked slightly older than Nick did, and his French blue long sleeve shirt showed a bit more sophistication as far as dress was concerned.

Jones began his testimony. He was, indeed, older than Nick by eight years. His job was that of a trim carpenter.

On November 22nd of 2002, he was working at the Sandstone home in Janesville. He'd arrived at work on 7:00 a.m. and was working on the inside of the home.

When shown Exhibit Three, Jeff identified the photo as showing the house next door to the one he'd been working on. There was also another house to the left of Jennifer's. He thought there was a finished duplex on the corner of Sandstone and Wuthering Hills.

On that day Jeff took his lunch at around 11:00 a.m. Something "unusual" occurred about 11:30 a.m. He'd heard some yelling. At that time he was in his car, a Chevy Cavalier, with the radio on and the windows down a crack. He heard what he thought was yelling, but he could not make out anything specific. The yelling went on a few minutes; he heard it a couple of times, but could not tell where it was coming from. At that point Jones got out of his car and asked his co-worker if he'd heard the yelling, but Nick hadn't.

Then, Jones testified, he saw someone leaving on the side of the house between it and the duplex. The individual went out to the street. He was wearing light colored "sweats", a dark black jacket and was carrying a bag. The bag was approximately two or two and a half feet wide and one and a half feet tall. He classified the man as being "average sized". O'Leary needed a clarification. Jeff thought that he was about five feet eight or nine inches tall.

My jurors five and six were looking at the defendant.

Are they sizing him up? He does fit the description given by both construction workers. The testimony of the two is nearly identical and that lends credence to both.

Jones then testified that the man had gone behind the duplex. He had not heard anything else unusual for the rest of the day.

On cross-examination, Daniel had the witness clarify that he'd seen just one bag, and that he hadn't actually seen the man exit the house through a door or anything else.

It appeared that the defense got little from Jeff Jones' testimony. The difference between his and Demrow's testimony was one bag. That didn't seem like too much to build a defense around.

The DA informed the court that his next witness would not be available for a few minutes. A short recess was called.

Daniel wanted a few minutes of the judge's time after the jury was out.

The defense attorney complained about the lack of a firm time range for the prosecution's case. He wanted to know what he was supposed to tell "his people" about when they could expect to testify.

Judge Werner firmly explained that it was too early yet to make an accurate prediction of when the case would be turned over to the defense.

The judge looked questioningly at the district attorney. David O'Leary said he thought he would be finished with his case by the end of the week.

The judge addressed Daniel and told him to tell his witnesses that they should be ready to testify on Friday.

At 4:40 p.m. Detective Martin Altstadt of the Janesville Police Department was called to the witness stand. The detective was middle-aged with a tanned long face. His brown hair was receding in the front. He wore a light green shirt with a dark green patterned tie. His dress, manner and voice were all very professional.

The officer had worked for the Janesville PD since 1970. He'd been a detective since 1985.

Altstadt had been assigned to Jennifer's case. He'd driven from the Sandstone Drive home on Sunday, November 24, 2002, to the Wal-Mart store in Minocqua. The witness had several maps on which he marked his route.

The detective reported that his average speed on the highway had been 71 miles per hour, while in town he had adhered to the speed limit. His trip had been completed in three hours and 20 minutes.

Detective Altstadt also reported that in the past month he had timed his drive from Craig High School to Sandstone. It had taken about ten minutes.

Folts asked the witness if he had viewed the surveillance tapes from the Minocqua Wal-Mart store. He had. Altstadt had noticed that there was something wrong. It became clear that there was an approximate one-hour time difference between some of the tapes. It had been determined that the difference had occurred because of a failure to adjust one of the cameras for the fall time change.

That aside, the defendant had been captured on tape in the entry, then coming through the exit doors. Bill had gone straight into the entry, then "abruptly turned" and thrust his hand into the garbage can. After that he had been seen coming in through the exit, at the courtesy desk, purchasing a candy bar and exiting through the entry door.

This man is an outstanding witness. His testimony is very precise and he appears very self-assured. Police officer or not, his testimony should carry a great deal of weight with the jury.

According to Altstadt, Bill was in the store a total of ten to twelve minutes.

The detective acknowledged that he had seized the security tapes from Wal-Mart. At present one of the tapes was still viewable, but the other could no longer be seen because it was old and worn.

In his cross-examination, the defense attorney wanted to know exactly how many miles it was from I-90 at Highway 14 to I-90 and I-39. The detective did not know.

Next, Daniel asked for the exact mileage to where the double lane ended at Highway 8 near Tomahawk. Again, the witness did not know the exact mileage, but thought it was about a fifteen-minute stretch on that road.

Detective Altstadt testified that he had kept records of his activities, and on November 23 he had conducted a search of Mr. Mereness' Janesville apartment. At that time he had seized a green and black Columbia jacket, some sweatpants and socks.

It seems once again that the defense is grasping at trivialities. The exact mileage is really unimportant if one knew the average speeds and distance traveled.

The cross-examination appeared to be another attempt to make the witness look unprepared and not thorough. In this case it would probably have little effect. This police detective was the most poised witness we'd seen thus far.

The prosecution next called Officer Ricky A. Larson of the Janesville PD. Ricky was wearing his blue police uniform. He was of average height and build, had short blond hair and a ruddy complexion.

Larson first testified that he'd been employed on the second shift of the Janesville Police Department for five years.

I knew Ricky as "Ranger Rick". Previously he'd worked as our school's police liaison officer. I'd known him to be forthright, fair and sensible. I'd also had Rick's daughter in class and she had been a top-notch student. I'd enjoyed speaking with Rick and his wife at Back-to-School Night and Parent Conferences. We shared many of the same values.

The night of November 22nd, Officer Larson had responded to 4219 Sandstone Drive. He'd been told the scene was a possible homicide.

When he arrived at the scene about 7:00 p.m., there were three other officers there: Hageman, Rau and Neighbor.

Rick went into the residence after a paramedic informed him that medical services were not need.

In other words, the victim was dead.

Larson observed the body with the paramedic who told the officer he should "contact the coroner's office". Rick did so.

Then Officer Larson assisted the coroner by taking photos, contacting the state crime lab and securing the residence.

To secure the residence, the officers used yellow tape outside the property lines. Officer Larson had also stationed officers in front of and behind the house.

The crime scene investigators had arrived about 11:00 p.m. and were on the scene until 4:30 a.m. At that point the police were allowed back into the house until 6:00 a.m.

Larson was shown a photo from one of the exhibits published earlier. It was of something on Jennifer's counter, a purse. It was of brown leather. Larson had checked the purse for identification and it had belonged to the victim. Other items in the purse had been a wallet with $18, a checkbook and some personal items. He did not recall if there were any credit cards in the purse.

Hmm. If there had been a robbery surely the perpetrator would have taken a purse that had been in plain sight.

O'Leary inquired about the gold earring that had been turned over to him. The witness explained that the crime lab investigators had given it to him to compare to the one the victim was wearing.

Larson next testified that the Janesville PD had seized the defendant's vehicle, but he did not recall the exact model. He had been involved in the transportation of the vehicle to the crime lab. On November 25th he had called a tow truck for the vehicle and he had followed in his squad car. He turned the car over to the state crime lab so they could look for evidence.

The state crime lab workers were also back on the scene at Jennifer's home on Monday the 25th of November. They had a new machine and they were going to try to lift shoe prints off the cement floor in the basement. Larson confirmed that on that date the scene was still secured with police tape and posted officers.

The DA thanked Officer Larson for his testimony and turned him over to the defense.

Under the same type of cross-examination used previously, the witness clarified that he had arrived at the Sandstone property between five and 20 minutes behind Officer Hageman. Hageman and Rau had done a sweep of the residence and taken themselves out into the kitchen area.

Officer Larson did admit that he had not checked to see if the front door of the residence was locked.

Next, Larson explained that a CSI had found the earring in the daylight hours on the cement front porch. He did not know if it had been in plain sight. He did recall that it had been a large, post-type earring.

The witness was not sure if there were muddy footprints on the porch. He also was unaware if the lawn at the house had been established or not.

The witness was excused.

At that point, Judge Werner spoke directly to the jury.

Some of the jurors had written a note to him. From the note it appeared that a few of the jurors might have been talking about the case. Werner spoke in a very firm voice, "Do not do that until you are deliberating." He announced that he was admonishing them for writing the note and for possibly discussing the case.

He proclaimed that "Court's Exhibit One" was the note. It appeared to have more than one person's handwriting on it. One request had been, "Can we see a bird's eye view of the house?" Another request was to see a house plan.

Defense attorney Tod Daniel made a motion for a mistrial.

What the hell?

Those of us in the family section reeled back as if we'd been slapped in the face.

Daniel's argument was that the jury had ignored the judge's directions from earlier in the day.

Judge Werner said he would take the motion under consideration.

I felt weak and dizzy. *How can this be happening? We cannot have come this far to have a mistrial declared.*

Next, the defense attorney renewed his request for the jury to visit the home in which the crime had occurred.

Werner said he would consider that as well.

Assistant DA Perry Folts said that they would be bringing in people to testify as to the house plan. They would have schematics of the house.

O'Leary cautioned the judge that notes from individuals didn't mean the jurors were discussing the case.

Daniel interrupted to say that the notes were on the same piece of paper.

Werner agreed, saying there were three different handwritings on the paper.

With that, Judge Werner recessed the court at 5:20 p.m. We would reconvene at 8:30 a.m. Wednesday.

As the family gathered in the hall outside the courtroom all eyes were on the attorney, Michael Judge. Someone asked, "Will he get a mistrial?"

"Probably not. But then, I said there was no way he'd get out on bail. I'm not sure I can predict what's going to happen here."

My evening's activities took place in a blur of panic and concern. I did my chores, ate something for dinner and called Jeff at our friend's in Iowa.

He was shocked to hear this latest twist in the case. He encouraged me to, "Hold tight and hope for the best".

"I don't know what else to do. It seems so unbelievable that this has happened. How could those jurors do such a thing?"

"Well, didn't you tell me Werner had said they could write him a note?"

"Yes, but he also told them not to discuss the case!"

"That's true, but maybe they all just wrote separate notes on the same piece of paper. That doesn't really prove they had a discussion."

"That's true. I've just got to hope that the judge doesn't rule a mistrial. I don't know if I can go through all of this again."

"I hope not, too. Now try to get a good night's sleep. There's nothing you can do about it."

"Well, that's for sure."

23

I was unable to take Jeff's advice. I'd gone to bed at 11:00 p.m. tired enough, but unable to sleep. I was so worried about the motion for a mistrial. Michael had said that if a mistrial was declared, the new trial wouldn't be rescheduled for about two months. So much emotional energy had been invested into preparing for this date, I couldn't imagine doing it over again. In addition school would have started; and I, undoubtedly, would have a very difficult time getting off for the trial. I felt desperate because I knew I had to attend the trial. I'd either have to take sick days and have a mental health professional write me an excuse, or I'd have to try to get an unpaid leave approved. Neither of those was a good option. My sick time had been wiped out when Josh had his accident four years before, and I had only just built back up to thirty days. I certainly couldn't afford to take the time off without pay.

I worried that my brother would be in the same predicament, although he had said he did not feel compelled to attend every minute of the trial the way I did. However, if he was faced with being unable to attend at all he might feel differently. All I could do was pray for a denial of the motion for a mistrial. I tried to push these thoughts aside so I could get just a small bit of sleep in the time left before the alarm shrieked.

I dragged out of bed at 6:30 a.m., threw on my chore clothes and fed my horses, dogs and cats. Even the usual joy I felt just being around my animals was absent.

At court there was a rather smaller gallery. Maybe the word hadn't gotten out about the possible mistrial. Maybe others were not worried as I was.

I sat next to Stephanie in the second row behind the prosecution. She volunteered to help me in my note taking if I needed it. "That would be great! Sometimes things do move a little too fast for me."

At 8:40 a.m. Judge Werner entered the courtroom. The bailiff called out, "All rise". We stood. I was holding my breath; a huge lump was in my throat. My palms were sweating.

Judge Werner talked quietly. He made his usual announcement about this being the "Matter of the State versus William Mereness."

Please hurry up! I can't take this!

After Werner noted for the record that the jury was not present he said that he had taken the motion for a mistrial under advisement and was ready to rule on that.

I could feel everyone around me draw in their breath.

He said the mistrial related to a concern that members of the jury wrote a note, which had been placed in the court file. In his opinion, there was no real indication of how much the jury may have discussed this matter. It might have been a fluke situation or they were possibly confused after coming out of the jury box. He repeated that he had admonished them and would continue to do so. Then he announced he was denying the request for a mistrial. *Thank God!*

Family members exhaled in unison while looking at one another in tremendous relief.

Daniel immediately spoke, "Can I make a record?"

Please, no.

Bill's attorney went on to say that he had found one reference in case law. In the Deer case of 1985 a note had been sent to a judge. The judge had conducted a voir dire of the jury to discover if there had been a discussion among them. Daniel believed the critical difference was that in this situation the three different handwritings on the note would or could indicate that there had been actual discussion.

Judge Werner asked to see the case. As the defense attorney handed over the document, he added he believed that if the topics in the note were being talked about it went to the credibility of witnesses early in this case. He then requested Werner conduct a voir dire of the jury.

Werner studied the case for about five minutes, then said, "Mr. O'Leary do you have any response?"

O'Leary countered that the State's position was that the questions asked by the jury were not prejudicial to the defendant or the State. Further, the judge had already admonished the jury and that should be sufficient. Finally, he indicated that back in 1985 the courts had been leaning toward letting jurors ask questions of the judge. The State's stance was that the proper remedy, which was to admonish the jury, had already occurred.

Daniel argued that there were credible differences with the Deer case. The distinct handwritings on the note indicated some discussion had taken place after testimony as to whether or not the witness could see the front door. The timing of the homicide was critical. If Mr. Demrow had had full view of the front door the homicide could not have taken place at 11:30

a.m. since he would have been able to see that door. The defense attorney was not saying he deserved a mistrial; but, certainly, a voir dire to discover what the jury had discussed was in order.

I was shocked when Judge Werner amended his ruling and determined he would hold a voir dire. He justified his decision by saying a lot had been invested in time and emotion in this trial. He would talk with each juror privately to avoid embarrassment and to find out "who wrote what" and "who said what". Werner concluded that he was taking a "better safe than sorry" approach.

My anxiety level shot back up. *Oh no, just when we thought we were out of the woods.*

The judge indicated that he, the attorneys, the defendant and the court reporter would recess to the conference room, which was on the opposite side of the bar and to our left. They would discuss what questions would be asked of the jurors.

Shelly, the victim-witness liaison, quickly followed to find out if she could be present. Apparently she could, as she disappeared into the conference room behind the others and the door was shut.

It was fairly easy for us to keep track of progress because after each juror walked in front of us to the conference room we could check our watches to see how long he or she was being questioned. After the juror was excused from the conference room, he or she took his or her rightful chair in the jury box. One by one they passed by, went into the conference room, then walked by again on their way back to the box. The entire process took over an hour.

We were all on pins and needles. I could feel my energy flagging. My poor night's sleep was taking its toll.

At 10:00 a.m. the final juror took his seat in the jury box.

Then my juror number 13 was called back into the conference room.

I leaned forward to whisper in Michael's ear, "What's going on?"

He spoke very quietly, "He's being dismissed".

"What?" I hissed as emphatically as possible without raising the ire of Mr. Bliss.

Mike replied, "Why else would they call him back in?"

Within moments, the conference door opened once again and everyone came out. As the judge, attorneys and defendant took their rightful places, my juror 13 came through the door in the bar and walked past us as he exited the courtroom. His face had a deep frown and his jaw jutted out. He looked angry.

The faces of family members reflected our anxiety.

Shelly must have read us accurately because she hastily whispered, "He's ruled against a mistrial. They were just talking about how they didn't understand directions and the house plan."

I inquired, "What about that juror who just left?"

"He talked about some murder case out East."

Judge Werner began to speak, "Perhaps Mr. Daniel's request for a viewing of the house would be helpful given the comments of the jury."

The DAs feared that no one had been doing anything with the house since that time, that there was nothing in it. It wouldn't look like it had. Since the prosecution would have maps and a floor plan and Mr. Daniel wasn't contesting the cause of death, what benefit would a visit have?

Judge Werner reiterated that Mr. Folts had said there would be schematics.

Folts responded, "Yes the state crime lab has prepared schematics of layouts of upstairs and downstairs."

Werner asked, "Along the line of the size of those maps?" He pointed to the maps that had already been posted on the wall between the witness stand and the jury box.

"Not that large," answered Folts.

Werner said that while he'd found the testimony of Mr. Demrow to be clear, it had become obvious in talking with the jurors that it might be helpful to check "what it would take to get them into the house". He cautioned he wasn't agreeing to nor denying the motion yet.

After a bit of persuasive talk by both attorneys, Werner said he would put the decision off until the afternoon. He told Mr. Bliss to call in the jury. He would tell them the one juror had been removed, he'd admonish them again, then take a break.

While the jury came back into the box my juror number 14 didn't know where to sit, since number 13 was no longer in front of her for the walk in. Werner gestured for her to sit in her regular place and said, "I will address that".

Judge Werner began, "First of all, I appreciate all of you being forthright with me this morning. I want you to know I have excused Mr. Carter today and that's a decision that I know about and the attorneys know about and that's all I'll say about that."

The judge then reminded the jury he'd told them in voir dire not to talk about the case and he was doing so again. Werner asked if the jurors understood. The panelists all nodded, their faces somber. It was obvious they had taken the incident very seriously.

Werner continued, "...please don't talk about any cases that you've heard about on TV that are aside and have nothing to do with this case, high profile cases, anything you read about in the newspaper or anything that you've seen on TV, "Law and Order", "LA Law", any of those types of things. It may restrict your conversation, but it's become apparent to me it's important you not talk about anything to do with law cases."

He further explained that the note system to the bailiff was for personal needs but not for the facts of the case.

The judge finished up, "Now you all indicated that you're happy to have breaks occasionally and I know we have not really gotten much accomplished as far as what you have to do here, but now we have to rearrange some witnesses so I'm going to take a break until about 10:35. Then we will get into the meat of the case again."

As soon as the jury was out, everyone in the family let out their pent up emotions. There was a great deal of sighing and head shaking as we all expressed tremendous relief. It had been a huge hurdle, but we'd made it over.

At 10:45 a.m. Bailiff Bliss again commanded us to stand. When the judge began his comments that we were back on the record the bailiff held up his right hand, stepped toward the judge and stopped him. Mr. Bliss addressed Werner loudly enough for me to hear, "We don't have the defendant."

Judge Werner thanked the bailiff and sat quietly. A minute or so passed before Bill entered the courtroom, head down as usual. For the first time I really took note of his clothing. He was wearing a dark suit, charcoal I thought. His shirt was white and his tie was dark. His attire was very professional looking.

I hope the jurors aren't fooled by his appearance.

Without a word to explain his tardiness the defendant sat down next to his attorney.

Judge Werner completed the preliminaries.

The District Attorney called Carolyn Hetrick.

In walked a middle-aged woman, petite in stature, with short gray hair. She was dressed "business casual" in a white, short-sleeved sweater and pleated slacks.

During Perry Folts' examination it was determined that Ms. Hetrick had been employed by Wal-Mart Incorporated for 11 years. She had been a regional manager for Sam's Club for a year and a half; she'd been Bill's immediate supervisor during that time. Bill reported directly to her by phone or fax at her office in Bentonville, Arkansas.

The witness explained that since Sam's Club was a division of Wal-Mart there was no crossover in the management between the two.

Hetrick knew of no scheduled remodel for the Minocqua Wal-Mart. Further, even if there had been a proposed optical department, Bill would have had nothing to do with it.

The next topic for the witness was Bill's itinerary for the week of November 16 through 22, 2002. Exhibit 46 was the schedule Bill had faxed to Ms. Hetrick. On it Bill had proposed to be in Duluth, Minnesota, on Wednesday the 20th, Appleton, Wisconsin, on Thursday the 21st and West Allis, Wisconsin, on Friday the 22nd. Additionally, he had a doctor appointment scheduled for Friday afternoon.

When asked if a conference call had initially been scheduled for Friday, the witness answered affirmatively. Ms. Hetrick then testified that the call had been rescheduled early in the week, so it would not take place on Friday, but on Saturday the 23rd.

Then, according to his boss, on Friday Bill had left a voice mail requesting Ms. Hetrick call him.

She had called him back on Friday, but did not remember at what time.

Folts questioned, "And what did he tell you at that time?"

"That something had come up. He couldn't talk to me on Saturday. Could he do it on Monday and I said that was fine."

Next Hetrick explained that it was her policy that if the district managers were changing their itinerary they were to call and let her know where they were going to be that day.

"And did you get a call then regarding his itinerary for Friday, November 22, 2002?

"No."

"So as far as you knew he was supposed to be going to the West Allis store on Friday, November 22nd of 2002?"

"Correct."

When Ms. Hetrick checked her voice mail on Saturday morning, there was a message from Bill indicating that it was Friday and he was travelling to Duluth.

"Is that the first notice you had received of that particular change?"
"Yes."

Further testimony revolved around Bill's expense account. Such items as lunch, gas, hotel and office supplies were included. Mr. Folts asked if a candy bar for Bill's nephew would be included, and the witness replied in the negative. However, if a candy bar had been reported as Bill's lunch, it could have been claimed. Snacks were not reimbursed, and there would have been no reason to keep a receipt for a snack.

At that time Folts paused and spoke to O'Leary in hushed tones. Then he inquired, "At any time about November 22nd or 23rd did you receive any inquiries from other employees requesting the whereabouts of the defendant?"

"Yes," Hetrick responded.

Daniel immediately and loudly said, "Objection, relevance".

After Werner sustained the objection, Folts said, "I'll be heard on this".

The jury was excused.

Folts explained that the testimony would tie into Janesville Police Detective Danny Davis' interview of Bill. It would also offer proof that Bill had varied his itinerary, and that that was unusual for the defendant.

Daniel argued that the question was designed to elicit hearsay testimony.

Werner let Folts go ahead with an Offer of Proof.

Ms. Hetrick told the court that two individuals had called about Bill's whereabouts, one from Duluth and one from West Allis. They'd indicated he hadn't shown up for his appointments.

After Daniel again argued that Folts was "obviously eliciting hearsay evidence", Werner sustained the objection and the jury was recalled.

What a blow to the prosecution! Hopefully the DA has subpoenaed the individuals who had placed those calls. That way the testimony would be direct and not hearsay.

As soon as the jury returned Folts said, "I have no other questions".

Damn. Now it'll be obvious to the jury that he'd lost his argument. They might think he'd tried to sneak something past the defense attorney. Not only did the jury not hear the damaging information, but now they might have a negative opinion of the DA.

Under cross-examination, Bill's territory was established. It was determined that some of his duties included interviewing eye doctors for his Sam's Optical Departments as well as working with inventories, associates and scheduling. When Daniel asked Ms. Hetrick if Bill's duties included the design of departments or planning, she firmly said, "No".

Daniel moved on to another line of questioning. He wanted to know the relationship between Sam's Club and Wal-Mart. Ms. Hetrick was clear that they had their own identities, but that employees from either facet could access a web site known as *Pipeline*. While Bill's boss agreed that job openings were posted on *Pipeline*, promotions were not.

It was confirmed that Sam's Club managers were allowed to use fax machines at Wal-Mart. But the witness disagreed with the defense's supposition that managers were encouraged to make stops at stores to make contacts.

Following was some very drawn out testimony about the rescheduling of the conference call. Daniel brought up distances to Duluth, Minnesota, the fact that Hetrick was in New York, and time zone differences. It made little sense to me and I hoped it irritated the jury a bit.

Ms. Hetrick also testified that Bill had had a company car. There were restrictions regarding personal use, and it was unacceptable for anyone other than Bill or another Wal-Mart employee to drive his company car due to liability issues.

The witness believed Bill had a gasoline credit card and a corporate Visa.

There were no additional questions for this witness.

This testimony sure puts some holes in Bill's various alibis. He's lied so much about Sam's Club and Wal-Mart; it was wise of the DA to have this official set the record straight.

The next witness for the prosecution was Elizabeth Patterson, known to me as Penny. Penny, middle-aged and quite tall, entered the courtroom wearing a dark pink T-shirt under a jean jumper with embroidery on it. Her long, curly blond hair was pulled back in a ponytail. She looked tired and nervous. I felt so sorry for her. I knew her to be a very sensitive person. I imagined the death of Jennifer had been stressful for her, and the act of testifying would add to that stress.

After it was established that Penny had been a French teacher at Craig High School for 28 years, and that she served as the foreign language department chair, the pertinent questions began.

Penny had known Jennifer since she'd been part of the interview team that ultimately chose Jennifer for the Spanish position.

Once Jennifer started her job the witness had had daily contact with her. Penny had wanted to be sure that Jennifer had all the materials she needed, and that she was comfortable with how classes were proceeding. While the witness did not share a classroom with Jennifer, the two did share a planning room along with several other teachers and aides.

Folts drew Ms. Patterson's attention to Thursday, November 21st. Penny had entered the planning room at about 1:30 p.m. She had been surprised to see Jennifer there, because Jennifer had a class at that time. Penny explained that Jennifer had been standing by her planning station with a phone receiver held away from her ear. Penny could hear an angry male voice emanating from the phone. The witness stated, "She mouthed to me, 'it's my husband.'"

Daniel objected immediately. It was hearsay again.

Folts wanted to be heard and the jury was, once again, excused.

A very long debate ensued as to whether or not this testimony was an exception to the hearsay rules. Both O'Leary and Daniel were vehement.

The DA had done his homework on this. He referred to State Stature 908.03 (1) and to State v. Weed, 2003 Wisconsin 85.

Impressive.

The defense attorney argued, "Judge this is clearly hearsay. She's being asked to basically identify a voice on a phone and then testify as to what someone else said. And again, it's the confrontation problem again. We're not, you know, in any position at all to confront this testimony."

Yes, because your client killed the woman who spoke those words.

Werner broke in, "...the declarant, Ms Mereness, is unavailable. There is no question about that. Counsel doesn't argue that."

The judge then talked about the "substantial corroboration as to the truthfulness of her statement" and referred to State Statute 908.3. He then directed O'Leary to give an Offer of Proof.

O'Leary did so, then Daniel asked questions of the witness.

Werner thought the issue had to do with the question of "particularized guarantees of trustworthiness" as in statute 908.45. Then both attorneys were able to make a record regarding that issue.

Finally, Werner was ready to rule. He talked a long time about legalities, but finally said that he did not believe the witness would have a reason to fabricate her testimony, "She has no personal state in this matter beyond the fact she was personally acquainted and talked with Ms. Mereness...I'm going to allow it. The objection is overruled."

After 20 minutes, the jury was recalled.

Hastily, everyone in the family sighed in relief and gave one another thumbs up. We didn't want to be admonished by the bailiff.

O'Leary continued with Ms. Patterson's testimony. It was repeated that Penny could hear a man's angry voice over the phone and that Jennifer mouthed, "It's my husband". Penny explained that while she was trying not to listen to the words, she could tell the tone was angry.

The prosecutor asked, "All you heard was loud, angry tone, male?"

"Yes, and speaking very fast."

The call went on for three to four minutes.

"Did she say something when she hung up the phone?"

"When she hung up the phone she said, 'My husband is wanting to know what he should do with my birthday card that his parents have sent me.' And she said, 'He has not yet told his parents what is going on.'"

O'Leary continued, "...you knew her for a while. Could you tell what her demeanor was while this was going on?"

"Yes, she was upset."

"How could you tell that?"

"Um, because she was shaky, because of the expression on her face."

After that Jennifer had returned immediately to her class.

On cross-examination Daniel established that Penny was not Jennifer's supervisor.

"She often shared her personal affairs with whoever would listen, isn't that correct?"

I wanted to jump up and yell, "That's not true! She didn't tell her family everything or we might have tried to do something to get her away from danger!"

"She shared with a few of us, yes."

"Intimate details, correct?"

"Yes."

"And she was quite an emotional person, is that correct?"

Penny paused. She looked very thoughtful then said concisely and clearly, "I would characterize Jennifer as very in control of herself. I wouldn't—I would not consider her to be an emotional person, no."

Wow! What poise! This is valuable testimony.

Daniel again stressed the fact that Jennifer had shared intimate details of her divorce. But when he asked Penny if she had characterized her divorce as friendly, O'Leary objected for hearsay reasons. The objection was sustained and Daniel's cross-examination was over.

On redirect, O'Leary clarified that Jennifer had been upset after the phone call. Then he established that Penny had spoken with Jennifer several times over the summer as well as almost daily after school had started.

The prosecutor inquired, "When is the last time prior to November 21st, the date of that phone call, that you talked to her about her divorce?"

"Probably a couple days before."

"At that time was she—did she act in any way upset?"

"Um, she talked matter of factly, but she was upset because she reiterated the loss of the baby that she had hoped to adopt."

Daniel renewed his objection "to comments allegedly made by Ms. Mereness".

The objection was sustained and the last portion of Penny's answer was to be stricken from the record.

The DA had nothing further for the witness. Penny was dismissed, as was the jury.

Judge Werner suggested the jury take a view of the Sandstone property "first thing in the morning". He asked O'Leary if his witnesses could be rescheduled. The DA explained that they were state crime lab experts, and he would call them during lunch to see if they could come at 10:00 a.m. instead of 8:30 a.m.

Court was in recess until 1:15 p.m.

As I went into the hall I saw Penny sitting on a bench next to another teacher, Katy Hess.

I patted Penny on the shoulder and said "Good job, I'm sure that was really difficult".

She had tears in her eyes and said, "I had so much more to tell, but they wouldn't let me."

"I bet you do. Lots of people do, but the district attorneys have to be so careful to stay within the confines of the law. It really seems like when Jennifer died, most of her words died with her."

Penny nodded in agreement, "I hope I made a difference."

"I'm sure you did."

24

Again, the family went to Bobby and Cathy's for lunch. Cathy and Patti very quickly set out the lunch items. I felt bad that I wasn't helping with that task and I told them so. They waved me off and told me not to worry about it.

As usual, I wasn't very hungry; but I didn't want to risk an upset stomach later, so I ate a sandwich and had a Coke. The caffeine had seemed to help before.

We talked a bit about Penny's testimony. Everyone agreed that she'd appeared sincere and completely believable. She had strengthened the case. The puzzle, as promised in O'Leary's opening statement, was being laid down, piece by piece.

At 1:15 p.m. court resumed. Judge Werner asked DA O'Leary if he'd had the opportunity to reschedule witnesses.

"Yes, I advised them to be here at 10:00 tomorrow morning so that we'll have time to do whatever we need to do."

Werner addressed both attorneys, "Counsel, I don't know what we want to do with Mr. Mereness, because he is in custody."

O'Leary responded, "…if he's gong to be transported it's going to be by the sheriff's department".

Werner clarified, "Clearly on a view the Court is the only one that will be talking at all if there's any discussion with the jury. I'm open to suggestions as to how you want to logistically handle his transportation."

Daniel inquired as to what type of guard Bill would be under that the jury would see.

O'Leary stated that if he were outside the courtroom he'd be in restraints.

Werner asserted he wasn't sure that's what Mr. Daniel would want.

Daniel agreed, "Correct. If the alternative would be we would waive his appearance, Your Honor."

The judge wanted to know if the defense attorney had talked to his client about that possibility.

He had and Bill was comfortable with it.

Judge Werner then asked Bill a number of direct questions about understanding his right to be present at the viewing of the house as well as his decision to waive it. Bill answered each question affirmatively. His voice was very firm and polite. He used phrases like "That's correct" and "Yes judge".

It's hard to believe that's the voice and demeanor of a cold-blooded killer.

I don't know what I'd expected: some sort of screeching or rasping, an arrogant rudeness toward the judge? I'd had prior conversations with Bill, but that was before he had committed murder. It had been easy these past ten months to attribute all evil qualities to Bill. When he had just spoken like a normal human being it caused me a great deal of discord. It was so contrary to what I'd been building up in my mind of this monster, this evildoer.

I wish I hadn't heard his voice.

At 1:20 p.m. Kathryn Hess was called as a witness for the prosecution.

Katy, as I knew her, had just been through another terrible trauma. While she and her husband Eric, a co-worker of mine, had divorced the summer of 2002, she had suffered mightily since he'd been diagnosed with ALS back in November.

The news had also been a huge shock to my teaching family at Marshall Middle School. Eric had always been a robust, stalwart member of the staff. We had been officially told of Eric's illness just a week before Jennifer's murder.

November had been a month of the most horrible news.

Eric and Katy's *had* truly been an amicable divorce. They just weren't as compatible as they'd once thought. Katy had been supportive of Eric throughout his struggle until his death in early July. I'd visited with her at the memorial service less than a month ago. She and I seemed to be bound together by these two tragedies.

About my age, with short, graying hair, Katy took the stand.

It was determined that she'd known Jennifer since Jennifer was hired at Craig.

On November 22, 2002, Katy saw Jennifer during their mutual preparation period between 9:00 a.m. and 9:50 a.m. The witness recalled it was about in the middle of that block of time when she had seen Jennifer in the school's front hallway. Jennifer's appearance was unusual, she'd been crying. In order to bring something positive to the situation Katy had complimented Jennifer on her clothes, which included a sweater with snowmen on it. During their conversation Jennifer requested that Katy check her makeup. It was smudged. The witness continued to speak, but I couldn't hear what she was saying over Daniel's repeated loud calls for an objection due to hearsay.

Folts again wished to be heard and the jury was dismissed. The attorneys and judge had the same basic argument they'd had over Penny Patterson's testimony. It wasn't quite as long, but the result was the same. The objection was overruled.

Another small victory.

Once the jury was back, Folts continued his direct examination, "What did Jennifer say to you at that point?"

"She asked me if her makeup was smeared because she had been crying."

"And what did you do then?"

"I told her that it was a little smudgy but it wasn't bad. It looked okay."

"Did you notice anything else about her eyes at that time?"

"They were very red. You could tell she had been crying."

"How was her demeanor otherwise?"

"She was very upset."

O'Leary thanked the witness, but she must not have heard him. She continued to speak, "Her face was very blanched, and her lips were very white like she had been crying. And you could tell she had—something happened, and that's why I had asked her."

Daniel wished for the last part of Katy's answer to be stricken.

It was.

On cross-examination, Daniel asked about Katy's desk's proximity to Jennifer's in the planning room. The two were a few desks apart.

Then Daniel inquired if Jennifer had told her anything about her new boyfriend, John Furgason.

Katy replied, "No".

With that, Kathleen Hess was dismissed. As she left the courtroom she looked sympathetically at the family.

At 1:33 p.m., the prosecution called Glenn Disrude. I also knew Glenn. He was the principal of Craig High School and I'd had some teacher's rights dealings with him when I was the president of our teachers' union. He had also traveled to Wisconsin Rapids for Jennifer's funeral. I'd found him to be a sensitive man.

Glenn testified as to his position and that as such he kept teachers' attendance records. He, of course, had known Jennifer and reiterated that she had been hired in January of 2002.

Jennifer's boss then said that according to his records, Jennifer had come to work on Friday, November 22, 2002. He was unable to say how long she had been there because he did not have the document he needed.

The prosecution supplied Exhibit 47, which was the school district's sub caller's report for that day. It indicated Jennifer had left school after third hour. That would have been after 10:52 a.m.

Mr. Disrude did not recall seeing Jennifer at all on the day she was murdered.

The next line of questioning concerned Exhibit 48, which was Christopher Mereness' schedule and attendance record for November 22, 2002. Since there was no indication Christopher was absent, the principal deduced the young man had been present at school the entire day. Christopher's lunch period was at 11:49 a.m.

Good. This will provide an alibi for Christopher in the event that Daniel tries to implicate Bill's son as "the real killer". Nothing is sacred here.

Daniel's cross-examination of Glenn Disrude was merely a recheck of Jennifer's schedule, hour by hour.

Janice K. Wexler was called by the prosecution at 1:45 p.m. Ms. Wexler was a very sharp looking, professionally-dressed woman. She appeared to be in her late thirties. Her dark hair was short and precisely trimmed. Her countenance exuded confidence, intelligence and efficiency.

I remembered that either Bobby or Cathy had told me in September that Jennifer had hired a "ball-busting" divorce attorney from Madison. I got the distinct impression that Ms. Wexler was just that.

As soon as Ms. Wexler took the oath and was seated, O'Leary told the judge he had a matter he needed to discuss outside the presence of the jury. Werner excused the jury "briefly".

The DA explained that Ms. Wexler was appearing today by subpoena and that she had been the attorney for the diseased, Jennifer Judge.

Judge Werner asked if Michael Judge was present. O'Leary indicated he was.

Werner instructed Michael T. Judge to step forward, inside the bar. Michael did so, standing slightly behind and to the right of the prosecution's table.

The judge asked several questions. Was he was the brother of Jennifer? Was he her co-personal representative? Had he waived the client privilege on behalf of her estate? Had he waived client privilege today for this witness?

Michael stood ramrod straight and in a firm voice answered each question in the affirmative.

Judge Werner then asked O'Leary if the other co-representative was in attendance. O'Leary indicated she was. Catherine Luchsinger was called forward.

As Cathy made her way down the pew in front of her family members, many reached out to place their hand on her arm in support.

She walked through the gate in the bar and stepped up next to Michael. Suddenly she startled and shifted to the left.

She realized she was standing right next to Bill and must've recoiled in sheer revulsion. I can't blame her.

Cathy answered positively to the same set of questions the judge had posed to her brother. She, too stood straight and tall.

I wish the jury could see them like this; Jennifer's family, good people torn by this heinous crime.

Michael and Cathy were instructed to return to their seats.

Werner asked if there was anything else at this time. Daniel said, "Not on privilege."

"Something else?" Werner queried.

"Yes, Your Honor. Based upon my previous discovery, my concern is that this testimony not be a litany of complaints that Miss Jennifer Judge had concerning her husband while we were processing a divorce. I trust the court can rely on its experience as a domestic relations attorney prior to taking the bench as to what that can turn into and how that can come out."

Wow, that's a challenge to Judge Werner about how to do his job.

Daniel seemed to become more agitated. He didn't want to hear about the lien on Minocqua, the restraining order, the plugging of the vent, that kind of "stuff" being allowed. He asked the judge to take judicial notice of the divorce file in this case. Daniel explained that it contained a petition by Mr. Mereness, a summons, etc. etc. He asserted that there had never been a filing of a restraining order though it was standard in this county. Almost on a rant, the defense attorney insisted this testimony not be a "sounding board for all the ills and complaints that Miss Mereness had through this attorney, which is again clearly hearsay." Daniel threatened, if that happened, he would call Mr. Holznecht to confirm that it had been the simplest amicable divorce settlement the judge would find.

Almost in unison, the family members began to shake their heads in disagreement. It was a good thing the jury wasn't in the box, or we'd have been admonished for certain.

O'Leary finally had a chance to speak. "His last comment, judge, is part of the reason Miss Wexler is sitting here today. The amicable divorce that he keeps waiving in front of this jury's face. This is an amicable divorce. This is an amicable divorce. He said it several times throughout the trial. I do not intend to introduce hearsay at this point. I don't intend to introduce conversations the victim had with Miss Wexler. I believe I am entitled to introduce the evidence that the defendant filed for the divorce, the date he filed for the divorce. The date that the real estate closing occurred according to her records was the day before. So he filed for divorce the day after the real estate closing, which will tie into some other witnesses we have later. We can and I do intend to ask about whether or not she gave any advice to her client about a harassment order. What advice she gave to her client on obtaining a harassment order against the defendant."

At that point Daniel interrupted, "If the purpose of this witness..."

O'Leary was terse, "May I finish my presentation?" He shot an agitated glance at the defense attorney.

"Excuse me. I thought you were done."

Not likely.

The judge stepped in. He wondered what O'Leary wanted to include as to the nature of harassment. He allowed O'Leary to offer proof.

Again, we would hear the testimony without the jury present, then Werner would rule on the objection.

After lengthy direct and cross-examinations Werner ruled that he would allow the testimony as presented in the Offer of Proof.

Once again, the family was ecstatic. But we had no time to celebrate, the jury was filing in.

I'm learning far more about trial law than I ever cared to.

Ms. Wexler said that Jennifer had retained her services as divorce counsel. While Bill had been the petitioner in a divorce action filed on September 17, 2002, Jennifer had wanted Ms. Wexler to file a response.

"And what is included in that response to the divorce petition, or what did you include in your response to the divorce petition?"

"I responded to the original petition by affirming those paragraphs that my client represented were true and correct and also indicated that some piece of information in the original petition was not correct in that it alleged there had never been a prior filing, and in fact there had been a prior filing for divorce so my response indicated that because as a matter of record that needs to be done."

Jennifer had filed for divorce in 2001, and then changed her mind. But this witness could not testify to that, as she had not been her attorney at that time.

Wexler continued, "I also alleged affirmatively the existence of two agreements—one executed prior to marriage, one subsequent to marriage—and the legal position that I believed they were both null and void."

We knew that Bill had "blackmailed" Jennifer into signing one of the agreements by promising in return to adopt a child. Since the divorce hadn't proceeded far enough, that information was also not available to share with the jury. I hoped they would be able to read between the lines and figure Bill must have been trying to pull a fast one since Jennifer's attorney had said the marital property agreements were null and void.

And that is what made Bill think he would lose the Minocqua property, sending him into a homicidal rage.

The district attorney wondered if the witness had filed a counterclaim.

She had. Wexler then explained what that was. "When someone wants to set the record straight and tell their version of the facts and--as I just explained--what was different from the original filing, they will do that in a counterclaim and also say, by the way, I do want a divorce. If the original filer changes his mind, it would give us a legal basis for us to move the matter forward."

The family knew Bill had been making overtures to get Jennifer back. She wasn't going to let him have any legal reasons for holding up the process.

And that would tell Bill that reconciliation would not be possible, more fuel for his rage.

On November 11, 2002, Ms. Wexler had filed a lis pendens on the Minocqua property, which would alert anyone looking at the property that there was a divorce action pending and that the property was involved in the divorce.

That would have been like pouring gas on the fire.

O'Leary inquired as to whether Ms. Wexler had advised Jennifer on harassment restraining orders.

"I did so twice. On October 15, 2002, and on November 4, 2002."

The DA wondered if Jennifer's attorney had filed a demand to obtain financial records of the defendant.

She had done so on November 11, 2002. The information would have been due back to her within 30 days. She had not received any information prior to being informed of Jennifer's death.

On cross-examination it was a real battle of wits and wills. Daniel asked many legally specific questions about the marital property agreements and Wexler more than held her own. It was obvious she knew the law. Daniel was not able to trip her up.

Janice K. Wexler had been an outstanding witness. She hadn't appeared at all intimidated by Daniel's bullying tactics.

Thank goodness Jennifer hired her. She's supplied excellent evidence in the case against her killer.

On redirect, O'Leary clarified the type of restraining order Wexler had suggested Jennifer obtain. It was stronger than the one that was standard in divorce proceedings and the charges for breaking it would have been criminal rather than civil. Ms. Wexler made a point of looking at the jury to emphasize that fact.

Jennifer's attorney was dismissed after nearly an hour on the stand. We were in recess for fifteen minutes.

As I left the courtroom I encountered Ms. Wexler in the hallway. After introducing myself, I thanked her for her excellent testimony. I assured her that every woman in that courtroom would remember her name should they ever require a divorce attorney. She laughed and indicated she didn't think she had been there for marketing purposes. As she departed I called after her, "But it was accomplished anyway!"

25

At 2:55 p.m. the State called Dr. Robert W. Huntington III, MD. I knew from Shelly's witness list that Dr. Huntington had been the medical examiner in this case.

He could not have looked more the part. It was as though he'd walked off a movie set. He had gray, unkempt hair and an unruly, gray beard. He wore a faded blue jeans sport coat and rumpled khakis.

While being sworn in, he leaned his elbow casually on the judge's bench. Actually, he wasn't sworn in the traditional way; he agreed to an alternative oath. The Court Clerk read: "Do you solemnly affirm that the testimony you will give in the matter now on trial shall be the truth and nothing but the truth under penalty of perjury?"

That's admirable. I'd always wondered about the traditional oath. It says, "So help me God". Where does that leave witnesses who don't believe in God? Besides, if there is supposed to be a separation of church and state, how can such an oath be legal?

District Attorney O'Leary asked how long the witness had been employed by the University of Wisconsin Medical School.

"A bunch of years now. I have been sort of creeping up the academic ladder since 1971."

Gosh, he was there when I was a student. What would he have been like back then? Too bad we hadn't met.

Daniel agreed to stipulate to Huntington's training and experience in the area of pathology so the testimony could move on to the autopsy.

I had anticipated the medical examiner's testimony would be graphic, but it would not have been possible to prepare for what I was about to hear.

His first step had been to "just look at what we've got without moving anything, removing anything. Just look."

Dr. Huntington had turned in the witness chair so as to be facing, looking directly at and speaking directly to, the jury.

This is effective.

"What's the purpose of that?"

"To see what you can see without disturbing anything, or disturbing as little as you can manage, so as not to dislodge, disconnect anything."

Oh boy, dislodge or disconnect. My stomach began to churn.

The DA wanted to know what he'd found at that point.

"Well, once she arrived in the properly sealed body bag, she was face down and there was a good deal of blood on the back of the head. So, when you just sort of moved the hair to one side or the other gently, what you saw was an X-shaped array of cuts sitting slightly to the right of the middle of the head, midline in the back of the head. Now, these were pretty sharp cuts in that skin, but it was equally plain that the skull underneath had been pretty badly smashed. So, in other words, you had to explain with something that would have an edge and still have mass, if you follow."

My head spun. Bile rose in my throat. *I can't get up and leave, but I don't want to hear any more!* I ground my molars together and steeled my nerve. *I must concentrate on my note taking and be a detached observer.*

Dr. Huntington was then presented with a series of exhibits, all photographs of Jennifer's injuries. He recognized Exhibit 53 as the X-shaped wounds he had just described. When asked if his hands were shown in the photo, Huntington candidly answered, "I believe so. At least the forearms are hairy enough to be me".

The tension was broken. He was charmingly intelligent and self-deprecating. We seemed to have another perfect witness.

Huntington explained that the photo accurately depicted the injuries, the well-defined sharpness of definition of the edges.

For Exhibit 54, Huntington explained that it showed the same wound after some of Jennifer's hair had been shaved off. "It shows very well the X-shaped cut."

With that comment he started to get up and leaned over to show the photo to Judge Werner. Werner held out his hand to stop him and said, "That's all right doctor, thank you."

The witness tried again, "If Your Honor wishes to see, by all means."

"I will look at them later."

"Okay."

What was that about? This man didn't seem to have an agenda. Had he showed photos to other judges at that stage of testimony? Did he want the jury to see the judge's reaction?

O'Leary continued with his direct examination. "The type of wound or the X-shaped wound, what does that indicate to you?"

"Cross cuts. Intersecting cuts." He used his hands to show the shape.

I bet the DA was hoping the doctor would say something about the personal nature of the wound, or the possible rage the attacker would have had to inflict them. But Huntington is being purely clinical.

What observations had the witness then made?

"Well, this was a clothed, reasonably well-developed and nourished Caucasian female; reasonable that there was blood around. Well, then, of course, after noting this I turned her over to look at the front side, and that's when some other head wounds became pretty evident."

Dr. Huntington paused for a moment while looking at a document in his hands. "Okay. Now, for purposes of accuracy I'm now referring to my autopsy report in this matter, WO2516F, autopsy by number. To my knowledge, counsel for the defense has been provided with a copy thereof, and I'm referring to that to be strictly accurate."

At that point, Judge Werner addressed Dr. Huntington, "And, doctor, could you just elevate your voice a little bit? You're tailing off a little bit at the end of your sentences."

Huntington whipped around in his chair, faced the judge, gave a quick salute and said, "Yes sir!"

This is one eccentric fellow! Hollywood could not have better cast him.

The medical examiner was precise and referred to "page three, fourth paragraph, for counsels' purposes". He explained that on the high right forehead there was a laceration, a tear in the skin one of three-eighths inches by one-fourth inch. He described another similar injury that was smaller and a bit to the right. Jennifer also had bruising near her right external ear.

Exhibit 56 showed a Y-shaped wound, bruising on the victim's right hand and another bruise at the base of the left thumb. It also showed an older bruise to the hand that the M.E. explained had nothing to do with this incident.

Moving on to Exhibit 57, Huntington reported, "That's a picture of bruising near the ear, and a very good one I might add." He clarified that the bruising was actually behind and below the ear.

That's where he hit her first, as she had made it out the door.

What had the doctor done next?

"Well, again, at the point of discovering these, she had been somewhat cleaned off and had been undressed. Well, after this sort of subtle look, after cleaning off, and then we looked inside the major organ bearing areas of the chest and abdomen and then looked in more depth at the head."

"Prior to looking at the head, did you find anything of significance in the other major organs that you examined?"

"She had some stomach contents, which people often do. That was just about it."

"And what did you find in your examination of the head?"

"Okay. Now what we found was that there weren't any fractures under the lacerations of the right forehead. There was blood in the tissue but no fracturing. Now quite by contrast, on the back of the head not only was the bone under that "X" fractured, but the fracturing extended forward and under the back side of the skull. In other words, it came down under the backside of the skull toward the ears, and that there were actual physical tears in the portions of the brain furthermost back in the head."

Several of us muffled our gasps.

This is unbelievable!

The doctor continued. "Both of these cerebral hemispheres, the hemispheres up high and in the cerebellum, the part of the brain that sits back and low, there were physical tears in those structures, and that again the back and low side of the skull was pretty badly smashed."

"What would those tears indicate to you, doctor?"

"Well, what it would indicate, of course, are that the force carried forward into the substance of the brain. In other words, that we were dealing with really powerful pure force to not only shatter that skull but to tear the brain."

It was so quiet in the courtroom I could hear people inhaling and exhaling. Many eyes had tears in them. The jury was riveted on Dr. Huntington.

The DA asked how many times Jennifer had been hit.

The medical examiner gave a thorough answer while referring to his notes. "I left out one bruise that we identified at the top of her head under the scalp with no skin injuries overlying it. There was that bruise there. So now you can try and imagine some weird geographies, you know, somebody hitting into a two pronged something or other to account for both the forehead injuries, but barring something really weird, it took two hits at least to make this wound in the back."

Dr. Huntington used his hands to point out different areas of the head where Jennifer had been struck, "We've got another hit to make this wound here. We've got another hit to make the wound at the top of the head. And again, barring some weird geography, we've got two separate wounds to the forehead, so that gives us six impacts to the head in addition to one to each hand."

God it was a horrible beating.

The witness continued, "Now, yes, sir, you can very well imagine that these wounds to the hands could have been caused by an effort to try and shield the head—do you follow me—and could presumably, in an attempt to strike the head, hit the hands at the same time, but you've got two impacts on the hands. So you've got a total of six impacts in the head, one on each hand, and that's all I can say. That's minimum you understand, because I don't know that some of the areas in the head weren't hit more than once."

The prosecutor asked if the hand wounds could have been defense wounds.

Dr. Huntington held his arms out in front of him, "Again, somebody trying to ward off incoming, stopping it with their hands, trying to. You follow me?" He was talking directly to the jury. They were enthralled.

O'Leary said he was going to show Dr. Huntington the weapons.

Daniel objected on the grounds of hearsay.

The District Attorney countered by saying Huntington had been told the hammer and hatchet were found at the crime scene

Werner overruled the objection.

Dr. Huntington agreed that the hatchet was consistent with the wounds on the back of the head. Holding the handle of the weapon with his left hand, he used his right hand to point out first the front edge and then the massive hind portion of the metal blade. Again, he directly addressed the jury, "Because you see, ladies and gentlemen, it's got an edge, but it's also got mass. In other words, if swung—the engineering term is a moment of torque—you've got a mass, and you're accelerating it, and so it has the edge, and it has the mass to account for the skin and the skull and brain injuries present."

The DA asked, "Would it also be consistent with the—I'm trying to remember how you phrased it—the cleanness or the edge inflicted in the wound?

"Quite."

"How so?"

"Edge."

"Straight edge, same length, size?"

"Roughly."

"The..." O'Leary's question was interrupted by his witness.

"Again, you understand, of course, if it was swung in such a way that the whole of the edge didn't cut in. You know, say one top edge or bottom edge lead, this wouldn't have to carry the whole of the edge for the wound to make it precisely the same."

"Were there any wounds that you observed inconsistent with the use of that axe?"

"Well, if for instance, the back end were used, you see, you then have a much wider edge and you could do the forehead lacerations with that. And if you hit her with the handle, I can see that one to deliver the one below the ear as well as the right hand. Okay. Therefore, no. In other words, not every hit has to be with the edge, but…"

It was the DA's turn to cut in. "I'm going to show you, doctor, what's been marked as Exhibit Number 40 and ask if you recognize what it is."

Huntington looked at a label on the weapon before answering, "It says four pound sledge."

"Would any of the wounds that you observed be consistent with being struck with that?"

Huntington cradled the weapon. "Well, again you've got a handle, so you could still do the one right hand and below the ear, and of course you've got a really blunt edge. The face is here, so you may make a laceration with that. I don't see how you can make this in back of the head with that."

"That "X" you talked about would be inconsistent with being struck with the sledge?"

"Right."

"What about the injury to the forehead?"

"You could do it with either one, I don't know, or something else, I don't know. It's just that we have no reason to look past these to explain the wounds."

"Doctor, when you were conducting your autopsy, did you note—and I draw your attention to page two of your report, doctor, under the initial view of wounding, second paragraph…"

"Uh huh."

"…blood smear or blood spatter on the body?"

"Oh, yeah."

"What did you note?"

"Well, there was a good deal of blood on the face, blood, of course, around the wounds to the back of the head, and again smeared around the body, sure."

"The blood spatter that you indicated on this, what does that indicate?"

"Blood flying."

"Does that indicate force?"

"Yeah. Again, it could be cast off. That is blood on something and then as it's swung the blood flies, or it could be direct and delivered from the wound. I'm not sure at all."

When the DA asked the medical examiner if he had found a hoop earring on the victim, he replied affirmatively. Huntington described the jewelry as a hoop earring in Jennifer's right ear. He had given it to the crime lab or the Janesville detective who had been present at the time or Madam Haverley, the deputy coroner who was also present. He said it had been reported to him that the other earring had been found at the scene.

Finally, District Attorney David O'Leary asked, "To a reasonable degree of medical certainty, did you form an opinion as to cause of death?"

"I did."

"And what is your opinion?"

"She was beaten to death, period."

There was not a sound in the courtroom. People were staring off into space. I once again had the feeling that I'd been punched in the stomach.

Daniel cross-examined the witness. He wanted to know how disturbed the body had been before it arrived at Huntington's laboratory. The expert said that the body had been disturbed as little as possible. There had been some blood in the bag as well as a bit of brain.

Dear God, this is too much. What is the point of this detail? Is the defense trying to prove that the body had been tampered with, and so the doctor's findings are unreliable? Who could doubt this man?

Next, Daniel wanted to know if Dr. Huntington could explain the sequence of the blows to Jennifer's body.

"Not accurately, but it was interesting—two things—one, when you look really around in depths below this X-shaped array there was some blood there but not all that much, and it would be reasonable—I will underline that, I'm not sure of this—but it would be reasonable that that was the final event in the sequence, the delivery of those blows to the back of the head."

"The blows to the forehead were made by a blunt instrument, correct?"

"Correct."

"Would they have in your opinion been fatal?"

"Possibly by a concussive—that is jolt—to the brain, and they stopped breathing by a concussive mechanism. However, in this particular case the blunt force coming in the back of the head was so powerful, and again there was enough blood on that to convince me that she was alive at least for awhile, when those hit that they could rather pale by comparison."

"There's also something called a mechanism of death, right?"

"Correct."

"In this particular case, it was the blows to the base of the skull that basically cut the brain that was the mechanics of death, right? She didn't bleed to death; she wasn't asphyxiated."

"Right. But you referred—you referred also to the brain report which also showed bruising well forward, including in some-in very vital territory around where the brain connects to the spinal cord, and we have good solid evidence of force delivered that far forward into vital structures of the brain. And in this particular case, I think that the mechanism of death was, in fact, the force that reached that far forward toward the breathing regulating centers, the heart regulating centers. In other words, the really vital territory."

At that juncture, Patti hastily left the courtroom.

I hope she's okay. Why is Daniel having Huntington go into such graphic detail? I thought he had agreed as to the nature of the injuries and cause of death? This is really not necessary.

Patti's departure had left a fairly large space in the front row between Cathy and her brother Tom. Because Bobby was due to arrive, a place had been saved for him. Now with Patti gone, there were two spaces.

Shockingly, a short, large-nosed man in a brown-striped, seersucker sport coat entered the courtroom. He walked to the front row behind the prosecution and sidled in front of Michael, Mavis, and Tom, then sat down between Cathy and Tom.

Stephanie and I looked at each other in disbelief, our mouths agape.

I knew I had seen the man in the courtroom a few times earlier in the week. He had always sat on the other side of the aisle, behind the defense. I had assumed he was just another local lawyer stopping by to see how the trial was proceeding. Other attorneys had briefly occupied seats in the back row behind the prosecution, or had sat on the side behind the defendant.

This man had boldly walked in front of Jennifer's family during testimony about the fatal beating of their daughter and sister and sat amid them. It was incredulous!

I asked Shelly, who was sitting to my right if she knew who the man was. She indicated his name was Lloyd Oberman, a local private attorney, who sometimes worked with Tod Daniel.

I nearly blew up. After whispering this information to Stephanie, we both tried to get Mr. Oberman's attention by staring at him. He never turned around. If it hadn't been such critical, serious, emotional testimony I would have tapped him on the shoulder and demanded he leave.

So we sat, feeling violated, and listened to the rest of Dr. Huntington's testimony.

Meanwhile, Patti returned to her seat and the front row was filled. She shot a glance at Oberman. He didn't react.

I noticed Cathy kept turning to look at entry door to the courtroom. I saw her mouth, "Come on, Bob".

I imagined my brother was overdue in his arrival. Clearly Cathy could have used his support during this testimony.

Momentarily, Bobby arrived. He saw that his usual spot was taken and stopped just inside the door. Cathy had also seen him enter. He gestured to Cathy, wondering where he should sit. She motioned him up to the front row. Bobby shrugged his shoulders and proceeded to move to his customary place next to Cathy. Mr. Oberman squeezed over toward Cathy's brother Tom so as to make room for my brother.

I don't think I could have been angrier. I felt like a mother grizzly protecting her cubs. I told Stephanie I would deal with Mr. Oberman as soon as I could.

Daniel continued his cross-examination of Dr. Huntington. He wanted to know if the bruising by Jennifer's ear could have been caused by falling against something.

The doctor thought that was possible.

"And there were some fabric patterns?"

"There was a suggestion that there was. There was sort of a repeating dot pattern that suggested fabric. In other words, an incoming something with a layer of—carrying a layer of fabric with it or again impacted into something with fabric on it, but that's a suggestion, okay."

"Or falling against a table."

"Yeah, or—but again something with fabric is what would be suggested by this sort of—this kind of a repeating dot kind of pattern."

So not really a table.

I thought the defense attorney had moved on. He wondered if falling could have caused the injury to the top of the head.

"That's possible, but again when you fall you tend to go more forehead or the back. A fall that strikes the top of the head, if you can do it now, it's not the most usual place."

"Well, if there would have been a fall against a table or some other obstruction, that's a possibility, correct?"

"That's a possibility, yeah."

Oh for Christ's sake! What difference would it make if she fell on a table or not?

"And then the defensive wounds as you refer to them on the hands, they could have happened at the same time as, say, the blows to the forehead, correct?"

"Or even, you know, some of the back stuff. Again, that's possible they were. I don't know that."

"Again, I think you indicated in your earlier testimony you believe the fatal blows are the blows to the back of the head which were struck while she was in a prone position, is that correct?"

"I think that's reasonable."

"Again, that's based upon how far into the brain cavity the laceration penetrated, is that correct?"

"Well, again that makes it—if she's resting on something, you see, it makes it sort of a—it makes it—see, the head's got no other place to go, so that would—again it would help explain why the skull fracture was so massive. Again, do I know that that's so, no. Is it reasonable? I think so."

"Okay. I guess, by comparison, if you're standing when you took the blows to the forehead and you get knocked over or knocked down that takes up some of that force, is that correct?"

"It takes at least some of it, and..."

An interruption by the defense attorney, "That—I'm sorry. Go ahead."

The expert witness deferred to the lawyer, "Go ahead."

"That would then cause someone to become unconscious, dazed, or lose their balance and go down, is that reasonable?"

"That's reasonable," Huntington emphasized while he was speaking to the jurors, "Please understand, ladies and gentlemen, I don't know. I have no way to measure what or how much it took to knock this lady out, and I've got no way to measure that in autopsy obviously. But it's reasonable she got staggered, or woozy or knocked out by some of these, in particular, forehead blows. I don't know that that's true, okay."

The defense attorney asked if the earring the doctor found on the victim was pierced.

He did not know.

Hadn't the expert noticed if an earring had been torn from the left ear?

Huntington had not noticed a laceration of the left ear.

What possible difference could it make what type of earrings she'd worn?

Mr. Daniel had one last question, "Is there any way based upon your examination, training and experience to place a time on Miss Judge's death?"

"No."

That seems odd. In movies, TV shows and books the medical examiner always estimates a time of death. But those are works of fiction; this is real life.

Under redirect, Mr. O'Leary asked one question. "Doctor, Mr. Daniel was talking about handling the body. It's my understanding at some point prior to transporting the body to your facility for an autopsy an attempt was made to remove some of the blood from her face so the family could identify the victim. Would wiping some of the blood away from her face in any way change your opinion?"

Huntington's reply was firm, "Not a whit."

26

Court should have been dismissed for the day. After such gut-wrenching testimony I was exhausted mentally and emotionally. I couldn't imagine anyone in that courtroom feeling otherwise.

Does a judge have the latitude to stop the proceedings for the day? If not, he should. This is incredibly cruel to the family. It can't be easy on the jury either.

We didn't even have a break.

The District Attorney moved Exhibits 47 through 58, the photos of Jennifer's body.

He then called his next witness. It was Paul Stein.

While Mr. Stein was making his way to the stand, our intruder, Mr. Oberman, got up and moved across the aisle to the end seat in the front pew. He was directly behind Tod Daniel and the defense table. Oberman removed his sport coat and draped it casually over the bar.

Bobby turned around to look at me. He raised his eyebrows and shoulders as if to say, "Who's that?" I pursed my lips, nodded, and put my right index finger up. He understood my meaning. I knew who the man was and I'd tell him as soon as I had the opportunity.

Mr. Stein reported that he worked as a manager of traffic for the Wisconsin Department of Transportation (DOT). In his twelve-year career, Stein has analyzed traffic on Wisconsin's highways for speed and volume. Traffic information was regularly gathered on the highways on the route from Janesville to Minocqua. There were several automatic traffic collectors connected to loops buried under the pavement. There was some explanation of how this worked, but it meant little or nothing to me.

If only Jeff were here. He could have given me the "layperson's translation" as he often did in technical situations. As an engineer he understood those things so well. It all seemed like magic and hocus-pocus to me.

However, the middle aged, gray-haired Stein appeared very knowledgeable as well as credible. He certainly looked the professional in a dark jacket, burgundy shirt and tie.

The DOT expert told the court that there were collection sites on I-90 just north of Janesville at Newville, and then further north at Cottage Grove Road, near the exit for Highways 12 and 18, and where I-90 and I-94 split. Further collectors were located along I-39 at Decorah, Endeavor and Coloma. The final relevant collector was located on Highway 51 near Pine River north of Wausau.

When Mr. Stein acknowledged that some of the collectors also identified the type of vehicle, most people in the courtroom looked impressed and slightly shocked.

Wow, "Big Brother" really is out there. I had no idea such data was kept. From the reactions I'd seen, many others in the courtroom felt likewise.

Stein answered affirmatively when Perry Folts asked if he'd been subpoenaed to bring data for the dates of Friday, November 22, 2002, and Sunday, November 24, 2002. The data was to cover the hours of 11:00 a.m. through 4:00 p.m.

When Folts began to question Stein about Exhibit 58, the data from the Newville site, Daniel interrupted. He asked for "a minute to look at this stuff". Werner granted a brief recess at 3:30 p.m.

I needed to stretch my legs and use the bathroom which was down the hall. I instructed Stephanie to keep her eye on Mr. Oberman, as I still intended to have a word with him.

I was approaching the bathroom when I heard Stephanie call my name. I turned around to see Lloyd Oberman between the two of us. He was headed for the elevator. I approached the interloper. Stephanie did the same from her direction. "Mr. Oberman?" I queried.

"Yes?" was his puzzled reply.

"Were you aware that the first two rows behind the prosecution were reserved for the victim's family?"

"Oh, so I shouldn't have been sitting there?" His tone sounded curious.

"Certainly not, it was really inappropriate."

"I apologize," he said mildly. I was not in the least convinced.

"Well, now you know," I said flatly, then turned and walked away. Stephanie followed me into the ladies' room.

We agreed that Mr. Oberman should have been aware of the situation, given his profession and familiarity with Rock County courtrooms. We weren't sure what was going on, but felt it might be some type of intimidation tactic by the defense. Of course there was no way we could prove such a thing, but it was extremely upsetting nonetheless.

Bobby was in the hallway looking over the rail to the floor below. He motioned me over. "Who was that man?" I explained and told Bobby of my encounter with Mr. Oberman. I was a bit concerned that Bobby would not be pleased with my actions. I needn't have worried. Bobby, too, was angry. He questioned, "You said he was a lawyer?"

"Yes, so I think he should have known better."

"Well, he's either stupid or up to something. I'll have a word with Mr. Oberman when I see him next."

It was a relief that Bobby had interpreted the situation the same way Stephanie and I had. I certainly didn't want to cause any friction within the family.

I wouldn't want to be in Mr. Oberman's shoes when Bobby catches up to him.

My brother could be forbidding when the occasion called for it.

We went back into the courtroom. At 4:06 p.m. Judge Werner was back on the bench. He asked the defense attorney if everything had been cleared up. Daniel responded affirmatively.

The jury was recalled and Perry Folts continued his examination of Mr. Paul Stein of the Wisconsin DOT.

After much specific data, it was summarized that traffic northbound on I-90 at Newville had averaged 72 miles per hour between the hours of 11:00 a.m. and 4:00 p.m. on Friday, November 22, 2002.

Mr. Stein's testimony also indicated that the speed on Sunday, November 24, 2002, was consistent with that of the previous Friday, except between the hours of 3:00 and 4:00 p.m. The average speed at that time had only been 64.7 mph. The witness testified that such a low average speed would indicate there had been some sort of "incident" that slowed the traffic at that hour on Sunday. There was no such indication for the day of the murder.

Ah, Folts is implying that traffic was actually faster on Friday when Bill drove to Minocqua than when Janesville Police Detective Martin Altstadt recreated the drive on Sunday. Hopefully, the jury is making the same connection. Bill had said it was a five-hour drive to Minocqua. Detective Altstadt drove it in three hours and twenty minutes when the traffic data from "Big Brother" showed the traffic, in at least one place, was slower.

Mr. Stein then gave testimony that the speeds for the Decorah site on I-39 south of the Wisconsin River were similar to those on I-90. Unfortunately though, some data was missing because on Sunday two lanes at Decorah "went bad". That meant that there was a failure of some kind and the data was not being collected accurately. A similar problem occurred at the Endeavor site on I-39.

Exhibit 62 was for the Pine River station on Highway 51, the last station on the route to Minocqua. This data was the most striking. On Friday the average speed was 79 mph, where Sunday's average speed was 68 mph. Mr. Stein said the Friday data would be considered an "outlyer". That simply meant people were in a hurry to get someplace. He was certain the equipment had been functioning properly.

Mr. Folts asked if someone had been traveling much slower than the average speed, would it have created a hazard?

Daniel objected due to speculation. Judge Werner overruled it.

Folts asked the question again.

Daniel objected due to no foundation. That Werner sustained.

Folts wished to be heard.

The jury filed out.

The ADA told the judge that in a statement to the police Bill said it took five hours to get to Minocqua. Mr. Stein could testify that at that speed it would have caused a hazard. Folts added sarcastically, "Unless Mr. Mereness wants to concede he didn't leave until 12."

Wow, that's a surprise. Folts must be getting near the end of his rope with Daniel. I can't blame him if he is.

The defense attorney argued that the answer would elicit a "personal opinion" from the witness.

Judge Werner sustained the objection. He reminded the DA that he'd said previously that the jury could use common sense in determining the effect someone travelling at a slower speed would have had.

Following that was a brief argument about Court's Exhibit Three, the judicial notice on Yahoo Maps. It was determined by Werner that the jury, given the average speeds reported by Mr. Stein, could use simple math to figure out how long it would have taken Bill to travel 247 miles.

These decisions hurt the prosecution, but they don't seem that vital. Surely by now the jury is well aware that Bill fabricated the time it would take to drive to Minocqua. The prosecution's done an excellent job of supplying data from the DOT and having a police officer testify to his actual drive time. We can't be in too much trouble here.

At 4:26 p.m. the jury was recalled.

Mr. Folts stated that he had no further questions for Mr. Stein.

Well, now the jury knows that he's lost his argument about the "hazard" of Bill driving so slowly as to take more than five hours to drive to Minocqua. I hope common sense will lead them to figure it out themselves.

On cross-examination, the defense attorney simply asked if Stein had one other data collection point summary in Exhibit 64. Stein agreed that there was an additional station at Coloma that had volume data, but no speed data.

The ADA moved Exhibits 58-62 and 64. Mr. Stein was excused.

The next witness for the prosecution was Anthony James Nelson. Mr. Nelson was a burly man with a bald head. It was not a surprise when he stated what his occupation was as of November 22, 2002. He had been employed by Wal-Mart as a District Loss Prevention Specialist. His looks reminded me somewhat of the Telly Savalas TV character Kojak. He sure didn't look like anyone you would want to mess with.

In his job Nelson had supervised seven stores with regard to theft and, consequently was familiar with surveillance tapes. He agreed that the Minocqua Wal-Mart was one of "his" stores and, as such, was acquainted with the manager Cass Wisco. According to Mr. Nelson, Cass Wisco had called him because he was having trouble finding someone on a tape.

When Mr. Nelson worked with the tapes in question he found some discrepancies. He determined that the switch on the VCR for daylight savings time had not been set. That meant that the time was incorrect by one hour. That same tape was also off about eight minutes when compared to the other tape Mr. Wisco had been searching.

After telling the court that he had been given a description of the individual he was looking for, the witness explained what he had observed on the tapes. Bill had come in the outer entrance door, turned abruptly and "started digging around in a trash can". This activity had been captured by the camera at the entrance to the store. Bill then entered the store through the exit door and went to register number seven and purchased a candy bar for 44 cents.

When ADA Folts asked how long Bill had been in the store before he'd made the candy bar purchase, Mr. Nelson responded, "Three to four minutes, maybe less".

From that point Bill was picked up by the camera at the service desk. The tape then showed the portion of Bill's body from mid-shoulder on up as he stood in Wisco's doorway talking with him for about four to five minutes. After that Bill came out of the offices and exited the store through the entrance door. The back of his head was visible on the surveillance footage.

Mr. Folts showed Nelson Exhibit Number 42. The witness identified it as the actual receipt from the Wal-Mart store. It did show the time of the candy bar purchase to be 15:34:32. To the layperson that meant 3:34 p.m. plus 32 seconds. Nelson concluded by saying the total time Bill spent in the Wal-Mart store was about twelve to thirteen minutes.

On cross, Tod Daniel asked Mr. Nelson to explain how the multi-flex surveillance setup worked. The security specialist did that, telling the jury that sixteen shots were taken at once, and that it continuously shot one area in 100^{ths} of seconds. The defense wondered if that resulted in a rather jerky film like the one in the Janesville store. Mr. Nelson put forth that he could not speak to the tapes from Janesville, as it was not one of "his" stores.

The attorneys were finished with Mr. Nelson.

District Attorney O'Leary next called James Martin to the stand. Mr. Martin testified that he has been employed by the Janesville Police Department for the past sixteen years, serving the past two as a detective. The witness had been assigned to Jennifer's case. His duty had been to track down phone records at Craig High School. He reported that he had checked various rooms with phones Jennifer had had access to.

According to Detective Martin, the extension to Jennifer's planning desk had a voice mail message left on it at 12:45 p.m. on November 21, 2002. That message checked back to a Sam's Club in Appleton, Wisconsin. When Officer Martin attempted to determine who had made the call, he had found that it had originated in the Optical Department. The head of that department was unable to specifically say who had made that call.

Hmm. I wonder who from the Wal-Mart Optical Department in Appleton would have a reason to call Jennifer? The jurors should be recalling that this testimony matches that of Penny Patterson. It proves that Jennifer had indeed had a call from Bill the day before her death. Then they should remember that Bill's voice had been very angry at that time, less than 24 hours before Jennifer's murder. This is damning evidence. Good.

When O'Leary asked if there were any other messages on Jennifer's work station phone, the officer responded, "Not that I can recall, none significant to the case".

Detective Martin then informed the court that he had been able to locate outgoing calls from Jennifer's workstation. A call had been placed from that phone on November 22, 2002. That call was traced to the phone of James H. Mereness, the father of the defendant. The call initiated at 9:28 a.m. and was eighteen minutes in duration.

This is good evidence too. It certainly corroborates the testimony of Katy Hess and could explain why Jennifer had been upset when Katy encountered her in the hall that morning. It was pretty complicated, though.

Should the jury members have been allowed to take notes? Hopefully, these connections aren't being overlooked.

The DA then directed his witness to step back to November 18, 2002. O'Leary asked if he had reviewed a voice mail from Jennifer's phone from that day. Martin responded affirmatively. The message was short and had come from a phone number checked back to William Mereness' cell phone.

Ah, good again. Proof that Bill had tried to contact her multiple times in the days before the murder.

The rest of Detective Martin's testimony dealt with his initial assignment at the homicide scene. He had first protected the scene and then he had custody of the body en route to the Mercy Hospital morgue. During the trip to the morgue, Martin had been told that the body would be cleaned up for identification by a family member. Jennifer's brother-in-law had attempted to make the identification but could not.

Of course, Martin's talking about my brother. Oh, that Saturday when he came to our house in the early morning. As shocking as the news of Jennifer's murder had been, when he'd told us that he'd been unable to identify the body that had been the single most horrific moment for me.

The witness testified that the bag with Jennifer's body was then re-sealed and sent to Madison. Detective Martin had accompanied the body to Madison.

O'Leary must be trying to repair possible damage done in the cross-examination of Dr. Huntington. Daniel had implied that the body had been tampered with before the medical examiner received it. Martin's testimony should reassure the jury that there had been a police officer present throughout the transportation of Jennifer's body to the morgue and then to the state crime lab.

Powerful waves of nausea consumed me. *What had my brother gone through?* I couldn't imagine it, didn't want to, except that perhaps that might help me be of more assistance to Bobby. Without doubt, I had never imagined anyone in my family would be called upon to do such a thing. It seemed that much of what we had gone through was part of some television program or movie. *These things did not happen to people like us!* But now I knew they did.

Daniel's tone during cross-examination sounded contemptuous to me. The questions seemed designed to make Martin look inept.

First, the defense attorney demanded to know the exact date on which Martin checked the phone records at Craig High School. The witness admitted that he didn't recall the exact date, but that it had been a few days after the homicide.

Had the detective checked all the records on the same day?

He had not.

Then the attorney for the defense said he "was confused". He wondered if some of the records had been from "downtown".

Daniel was referring to the Educational Services Center for the School District of Janesville, which was located in the downtown area. Those of us involved with the district simply referred to it as "downtown". Since the defense attorney had been a school board member at one time, that term would be familiar to him.

Martin agreed that some of the records were from the Educational Services Center.

It was then established that Martin had first checked the phone records on the 25th of November 2002. Daniel emphasized that the 25th was the first business day following the death.

He's going someplace with this. I hope it isn't too damaging.

Detective Martin testified that he had looked at printed records for phones Jennifer had access to, including the one in her planning room.

Daniel asked for an exact number of phones, but Martin couldn't say without looking at his notes, which he did not have with him. But he knew it had been more than one phone.

Why the hell doesn't he have his notes with him? Isn't that standard procedure in such a situation? Did somebody drop the ball in preparing the witness?

Daniel pressed on. Was Martin sure that each person in the planning room had his or her own phone number?

He was.

After Bill's lawyer asked for Jennifer's phone number and Martin gave it, Daniel summarized, "It is your testimony that no one shared that number".

It was.

The defense attorney wanted to know what other phone numbers Martin had checked. The detective told the court that he'd checked several classrooms in proximity to Jennifer's, as well as others in the planning room.

Then Daniel inquired as to exactly how many total calls had been attributed to Jennifer's phone. For a second time, Martin could not say without looking at a printout.

And damn it why doesn't he have that?

Daniel asked for Martin to give a best guess, which was less than twenty. The detective thought there had been four other phone messages in the five-day period preceding the murder. That number was roughly the same for all the phones he had checked.

The witness then indicated that it had been difficult to interpret the phone records, as some were incoming calls, others voice mail and still more were outgoing calls. A phone technician from the ESC had explained all of that to him.

Daniel zeroed in, " You made a judgement about the calls significant to the case."

"Yes."

"Only those to Mr. Mereness or his parents?"

"Yes."

"Only three days after the death?"

The detective seemed to understand that it looked like he had made assumptions. His response was more sheepish than bold, "Yes."

Then Daniel again did what I had feared the most. He brought Jennifer's character into question. Had Martin known that Jennifer had a Yahoo personal page?

Martin responded that that had not been a part of his investigation.

Should it have been?

Daniel continued. Had the detective known Jennifer had a personal ad in *The Janesville Gazette?*

The detective again responded that that had not been a part of his investigation.

Should it have been?

Had Martin been aware that Jennifer had been involved in a new relationship?

Martin responded as he had for the two previous questions.

Daniel dealt the final blow. Had Detective Martin made his judgement about calls significant to the case before any fingerprint evidence was in?

Martin had to answer, "Yes".

The defense attorney had made his point. "Nothing further."

At 4:55 p.m. a five-minute recess was called.

In the hall, the family was subdued. Everyone wondered how much damage the cross-examination had caused. At the very least, Detective Martin and the DA, because he was in charge of the court case, looked negligent in failing to have the case notes for the witness to refer to. At most, it looked like the police officer had jumped to conclusions to the exclusion of other possible perpetrators. In that case Bill had been railroaded, and Daniel's assertions that the real murderer was still out there could possibly be true.

Of course, we all knew that Jennifer had called the police before about Bill. We knew she'd suspected him of stuffing her vent with putty and stones. We knew that Jennifer had told other teachers that she was afraid Bill would try to kill her. We clearly understood why Detective Martin had been so concentrated in his judgement about relevant phone calls. Unfortunately, the jury knew none of this, and due to hearsay rules, would probably not hear any of it.

This is a dark time. Daniel did a good job of taking advantage of the situation. Hopefully, the jury will yet have such a preponderance of evidence pointing to Bill, and only Bill, that they'll see that Detective Martin acted appropriately.

Everyone in the family had talked at lunch about the upcoming witness. All were hopeful that he would provide testimony that would be significantly damaging to the defendant.

27

At 5:10 p.m. the prosecution called Christopher Mereness.

Finally, Christopher could enter the courtroom. He approached the witness stand wearing khakis, a white and dark blue checked shirt with a navy T-shirt underneath. He looked very young. The white necklace of shell or stone would have given away his age if his face hadn't. He was very thin and vulnerable-looking.

Bill's son was sworn in.

Christopher gave his date of birth as December 12, 1984.

He turned 18 three weeks after the murder. What a tragedy for this young man. Will he wonder his whole life if he has inherited some sort of "killer" gene from his father? Hopefully not.

His mother, sisters, aunt and uncle had been very supportive of him all week. He had also seemed close to his grandfather when they had been together during preliminary court proceedings.

Perhaps that will be enough to help him overcome these troubles.

Christopher identified the defendant as his father.

What a painful task.

Bill's son then explained what the living arrangements had been in November of 2002. They'd had a one-bedroom apartment on Morningside Drive in Janesville. His father had been the primary user of the bedroom; Christopher had slept on the couch in the living room.

ADA Folts asked if Christopher and his father had shared clothes. The young man explained that since laundry had only been done once a week, his dad sometimes borrowed his socks. Otherwise, there was no sharing of clothing.

Folts inquired about gray sweatpants. Christopher testified that his father had owned two pair.

Folts bent over and picked up a brown paper grocery bag. He wrestled with the bag to open it. The activity made a great deal of noise in the hushed courtroom.

The ADA pulled out an item, pronounced it to be Exhibit Number 68, and asked Christopher to identify it. Without hesitation Christopher said they were a pair of gray sweatpants that had been kept at the cabin in Minocqua.

Folts inquired, "Who wore them?"

"Primarily, Jennifer."

"Anyone else?"

"Occasionally my father."

Folts picked up another paper bag. Once again the noise caused by opening it was incongruous with the courtroom quiet. The attorney pulled out an article, identified it as Exhibit 69, and requested of Christopher, "What are these?"

"Gray sweatpants."

Folts inquired, "Have you seen them before?"

"Yes"

"Where?"

"In the Morningside apartment." That pair of sweatpants had been kept in a drawer in the bedroom, his father's bedroom.

Folts then asked, "Did your father own any other gray sweatpants?"

"Not to my knowledge."

"Any other color sweatpants?"

"No."

Christopher's answers were very precise and firm. He was doing an excellent job. He had to be incredibly upset and nervous, but it didn't show. He was keeping his focus on Perry Folts.

The defendant's son then identified Exhibit Number 71 as being a pair of tennis shoes his father used when he cut the grass on the property in Minocqua. According to Christopher, his father also had a brand new pair of the same style that he didn't wear much.

The ADA wanted to know if the other pair was as worn as this pair, Exhibit 71.

Christopher's confidently replied, "No".

Folts next held up Exhibit 40, which Christopher identified as a hatchet.

That looks like the sledgehammer. I thought the hatchet had been Exhibit 39. Are Christopher's nerves causing him to misspeak?

The ADA seemed to notice the error, "You call that a hatchet. Okay. Have you seen that before?"

He had. It had been in the toolbox up in the garage in the Minocqua residence. He had seen the item again when Jennifer was moving out of the Minocqua cabin and back to Janesville at the end of the summer of 2002. It had again been in the toolbox, which was subsequently kept in the garage, at the house on Columbus Circle.

Folts wanted to know when Christopher had last seen that item.

"The last time I saw the item is when we were moving out of Columbus Circle in the end of August or September, and we had put that on the moving truck, and my dad had told me to keep that toward the front because we put a lot of clothes or a lot of our stuff in the moving truck and he wanted to keep it toward the front so we could get it off."

Folts inquired, "Who took it off the moving truck?"

"That I do not know."

Bill's son also did not know to which residence the weapon had been taken.

The questioning took a different direction.

"Now, do you know if the defendant owned a Columbia-brand coat?"

"Yes, I do."

"What color coat did he own?"

"He owned a green Columbia-style jacket, green and black."

Exhibit 66 was taken from another paper evidence bag. What did the witness think it was?

"This is a green and black Columbia-style jacket."

"That looked like the one the defendant owned?"

"Yes."

The Assistant DA wanted to know where that coat had been kept. According to Christopher it had been hung in a closet between the bedroom and bathroom of the apartment on Morningside Drive.

The defendant's son testified that there was another coat that had been stored in that same closet. It was a royal blue and black coat that Christopher never wore. Folts wanted a clarification. Had the witness ever worn the liner of that blue and black coat? Christopher answered affirmatively and stated that the liner of that particular coat was black. He had left that lining to the Columbia-type jacket at school.

Folts brought out yet another brown paper bag and noisily produced Exhibit Number 65. Christopher identified it as the lining he'd worn and left at school.

Bill's son then testified that the last time he'd seen the outer part of the blue and black coat was on "the last Wednesday before it happened". It had been in the closet on November 20, 2002, the same closet his father's green and black coat was kept.

The ADA continued asking questions about the black and blue coat. He wondered why Christopher never wore the outer part. The young man explained it had been too big and he hadn't ever liked it. His dad had told him he could wear his coat, the green and black one.

Would Christopher have been surprised if his father had bought him a coat like the black and blue one?

He would.

Did Christopher's father know he didn't like that coat?

Daniel objected because the question called for speculation.

Folts restated, "Did you tell him you didn't like it?"

"Yes."

The point had been made.

Another bag yielded a new-looking Columbia jacket. Christopher explained that the exhibit was similar to the one he disliked, but these sleeves were grayer and the blues were different. The blue on the disliked coat had been more "purplish".

The next line of questioning concerned the separation of Bill and Jennifer. Christopher testified that it had occurred in mid-September of 2002. At that point Jennifer moved to the home on Sandstone.

Christopher had gone to Sandstone once with his father.

Had his father ever been allowed inside the Sandstone residence?

"Not to my knowledge."

The testimony moved to the closings for the houses on Columbus Circle and Sandstone. Christopher attended both of those events with his father and Jennifer.

"What happened at the closing?"

"At the closing they closed on Columbus Circle, and my dad had received a check for, I believe, $20,000. He tried to go cash that check; but they would not cash that check at that bank, so he came back to the room for the closing of the house and said, 'Jennifer, I know what you have been doing; I know what your plan is, I'm divorcing you.'"

"He announced that at the closing of the Sandstone property."

"Yes, he did."

I looked at the jurors. If they were surprised or shocked they did an excellent job of hiding it. I could only hope the testimony had impacted them as much as it had me when I first heard it. It had seemed to be unusually cold and cruel treatment.

Perry Folts then transitioned to Christopher's recollection of the day of Jennifer's murder.

Bill had awakened his son at 6:15 a.m. Father told son that he was going to Duluth and that he also had to let Christopher's Uncle Jim into the cabin up north. Bill instructed Christopher to find someplace to sleep that night because he would be back "late or not at all".

The ADA inquired, "And did you normally stay over at friends' houses?"

"No, I did not."

"Why not?"

"My dad was against that. I had called—I had called him up sometimes and asked him if I could sleep over, and he said no."

According to his son, Bill had left the apartment at 6:30 a.m. only to return about fifteen minutes later. Christopher was surprised because he'd assumed his father had gone to work.

"After he came back, what did he do?"

"He'd come in, and he said, 'What—are you going to school today?' I said, yes, but it's only 6:45, 7:00 and I walked outside and smoked a cigarette, and I noticed he was vacuuming the living room, cleaning the house."

At about 7:15 a.m. Bill took Christopher and his friend Justin to school. Father and son had no further conversation.

The defendant's son testified that he had attended all his classes that day. He also related that he had seen Jennifer at school.

That night Christopher had tried to reach his father on his cell phone about 7:00 or 7:30 p.m. His attempts to reach his father from his friend's cell phone were unsuccessful.

"Did you ever that evening of November 22nd of 2002, receive a phone call from your father?"

"No, I did not."

"At some point were you able to make contact with your father?"

"Yes, I was."

"When was that?"

"I'd say roughly 12:00, 11:45 at night."

"And how did you make contact with him?"

"I called him on his cell phone."

"You have been to the cabin at Minocqua."

"Yes, I have."

"Is there cell phone service at the cabin?"

"Not at the cabin."

The ADA had no further questions for Bill's son.

Daniel began the cross-examination. The questioning was so fast and furious I had difficulty keeping up with my note taking.

The defense attorney's tone seemed contemptuous again. It was as if he was trying to goad Christopher into losing his composure.

It won't be easy; he's going to have to put in a lot of effort here.

"Mr. Mereness was your dad and Jennifer was your stepmother. Were your dad and Jennifer married when you moved in with him?"

"Yes."

"They were married?"

"Yes."

Asked and answered!

"Was this before or after the first divorce? The one that Jennifer started."

"I did not know that Jennifer started a divorce."

"So you were not aware of that, correct?"

"Correct."

Will every question be asked twice?

The black and blue Columbia coat was the next topic. "And it's a fact, is it not, that the blue jacket that you wore the lining of actually belonged to Jennifer, is that correct?"

"That is correct."

"And that she had wanted it back, is that correct?"

"That is not correct."

The defense attorney moved on. "What was your father—strike that. Okay. You came to Janesville because you were having some problems living with your mother up in Fox Valley, is that correct?"

"That would be correct."

"And sometime prior to November 22nd you told your father that Jennifer confided in you that she was going to divorce him after the adoption..."

The DA objected on the grounds of hearsay.

Judge Werner overruled the objection.

Christopher answered, "Yes I did."

"And for what reason would you do that?"

"There was no reason."

"Did she, in fact, tell you that?"

The prosecutor objected again, but the exchange was so quick and Christopher so focused on the defense attorney that he had already answered when the judge sustained the objection.

The defendant's son had shrugged as if it hadn't been a big deal, "There was no reason that I told him that. I--she told me, I told him."

Daniel had gotten his answer.

"She asked you to keep it in confidence, didn't she?"

This time the objection and ruling came in time, Christopher did not have to answer that question because it was hearsay.

What does all of that prove? That Christopher had been an agitator and had contributed to the hostilities in the relationship? Even if that was so does it make his testimony unreliable?

The next line of questioning concerned Bill's clothing on the 22nd of November. The son testified that his father had worn a brown leather jacket, khaki's, and a plaid long-sleeve shirt. When asked about footwear, Christopher said, "That I do not know".

The next exchange between defense attorney and the defendant's son appeared to be even more adversarial.

The gist of it was that Daniel insisted Bill had known his son's work schedule; they had made plans. "...He was going to complete his work in Duluth Saturday morning and be back to get you Saturday night, isn't that correct?"

"That's not what he told me."

Christopher looks a bit ruffled, but he's parried Daniel's attacks fairly well so far.

"Okay. At what phone number do you say you contacted your father on the night of the 22nd?"

Christopher related the cell phone number.

"Okay. That's the one you used, correct?"

"I used my friend's cell phone and that was the number for my friend's cell phone."

We're back to double questions.

"Okay. And what number did you use for your father?"

The witness supplied another number.

"And that you're saying is his cell phone."

"Correct."

"You're saying he answered that cell phone at 11:45 or midnight of the 22nd of November, is that correct?"

"Correct."

Daniel was finished with the witness.

On redirect, Perry Folts guided the defendant's son through an explanation that on one of his visits to Jennifer, Bill had returned to the apartment with the black and blue jacket. Bill had said Jennifer wanted Christopher to have it because he hadn't a winter coat of his own.

It was re-established that the last time Christopher had seen the black and blue coat was the Wednesday before the murder. It was in the closet of the Morningside apartment between the bedroom and the bathroom.

Folts completed his redirection. "Now, after he dropped you off at school you don't know what he did after that, do you, personally?"

"No, I do not."

Christopher was dismissed from the witness stand.

If Bill's son had made his way directly to the courtroom door, he would have passed within inches of his father. Instead, Christopher walked in a deliberate arc as far away from his father as the position of the prosecution's table would allow.

Wow, I hope the jury saw that.

The son did not look at the father. It was a very powerful statement.

The jury was excused for the day at 5:40 p.m.

After they had filed out, Judge Werner directed the attorneys to be in court at 8:30 the next morning. At that time he would instruct the jury about the viewing of Jennifer's house.

Daniel wanted to know when he could advise his witnesses to be ready for their court appearance. "We're still on—I'm still on at 1:30 Friday?"

Werner deferred to the prosecutor.

"I have—depending how long the view takes, I have my crime lab witnesses. All four of them are going to be here at 10:00 tomorrow ready to go. If we go through tomorrow like we did today, I'm expecting to finish up Friday morning. That's the best I can tell you, Your Honor."

"All right. Fair enough." The judge looked to the defense attorney. "Does that answer your question?"

"I'm still okay."

The family left the courthouse, commenting that most of the day's testimony had been pretty damaging to Bill. We were all so exhausted; we did not linger, but said our good-byes and went our separate ways.

I was drained, but still had animals to care for, dinner to prepare and eat, and calls to place to my dad and Jeff.

It was still extremely hot out, over 90 degrees. The heat was taxing what little energy I had left, so I did my chores as quickly as I could and retreated to the air-conditioning in the house. I called my dad while I prepared a salad. I reported the day's proceedings and found out that my mom had had an okay day in the nursing home. She had, of course, asked him when she could come home. I could tell that was hard on him.

After I finished eating I called Jeff.

It was of some comfort that he'd had a safe day's travel and arrived in Cheyenne without incident. It would have been unbearable if something had happened to him.

After filling him in on the events at court we admitted we were both tired so we cut our conversation short.

I fell into bed about 11:30 p.m. and, thankfully, went to sleep without much trouble.

28

It was nice to have an extra hour to sleep. For the first time in days my eyes weren't burning.

I'd been tempted to drive over to Jennifer's house and spy on the jurors as they had their tour, but I didn't want to do anything that might jeopardize the proceedings. For all I knew, it would have been considered jury tampering and a mistrial would be declared.

As I went about my morning tasks I imagined what the 15 were experiencing during their visit to the murder scene. I supposed the position of the body had been pointed out, as well as blood spatter. The entry window would have been a place of interest, as would the ransacked bedroom. Otherwise, they were probably just allowed the chance to take in the layout of the house so they could put some pieces together from prior testimony. Having the house plan in their memories could also make future evidence more understandable.

Judge Richard Werner leads jurors on a view of the murder scene
(*Courtesy of The Janesville Gazette*)

Ordinarily, my dad felt too rushed to be in attendance at the start of a day's session. But with the later start time he felt he could be there.

He had come with his good friend, Orv. They were both quite nervous about going through the metal detectors. In an effort to diffuse some of the tension my dad made some clever quips to the security guards about weapons. They were not amused. I quickly hustled him from the area, telling him this was definitely not the place for humor. He was contrite.

When we entered the courtroom I indicated Dad and Orv should sit in the second row with me. They refused, saying they didn't want to take anyone's place. Instead they sat in the third row. I quickly gave my dad one of my seat cushions since I knew with his bad hip he'd be hurting in a matter of minutes.

Cathy, Patti, Tom, Mavis, Michael and Stephanie were all there as usual. Stephanie sat next to me so she could be my note taking assistant again. I had really enjoyed sitting next to her. Not only did she help out with notes; she had a quick mind and we had some interesting conversations about the proceedings. It was sad that it had taken this tragedy to allow us the opportunity to really get to know one another.

Penny Patterson arrived and sat next to my dad. Since she had already given her testimony she was now free to attend the rest of the trial. I completely understood her desire to be there.

A few minutes later, Perry Folts entered with a cardboard box about the size of a card table. He set the box down near the prosecutor's table. From the box he proceeded to remove, one at a time, what appeared to be five large floor plans.

The defense attorneys and the defendant had taken their places at their table. Bill's gaze had been fixed straight ahead. Once seated, he held his head erect and looked directly forward toward the witness stand. He never even glanced out into the gallery. For that I was grateful. I wouldn't have wanted to make eye contact with him.

At 10:26 Judge Werner entered the courtroom and announced the case. He then instructed the bailiff to bring in the jury.

The prosecution called Gerald Kotajarvi.

The witness appeared to be in his 50's. He had brown hair and a bushy brown moustache. He wore glasses, a black suit, white shirt and dark tie. He looked remarkably like Mike Holmgren, the former coach of our Green Bay Packers.

Mr. Kotajarvi had impressive credentials. He'd been employed by the Wisconsin State Crime Lab since 1992. Prior to that he'd worked for the Michigan State Police for 27 years.

The duties in both positions were similar. The witness explained that he received evidence and processed it for identifiable fingerprints. He also worked crime scene investigations. Over the years Mr. Kotajarvi had received intensive training in latent fingerprint identification from the Michigan State Police, the FBI and the Royal Canadian Mounted Police. He had also been an instructor at both the University of Michigan and Michigan State University. The witness estimated that he had worked with "hundreds of thousands of prints". He'd also testified as an expert witness approximately 100 times.

There could be no question that this man was an expert in his field.

On November 22, 2002, Mr. Kotajarvi had been called to Sandstone Drive in Janesville. He had been one member of a three-person team assigned to handle the crime scene investigation at that site. One of his tasks had been to prepare drawings of the scene.

Assistant District Attorney Perry Folts asked the witness to identify Exhibit 72, which was one of the large schematics. Kotajarvi told the jury that it was an enlargement of his sketch of the overview of the inside of the home. It was not to scale, as it was a crime scene sketch. It showed items in the home, the general layout and where the victim had been lying.

Folts wanted to know where the victim had been found. Kotajarvi pointed to the sketch while he explained that she had been in the entrance to the home at the top of the basement stairs.

Next, the ADA inquired as to the items in the kitchen. Again, referring to the sketch, the witness pointed out two briefcases, sunglasses, a cell phone, the breakfast bar with papers on it, a chair with a jacket on it, some more papers and a purse.

Continuing the walk through his sketches, Kotajarvi showed the laundry room, which had contained a cage with two small dogs. There had been another dog in a cage in the dining room by the patio door.

The witness moved on to describe the master bedroom. It had been "ransacked" with clothing on the floor, dresser drawers open, the bed unmade, the mattress moved off of the box spring about five and one half inches, a neck pillow on the bed, other pillows on the floor as well as on the bed.

Those Judge girls and their neck pillows! Cathy had introduced them to me. She'd given me what we called my "bone pillow" because of its shape. It had served its purpose well, easing strain on my neck while riding in the car, or lying on the couch or in bed. I'd loved it. I never knew Jennifer had one too, but it made sense.

How strange the smallest of things that pop into consciousness and jab at my emotions.

Folts showed the witness Exhibits Eight, Nine and Ten. They were identified as photos of the ransacked master bedroom, which echoed what Kotajarvi had pointed out in his sketch, Exhibit 72.

According to the crime scene investigator, Exhibit 73 was an enlargement of his sketch showing how the victim had been found. She had been partly on the vinyl floor and partly on the carpet. Her body had been face down. When Kotajarvi arrived at the scene, the front door was unlocked and the laundry room door had been closed.

The witness' drawing also showed spots on the wall that depicted blood spatters.

Exhibit 74 was Kotajarvi's drawing from the perspective at the top of the stairs. It showed the keys to a Ford were found on the second step going down to the basement.

Oh my God! A slow motion scene of the attack played in my head.

Jennifer came home and set her school bag and purse on the breakfast bar. The TV was on which caught her attention. On the way to the living room to inspect she walked through the foyer and past the basement steps. Bill charged up those stairs with the hatchet in one hand and sledgehammer in the other. He let out an attack yell. Jennifer heard him, caught sight of him, then dropped her keys and ran for the front door. She got the door open. That's when the construction worker Jeff Jones heard her scream. She was a step outside when the first blow struck her in the forehead. Stunned and weakened, she was pulled back into the house where Bill beat her to death. Outside one of her earrings had come off. Had a blow from one of the weapons knocked it off? Or had Bill ripped it out when he clawed at her to haul her back inside? Only one living person could answer that question.

The witness continued with his description of Exhibit 74. The victim had been wearing blue jeans and a black sweater.

With snowmen on it.

The weapons had been found next to Jennifer's head, as were her brown, cloth-like shoes.

Why had Bill taken the time to place the weapons and her shoes near her head?

I searched my imagination for what I'd feel if I struck someone out of anger or hatred. *When the person fell I would drop the weapons from my hands, drained of the emotion that had propelled the attack.*

What was the significance of Bill's actions? Maybe a profiler could answer such a question. Had a profiler been consulted in this case? Did Rock County have access to one? Perhaps we would see one on the witness stand yet. The killing sure seemed to indicate a personal relationship. Would the jury hear about that?

As I returned my focus to the witness, he was describing Exhibit 75, another enlargement of one of his crime-scene sketches. It was of the basement of Jennifer's home. It showed the stairway and a small landing with a door. The door swung inward. Kotajarvi pointed to where the mechanicals of the house were located. He also indicated the egress window, which was "big enough for someone to get out of". In the room there were also numerous moving boxes, some partially unpacked, a television, a broken screen, a Tupperware container, some footprints and many pieces of glass.

Exhibit 76 showed the broken window screen and the window, which measured 43 by 24 inches. The sketched pieces of glass were representative of their actual size. This drawing also showed the boxes, Tupperware and the windows on the west wall.

The next sketch, Exhibit 77, showed the window with its modern-type window well. The bottom of the window well contained pea gravel and a large rock.

The rock Bill presumably used to break the window and gain entrance. But why would he have taken the time to throw it back outside?

At that point the enlarged drawings were admitted as evidence.

On further examination, the witness indicated that in the course of his investigation latent fingerprints had been found. Some were located around the body, in the laundry room, in the master bathroom and on the master bedroom door. There had been a total of 17 latent prints lifted from the scene.

Folts asked Kotajarvi to explain a bit about fingerprints. The expert explained about the ridges and pores that allowed traces of our fingerprints to be left on surfaces.

Wow, it sounds just like the fingerprint lab my students do. It'll sure be hard to do that lab after all of this.

At that point, Mr. Daniel asked the witness to slow down.

The crime scene investigator continued, slowing his delivery a bit. He was still going fast. It was a typical case of an expert explaining something he or she understands very well to a group of lay people. I could tell he was trying to keep it simple as he talked to the jury.

Mr. Kotajarvi explained that a fingerprint was a reproduction of the "friction rich" skin, but you couldn't see it. So on something like a table, powder had to be used to make it visible. On paper, chemicals brought the print out.

It was determined that in order to leave a print a person would have to have bare skin; he or she could not be wearing gloves.

Jeez, I sure hope these people know that!

The CSI began explaining to whom the fingerprints found in the house had belonged. One of the prints on the master bedroom doorknob compared to the number two digit of the right hand of Mr. John Furgason, his index finger.

Daniel interrupted. He wanted to know what Mr. Kotajarvi was reading from.

It was the report the witness had made.

The defense attorney wished to know the page reference.

Kotajarvi obliged.

Folts then inquired if any of Jennifer's fingerprints were found on that doorknob.

The expert checked his report, "No sir."

Testimony continued. There were no prints found on the front of the home's exterior door or on the exterior garage service door. Jennifer's prints had been found on the clothes dryer, the toilet handle in the master bathroom, a drinking glass in the kitchen and on the kitchen sink.

Folts emphasized that even though Jennifer lived in the house her fingerprints had only been found in four different places.

Ah, he's implying that the murderer must have taken the time to wipe down many surfaces in the house. If the jury is following carefully they will know that Jennifer must have been outside the front of the house at one point, yet her fingerprints weren't found on the door at all. Likewise, her prints were not found on her own bedroom door, but John Furgason's were. John, who entered the master bedroom when he first arrived at her house. John, the first person on the scene to touch the doorknob after it had been wiped clean.

Mr. Kotajarvi also stated that additional fingerprints matching John Furgason's were found on the dryer, toilet bowl rim, and on the master bedroom phone.

That means despite having lived there, Jennifer had left fewer fingerprints than Furgason. That was not realistic. Someone must have done an outstanding job of wiping the place down. Someone who was very meticulous.

The witness appeared to be tired. He removed his glasses and rubbed his eyes. After replacing his glasses, he focused on the ADA again.

Folts wished to know if Kotajarvi had examined the foyer, front door and exterior of the house.

He had. He'd found blood spatters in the foyer and, most unusually, blood spatters on the exterior surface of the front door. It was a door that opened inward. But there was also blood on the wall behind where the door would have opened up.

That would indicate that Jennifer had been struck when the door was open and also when it was closed. That was the only explanation for blood to be in both places. I replayed my version of the crime; it fit perfectly.

The crime scene investigator also had found some blood spatters on the front porch.

After examining Exhibit 27, a photograph, Kotajarvi recognized the light socket on the exterior wall with three blood spots staining that wall.

Exhibit 28 was a close-up photo of those same blood spots.

Folts showed Exhibit 78 to the expert. That photo depicted the west wall and the north end of the basement. A piece of particleboard the crime scene investigators had put up when they left the scene was visible.

Undoubtedly, the piece used to cover the hole in the egress window.

The photo also showed some markers the crime lab workers had set on the floor near what they believed were footprints. In the background the witness identified other items like the storage boxes and the television.

The ADA stopped the witness with a question about the markers on the floor.

Mr. Kotajarvi explained that they had put the markers down that night because they had planned to come back and do electrostatic prints of the footprints.

This man is a seasoned professional. His testimony flows so smoothly.

Folts next showed the CSI the axe, which he identified as "one hickory forge camp axe". He then showed the jury where the crime lab investigators had made their mark on it.

Kotajarvi then pointed out his own initials on the "four-pound roughneck hammer".

The next piece of evidence had been marked "B-1" by the crime lab workers. It was a clear drinking glass that had been found by the kitchen sink.

The witness then identified additional items from the murder scene: a brass doorknob from the master bedroom, the front exterior door of the house, the garage service door and the basement screen from the west wall.

All of that evidence had been examined for latent prints. One print had been found on the screen, it matched a Fredrick W. Hookham. The witness testified that Mr. Hookham had been one of the construction workers who had built Jennifer's house.

The Assistant District Attorney began removing brown paper wrapping from a large flat object. Again, the noise was very loud and intrusive. After the dramatic unveiling, the object turned out to be a window screen with a bent frame. The screening had a gaping hole in the middle of it. The expert witness identified Exhibit 79 as being from the window in the west wall of the basement. It carried one of the state crime lab tags bearing their number and Kotajarvi's initials.

Folts inquired, "You weren't able to identify any prints that belonged to the defendant?"

"No."

"Does that mean he wasn't there?"

Daniel objected. The ADA was calling for a conclusion.

Judge Werner sustained the objection.

Perry Folts tried again, "Does a person always leave fingerprints?"

Again the defense attorney objected. This time he claimed the question had been "asked and answered".

Sustained again.

The prosecution had no more questions for the crime lab expert.

Exhibit 80 was the first concern from the defense on cross-examination. Mr. Kotajarvi identified it as two reports that had been prepared and signed by him. One was from February 12, 2003, the other from March 17, 2003.

Had the witness generated any other formal reports in the case?

Kotajarvi leafed through the papers in front of him, "I don't see any".

At that the defense attorney took a small stack of papers and distributed some of them to the DA. There was an exchange of murmured remarks between Folts and Daniel before Daniel took the rest of the papers to the Court Clerk for marking. As the witness told the jury that there was only one file at the state crime lab, the defense attorney handed him the papers that had just been marked as Exhibit 81.

Kotajarvi identified it as the handwritten, crime scene worksheet that had been prepared by team leader Nick Stahlke.

The crime scene investigator explained that Stahlke had served as the team leader for the investigation at the scene of Jennifer's murder. According to lab policy, the leader position was rotated among the investigators in the department. It did not mean that Stahlke was Kotajarvi's boss, just that Stahlke had directed the investigation in that particular case.

Daniel purported that Mr. Stahlke was not available to testify at trial because he was in Afghanistan. Kotajarvi concurred and indicated that Stahlke would likely be gone for "some time".

At first Kotajarvi did not recognize Exhibit 83. He looked puzzled as he examined another set of papers. Shortly, he apologized and told the court that it was a set of handwritten notes from the day after the murder. They had been written when the team had gone back to the crime scene in daylight to do the electrostatic lifts of the footprints found there.

The defense attorney put forth that all the notes had been written down as the investigation took place and then reviewed.

The witness agreed.

Then it appeared that Daniel was trying to confuse the crime scene expert or make him look inept. The defense attorney kept referring to the notes as "his". Kotajarvi tried to clarify that some of the notes were indeed his, but some were Stahlke's. Daniel kept referring to the two sets as one. The witness kept continuing to differentiate between them. The two men parried back and forth. Daniel finally gave up.

Good for Kotajarvi. This guy isn't going to be tricked into anything. He's a real pro.

The next topic consisted of all the tasks, besides collecting fingerprints, that had been performed by the witness at the scene. Mr. Kotajarvi explained that he had observed, made drawings and assisted in the taking of the electrostatic prints.

CSI Kotajarvi testified that he had seen the blood stain near the patio door and assumed that it had been taken into evidence, but he had not collected it himself.

The expert agreed that the west bedroom had been "ransacked", but the other bedroom had not. The other bedroom contained unpacked boxes. It also had a computer table in the northeast corner.

As for the front door of the residence, Kotajarvi explained that it had a deadbolt lock, but he could not recall if it also had a lock on the doorknob. In any case, the door had been unlocked when he checked it.

Thank God. A witness who checked to see if the front door was locked! If Jennifer had attempted to flee, she would probably have had to unlock it. Had the time it would have taken her to do that been the difference between life and death?

Still, the defense can argue that the police officers who were first on the scene unlocked it during their sweep of the home.

The crime scene investigator recalled the dogs being in their crates, but was unsure if the crates had been soiled or not.

Oh no, here we go again with those dogs and their bowel habits. This is becoming "The Dog Poop Defense".

Gratefully, the defense attorney moved on.

Mr. Kotajarvi explained how the footprints in the basement had been found. After he secured the basement window on the night of the murder he looked back and saw the prints because they had been illuminated by the light coming from his flashlight. The team had then "sidelit" the basement floor; they shined their flashlights from the side to make an exact location of the footprints. After that Nick Stahlke marked five locations to come back to and lift along with other identifiable footprints.

The following day the team had made seven or eight electrostatic lifts, where the five markers showed prints entering the house, as well as other footprints up the stairs.

Daniel was concerned that the crime lab investigators had made "a path" of lifts, not just the marked area.

There's no question here. Isn't O'Leary going to object?

The defense attorney switched topics. He wished to know about the fingerprints on the bathroom toilet. Was there evidence that someone had thrown up in there?

"Yes sir, I made that remark to a police officer."

Daniel started to suggest that it would be reasonable to assume that the vomit had come from the perpetrator, but Folts cut him off with an objection. The defense was calling for speculation.

The judge sustained the objection.

The defense attorney took a different approach.

Hadn't the witness had a career in crime scene investigation for 37 years? Wasn't his job a combination of science and art? Could he "rely on that experience to form judgements"? Didn't his job have an intuitive aspect to it?

Kotajarvi agreed to all the suppositions.

Daniel continued. Since the witness had a great deal of experience wouldn't he be able to draw conclusions that someone was sickened and then threw up in the toilet?

The witness sat silent for a few seconds before replying tentatively, "It could have happened".

If Daniel had been hoping the jury would buy into his "Random Burglar Vomits After Heinous Murder" theory, this was not the witness to convince them. While Mr. Kotajarvi had verbally agreed with the defense attorney, his body language; head tilted, eyes skyward, mouth pursed to the side, hadn't been in concert with his words.

The witness did wholeheartedly agree that there had been no evidence that anyone had attempted to clean himself up after the murder. Nor had there been any evidence that anyone had tried to wipe up blood, or clean up or move the victim.

The next few minutes of testimony were about blood spatters and drops. Kotajarvi clearly stated that he had never been trained in blood spatter analysis and that he would not perform that task at the scene of a crime. He did, however, agree that there had been directional blood near the body. There was also blood near the patio door, on the wall near the baseboard, farther up the wall and across the exterior of the front door. The witness thought that such evidence would indicate the door would have been open in order for the blood to be on the outside of the front door.

Daniel inquired about the earring that had been recovered from the front porch. Kotajarvi stated that Nick Stahlke had done that. He denied Daniel's supposition that he had been the one to see the earring first.

Next the defense attorney asked the fingerprint expert to tell the jury "chronologically or geographically" all the things he had done to get the 17 fingerprints he had lifted from the residence.

It had been Mr. Kotajarvi's decision that night to start where he believed Jennifer had entered her home. He thought she would have gone to the end of the kitchen counter and laid down her purse. He ended his efforts near the body. He had covered the kitchen, laundry room, foyer, spare bathroom, the victim's bedroom and bathroom.

According to the investigator the rest of the house had not been disturbed and there were some surfaces that were not conducive to latents such as the hand railing down to the basement, wood trim and door. The exterior doors had been removed and tested at the lab; the team had taken them along with the axe, hammer, glass, brass doorknob from the master bedroom door, and the window screen. He had wanted to process those items under full light and use super glue and laser poly light.

Daniel interrupted; he was confused as to the reason Kotajarvi hadn't been able to retrieve more prints from the objects he'd taken to the lab.

The witness explained that he couldn't lift reliable prints from the axe and sledgehammer because they were saturated with body fluids; they were covered in blood. He had been unable to get prints in liquid. After the serologist had finished with the weapons, Kotajarvi had used a poly light, dye stain and super glue to no avail.

If that was an attempt to make this man look incompetent it sure failed miserably.

The defense attorney asserted that after he had recovered the 17 fingerprints, Kotajarvi had compared them to standards.

The witness agreed.

"From whom" had he obtained standards?

The expert began his response, "Mereness, Jennifer, John Furgason..."

Daniel cut across him. Hadn't Kotajarvi had complete sets of fingers and palms for all three of those individuals and hadn't he compared the prints from the scene with those standards?

"Yes," the witness replied mildly.

The defense attorney again supplied the information. Hadn't Kotajarvi found Jennifer's prints as well as Mr. Furgason's?

Again, the response was flat, "Yes."

"But Mr. Mereness' didn't match any?"

Still using a controlled monotone Kotajarvi said, "Correct".

Daniel wished for a clarification. Was there "something" referred to as identifiable but unidentified?

Oh, here we go again down the "Random Burglar Murderer" road.

The witness began his explanation that the term meant that a print was identifiable in sufficient detail and clarity to match...

Another interruption by the defense attorney. Wasn't the latent such that by looking at it you could make a comparison?

"Yes," agreed the witness a bit tersely, "And an identification".

Daniel laughed aloud.

How bizarre! It's as if Tod's being condescending to the witness because he's being overly concise. It looks like the witness is annoyed because the defense attorney keeps trying to supply the testimony. Kotajarvi wants all present to know he's the expert and can speak for himself.

During the skirmish between the two men I could hear from behind me my dad repeatedly sighing deeply. It had always been his habit to do that when he was frustrated, and he evidently interpreted Daniel's efforts as I had, and as it appeared the witness had.

Hopefully, the jury is seeing it the same way.

How many latents did the witness have at that stage, after eliminating those of Jennifer and John?

Kotajarvi thought there were perhaps 20.

Daniel continued to supply the better part of the testimony, with the witness left to agree or disagree. Wasn't the next step to ask for more standards?

"Yes."

The defense attorney wondered why.

It was for the purpose of elimination; to try to identify any remaining prints. He'd asked for the prints of people who had worked on the home.

Another interruption. Could we use the screen as an example of that?

"Screen and toilet, yes."

Daniel asserted that the witness had focused on the screen and the toilet. Weren't they examples?

They were.

Hadn't the witness wanted to look at the screen and whomever allegedly installed the screen?

He had.

More supposition. The police had sent the installer's prints to the lab and Kotajarvi assumed he wasn't the perpetrator.

It was the witness' turn to cut in, and he did so sharply, "I don't know if he's the perpetrator. He installed the screen."

Touché!

Mr. Kotajarvi tried to explain why he had 10 unidentifiable prints from the screen. He couldn't match them to each other because he didn't do latent to latent identification.

The defense attorney asserted that each one of his own fingerprints was different from the other.

"Yes."

And each section had it's own pattern?

"Yes, individual to that person and that finger."

Daniel concluded that by seeing one of his fingerprints it would not supply the expert with information about the others.

The witness agreed.

Another conclusion, "So you can't go from a latent to latent. You can't draw conclusions?"

The witness admitted that there were people who did just that, but he had never been trained to do so.

Is that meant to show this witness was, after all, incompetent?

Bill's lawyer wanted to know how many identifiable but unidentified prints he had found on the exterior garage door.

Kotajarvi did not believe he found any. He checked through his notes. "No, I used black powder and super glue but didn't identify any on either exterior door."

Daniel was scrutinizing the report in front of him. He was sorry, but to him the doorknob was part of the door.

Are we exposing ineptitude again?

"I did take the doorknob units apart and off the door so we could put them in a smaller chamber to be processed."

Check.

The expert agreed that there had been identifiable but unidentified prints on both the doorknobs, that to the exterior garage service door and the other to the master bedroom.

Had the witness found such prints in any other place?

He had. There were some on the washer and drier and on the toilet in the bathroom east of the body.

"On the stool?"

"It was on the cover, I believe."

"That's where Furgason's palm prints were, right?"

"His were on the rim of the bowl water container; but the tank itself, cover on the tank, there were palm prints that were not identified."

"Maybe I'm losing it again. Mr. Furgason's were right on the bowl, right?"

"Yes."

Is this a bit of a miscommunication or is the witness making the defense attorney work real hard to get the exact answer he is looking for?

Not yet satisfied, Daniel put forth that many people in the service or in certain jobs have their fingerprints on file. Could the witness please explain?

Is he trying to make the witness look like he hadn't worked hard enough to find out whose prints had been at the scene? Is he suggesting there was a conspiracy to frame Bill since Detective Martin had already been "caught" jumping to conclusions about Bill?

Kotajarvi explained that when ordinary people were fingerprinted, their prints remained in an FBI file that was non-criminal. If someone had been arrested those fingerprints were generally kept by county, unless the crime had been a felony. If that was the case they were stored permanently in state records.

The defense attorney seemed peeved. Didn't the FBI have a repository somewhere?

Expert witness Kotajarvi's tone was a bit condescending. The unidentifiable prints he'd found did not qualify to run through the FBI's system. The computerized system contained only the prints of felons, not of people who'd been printed to obtain a liquor license or any other reason.

Checkmate.

The cross-examination was complete.

ADA Folts wished to redirect. He put forth that there was no way anyone could tell how long identifiable but unidentified prints had been on an object. There was no way of dating them, they could have been left from manufacturing, distribution or building.

The witness agreed wholeheartedly, "Yes, yes, yes."

Folts pushed further. There would have been no way to know if such prints had been left by the murderer.

The defense objected, there was no question.

Wow, talk about the pot calling the kettle black! Daniel had been doing that very nearly the entire trial.

A question was formed. Could the witness tell why the prints were there? Couldn't they have been from a family member helping her move?

Another objection. The ADA was calling for speculation.

Folts cut in, annoyed, "Your Honor, he's been examined by Mr. Daniel as an expert and allowed to speculate on other matters. I think it's appropriate at this point."

This is getting nasty.

Judge Werner overruled the objection.

The witness answered. The print could have been from anyone.

Wasn't it possible that whoever vomited could not have been involved in the homicide?

It was.

The person could have been sick earlier in the day and simply vomited. Mr. Furgason testified he'd been sick earlier in the day and a palm print would have been consistent with that, wouldn't it?

"Correct."

The prosecutor continued by saying there had been a lack of cleaning up; it hadn't appeared anyone had washed up in the sink.

The witness hadn't seen any such evidence.

We could then conclude that the murderer left after the murder.

Daniel objected, there was no question.

The objection was overruled.

"I don't know," answered the expert.

He's not going to make anybody's case. He's testifying strictly as to the evidence. That's good. It'll be less likely Bill will have grounds for an appeal.

Folts pressed, couldn't it be just like the speculation about the vomit?

"I suppose."

Wow, that's as good a gift as we'll get from this fellow.

The ADA must have been thinking the same thing, as he moved on. Hadn't the witness checked a number of other surfaces like the handrail to the basement?

"Yes."

Had he found latents there?

"No."
Was that unusual?
"No."
Did he always find the murderer's fingerprints at the crime scene?
Daniel nearly shouted, "Objection!"
Overruled.
"No."
Kotajarvi had turned the footprints over to a footwear examiner?
"Correct."
Folts wanted to know if the witness recognized Exhibit 84.
"Yes, it bears our lab emblem. It's broken glass from the basement. It has Nick's initials on it."
The prosecutor pointed to something on the exhibit. Was that the number from this case?
"Yes."
Folts wished to move Exhibit 84 into evidence.
Daniel objected.
Werner needed a clarification. Was the defense attorney objecting to the admission of the exhibit?
"Yes."
Judge Werner seemed confused. "You object to it, did you say?"
"Yes."
"We'll deal with that later then," added the judge.
"I have no other questions, thank you," Folts said.
The defense wished to recross-examine the witness. "You've got unidentifiable fingerprints there, correct?"
Folts lodged an objection. "Been asked and answered."
"Sustained."
Daniel argued, "Judge, this is following up on Mr. Folts' question about whether or not you always get the print of the murderer."
Folts defended himself, "That question still has been asked."
Werner was decisive, "It has been asked and answered. I will sustain the objection."
Daniel rephrased his question, "You don't know if you got the print of the murderer or not, do you?"
"No sir."
"Thank you."
At 11:52 a.m. the judge called for a recess until 1:30 p.m. The jury left the courtroom.
Judge Werner inquired of Daniel, "Want to be heard about 84? Exhibit 84?"

"No."

"You objected to it."

"Correct. I will withdraw that objection."

"I'll receive 84."

What the heck was that all about? Some sort of grandstanding in front of the jury?

There was a long debate over exhibits that had or had not been entered into evidence. It involved the judge, the opposing attorneys and the clerk.

When the problem finally seemed resolved, Werner asked, "Are we able to recess at this time?"

Daniel was snippy, "If you say so, Judge."

Wow, what is going on here? I must have missed something.

29

At lunch everyone agreed it appeared that something had transpired between Judge Werner and Daniel that had left the defense attorney a bit testy. But no one seemed to have an idea of just what had occurred; it was puzzling

As we were all settling back into our seats Bailiff Bliss came to stand in front of our section. He told us in the very strictest of terms that there was to be no further loud sighing while the jury was present. We were on short notice. If the behavior continued, someone would be told to leave the courtroom.

Everyone's face reflected surprise, shock and hurt at the admonishment, especially Mavis'. Then the family members, except for my brother, looked quizzically at one another trying to find out exactly who had done such a thing. Obviously they'd all been oblivious to my dad's sounds of frustration. Bobby gave me a knowing look. I turned to check on my dad, but he seemed as puzzled as the others. I was sure he hadn't even been aware of his responses. Even knowing exactly what the problem had been; I, too, was surprised that such a minor thing could upset the bailiff.

How was I going to get my dad to stop such an unconscious action? If he isn't even aware that he was doing it, how could he monitor himself? If he gets thrown out of court he'll be embarrassed beyond imagination!

I quickly turned to my dad and spoke as quietly as I could, "He's talking about you, Dad."

"What?" was his incredulous reply.

"You always sigh when you're frustrated, I'm sure you weren't doing it on purpose. But you've got to try to watch yourself."

"I didn't even know I was doing it." He looked as if he didn't quite believe it had really been him.

"I know. But apparently it's not allowed, so try to beware from now on. We don't want to see you get kicked out, we've already had that happen to one member of the family." I grimaced.

"Oh boy, I don't want that." He shook his head as if to say this was all way too much to manage.

"You'll be okay. I'll try to give you the evil eye if I suspect you're getting frustrated."

"Well, that'd be just about every time Daniel opens his mouth."

"Then I guess you've got it figured out."

"Yeah, I guess."

At 1:40 p.m. Judge Werner proclaimed that court was back in session.

Quickly, before the judge could ask for the jury, the prosecution had "one quick request".

Mr. Folts had been contacted by Christopher Mereness during the lunch recess. Folts reminded Werner that Christopher had testified on Wednesday, was cross-examined and released. He had since been resubpoenaed by the defense. Christopher wanted to know if he could come into the courtroom.

Werner addressed Daniel, "Was he called by you, Mr. Daniel?"

"Yes."

"Then we will deny access at this time."

Again we wore the same surprised look: eyes wide, mouths agape. Family members looked at one another for an explanation of this latest development. But there was no time to talk; the jury was entering the courtroom.

What a snake! Daniel's already had his chance to question Bill's son. This has to be a ploy to keep him out of the courtroom for the rest of the trial! I'll bet he doesn't want the jury to see Christopher siting with the victim's family. Even though his ex-wife and daughters are sitting with us the jury doesn't know who they are. Since Christopher has testified, they know who he is and his presence with us will be a constant reminder to the jury of how he feels about his father. Poor kid. He's got to be awfully upset. At least his Aunt Sallie will be out in the hall with him. She'll offer him some support.

The prosecution called Steven J. Harrington.

Mr. Harrington was short of stature. His hair was dark, but he had a bald spot on the top of his head. He wore glasses and a navy sport coat, white shirt and red printed tie. Mr. Harrington's expression suggested he was a strict and conventional man.

After being sworn in the witness told the court that he was an employee of the Wisconsin State Crime Lab. As such, his duties included the examination of fingerprints, footprints and crime scenes. He routinely examined objects for fingerprints, palm prints, shoeprints and tire prints. Then he compared the various prints to known standards.

Harrington's credentials included 28 years in the Crime Information Bureau, four as a fingerprint examiner. He'd taken courses from the FBI and other federal departments. In the 1990's he'd specialized in latent prints, footprints and tire prints. He had testified in about 200 different trials.

In this case, the witness explained, he had been called upon for his expertise in footwear impressions.

According to the expert, footprints from Jennifer's basement and stairs had been photographed and lifted. Lifting was accomplished with transparent adhesive tape or with electrostatic lifting. The electrostatic process involved passing an electric current through the lift using a metal background. That allowed for a static charge to cause the dust in the print to be attracted to the plate. Unfortunately, over time, an electrostatic record could be damaged, fade or collect dust. To make a more permanent record, photography was used. Photography could also be used to enhance the prints in terms of contrast.

Talk about technical. Hopefully, the jury's going to understand this enough to make use of it, if they've not been turned off already by the jargon.

District Attorney David O'Leary took a set of photos to the Court Clerk to be marked. He then showed them to the three men at the defense table. The photos were examined briefly and Daniel murmured something to O'Leary. The DA whispered something back.

Several minutes of silence ensued as the defense studied the photographs.

After another exchange of murmured remarks between defense and prosecution, the prosecutor took the photos and approached the witness.

Mr. Harrington identified Exhibits 85, 86 and 87 as black and white photographs of electrostatic lifts that had been taken in this case. Also, on Exhibit 85 were notes handwritten by the witness himself. The notes were on the outside margin of the photo. They were significant in that he'd assigned a case number, M022583, and written his initials. He had also made some notations for his own benefit as to which impressions he'd compared to left or right shoes.

The prosecutor wished to know if the footprints in the photo were identifiable.

According to the witness they "had value" and were "potentially identifiable".

This is a very precise, regimented man. He makes Kotajarvi look like a schoolboy.

Exhibits 86 and 87 had similar information in the photo margins. Those prints were "identifiable for comparison purposes".

The footprints in all three exhibits had been compared with Exhibit 71, which were a pair of athletic shoes Harrington had examined in this case. In his expert opinion, the footwear in Exhibit 71 could be eliminated.

Surely, this isn't the answer O'Leary had been expecting. If so, this man wouldn't have been called by the prosecution, but for the defense. How will O'Leary try to get the advantage back?

The prosecutor went into detail. He wanted to know if the shoes in Exhibit 71 were fairly worn.

The response was precise, "Significant wear is present."

O'Leary waded a little farther into the potentially dangerous waters. Were the patterns on the bottom of Exhibit 71 similar to the patterns in the lifts? Wasn't the tread similar?

Daniel objected. The question was irrelevant because the shoes had already been excluded.

O'Leary wanted to be heard on the matter.

Judge Werner excused the jury.

As soon as the door to the jury room closed, O'Leary argued that he was trying to "make a foundational understanding". The comparisons in the shoes in Exhibit 71 had been excluded because of wear, not size or style. Further, Christopher had testified that Bill had a pair of shoes like Exhibit 71, only newer.

Werner commanded, "Give me proof".

Harrington agreed with the DA that it was common for different brands of shoes to have different treads. But he did not know the brand or tread comparable to the photographic images or Exhibit 71.

O'Leary pressed. Didn't the general tread design in the photos match Exhibit 71?

"Some are consistent with the tread design."

The prosecutor pointed to something the footprint expert had written in the margin of Exhibit 85, "right except for wear not corresponding". Did that not mean that the shoes in Exhibit 71 had tread that was more worn than those that made the impressions were?

The witness was extraordinarily precise. His words were clipped, "In the corresponding area there is dissimilar general wear between the shoes and the impression on the photograph."

The DA would not give up. "The center of that tread wear has a fairly distinct design, correct?"

"Yes, it is distinctive in the photographs."

"Is that tread design in the center of that tread mark consistent with the tread mark or the tread on Exhibit 71?"

The defense attorney had an objection, the question was irrelevant.

Since it was an Offer of Proof, Werner allowed the question.

Harrington responded, I would not say that it is consistent or inconsistent."O'Leary needed a clarification.

"I would say that the—again, the general wear on the tread design does not correspond between Exhibit 71, the shoes and the photograph."

The district attorney sounded frustrated. "Correct. I'm talking pattern; I'm not talking wear design. I'm talking as a pattern is the pattern contained in this exhibit consistent with the pattern of this brand of shoes contained in Exhibit 71?"

Huh? Now I'm confused. O'Leary keeps interchanging the terms pattern, tread and design. He should take a deep breath and define each of those terms and then restart his questioning. The witness seems most concerned about being precise, but O'Leary probably thinks he's being difficult.

To make matters worse, Daniel objected again. He felt the question had been asked and answered.

I don't even know what the question is!

Fortunately, Werner overruled the objection.

Maybe the judge is as confused as I am and wants this to be sorted out one way or the other.

It seemed the DA was trying to get the witness to say that the shoes in Exhibit 71 had been excluded because of the amount of wear they had, not because of the tread design. However, O'Leary hadn't been able to pose the question accurately enough for the expert.

Harrington answered, "I would say the overall tread design is consistent with and cannot be distinguished between."

Finally!

The prosecutor forged ahead. Could the witness eliminate the shoes in Exhibit 71 based strictly on size?

He could not.

"So," the DA summarized, "The elimination of the shoes in Exhibit 71 was primarily due to wear?"

"That's correct."

The witness then explained that there were four separate tread designs present in the photos. He could not say how many different pairs of shoes would have a consistent tread pattern with those in Exhibits 85 through 87, nor could he determine what brand those shoes might have been.

O'Leary indicated he was finished with his Offer of Proof.

Judge Werner thought that there was enough to prove beyond reasonable certainty that the shoes in Exhibit 71 had not made the impression. There was sufficient detail in terms of general wear to eliminate those shoes. Therefore, he was going to allow the jury to hear the witness speak about tread pattern and size.

The jurors were brought back in.

Fortunately, all the confusion in the Offer of Proof was avoided. Harrington was able to succinctly tell the court that the shoes in Exhibit 71 had been excluded because of wear, not tread pattern or size.

Whew! That was brutal.

In his cross-examination, Daniel had the witness explain that there were "a minimum" of four different tread designs in the photographs and that he didn't know how many sizes were represented. Size of shoe could not be determined by tread impressions alone.

Then Bill's attorney asked if the photos were going to be published to the jury.

Werner replied, "We'll get to that."

Daniel told the judge it would make a difference in what he was going to ask.

There was no response from Judge Werner. He'd answered the question.

This man knows exactly how to handle the defense attorney. It's a great asset for this trial.

Daniel then launched into a diatribe about how people walk: first striking the heel, then rolling to the toe, etc. He wished the witness to concur.

Harrington did not.

It seemed important to Daniel that he prove the point about full versus partial shoe prints.

The witness did say that the way a person walked could have a determination on whether they left a full or partial print.

Harrington then told the jury that he could not determine the brand of any of the shoes that had left the prints.

Could he estimate how many "thousands or millions" of shoes could have the same pattern?

He could not.

The witness was excused.

Exhibits 85, 86, and 87 were moved into evidence.

I wasn't quite sure where this witness had left us. It was hard to separate what had transpired during the jury's absence from what had happened in their presence. At worst, it was probably a long time spent on a neutral outcome.

30

The prosecution next called Curtis D. Knox to the stand. Mr. Knox's appearance presented quite a contrast to that of Mr. Harrington. He looked to be in his 30's, was blond and had a friendly countenance. He wore a dark green suit with a green shirt and a patterned tie.

The witness explained that he was employed by the state crime lab in Madison. He'd been a DNA analyst for about six and a half years. His duties primary involved examining evidence with the objective of finding biological materials that might give him DNA. If he found DNA then he would make a profile and compare it to victim's or suspect's to see if they did or did not match. Knox's training had begun at the University of Iowa where he obtained a degree in genetics. He then interned with the FBI in Quantico, Virginia. The witness had learned DNA analysis at a crime lab in Louisiana. He had previously testified as an expert witness about 20 times.

In this case Mr. Knox had been given a large number of items to search for DNA.

He had not gone to the scene, but processed the evidence that had been brought back to the lab. That evidence had included shoes, blood, a sexual assault kit, as well as vaginal, cervical and oral samples. Additionally, he'd examined fingernail scrapings, pubic hair, a sweater, a turtleneck shirt, William's glasses, a watch and a necklace. The witness had also tested the hatchet and sledgehammer, stains from the scene, a drinking glass, a Ford Taurus, sweat pants and a ball cap from the car. Garbage, paper towels, tissues, a file organizer, socks, a washcloth and another pair of sweatpants were studied as well.

Wow, it sure looks like the investigators did a thorough job.

The prosecutor wanted to know what the witness had been looking for.

Mainly, he'd been searching for blood, semen…

O'Leary interrupted his witness. Had he found any semen?

"No."

So the tarnish Daniel had put on Jennifer's reputation just came off. She hadn't had sex recently. She also hadn't been raped by that marauding intruder.

Had Mr. Knox draw any conclusions from his testing?

The expert attempted to summarize as best he could. The blood items that were consistent with Jennifer's were from the hatchet, sledgehammer, a swab from the scene and the pair of jeans. The only thing not consistent with Jennifer was the sweat pants from the car. One stain had been consistent with both William and Jennifer.

Knox had tested the fingernail scrapings and found some blood and fibers but no tissue. The blood was not foreign to Jennifer and the fibers were consistent with her clothing. He then cautioned that he was not a fiber analyst.

The district attorney wanted to know if the witness had found any DNA belonging to the defendant.

He had. It was on his watch. Also, there was a partial match from the baseball cap and from the washcloth. The washcloth evidence would be consistent with one out of 93 people, while that on the cap would match one in one million.

The DNA from the paper towels and facial tissues in the garbage from the cabin were not consistent with William or Jennifer, but did have factors in common with Mr. Mereness.

O'Leary wondered if those samples could have been from a brother of Bill's.

"Yes."

The DNA on the sock hadn't matched either Jennifer or William, but it was consistent with a close relative of William's such as his son or father.

The district attorney wanted to know how DNA was left by a person.

His expert explained that there were a number of ways for that to occur. The most obvious would be from cutting oneself or an attacker. If a person left tissue, saliva, semen or blood then he could recover DNA from that.

On cross, Daniel wanted to know how many standards had been provided for Mr. Knox to compare his samples to.

He'd only received standards from Jennifer and William.

The defense attorney was puzzled. Hadn't Knox been given standards from any other family members?

"No."

Had he received any for Mr. Furgason?

"No."

Why doesn't the DA object? The question had been asked and answered.

Had the witness examined the Ford Taurus himself?

"Yes."

Had he been looking for blood?

"Yes."

The defense attorney asked the same basic question again, "You went through it looking for blood?"

"Yes."

Daniel asked the DNA expert to describe the process he'd used in the car when looking for blood.

He first had done a visual exam with a bright light. Since blood tended not to show, a bright light at an oblique angle could reveal contrast for transfers of very light amounts…

An interruption. Bill's attorney wanted to know what a transfer was.

An example of a transfer would be if someone got blood on his or her pants and then sat on something.

The defense attorney supposed that if there had been a bloody scene and a person got into a car some of the blood would transfer.

The witness agreed.

Then he continued describing the process he'd used. If he saw a light red or brownish color he'd test it further with a presumptive test.

A clarification was required.

Knox explained that he would test the stain with a chemical: phenol thalline. He'd wipe the stain with a sterile swab. A positive reaction would be bright pink. If it were negative, there would be no color change. By presumptive he'd meant he presumed it was blood but couldn't say for certain. If the test turned out positive he'd have taken it to DNA.

Daniel drew a conclusion. Negative meant there was no blood and that would be an exclusion.

Knox affirmed the statement and added to it, "Yes, anything I thought was blood I'd then test."

He'd finished the exterior of the car then processed the interior with the bright light to check for stains of the right color.

After that he took one last test. He sprayed the chemical luminol onto the interior. Luminol made blood fluoresce. Anything that glowed would be identified for further testing.

Had the witness done that with the Taurus?

Good grief! Isn't that what he just said? Why doesn't the prosecution object to these repetitions? Hopefully the jury's as annoyed as I am.

"Yes." Knox had sprayed the seats, floor, wheels and dash with luminol.

Bill's lawyer inquired as to how much blood would have to be present for the witness to find it.

Not very much. It would have been just a matter of spotting it. It could have been as small as a pinhead. If he could discover it he could do DNA testing. The stain could be very obvious or just a light swipe across.

Did he then extract the DNA?

It depended upon whether it was found on fabric or a dashboard.

Again, Daniel repeated a question. How much did he need to test?

Not much. Especially if the stain were new and hadn't been subjected to environmental damage. A spot the size of the head of a pin might be enough.

We heard this already.

Next the defense attorney wanted to know if Knox had written a report that was dated March 6.

He had.

Had the report listed all the things he'd tested?

"Yes."

And it told if he'd found DNA?

"Yes."

Daniel took the papers he'd been looking at to the Court Clerk. After she stapled them, the attorney showed them to the witness.

Knox said it appeared to be a copy of his report.

The defense attorney went through a number of items like the washcloth and sock that had already been discussed. The witness confirmed Daniel's assertions that Bill's DNA was not found on them.

Why doesn't the prosecution object to all of this repetition? Do they know it will actually help them because it only serves to irritate the jury?

Bill's attorney summarized Knox's findings. There was nothing at the scene that contained Mr. Mereness' DNA.

The witness agreed.

There was nothing in the vehicle that contained Jennifer's DNA.

"No."

There was none from Mrs. Mereness and two from Mr. Mereness. Could he describe them?

They were on a tan cap. They were small dots about one to two millimeters.

Could the witness show the size of the dots using his fingers?

Not really.

Daniel's expression indicated he was pleased with his cross-examination.

The DA wanted to redirect.

Was he correct in thinking that blood evidence was very fragile?

Somewhat, it could survive sometimes or be destroyed very quickly.

Could it be destroyed by water, washed away when washing glasses in a sink?

"Yes, certainly."

The witness then agreed that if a person was wearing gloves he was less likely to leave tissue or DNA.

O'Leary held up Exhibit 39. Did Knox recognize it?

Yes, it was the hatchet submitted to the crime lab.

Had he examined it?

He had.

Was there any unidentified DNA on it?

No, only Jennifer's.

How had he taken the DNA from the hatchet?

He'd used sterile Q-tip like swabs.

If there had been more than one person's DNA would he have found it?

Given the amount of Jennifer's blood, it had saturated the axe, it was unlikely that he could have picked up any other DNA. Her blood could have wiped it out.

The district attorney was finished with the witness.

Bill was certainly very thorough in his actions. He made sure there would be no DNA link to him. It certainly indicated thoughtful planning and meticulous action.

At 2:40 p.m. Kenneth Olson was called to the stand.

Olson's face was clean-shaven and nicely tanned, his hair was dark brown. His expression indicated he was likely an amiable fellow. He wore a gray suit with a white shirt and burgundy tie.

The new witness had been a member of a trace evidence team for 23 years, a unit leader for 11. He analyzed a variety of materials including paint, glass, fibers, metals, plastics, oils and others that did not fit into other units at the lab. His education included a bachelor's degree in chemistry as well as numerous training sessions and workshops in different areas of study. He'd testified as an expert about 150 times.

Could Mr. Olson tell the Court what trace evidence was?

It was small types of evidence in a transfer situation. A lot of his work was done under stereomicroscopes so he could find things that needed to be compared to known items. He might find a piece of glass on someone's clothing and compare it to a known quantity to see if there was a relationship. When a pane of glass was broken, the glass would travel with the direction of force. But glass was elastic, so it would also come back in the direction of the force. Particles would move in different directions.

What did the witness look for as evidence?

If the police suspected someone broke a window and they found that individual they could bring in the clothing and shoes to find glass.

Could the glass sometimes transfer from the clothing or shoes?

"Yes, it's called a secondary transfer."

Was Olson familiar with Jennifer's homicide?

He had worked on it and had been provided with some known glass samples for comparison.

The witness identified Exhibit 84 as a white pillbox with their lab case number on it. It contained a known glass sample from broken glass at the residence.

Had Mr. Olson examined an automobile?

He had. A 2002 Ford Taurus that belonged to the defendant had been the subject of his examination. The crime lab worker first visually noted the condition of the car then had taken a modified shop vac with a filter trap and swept different areas in the vehicle. He'd used a new filter in each area of the car. Knox had concentrated on the driver's compartment and used one filter for the seat and another for the floor area. He also swept the passenger floor and seat as well as the back seat and floor.

The trace evidence expert then examined his findings under the microscope.

Had he found any evidence?

"Yes." From the front seat and floor of the driver's compartment he'd found two small microscopic glass pieces that were about one millimeter by one half millimeter in size.

When the witness compared glass samples, what did he look for?

Similar color first. When he found differences he stopped his analysis. But if there were similarities in color he went on to density. The pieces he'd found had been too small for density tests so he'd moved on to check the refractive index.

The prosecutor halted his witness. He needed him to explain what refractive index was.

Mr. Olson spoke slowly and clearly. If a pencil was placed in a glass of water and looked bent, that was an example of refraction. Glass fragments would refract similarly and that could be measured. The refraction index was based upon how the glass was manufactured, it's ingredients and how it was cooled. Even the same manufacturer would produce batches of glass with different refraction indexes because of the factors he'd mentioned.

As for the glass in this particular case, had the witness found the color in the glass from Jennifer's window to be similar to the shards found in Bill's car?

He had.

Since the pieces were too small for density tests, Olson had moved on to test the refractive indexes.

Had there been similarities in that regard?

There had. The witness confirmed that the pieces of glass in Bill's car could have come from Jennifer's window.

Just a tiny little slip up in the clean-up phase.

For his cross-examination Daniel went into a long dissertation about tempered glass, continuous flow, rolls, the addition of ingredients and how glass making was like making paper pulp. He wondered if there was a database on glass.

Mr. Olson said there was no such thing.

Daniel asserted that there was no way to even "guesstimate" how many pieces of glass in Janesville or in Wisconsin were consistent with the shards in Bill's car.

The witness agreed.

The defense attorney was finished with the witness.

No harm done here. This witness proved that the glass could have come from Jennifer's window, no one had ever contended that it positively had.

The Wisconsin State Crime Lab was released by the Court.

At 3:23 p.m. Richard Boyd was called by the prosecution.

The middle-aged Mr. Boyd had a distinctly more casual look than the witnesses from the crime lab had. His green suit was rather rumpled and he wore a white T-shirt rather than a dress shirt with a tie. He was tanned, had brown hair and wore glasses.

Mr. Boyd testified that he had been the director of network operations for U.S. Cellular for the past six months. Prior to that he had worked for Sprint. He'd been in the cellular field for eight years and in communications for 30 years.

In his duties for U.S. Cellular he was in charge of 200 running switches. Switches, Boyd explained, were devices that calls came into and went out from.

The prosecutor backed up to review the witness' education.

He'd had training in the United States Air Force, including on Air Force One. He'd attended the Harvard business school and had done a "little bit of everything". Most of his training specific to his duties at U.S. Cell was acquired while working for Sprint.

The witness began a "simple" explanation of how a cell phone worked. It was really nothing more than a two-way radio that talked back and forth through switch sites. After a user dialed a number, a message went to a cell site then went back to a switch site. If the user was valid, the switch okayed the call then routed it to a location. All of that activity took place in milliseconds.

The ADA wanted to know where switch locations were.

Boyd said that in a major location there would be several hundred cell sites. A cell site housed equipment that the handset talked to. It was out in a region or network that allowed handsets to have communication back and forth. Each cell site typically contained three antennas. Unlike radio, which broadcast in all directions, the cellular antenna needed to be focused toward different geographic directions.

Yikes, this is getting really technical. If only Jeff were here to translate for me.

Folts referred to one of several large, brightly colored maps that had been affixed to the far wall between the witness chair and the jury. The judge and the witness had to crane their necks to look at the maps, while the attorneys, defendant, jury and gallery had a straight-on view of Exhibit 91.

Mr. Boyd recognized the exhibit as a geographical map of a cell site around Janesville. The colored triangular areas, blue, green and yellow, indicated the area serviced by the three different antennas.

Had Mr. Boyd run a check on the cell records relating to a particular cell phone number?

He had.

Did the witness know to whom that account belonged?

He did; it was William Mereness'.

The record of incoming and outgoing calls on November 22, 2002, began at 6:46 a.m. That first call was an incoming call from the East Milwaukee-Somerset cell site. The next activity was an outgoing call at 7:34 a.m. which utilized the Milwaukee-Somerset Z sector which faced west and was represented on the map by a pink color. A third call was incoming at 7:43 a.m. It had come from the X sector of the Janesville Mall site, represented in gray. At 7:46 a.m. there had been an outbound call to Bentonville Arkansas that was again from the Z sector of the Milwaukee-Somerset site. An incoming call had come through at 8:11 a.m. That particular call was from the Milwaukee-Somerset X sector, shown in blue. At 9:17 a.m. an incoming call off the Janesville Craig X sector had been logged. That area was represented on the map by the color orange.

I needed to shake my head. *This is too much technical information for me to process so quickly. Between this cell phone stuff and that about the traffic, we can really be tracked by the authorities. Is it 1984?*

The witness continued to account for Bill's cellular phone activity on the day of the murder. It was of a significant volume all morning. Of particular interest was a 10:50 a.m. call outbound from the Milwaukee Somerset X sector because it was followed by no activity until 12:10 p.m. At that time, the call was from an Edgerton site, which was north of Janesville. A 12:20 p.m. call indicated Bill's handset had moved out of his home Janesville area and into the Madison area. Subsequent calls tracked Bill's movement from Madison to Stevens Point, Wausau and at 14:57 at Rhinelander.

This is an exact record of his movements during that day. This is truly damaging evidence. Praise to Big Brother.

Mr. Boyd also provided evidence that, as Christopher had testified, Bill had had an incoming call a little before midnight. It had originated from Christopher's friend's cell phone.

On cross-examination, Daniel requested the witness be patient with him. He'd thought he'd understood the cell process the other day, but apparently he hadn't.

Is this designed to illicit sympathy and empathy from the jury? No doubt some of them are having problems digesting all the technospeak. Will his admitted frustration cause them to identify with the defense attorney?

The thrust of Daniel's argument was that a person needn't actually have a cell phone in his or her possession in order for an incoming call to be logged. If a voicemail was received it counted as a connection.

It seemed that since he couldn't argue with the validity of the information this witness had provided, he would suggest that Bill didn't even have his phone with him. The phone record really only told where the phone was, not the owner.

Yes, quite possibly the random burglar who'd thrown up in Jennifer's toilet had taken it in order to frame Bill. Hopefully, the jury will remember what the judge had told them about "reasonable doubt".

31

Karyn Dexter, the next witness for the prosecution, was a very young-looking woman. Her clothing was typical of someone of her generation. She wore khaki slacks and a black blouse with a light pattern on it. Her medium-length, ash-blond hair was tucked behind her ears. Her manner alluded to a hint of nervousness.

Karyn told the court that she had been the assistant manager at Scheels All Sports in Appleton for almost two years. She recalled an encounter at work with an individual who had requested the cancellation of a receipt and the issue of a new one.

When asked to identify that individual Ms. Dexter pointed at Bill.

The witness was shown Exhibit 96. She testified that the exhibit consisted of three store receipts. The first was an original receipt, the second showed a void of the first transaction and the third was the "post void transaction".

The original receipt indicated the purchase of a jacket with cash and check on November 24, 2002. The jacket style was a "Double Whammy" by Columbia, which meant it had two layers. The inside fleece layer could be zipped to the outer shell or the two components could be worn separately. The coat was a size large and had been purchased at 10:58 a.m.

The Scheels employee then positively identified the coat in evidence as the coat she had sold to Bill on that day.

The next contact Dexter had with the defendant was at 11:40 a.m. that same day.

O'Leary asked, "And what type of contact did you have with him?"

"Basically, he came back into the store, told us that he had the rest of the cash and would like to get his check back because he was going to be closing the account and didn't want it to bounce. So what we did in that situation is we did a post void. Basically, what that means is we take that transaction, the initial transaction, out of the computer, and re-ring it. So we gave him his check back. He gave us the rest of the cash. We re-rang the transaction, gave him a new receipt and the two copies of the post void receipt is what spit out."

Miss Dexter had a further contact with the defendant.

"I'm not sure of the exact time but it was shortly after we closed. I'm going to have to say probably 7:00 p.m. He called and asked if there was a receipt of that post void that he should have gotten."

"And so I told him, you know, what information was on that receipt. And he asked if he could have a copy of it."

How had the witness responded to that request?

"I told him no because, generally, we do not give out receipts of the post void because there is no pertinent information that the customer would need…"

"And was he satisfied with that response?"

"No, he wasn't"

"What did he say?"

"He asked me, you know, what was on the receipt so I told him, you know, what information was on that receipt. And he asked if he could have a copy of it. And I said yes."

"And did you give him a copy of it?"

"I made a copy of it. And put it on my bulletin board and he came and picked it up the next day."

"So the 25th of November is when he came and picked it up?"

"Correct."

"Did you speak to him at that time?"

"Very briefly. He came in, found me, I got the copy of the receipt, gave it to him and he left."

"Did he say why he needed that receipt?"

"No he did not."

On cross-examination it felt like Daniel was challenging the witness. He asked many specific questions about the receipts, all of which Dexter answered. Bill had originally paid for the coat with a combination of $125 cash and a check for $42.95. One of the receipts had indicated that the coat purchased was blue and gray.

Daniel wanted to know if Columbia made a blue and black coat. The witness was sure that they had "somewhere along the road".

I knew from our skiing experiences that Columbia changed their colors every year. That way, skiers could tell which individuals on the slopes were right up to the minute in fashion. We rarely were.

Bill's lawyer and the witness went back to a discussion of the receipts. The check had not been tied to the receipt in the first place. She'd voided out the original transaction and issued a receipt for that. It was not store policy to give the post void transaction receipt to the customer because it didn't have much information on it. It was finally determined that Ms. Dexter had simply filled out the necessary paperwork to get Bill's check back to him in the easiest way.

At that point, Daniel stopped his cross and was talking to Bill.

The defense attorney turned back to the witness. "Miss Dexter, do you recall giving testimony in a related matter back on March 14th of this year?"

"Yes, I do."

"And we did that in Appleton, correct?"

"Correct."

Daniel then addressed Judge Werner. "Judge, I plan on reading page 15, line 11 through page 16, line three, and then page 16, line 10 through 17 of that deposition."

O'Leary interjected, "Does the Court have a copy of this?"

"No," replied the judge.

O'Leary said the prosecution did not have a copy either.

The defense attorney continued, unabated, with the witness. "Do you read and write English?"

Wow, that sounds like an indictment of the witness' apparent intelligence.

"Yes." Dexter's voice revealed annoyance.

"These are the questions that I asked you and these are your answers. If you read along to make sure that I'm reading it accurately, okay?"

"Question: All right. So Bill Mereness brought a jacket to the register to purchase? Answer: Uh-huh. Question: Okay. Can you describe the jacket? Answer: The jacket was royal blue and gray Columbia Double Whammy jacket. Question: Okay. Royal blue is kind of a vivid…Your answer was Uh-huh. Question: bright blue. Your answer was Uh-huh. Question: Correct? Answer: Uh huh or ahum. Question: You got to say yes. Answer: Correct. Yes. Question: And this would be a medium gray? Answer: Yes. Medium gray. You know, a darker gray like this color gray that is in my jacket."

Daniel addressed Miss Dexter, "Do you recall those answers to those questions?"

"Yes, I do."

"And line 11, excuse me, line 10. Again, I'm asking the questions and this is your answers. Okay. And I think in getting ready for this deposition you indicated that Columbia doesn't make a jacket accented in red? Answer: Not that I'm aware of. It's always possible there could be one, because they make numerous styles of jackets. But, as far as I am aware, we do not carry one that was that exact shade of blue with black. It was blue with gray."

The defense attorney was speaking to the witness again. "Do you remember that answer to that question?"

"Yes, I do."

"I have no further questions. Thank you ma'am."

Is this supposed to show the witness is a perjurer? Is she lying on the stand today about the exact shades of blue and black so as to make Bill look guilty? Is she a part of the conspiracy to frame him?

On redirect O'Leary acted as if a tempest had been made in a teapot. He even shook his head a bit.

"The defendant's attorney asked you if you ran the check through your register at your store. Do you normally or is it a normal practice to take identifying information when individuals give you checks?"

"What we require when a person writes a check is to see their driver's license, and the information that we require on the check is the driver's license number, birth date, date of expiration of the license, and phone number and address."

"Was that done in this case?"

"As far as I'm aware, yes. I can't recall specifically but.."

"Would that information be contained in your business records normally for someone who wrote a check? Is it normal for you to keep that information in your records somewhere?"

"Not specifically, no. We take the checks and the checks will then go to the bank."

"That information is contained, you put that on the check?"

"Correct."

"Not into any kind of system you have?"

"No."

"No further questions."

Judge Werner called for a ten-minute recess.

During the recess we all discussed the coat buying incident. It was the general feeling that finding this young lady had been a good piece of detective work. But Bill had actually distinguished himself by making such strange requests of Ms. Dexter. If he had simply left the purchase, as it had been originally, he might have gone unnoticed.

My mother's words swirled in my head, "Oh what a tangled web we weave when first we practice to deceive."

After 20 minutes had passed and we were deep in conversation, we heard the bailiff command, "Order!"

I nearly jumped out of my skin. We righted ourselves in our seats and clamped our mouths shut like naughty children.

What command this man has! Just knowing he can banish us from the courtroom keeps us on our very best behavior.

The jury was brought in.

After the next witness, a Glenn Schaepe, was sworn in Judge Werner addressed the defense table, "Something we need to take up at this time, Mr. Daniel?"

"Yes, please."

"All right. Ladies and gentlemen. Sorry to bring you in, but I do need to excuse you right at this point in time."

The jury filed back out.

Hmm. That's odd, to bring the jurors in just to turn around and have them leave. Maybe the jury had to see the witness sworn in before Daniel's concern could be addressed.

"Judge, Detective Schaepe had contact with Mr. Mereness on November 23rd and there is a tape of that contact. And I'm looking, these things aren't numbered very well. There are a couple of occasions during that contact that he asks Mr. Mereness about whether or not he had ever been arrested before. And I would ask that the witness be admonished not to discuss that portion of his interrogation in front of the jury."

"Mr. O'Leary?" queried the judge.

"I don't intend to ask him about convictions. I know..."

Werner interrupted the prosecutor, "Well, this is arrests."

"Or arrests, I'm sorry. I don't intend to ask him about arrests. I don't also intend to ask him about some of the information there that involves whether or not his son had ever been arrested. Also, whether or not he was involved in any kind of domestic violence incidents with his wife or previous wife. I don't intent to go into those areas."

"Those are the areas you were concerned about, Mr. Daniel?"

"Yes, Your Honor."

Werner turned toward the witness. "Officer, I am going to direct that you not mention anything about interrogation of the defendant in this matter, about him ever being arrested, his son ever being arrested or any involvement that he may have had with domestic violence incidents with his previous wife and Jennifer Mereness, victim in this matter. Do you understand that?"

"I understand."

The jury was recalled.

As the panel was entering I took notice of the man on the stand. He was middle-aged with glasses. His face, like so many other witnesses', was tanned. He had gray hair and a large moustache. His dress shirt was off white and his tie was patterned. He wore a gold badge on the left breast of his gray sport coat.

Schaepe began his testimony by saying that he'd been employed by the Oneida County Sheriff's Department for 25 years and had been a detective sergeant on the force for the past 15 years.

The officer had contact with Bill on November 23 of 2002, at the request of the Janesville Police Department. "Bill had been found and he was stopped and I interviewed him in my vehicle, an unmarked squad."

"Part of that purpose was to notify him about the death of Jennifer Mereness his wife?"

"Yes, it was."

"Do you know what approximate time it was that you met with the defendant?"

"I believe it was around 6:15 a.m."

"And where was it that you met with him?"

"The intersection that it was near is Squirrel Lake Road and Highway 70 West which is west of the town of Minocqua. It's in the township of Minocqua. It was actually on Squirrel Lake Road, little south of 70."

"Still in Oneida County?"

"That's correct."

"Where was Mr. Mereness sitting when you were talking to him?"

"When I talked to him initially he was in his vehicle that he had been driving. I asked him to... come up to the vehicle that I had parked there which was an unmarked squad, a truck. And I asked him if he could join me inside the truck and he did that. He was in the passenger seat front."

"And at that point did you advise him that his wife was deceased?"

"Yes. I first established who he was. I identified myself and asked him if his wife was Jennifer Mereness. He told me that she was. And I told him that she was deceased."

"And what was his response?"

"I think his first response was, 'What?'"

"What did he say?"

"I believe he may have said something else right after that. 'What happened?' I believe. And I told him that, I believe I told him that...it was an intentional act and it was not an accident."

The officer then asked the defendant when he had arrived in Minocqua.

Bill had explained that he'd arrived at Wal-Mart about 3:00 p.m. He'd come to Minocqua to let his brother into his residence at Pier Lake Road.

As Schaepe had Bill go through his activities on the day of the murder, something the suspect did caught the officer's attention. Bill produced a receipt for a candy bar he'd bought at Wal-Mart.

That should strike the jurors as odd and suspicious behavior.

The DA showed the witness Exhibit 42. Did he recognize it?

Schaepe confirmed that it looked like the receipt Bill had shown to him.

"What do you recall about him or what do you recall about the receipt when he showed it to you?"

"Well, what I do recall is the manager's name on it. I said that out loud as I read it when he handed it to me. I believe I said out loud the store number which is 2510. I believe I made reference to the item that he bought, 44-cent item, candy bar. The date on it. I brought that to his attention. I said that out loud. The phone number. The exchange was 356. That's the exchange for the Minocqua area. I brought that to his attention."

The time on the receipt had been in military time. It had said 15:34, but the officer had read it to Bill as 3:34. Bill had agreed with the time and also reported that he'd bought the candy bar for his nephew, Ryan.

"After that you asked him whether or not Jennifer was living by herself at her home, is that right?"

"I did. After I took the receipt and put it away."

"What did you do with the receipt?"

"I had a notebook that was opened. And I have a flap and I stuck the receipt into the flap of the folder so it wasn't visible anymore."

"So you were holding that and then you continued on the conversation with him?"

Schaepe confirmed that he had then inquired about Bill's wife; where she lived and if Bill had visited her there.

The defendant thought that he'd been to Jennifer's house a handful of times, perhaps five.

O'Leary asked the witness if he'd inquired about the last time Bill had seen Jennifer.

He had. "He didn't answer the question initially. He told me about, I think, phone contact that he had with her, but he told me that the phone contact was when she called him on Friday morning, and I believe he said first 8:00 a.m. and then he said between 8:00 and 9:00 a.m. that morning."

"Did he then answer your question about when's the last time he saw her?"

"Yes, he had stated it was the previous Sunday, and I looked at a calendar that was hung right next to me in my truck. And I pointed out the

17th to him, and he said if that is the date of Sunday that would be correct because he was talking about it being the 17th of November."

"Did he say what the purpose was of his having that contact with her?"

"The phone conversation or the personal?"

"Start with the phone conversation."

"Phone conversation he said it was a return phone call to him. He had left her a message. He said he talked to her about property that was left at the old house that they hadn't received or he hadn't received. Some of it was hers, some of it was his. He also said that the person who then bought the house she knew and they were going to talk about the return of those items. He also said that he wanted to talk to her about a birthday card that he had for her that came from his parents."

The topic of conversation went back to Bill's activities on the 22nd. He'd gotten the call from Jennifer on his cell phone when he was leaving his apartment. He was going to the gas station to use the phone there.

Schaepe wondered why Bill hadn't used his cell phone for the call he needed to make. Bill had explained that he didn't use his cell phone for his work at Sam's Club. He'd needed to call his voice mail. After that he'd returned to his apartment because he'd forgotten the laundry he'd intended to wash up at the cabin. When he was at the apartment he did some cleaning.

This sounds quite rambling and even a bit nonsensical. It must have struck the officer as such at the time.

I looked at the jury. Juror number 15 was looking intently at Bill while the witness continued to detail his conversation with Bill on the early hours of November 23, 2002.

According to Schaepe, the defendant subsequently told him about a telephone conference call that had been rescheduled. Bill had then left Janesville for Minocqua about 10:00 a.m. He'd stopped at a wayside near Westfield and then gone directly to Wal-Mart in Minocqua.

O'Leary wanted to know if that had made sense to the witness.

Daniel objected. The question was irrelevant.

Judge Werner sustained the objection.

The district attorney rephrased. Had the sergeant asked the defendant why he'd chosen that route to Minocqua?

He had, and Bill had said it was because he'd wanted to see his friend who had been promoted to manager, to see the store remodel plan and to look at the floor plan.

Had the receipt come up again during the conversation?

It had. About halfway through the interview Bill had asked if he could have his receipt back.

O'Leary wondered why he'd done that.

The defense attorney objected, it was irrelevant.

The judge overruled the objection; the witness could answer the question.

According to Schaepe, Bill had said that he kept all receipts because of protocol.

Protocol or not, that's a rather strange thing to be worried about when you've just been informed of your wife's death, a receipt for a 44 cent candy bar. No wonder the police were suspicious. Who wouldn't have been?

Next the officer related some discussion about the key to the Minocqua cabin. It was quite confusing. It seemed that even though Bill had been in Appleton where his brother lived on Thursday, he'd failed to give Jim the key, making it necessary for Bill to meet him in Minocqua on Friday.

The district attorney wondered what the defendant's demeanor had been during the conversation.

"I thought he was quite calm and nonemotional. There was some emotion, there was some emotion or surprise, you might say, when I first told him that Jennifer was deceased. But I also told him that it was an intentional act. And his response wasn't much different. And then, third, I told him that someone's responsible for a murder. And I felt that as I proceeded with those three different ways of wording it, that I would get more of a response than I did. It was very little response and his response that he did have dissipated very quickly. And most of the conversation that I had with him was very calm and collected."

Bill had agreed when the sergeant asked him if he would go to the Sheriff's Department. The defendant had expressed concern about being able to drive, so Schaepe had offered for an officer to drive his car. Bill then decided to go ahead and drive himself.

Once at the Oneida County Sheriff's Department, Sergeant Schaepe shared his thoughts with Janesville Police Detective Dan Davis. It was determined that Bill would then be questioned by the Janesville PD in the interview room. That conversation was taped as well as monitored a good deal of the time by Schaepe from his position in the resource room. Schaepe had not observed the entire interview because he had been busy making phone calls. He'd checked on Bill's whereabouts for Friday in addition to the plans he'd had for Friday and Saturday. Calls were placed to individuals from Wal-Mart and Sam's club in Duluth and Appleton.

When the Oneida County officer explained that he'd contacted Bill's supervisor, Ms. Hetrick, the DA wanted to know if the supervisor had said where she had expected Bill to be during the times in question.

The defense objected due to hearsay.

The objection was sustained.

The witness also had contacted Cass Wisco and a person in loss prevention at Sam's.

That would likely have been the very imposing Anthony James Nelson.

Later, Schaepe went into the interview room to ask Bill additional questions. "I asked him questions dealing with where he had planned on being that particular day, the voice mail that he had left on his voice mail, the city that he would be driving to on that day, his intentions."

"What did he say?"

"He said that he did leave a message on his voice mail indicating on Friday that he was en route to Duluth, but he stated that didn't necessarily mean that he was going to arrive in Duluth on Friday."

Next was a long, protracted argument about Bill's choice in his route to his home on Pier Lake Road. There were several objections and Judge Werner instructed O'Leary to "lay a foundation."

Schaepe responded, "He said he went Highway 39 or 51, I think 90 up to that point, but 39/51 which goes north south, north right to Minocqua. He said he went into Minocqua, stopped at the store there. And then went to the cabin. I don't know if we specifically talked about the route that he had taken. The easiest route would be to take Squirrel Lake Road south. If he was going directly to his cabin from Janesville, the easiest route though would be a different route and that's what I questioned him about."

"What would the route you're talking about be?"

"Driving 51 to Highway 8. 8 runs east and west. And that goes in the direction of Tripoli, Wisconsin, which is still Oneida County and at that point there is a road, Willow Road, that turns into Pine Lake Road and then goes to East Pier Lake Road and that would be the easiest route to take."

"And why did he say he didn't take that route?"

"I'm not sure if that question was asked him directly."

"Was the route that he took going up to the Wal-Mart longer?"

"Yes."

But he had to go to Wal-Mart in order to establish his alibi by being captured on security tapes, by making a purchase and by talking to his so-called friend Cass Wisco.

Daniel began his cross-examination of the witness by asking how many contacts he'd had with Bill.

Schaepe recalled the meeting on the roadway on the 23rd, a second at the sheriff's department and others when he executed a search of the house and septic tank.

The defense attorney wondered if the officer had known the defendant prior to November 23, 2002.

He had not.

So when the witness had made comments about Bill's reaction and affect he had nothing to compare them to.

Schaepe agreed.

The next line of inquiry surrounded the search for Bill in the early hours of November 23.

The witness explained that he'd received a call on the weekend. He was asked to locate Mr. Mereness by looking for his car at the Pier Lake Road residence. If Bill hadn't moved from the Pier Lake location Schaepe probably wouldn't have confronted him. At that time, Schaepe contacted the Janesville PD who requested he stop Mr. Mereness and inform him of his wife's death. He was also to question Bill about his whereabouts and activities.

Schaepe said Bill's vehicle had actually been located prior to 3:00 a.m. by a Deputy Young who also worked for the department.

What? When did that occur? I thought it was around 6 a.m.

Schaepe had instructed Young to stop Mr. Mereness before he left Oneida County. Young was to approach Mereness and advise him that another officer had something important to tell him.

Next was a long, heated discourse between the witness and the defense attorney about where and why the defendant had been stopped. There were numerous objections and references to testimony given on June 30, 2003.

Ultimately, it was determined that Bill had been stopped when he was at a "T" in the road. Had he turned left from that location he would have gone into Price County. A right turn would have resulted in Bill staying in Oneida County. So, Officer Young had stopped Bill before he made a choice. The stop was not an actual traffic stop, as for speeding, even though some of the reports written by others about that night referred to it as a traffic stop.

Schaepe testified that when Officer Young had done as he was instructed, he believed Bill had asked him if the news was about his son or his mother. The witness did not know if Young had responded to Bill or not.

Since the answer had already been given, it was a bit late when the prosecution objected that the information about Officer Young was hearsay.

The witness reiterated that he had not wanted the deputy to tell Mr. Mereness about the death of his wife.

Is that because it was important for Schaepe to note Bill's reaction to the news about Jennifer?

It had taken Schaepe about 10 minutes to get to Bill's location.

Deputy Young had initially used his emergency lights when stopping Bill, and there had been another police vehicle on the perimeter.

Daniel purported that Bill had been a suspect at that time.

Sergeant Schaepe didn't know whether he had been or not.

The defense attorney asserted that information had been withheld from the defendant and that he'd had to "sit and stew" for 10 minutes.

The prosecution thought Daniel was being argumentative.

The defendant answered before the judge could rule, "I was the one that wanted to see his reaction to the statement that 'Your wife is deceased'."

I knew it!

Schaepe also stated that he didn't know what the defense meant by "left to stew".

Tod does appear to be argumentative. It seems as if he is implying that the Janesville and Oneida authorities conspired to put Bill in a very disturbing emotional situation.

Had Schaepe told Bill he was taping their conversation in the car?

He had not.

Daniel seemed perturbed. "And during this conversation you did not feel an obligation to be truthful to Mr. Mereness, isn't that correct?"

"I don't know what you mean by that."

"It's getting really late. I think I asked you about a deposition, didn't I, date and things?"

Werner interceded, "No."

The defense attorney continued, "Do you recall giving a deposition in a related mater on June 30th of 2003? I didn't do that before?"

"You did mention it."

"I was going to say. Detective, I'm going to show you what's been marked Exhibit 97. That's a deposition. That's a transcript of the deposition, okay?"

"Okay."

"On page 48, line 15 this is me asking the questions and you giving the answers. We on the same page?"

"Yes."

"Question: And that was just a description to locate the guy, right? I'm asking anything about the incident that would have been noteworthy other than Jennifer had been bludgeoned to death, that Bill was her husband

and they wanted Bill's whereabouts on Friday. Answer: Yeah. Again, it's difficult for me to think of when I received some of this information. But I know in the transcript he even asked me about the house or we talked about the house. And I was serious. I mean, you know, we don't always have to be truthful, I guess, when we're talking to a, you know, a person who I maybe will suspect or suspect that he's, he's involved now in a murder, but I'm not sure.'"

What the heck was that all about? Did Daniel think Schaepe'd felt remorse about not telling Bill that he was recording the conversation?

So, the defense attorney wondered, how long were the two of them sitting on the road with the witness surreptitiously recording the conversation?

It had been about an hour.

"Okay, is there some reason you didn't go into the department where you have videotape, you have lighting, you have heat and air and some amenities?"

"I'm very comfortable sitting in the vehicle out there asking questions and he was not under arrest. I wanted to talk to him, get a feel for him. And asked him some questions on his activities."

"At that point you knew Janesville police were coming to Rhinelander, right?"

"Yes."

"So you knew that you were going to end up in Rhinelander, correct?"

"Not necessarily, no. As a matter of fact Janesville was coming to my location initially."

"What changed it to Rhinelander? For the record Rhinelander is the county seat of Oneida County, right?"

"That's correct. The change came when I received a phone call while I am interviewing Mr. Mereness and it was Lieutenant Davis. And I had asked him if I could call him right back. After that I talked to Mr. Mereness for a bit more. Then I told him that I had a phone call that I would like to make privately and I would like him to go back to the car. And then I called up Lieutenant Davis again and I spoke to him of my interview that I had with Mereness. And I suggested if he would like I would ask Mr. Mereness if he would like to come to the Sheriff's Department where they could interview him."

"Did you advise Mr. Mereness of his constitutional rights not to talk to you?"

"No."

The witness agreed that as per the Janesville police, their conversation had centered on Bill's whereabouts on Thursday, Friday and Saturday.

And the defendant had provided a chronology?

He had.

A receipt was produced by Mr. Mereness and retained by the witness?

It was.

The sergeant concurred with the defense attorney that when he invited the defendant to the sheriff's department Bill had expressed a concern about his ability to drive. It had been arranged that Bill would flash his lights if he needed assistance.

Had a videotape been made when the Janesville police interviewed the defendant in Rhinelander?

"Just about all of it."

Daniel appeared to be angry in his demand to know, "What's not videotaped?"

"Him walking into the lobby and probably my introduction and what proceeded after that."

Schaepe thought that those aspects of the situation might have been captured by the department's security camera.

"But the process is on videotape other than amenities and introductions?"

"Right."

"Did you know Mr. Wisco's hours of employment at the Minocqua store?"

"No."

"Could I have a second, Your Honor?"

Werner granted the request.

Daniel studied various papers on his desk for a few minutes.

"I have no further questions, Your Honor."

The DA wanted to redirect.

It was clarified that the conversation on the side of the road had begun about 6:18 on the morning of November 23. It had not been in the middle of the night. The witness didn't know why he had 3:00 on his mind.

But Daniel hadn't seemed to notice it anyway. Probably best to set the record straight, though.

Had the defendant been required to accompany you back to the sheriff's department?

No.

Why had the witness put Bill's candy bar receipt in his folder?

It was of possible evidentiary value.

What had happened when the defendant asked to have the receipt back?

The sergeant had given it to him.

"Are you required to read constitutional rights to every single person you talk to?"

"Objected to as calling for legal conclusion, Your Honor."

Werner sustained the objection.

"How long have you been a detective?"

"15 years."

"And in that time over 15 years have you interviewed certain people?"

"Interviewed lots of people."

"How many times have you interviewed people?"

"I would say thousands."

"And in those thousands of interviews did you read constitutional rights to every single one of the persons?"

"Absolutely not."

"Have you had training and experience about when you are required to give constitutional right to..."

Daniel interrupted his foe, "Objected to as irrelevant, Your Honor. We are taking..."

Next Werner interrupted, "I don't think so. Overruled. You may proceed."

"Yes I have received training."

"What type of training have you received?"

The defense attorney spoke again, "Ask my objection be continuing on in this line of questioning."

"You may have continuing," responded the judge.

The witness answered, "We have training in many different areas. One of them is legal updates and when it is necessary to give a person his Miranda warning."

"And have you had opportunity to testify in courts before on Miranda issues?"

"Many times."

"And do you know when it's required to give Miranda to an individual you're talking to?"

Another objection. "Objected to foundation, Your Honor. The Supreme Court can't unanimously agree."

The objection was overruled, "This is within his scope and knowledge."

Schaepe answered the question, "Yes."

"When do you have to give Miranda when you're interviewing someone?"

"When he is in custody and I asked him questions."
"Was the defendant in this case in custody?"
"Definitely not."
"After you finished talking to him did you take him into custody at that time?"
"No, I did not."
"What did you do with the defendant?"
"I asked him to, I asked him if he would be willing to come to the Sheriff's Department and talk to me and he voluntarily said yes to that and then voluntarily followed me there."
"And after you finished your second round of interviews or the interview at the department did he--was he taken into custody at that time?"
"No he was not."
"Was he released?"

Oh God, don't say released! That makes it sound like he was in custody!

"He was released after Janesville had gone to his cabin, yes."

Oh dear. That will fall on fertile ground.

"Is it highly unusual in your experience and background to want to personally notify a husband that his wife has been murdered?"
"Yes. That's--I've done that a number of times."
"That's not unusual?"
"Could you ask the question again?"
"Is it unusual for you to want to go and personally notify a husband that his wife had been murdered?"
"Objected to as irrelevant, Your Honor."
"Overruled."
"It's not unusual for me to want to make that interview myself or that notification."
"Is it also unusual for a deputy who pulls a car over in your county to receive a backup squad?"
"No, I would say it's not unusual."
"No further questions, Your Honor."

The defense attorney wished to recross examine Detective Schaepe.
"Backup is a safety issue, correct?"
"Yes."
"All right. So if you're going to notify widow Jones that her husband was killed in a car accident you don't bring backup, do you?"
"Generally not."

"All right. And you used the language he was released after Janesville went to search his cabin. That's your language, correct? He was released. Do you want it read back?"

Uh oh.

"That was the prosecutor's language and I agreed with it, though."

"Judge could we have that read back?"

"I think that's what he said, Mr. Daniel."

"All right."

Werner clarified his statement, "Or that was at least the word that was used by either Mr. O'Leary or the witness, but the witness affirmatively acknowledged that release was the verb that was used."

Daniel had a concern. "Judge, there are two more subjects to deal with this witness. And it's after 6:00. This is our fourth day."

"I will be glad to recess at this point."

Daniel thanked Judge Werner.

The judge reminded the officer that he was still under subpoena. Then he dismissed the jury.

Wearily we filed out of the courtroom. We were too tired to discuss the day's events. We plodded to our cars and went our separate ways.

After I'd revived following chores and a bit of dinner, I was wishing for someone at home to discuss the proceedings with. Instead, I replayed the day in my mind. Overall, I concluded it had been an excellent day for the prosecution. The defense's attempts to malign the authorities had seemed somewhat futile. Had the trial taken place in the '70's, when everyone had been suspicious of "The Man", things might have been different. But in the post 9-11 world the actions of the police seemed reasonable.

32

At 8:30 on the morning of Friday, August 15, 2003, Judge Richard Werner announced that court was in session in The State of Wisconsin versus William Mereness, case number 02CF3911.

How many times had I heard that pronouncement already during this trial? It has certainly gotten under my skin. I'll probably be repeating it in my sleep before too long.

Before the jury was called in Daniel had an exhibit for judicial notice. It was the U.S. Naval Observatory's Astronomical Applications Department sun and moonrise data for November 22, 2002.

Now what in the world is this about? Is Tod planning an astronomical defense?

The judge deferred to the prosecution.

"Offhand, I would—I was just handed that this morning, judge, so I have had no chance to verify anything, but…"

Werner interceded, "I will withhold ruling on that until you have had a chance to look at it."

The jury was called in along with the witness from the previous evening, Officer Glenn Schaepe.

Daniel continued his recross of Mr. Schaepe.

The defense attorney wanted to know what time the authorities finished with their interview of Mr. Mereness at the sheriff's department.

"I think it was after the noon hour."

"So now approximately six and a half hours had gone by between the time Mr. Mereness had been stopped and finishing whatever was done at the sheriff's department, correct?"

"That would seem accurate."

Schaepe then testified that at that point he had returned to his home.

Daniel continued, "All right. Do you know where Mr. Mereness went?"

"Yes. He went with officers to his cabin on East Pier Lake Road where he agreed to allow them to search."

"The car was searched before he left the sheriff's department, isn't that correct?"

It was.

"Was anything taken from the car at that point?"

The witness had not been present for the search, but he did not think anything had been taken.

"And again, just to keep this clear in everyone's and the jury's mind, this was all occurring on 23, November of '02, correct?"

"Yes."

The defense attorney wondered if Schaepe had had further contact with Mr. Mereness on November 23rd.

He had not.

"Do you know whether or not anyone else from the Oneida County Sheriff's Department would have had contact with Mr. Mereness after the 23rd?"

"After?"

Daniel's tone was snappish, "Anybody else from the Oneida County Sheriff's Department have contact with Mr. Mereness on the 23rd?"

"I had asked Deputy Gardner to assist Janesville officers and to be there when they searched the house."

And how had the various authorities and Bill been transported to the house?

Schaepe indicated that all had driven separate vehicles.

So they hadn't transported him in a squad. If they had I'm sure the defense would have jumped on that.

"All right. Do you know what time the police officers released Mr. Mereness?"

Don't fall for it! They never had him in "custody" so they couldn't have "released" him!

"You use the word release again."

Good catch!

Again, the tone was snappish, "That's your word, sir."

"I think it was the district attorney's word and I agreed with him, but after I did I didn't think that that was the appropriate word."

Wow!

Daniel looked displeased, "Judge. I would ask this be stricken. Do you understand the time frame? I'm just asking you for a time."

Judge Werner addressed the witness, "All right. What time was this completed officer, do you know?"

"I haven't reviewed reports to indicate when they were done with him. I do not know."

The defense attorney seemed satisfied enough to move on. He wanted to know if Schaepe had anything to do with a search of Bill's cabin on November 25th.

"It was a couple days after the 23rd. 25th does sound correct. I mean, I don't know that specific date, but the Janesville Police Department had a search warrant for Mr. Mereness' house on East Pier Lake Road, and I did assist them on that occasion."

Looks like Tod's got this fellow rattled a bit. Can hardly blame the poor guy, it's been antics with semantics before to his peril.

The witness explained that nothing of evidentiary value had been found in the search of the cabin. His role had been perfunctory as was standard when one county executed a search warrant in another, although he had videotaped the residence and its perimeter.

Had the officer been involved in the case in any other way?

He had. He'd gone to A-1 Septic and talked to the owners there.

"How is it you went to A-1 Septic? I understand there are a number of septic pumping organizations in Oneida County."

"There are a few I believe. I believe that I was told it was A-1 Septic, and I checked with them, and they had confirmed that they had pumped Mr. Mereness' septic."

"And they pumped it at Mr. Mereness' request, is that correct?"

"That's correct."

"That's because they suspected that the septic system was frozen, is that correct?"

"Mr. Mereness told them that he suspected it was frozen."

Another good catch. Instead of making it look like the company had made the diagnosis on the septic, it was Bill; he'd wanted it pumped.

"And it had been a relatively common problem in Oneida County last winter, correct?"

O'Leary objected due to speculation.

Werner allowed the defense to lay some foundation, which solved the problem of speculation. A lot of septic tanks and fields had had problems with freezing that winter.

So Bill was justified in his request to have his pumped.

Daniel wished to know what Officer Schaepe did after he spoke to the owners of the septic business.

"I went out to the field where they dumped the effluent the following day."

"All right. Again, English is a wonderful language, but the following day you went to the field where they pumped the effluent, correct?"

He had. *Hadn't he just said so? Should O'Leary have objected stating "asked and answered"? Maybe that would be playing into Daniel's hand. This is almost as much an exercise in psychological jousting as it is about the facts.*

"They pump the stuff the same day they collect it, correct, or at least they try to?"

They do.

The witness explained that the septic had been pumped on the 16th of April and he checked the field on the 18th. It had been a large field of around 80 acres. Part of it was routinely used by A-1 Septic to pump out their trucks.

Bill's effluent had been mixed with that of two other customers while still in the truck. And Schaepe had no idea how many other loads had been dumped into that same field.

So anything that was found could not be positively linked to Bill. It could have come from the other two residences, or already been in the field. But who else would have cause to flush items that would have a connection to the murder? The situation was speculative at best.

Had the officer recovered anything from the field?

"I recovered two cloths. One appeared to be a dishcloth and a washcloth, both measuring about 11 by 11, and I also recovered two latex gloves."

Who would flush cloths and latex gloves down the toilet and into their septic system? We don't even dare use colored toilet paper for fear that it would goof our septic up! But does the jury know how fragile septics are? Will someone tell them?

The witness turned the items he'd found over to Detective Erik Goth of the Janesville Police.

Next a very long protracted exchange raged between Schaepe and Daniel. It was very hard to follow because of all the references to exhibits, search warrants, affidavits for search warrants, returns of search warrants and the witness being required to read from those documents. My two pages of notes were the most helter-skelter I'd taken throughout the trial. It appeared to be a real test of wills between the two men. However, I thought the gist of the testimony indicated that a subsequent search of the Minocqua residence in April turned up no items that specifically matched those that had been found in the septic field.

So, Bill didn't have any other blue latex gloves in the house. And the wash cloth and dishtowel didn't match others in the house. That doesn't really prove anything much. Most people don't have latex gloves on hand, nor would they necessarily have a matched set of washcloths and dishcloths, particularly at a second residence.

Detective Schaepe was finally allowed to step down.

Mr. Folts had a matter he wished to take up outside the presence of the jury, so they were excused.

But first, Judge Werner wanted to deal with Daniel's exhibit containing astronomical data. "Mr. Daniel, I was looking at your exhibit that you marked as 99. And maybe I'm reading this wrong, but it talks about this information for the sunrise and moonset and what have you for November 11, 2002. Am I reading that incorrectly?"

Daniel responded rather flippantly, "Junk in, junk out. Huh?"

The judge's tone was serious. "I don't know. I may be wrong."

The defense attorney continued as if the matter were a trifle, "Yeah, thank you. We did it European style. It doesn't work there."

What is he talking about? European style? Is that some sort of joke? In a murder trial?

Werner explained that he would make Exhibit 99 part of the record, but he would not receive it as part of the judicial record.

There was no argument from the defense, just a request for a short recess.

During the break we discussed that while we'd had only about a half-hour of testimony things had gotten quite contentious. If the day continued in this manner it would be exceptionally stressful. We all hoped for a rather smoother feeling-tone when court resumed.

Our wishes were in vain.

Within 20 minutes we were back in session, with the jury still out of court.

Mr. Folts began, "Your Honor, our next witness would be James Mereness, and he has four prior convictions that would be inquired into. And I believe the proper procedure is we should have him in here, advise him he may be asked about those convictions, and that if he answers truthfully he can be asked how many times, and if he answers truthfully then that would be the extent of the inquiry into the prior convictions."

Werner responded, "All right. Mr. Daniel?"

"Judge, two matters with reference to that. His convictions, judge, go back to 1997, and they all involved some sort of assaultive behavior."

Folts interjected, "Your Honor, I would have to take issue with that. One is the violation of a...."

Daniel cut across, "Excuse me. I didn't interrupt Mr. Folts, and I would expect that courtesy."

Folts' tone indicated annoyance, "I would expect *he* relay the information truthfully to the court."

Judge Werner sounded like a parent with quibbling children as he first addressed Daniel, then the ADA. "I will hear you, then you can tell me what you have to say, Mr. Folts. Go ahead."

"Judge, the 1997 conviction is for a violation of an injunction, a domestic situation. The third conviction again is in 1999, and that is a conviction for a battery. The fourth conviction is in the year 2000, and that is a conviction for obstructing or resisting."

Oh boy, I didn't know Bill's brother had a criminal record. I hope it won't be too damaging to his credibility.

The defense continued, "Also, Your Honor, Mr. Mereness' deposition was taken in a related matter on March 13th of 2003, when he was asked whether or not he had ever been convicted of a crime and he said yes. And I asked him, okay, and what have you been convicted of. Misdemeanors. Question, when was the last one and for what? He says I don't know, and he indicated it was four years ago, bail jumping or whatever. I don't remember. It's been four years. All right. And this is...is that...was this one time you got convicted of a couple misdemeanors? Answer, couple, I got convicted of a couple different times. Further...further down the question, Your Honor, he was asked, did any of these involve crimes of domestic violence. The answer was yes. Question, so it would be a violation of a criminal statute for you to possess a firearm, isn't that right? Answer, I'm not sure of that."

So Tod actually thinks the jury should hear of Bill's brother's prior act of domestic violence, but they shouldn't hear about Bill's? It seems a little ironic that this witness would be expected to be held to a higher standard than the defendant is. Hopefully Judge Werner will disallow the information.

Daniel was not finished yet. "Judge, I think that creates a credibility issue that would be relevant with reference to the nature of the crimes, Your Honor. The violent nature of Mr. Mereness', James, Jr. Mereness', background is relevant in this particular case in that on the--this is evidence that will establish that on Wednesday, 27 November, at the Appleton residence Mr. Mereness, Jim Mereness, Jr. threatened William Mereness with physical harm and, in fact, threatened to kill him, and the, that, so the propensity, character trait, or whatever for violence is established with these convictions and would substantiate the allegations that he made these threats against William two days before the incident involving the bathtub and the car collision, and they go to the circumstances surrounding. Also, Your Honor, the discussion of that confrontation was witnessed by LaBelle, was initially denied, and then Sallie corrected her, and James, Sr. would be expected to testify to that confrontation. So, it's relevant on the testimonial trustworthiness. And I'm not plowing old ground, but it's relevant for the jury to make a determination of the testimonial trustworthiness of, I'm going to screw up his name again, the detective from Appleton, Helein's testimony as to Ms. LaBelle Mereness' alleged statement concerning the conversation that took place in the bathtub. The jury has, is entitled to have, all of the circumstances surrounding LaBelle Mereness' testimonial trustworthiness and the dynamics of her statements to Helein which again, judge, was a conference between the detective, LaBelle, James, Sr., James, Jr., and Sallie. So, I guess, if Mr. Mereness' false swearing had to do with his character traits with reference to credibility, four convictions involving violence over a rather short period of time would certainly be relevant evidence on his propensity and would create an issue as to whether or not it's a credible story that he did, in fact, threaten Mr. Mereness' life, Mr. William Mereness' life".

Deliver us, please!

Still not done, Bill's lawyer continued, "The other issue, Your Honor, is that with the injunction conviction I believe he's not allowed to possess a firearm, and at the time that the police came to the cabin in Minocqua on the 23rd he was possessing a loaded shotgun, and I think that caused some problems with him and the police and changed the nature of the dynamics."

Mercifully, Judge Werner interrupted the diatribe, "What day was that?"

It had been on the 23rd of November.

Folts was finally allowed to have his turn.

"Starting from last and going to the beginning, possession of the firearm has absolutely no relevance to this particular case, Your Honor.

"As far as the deposition is concerned, there's absolutely no record that he was ever admonished or told of, as far as the procedure was concerned, regarding prior convictions. I think it's clear from a reading of the entire transcript that he attempted to answer the best he could. However, he was not admonished either by Mr. Daniel who deposed him in a civil proceeding in this matter or the court reporter at that time.

"This is an example or an attempt to bring in prior bad acts or Whitty evidence. There's been no notice. There's been no hearing. It would be improper to do it simply by notice of conviction since it would be the facts that would be important, not simply the nature of the convictions, and we would need a hearing for that particular purpose. I think we would have to look into the facts of those particular cases. Again, we have had no notice. Mr. Daniel has known of these convictions since March 13th of this year and has made no attempt to notify the Court that he wanted to do this, nor the State.

"I think frankly, judge, for all of those reasons that the normal procedure should be followed. Mr. Mereness will be asked if he's ever been convicted of a crime and how many times and, assuming he's answered truthfully, that that would be the end of it.

"I assume if the Court decides otherwise and the battery convictions, for example, which I think are the only ones that would be relevant, which would come in for propensity of--of violence, I think that turnabout is fair play and we would ask the defendant's conviction for battery come in to also show his propensity for violence."

Praise be! He's perfectly right to expect at least equal treatment of witness and defendant.

A very lengthy and scattered discussion ensued between prosecution, defense and the Court. Daniel kept referring to a report by Detective Goth about the confrontation between the brothers, that James, Jr. had violated his oath during his deposition and that the prosecution was trying to force Bill into waiving his "constitutionally protected right to silence". Folts, naturally, thought otherwise.

Werner finally tried to summarize, "All right. I'm ready to rule on this issue. First of all, I think, and this is just my thought process, there's three separate things we're talking about. We're talking about these convictions and how they're going to come in or to what extent they're going to come in, the issue about this confrontation between the defendant and his brother, and the issue about this loaded gun."

Yes! He's got it sorted out. Now if he'll just rule in our favor.

"And first of all, as far as the confrontation between the defendant and his brother, it seems to me that that's clearly something that should be allowed to come in. If something comes up during the course of it being disclosed or testified to, we'll have to deal with that as it comes up; but it seems to me that that's clearly something that these two will--certainly the brother was a party to this confrontation, and he ought to be able to relate it. It won't be hearsay. So I think that should be able to come in."

Fair enough. Jim will be able to explain the nature of the argument between the brothers. If Bill wishes to tell his side of the story, he'll need to take the stand.

"The issue relating to the prior convictions, the normal procedure is have you been convicted of a crime, the answer is yes, then the next question is how many times. If he answers that correctly, the usual procedure is that's the end of it."

Daniel disagreed at length for the same reasons he had previously.

Werner seemed as if he'd reached the end of his rope, his voice was taut, "All right. Section 906.08, and this gets to the same place, it talks about whether it's probative of truthfulness or untruthfulness I think. That's the issue here, I think, and I ruled I thought the issue concerning the defendant was probative of his truthfulness because it is a conviction for false swearing in a divorce proceeding. And this testimony I don't think is probative, the fact that he has convictions for two batteries, obstructing, and an injunction violation is probative of truthfulness or untruthfulness, and on that basis I will not allow that testimony."

Thank goodness. The witness was not going to be put on trial.

The judge concluded his ruling. "And as far as the business about the loaded shotgun, I really think that that is an issue raised more to confuse the jury. I don't think it's probative."

Wow, this is more than I had dared hope for!

33

At last. We're finally going to hear what Bill's brother has to say.

Before the jury was called in Judge Werner needed to go over Jim's upcoming testimony about his prior convictions.

Werner first asked if the witness had ever been convicted of a crime. Jim answered in the affirmative.

"And then the next question would be how many times."

"Four."

The jury was called back into court at 9:44 a.m. The wrangling over this witness had lasted nearly an hour and a half.

James Mereness, Jr. first supplied some basic information. He'd recently moved to Black Creek, he had two children aged 22 and seven and he was the younger brother of the defendant, by two and a half years.

The content of the testimony became more specific. The brothers had had an off and on relationship for the past couple of years. He himself had been convicted of four crimes. He'd been invited to go hunting at Bill's cabin in Minocqua in November of 2002.

Final plans for the hunting trip had included Bill dropping off the key to the cabin at their parents' house on Thursday, November 21. Bill hadn't dropped off the key so Jim had telephoned his older brother. Bill told Jim that he'd forgotten the key so they should meet at the cabin on Friday and Bill would let Jim in.

Folts inquired, "Was it originally planned that he would join you on that hunting trip?"

"Not originally."

"Did you tell him that you were taking your son?"

"Yes, I did."

"How did he respond to that?"

"He didn't like it in the beginning, but then toward the end it was fine."

During the phone conversation had Bill asked his brother to do anything specific on Friday?

"Yes. He told me to call him specifically between eight and ten Friday morning."

"Did he tell you why to call him between eight and ten?"

"I don't really think so. I thought it was kind of strange that he had a specific time that I was supposed to call."

Daniel objected.

Werner sustained the objection and directed the last part of Jim's answer be stricken.

The prosecutor continued. "Did he tell you anything else about what you were to do the following day?"

"Pick up groceries at a certain place."

"Where did he tell you to pick groceries up?"

"In Tomahawk at the IGA."

"Did he tell you anything else about the groceries?"

"Yeah, he told me to pay in cash and get a receipt."

Bill also told his brother to get the groceries between four and five Friday evening.

Folts wondered if that seemed unusual to the witness.

Daniel objected to the question as irrelevant.

The objection was sustained.

The ADA moved on. "Did you have contact with the defendant on November 22nd of 2002?"

He had. He'd called Bill between 6:30 and 6:45 a.m. The call had been placed from Jim's ex-wife's house to Bill's cell phone.

"And how did he respond when you called him at that time?"

"He said I was calling too early."

"Were the groceries mentioned again at that time?"

"Correct."

"Did you go through the same sequence at that time as far as the groceries were concerned?"

"Yes. And then I asked if I could pick 'em up like in town, Cub Foods, or if I could pick 'em up early. He said no."

"Why did you ask him about Cub Foods?"

Daniel objected, the question was irrelevant.

Sustained.

"Groceries cheaper in Appleton than in Tomahawk?"

Daniel objected. The question was beyond the competence of the witness and was irrelevant.

Again the objection was sustained.

Despite these objections being sustained, Folts has made his point. The jury should deduce that it made no sense for Bill to specify where and when groceries were purchased. Unless he was building an alibi.

Bill's brother testified that he had left for the cabin between 7:00 and 7:30 Friday morning. He'd called Bill about 10:00 a.m. to verify his route. He'd, subsequently, received a voice mail from Bill that had been time stamped 12:10 to 12:15 p.m.

Just after he'd beaten Jennifer to death. Talk about dissociative!

The voice mail had indicated that Jim could go ahead and pick up the groceries early. Everything was fine and he didn't need the receipt. Also, Bill had estimated he would arrive at the cabin around 3:00 p.m.

Everything was fine? Minutes after you've bashed in someone's skull with a hatchet? He is a sick man.

Jim and his son had arrived at the cabin around noon and waited for Bill's arrival, which was around 4:00 p.m.

The prosecutor inquired, "When he arrived, how did he look?"

"He looked tough, looked stressed out. I asked him that, stuff like that."

"When you say tough, what do you mean by tough?"

"Like he had the whole world on his shoulders and stressed out, and he said it was because he was driving too much."

Folts wondered if Bill had had anything to take into the cabin.

"He had a box of laundry."

A box of laundry? Who keeps their laundry in a box? I've seen baskets and bags off all sorts, but never a box. That should strike the jury as peculiar or, perhaps, suspicious.

Bill had shown his two relatives around the house, and James and his son began "hauling" their things into the cabin.

"Okay. What did the defendant do after he was in the cabin?"

"He had the box of laundry. He went downstairs with the box of laundry."

"How long was he downstairs with the box of laundry?"

"About half an hour."

"Did you ever go down the basement when he was there?"

"My son did, and I did."

"And what happened when you went down the basement?"

"First my son went down there, and my brother got agitated. He yelled at him. He wanted Ryan to get upstairs. I was upstairs then, so I yelled downstairs, and I told Ryan to come back up."

About 15 minutes after Jim had gotten his son upstairs, Bill called Jim downstairs.

After the two returned upstairs they made dinner.

Later in the evening, Bill informed his brother he needed to make a phone call and "get some air". The three had left the house in Bill's car and driven into a town Jim had assumed was Minocqua.

Jim explained that cell phones didn't work near the cabin and that even though there was a place on the road they usually worked, that night Bill's hadn't. So they'd driven to a pay phone. Bill had said he was calling his son, Christopher, but the witness did not know if Bill had been able to reach him.

The line of questioning changed to Bill's appearance upon his arrival at the cabin.

Jim responded, "He was wearing a leather jacket, khaki pants, and a plaid shirt and glasses and a pair of loafers."

"Did you notice if he had any injuries?"

"I noticed he had like scratches on his forehead."

"Later did he change clothes?"

He did. "At one point he came down in a white T-shirt and underwear, and then I believe he went back up and put on a pair of jogging pants that night."

"Now after he changed his clothes, did you notice if he had any other injuries?"

"Well, I noticed when he went up to the bedroom he was limping, and I commented on that."

"What did he say?"

"He said he had something in his pocket, and I just left it at that."

"Did you notice something else beside him limping?"

"I noticed he had scratches on his arm."

"Does your brother wear glasses?"

"Yes."

"Did you notice anything unusual about his glasses?"

"Like when we were cooking dinner, he took his glasses off and washed 'em a few times."

"Did you ask him about that?"

"I don't remember if I did ask him, but I thought it was kind of weird."

"Okay. How was he washing them?"

"He was standing by the kitchen sink and running them under water and wiping them off with a rag on a roll or like a towel."

A towel or rag that ended up in the septic system?

Then, according to the witness, Bill found another pair of glasses in a drawer near the snack bar and changed them with the ones he'd been wearing.

Jim did not know if his brother had left the house at any time during the night.

At about 5:30 a.m. on Saturday, Bill had come into Jim's room and advised him he was leaving to go to Janesville to take Christopher to work.

Bill then returned to the cabin with the police officers around 3:00 p.m. At first Jim had thought it might have been Jennifer coming into the cabin, but then he saw the police officers and Bill.

The police asked Jim to take Ryan and step outside the residence.

The police were at the cabin for about one hour. During that time they questioned Jim and Ryan separately.

Folts wanted to know if after the police left Jim had had a discussion with his brother.

He had. "I asked him, you know, if he did it, and he said no. And, you know, I said, you know, I can't believe it happened, and I asked that and, you know, he didn't really show much emotion with, you know, your wife being bludgeoned to death. When I first heard the news, I had tears in my eyes, and my brother showed no emotion at all. And I mean, she was my sister-in-law."

Later that evening, around 9:45 Jim was awakened by a knock on the door of the cabin. He thought Bill was in the master bedroom, but had no idea if he was awake or not. Bill did not answer the door, so Jim got up, looked out the window and saw a car pulling out of the driveway. The vehicle had not appeared to be a squad car, but just a "regular vehicle".

Jim went to talk to Bill up in the master bedroom. "I said to him, you know, why didn't you answer the door. You know, I mean, your wife's just been murdered or been bludgeoned to death and why didn't you answer the door, and I said it's not my responsibility to answer the door, it's yours."

The ADA asked, "And what did he say?"

"He said, you know, fuck the cops, and you know, I mean, he said how do you really know if Jennifer's dead, you know, how do you know the police aren't lying to us?"

This is very damaging testimony. Bill was acting quite strangely at that time.

At about 10:30 p.m. when Jim saw Bill in the kitchen picking through the junk, Jim asked his brother why he was doing that.

Folts inquired as to how Bill had responded.

"He said, I need this stuff, you know, out of the junk. You know, I need this stuff."

"Did he take anything out?"

"Yes, he did."

The ADA wanted to know if Jim had been able to tell what Bill had removed from the trash.

"I'm not sure what it was, but it was like softball size because he had his palm open. And I said why do you need something like that, and he said he just needs it and told me to go to bed. And I just stayed up and talked to him."

"What were you talking about?"

"I asked why he needed that, and he said he needed it for his business and took it upstairs in his master bedroom."

After that Jim had gone back to bed and fell asleep for a few hours. About 1:15 or 1:30 a.m. he heard the front door.

"What did you hear?"

"I heard the front door shut. I heard the deadbolt lock or like turning the lock to lock the door, and what I did was I just laid on the floor. I was laying on the floor that night with- with- with my arm over the threshold and my son over on the bed. That way if anybody would have came through the door it would have hit my arm, and it would have awoken me if they had came through."

How terrifying that must have been. He didn't know if Bill would try to harm them or if someone else had killed Jennifer maybe that person would come to the cabin after Bill. And he had his young son to protect.

The two brothers were both up at about 6:00 Sunday morning.

"He was going to leave. I mean, I talked to him. He wanted to leave early--earlier than me. I kept pleading with him, you know, I have a quarter of a tank of gas, come on, please stay so I could follow you out of here, and he said, no, he had to go, get back to Janesville."

"You wanted to follow him because you weren't sure of the directions."

"That's right. And I only had a quarter of a tank of gas in my tank. If I took one wrong turn, I don't know where I would have ended up, and I probably would have ran out of gas."

"So what happened?"

"My brother left. I left my son sleep. I packed some of my stuff up in my truck. I woke my son up, asked him if he wanted anything to eat, he said no, dad. He said what's going on, and I said we're leaving, buddy, and I said I want to get out, get back home. And then we packed the rest of our things up. My brother gave me specific duties to do, that I had to clean the place up. I had to vacuum. I had to clean the refrigerator out and take all the junk with me and throw it in a garbage dumpster at my parents where I was living."

"Did you take the junk?"

"Yes, I did."

"Did you eventually do something with that?"

"Yeah, I gave it to Detective Goth. Yes, Detective Goth."

"Did you volunteer that to him, or did he ask you for that?"

Daniel spoke, "Objected to as irrelevant."

The objection was sustained.

After Bill's brother completed his cleaning duties he and his son got into his truck, Jim started it and was just about to back out when Bill returned. Bill said he "felt sorry" for his brother and had come back so he could lead him out and find him some fuel.

They did not leave immediately because Bill had to go in the house for "a minute".

After a couple of minutes Bill came out of the house with a pair of gray sweatpants and a pair of white tennis shoes with a blue stripe. The witness was asked to compare the shoes in Exhibit 71 with the shoes he'd seen Bill remove from the house. "They look like it, but they were newer."

Folts wanted to know if the plumbing had ever stopped working while Jim had been at the cabin.

It had, but Jim had no idea why.

Maybe it was clogged with towels and latex gloves?

Next Jim and Ryan followed Bill into Tomahawk and got gas. They had a discussion. Bill wanted to borrow cash from Jim to buy a Columbia jacket for his son, Christopher. Jim declined to lend the money.

After purchasing drinks the discussion about borrowing the money was renewed. If Jim could lend Bill the money they would stop at Kohl's in Appleton to buy the Columbia jacket. They decided to do so.

In the parking lot at Kohl's Jim agreed to lend Bill $105. Then he asked Bill why he didn't just write out a check or use a credit card. Bill said he didn't want to use a credit card and didn't want to write a check because it was from Janesville and he didn't think Appleton would cash it.

The ADA asked, "So did you give him any money?"

"Yes, I gave him $105."

"Did he give you a check?"

"Yes, but I had to almost get on my hands and knees for it. I mean, you know, he didn't want to write me out a check but, finally, I convinced him to write me out a check."

The witness then identified Exhibit 104 as the check Bill had written to him on November 24, 2002, for $105.

Next Jim identified Exhibit 103 as the receipt for the groceries Jim had bought at the Tomahawk IGA on November 22, 2002.

Folts wanted to know what had happened to that receipt.

"I kept the receipt because my brother wanted me to, and I gave it to him. And he said he didn't need it anymore, and he threw it away in the garbage."

He didn't need it anymore? Was that because he'd established a better alibi with the stop at Wal-Mart? Why else would he no longer need a receipt he'd previously required?

The next contact Jim had with Bill was on Monday. Bill had wanted Jim to go to Scheels and pick up a receipt for the Columbia coat. Jim had declined.

He'd wanted Jim to go so Bill wouldn't be able to be identified by the clerk. Jim must have been suspicious enough to stay out of the questionable situation. Good for him.

The prosecutor moved on to another subject, "Do you remember having a discussion with your brother about his previous divorce?"

"Yes I do."

"What did he tell you?"

Before Jim could answer Daniel spoke, "Objected to as the form of the question as to time, place and I would like to be heard if we're talking about the first one."

Huh?

After a bit of discussion, Werner excused the jury at 10:22 a.m. so Folts could make an Offer of Proof.

"Mr. Mereness, when was it that you had this discussion with your brother about his first divorce?"

"I had it when I was going through my own personal divorce. I was living with him at that time."

"And when were you going through your divorce?"

"In '99."

Daniel interrupted, "This was his first divorce? I didn't catch that, Your Honor."

Werner was concise, "When this witness was going through his divorce in 1999."

Folts continued, "What did he tell you?"

"He said he got fucked once, he won't get fucked again, he's got a better plan this time."

I perceived a slight intake of breath throughout the courtroom.

Folts spoke, "Your Honor, that would be the extent of what I would be asking him."

The defense attorney argued long and hard for the judge to bar the testimony. His major points were that the discussion had occurred in too remote a time, and that the comment about a better plan could be "interpreted a hundred different ways". He also wondered if the burden had been shifted. "I have the burden beyond a reasonable doubt and they're cross-examining state crime lab witnesses on possibilities and wild theories, about a--in 1999 he had a plan planned to commit a homicide in 2002. They're going to allow that kind of speculation."

Werner reacted, "...And first of all, I think that it is relevant to the point that this is a homicide matter. It relates to a situation wherein the parties--the defendant and the victim, his wife were in a divorce. I don't know how it's going to end up being characterized. It's been characterized as being amicable and somewhat less than that, so I think it is relevant in that regard. The question I have is whether it's unfairly prejudicial to this defendant to let this testimony in. I think that this can adequately be cross-examined and argued that other plan could mean marital settlement agreement, which has been admitted into the record, or Mr. Daniel has even argued get a better lawyer or what have you. So I'm going to overrule the objection, and I'm going to admit it."

Praise be!

Daniel argued a bit more, but Werner wouldn't budge.

The jury returned and heard how Bill wasn't going to be "fucked again". Some of the jurors shifted their gaze from Jim, the witness, to Bill, the defendant. Those jurors kept their faces neutral, but they'd been moved enough to change their focus.

That had a powerful impact.

The ADA returned to his discussion of Monday, November 25, 2002. After Jim had refused to pick up the receipt for Bill, the two had met at their parents' house that evening.

"And what was the nature of the contact at your parents' on Monday?"

"I believe on Monday there he asked if I said anything to the cops or anything about the receipt. I said I didn't. Stuff like that. We exchanged words."

"When you say that you exchanged words, what do you mean?"

"Well, I wanted him to leave, you know."

"Why did you want him to leave?"

"Well, I--I didn't want him around, you know, because we didn't know if he was guilty or innocent, and let him work out his own problems. My mother was in ill health, and I just wanted him to leave myself, my dad, my mother, my sister alone. I was up there when the police arrived, and I didn't want no part of and my family didn't want no part of that."

"When you say that you exchanged words, you told him to leave, were you yelling at him?"

"Well, I raised my voice and stuff."

"Did you threaten him?"

"No, I didn't."

"But you were upset, correct?"

"Yes, I was upset. My mother was there too."

"Now, you mentioned your mother. What has happened to your mother since this started?"

"She's passed away." Jim's eyes filled with tears and his voice was shaky. His hand went to his chin. He was trying to maintain his composure.

"When was that?"

"January."

"Of this year?"

"Yes."

Brilliant. Folts was able to get into testimony that Bill's mother had been fragile and that Jim quite likely blamed Bill for her death.

"Did you have any other contact with the defendant after Monday night?"

"Yes."

"Where and when was the next contact?"

"I believe it was when I picked him up when the cops took him to get the DNA."

Jim explained that on Wednesday, November 27th, he had gone to pick Bill up at the hospital where the police had taken him for the test.

"Was he reluctant to ride with you?"

"No. He was actually glad I was there to give him a ride."

So the rift had not caused the brothers to be estranged.

"When was the next time then that you had contact with the defendant?"

"I believe it's when he tried to commit suicide."

"And when was that?"

"I don't remember the date. I was talking to my sister on the cell phone though, and I heard the sirens from my parents', and I said to her, I said…"

Daniel cut in, "Objected as to hearsay, Your Honor."

Folts clarified, "He only said what he was saying."

Werner directed the witness, "You can only say what you said."

Bill's brother continued, "That's what I was trying to say, what I said. I said to my sister it's your brother, I know it is."

Daniel objected again. The testimony was irrelevant.

That objection was sustained.

But the jury heard it anyway. Now they know what Jim thought of Bill's mental state at that time.

The witness explained that on Friday, November 29th, Bill was hospitalized. A second reference to suicide was objected to and stricken from the record.

No matter, they already heard Jim say it the first time. Daniel hadn't asked for it to be stricken then, so it will remain in the record.

The prosecutor asked, "Did you see him at the hospital?"

"Yes, I--my sister, myself, and my mother went to see him."

"Was he in any condition to speak to you on that Friday?"

"I assume he was playing possum."

What did he just say? Everyone in the family had to stifle the urge to laugh out loud. We bit our lips and avoided looking at each other so we didn't lose it.

This man sure knows his brother.

Daniel requested that Jim's response be stricken. It was.

But the jury heard it and quite likely saw our reaction as well. It would be hard to erase that from their memories.

Jim then explained that he had seen Bill once again at the hospital. Bill had called a family meeting.

"And what did he say during this family meeting?"

"Well, he said he was good to us and we should be standing behind him. We told him we don't know if he's guilty or innocent but, you know, we just don't want to get involved, and he was like laying guilt trips on us."

After that he'd seen Bill at the hospital every day until he was taken to Janesville. He'd gone daily to take their mother because she had wanted to see her eldest son.

Mr. Folts had no further questions for the witness.

The court was in recess until 11:00 a.m.

The cross-examination of James Mereness, Jr. took nearly two hours. It was mainly a grueling rehash of the examination by the prosecution. I could only guess that the defense attorney hoped the witness would contradict himself at some point and become discredited. However, there were a few notable exchanges.

At the beginning of the cross, Daniel had the witness explain the family relationships, and that Bill had moved away from the Appleton area while

Jim and Sallie had remained. It was established that Jim and Sallie had a closer relationship than Bill had with them or with their parents.

Daniel attempted to have Jim characterize Bill's personality, "Bill has never been an emotional person, has he?"

"Not really, no. I said no. He has nerves of steel. He's a cold person."

It was also established that Bill was aloof, didn't make a lot of close friends, stuck to business and was very meticulous. The witness did not confirm Daniel's supposition that Bill kept "receipts of everything".

Later in the cross-examination Jim confirmed that when Bill arrived at the cabin his clothes were all clean and undamaged.

As to the unloading of Bill's car, Jim assisted to a degree. Jim had had a chance to observe the interior of Bill's vehicle and the trunk and he'd noticed nothing unusual. Bill hadn't attempted to keep his brother from seeing any part of the vehicle, but he did not allow Jim to touch the box of laundry. Bill took that downstairs.

Daniel posed an interesting question, "And you took 'em out of the dryer, right?"

"Because he wanted me to."

"Well, for whatever reason," Daniel snapped.

"Yes."

"And you folded them?"

"Yes."

"And what was in the laundry?"

"It looked like, to me, Christopher's stuff, like T-shirts, underwear, socks. That was it."

"No pants--excuse me--slacks, no shirts, no jacket, no anything like that, correct?"

"Correct."

What a relationship. Your brother comes to visit and you have him folding your clothes. Weird. Unless, of course, you need a witness to testify as to what was and wasn't in the laundry.

Friday's evening meal was a topic for discussion, "What did you have for dinner?"

"Hamburger, beans, I think maybe a vegetable, but I'm not for sure on that."

"And while he was frying the hamburger, he washed his glasses a few times, is that correct?"

"Correct."

"When you fry hamburger it spatters grease and moisture coming out of the hamburger, isn't that correct?"

"Correct. But he put a top on the cover because he don't want the grease on the oven. I had specific directions, if I made breakfast sausages I had to put a cover on."

Ha. He'd hoped to provide a reason for Bill's washing his glasses, other than to remove the blood that got on them during the murder. Wasn't going to happen.

Later still, the defense attorney made a statement about the late night knock on the door; "You believe a police car came to the house the 23rd at 9:45."

"I don't know who was at the house at 9:45. I have no idea. There was a knock at the door. My brother didn't answer."

No help here either. Jim wasn't going to provide evidence that the police were harassing Bill.

Daniel wanted to discuss the trash. "...Did you look for and take all the garbage?

"I took everything..."

"All right. And that was turned over to the Janesville Police Department, is that right."

"That's correct."

"And when did you do that?"

"Sunday, Sunday night."

"Someone from the Janesville Police Department saw you Sunday night?"

"Yeah. Because we called the police, and Officer Goth came to my apartment and questioned me, and I told him to take it because I didn't want no part of it."

"Had you already thrown it away?"

"No. It was in the back of my truck."

There was a long discourse about the conflict between the brothers. Jim reiterated that he didn't want Bill around their parents, and he'd been angry with him for involving Ryan in Minocqua.

Daniel proposed a theory, "All right. You were also angry with him concluding he somehow was involved in doing this, isn't that correct?"

Jim's tone was strong and full of emotion, "Well, I figured I was going to be his alibi. He wanted me to be his alibi. I just didn't want no part of anything. I wanted him just to leave us alone, deal with his own problems."

So, apparently, Jim had already decided Bill was guilty to some degree. That should bolster Daniel's argument that Bill felt abandoned by his family when he made his admission to his mother and then tried to kill himself. But that would be, at a minimum, neutralized by Jim's assertion that Bill was using him as an alibi. That made Bill look even more manipulating than he had before.

Daniel asked if the witness had been drinking alcohol on both the 25th and 27th of November. Jim denied it.

Was this an attempt to discredit Jim, because he was a drinker?

As for Bill being "fucked" in his first divorce, Daniel wanted to know the entire statement.

"He said I got fucked once, I will never get fucked again, I got a better plan the next time."

"Did he say whether or not that better plan was to get a better lawyer?"

Folts objected. "I'm not going to let defense counsel be testifying for him."

The jury was excused and after a several minute skirmish, Werner did rule that he'd allowed this testimony in the first place on the supposition that Daniel could cover the other possibilities on cross-examination. The defense could continue.

"Did he say whether or not that plan was a marital property agreement?"

"No, he did not."

"Did he say whether or not that plan was to get a better lawyer?"

"No."

"Did he say whether or not that plan was to settle earlier?"

"No."

"He didn't say what that plan was, did he?"

"No."

After Jim agreed that there were, indeed, a number of possible interpretations for Bill's comment the cross-examination was over.

The redirect and recross offered a chance for each side to leave particular facts and thoughts in the minds of the jurors.

Bill's brother was dismissed and the court was in recess at 11:59 a.m.

At lunch everyone agreed that Jim had been a valuable witness for the prosecution. Despite Daniel's attempts to trip him up and discredit him, he had retained his poise and seemed a very credible man. His demeanor gave the impression that he had been egregiously affected by this whole horrible affair.

34

At 1:30 p.m. court was back in session. A bit of legal business needed sorting out before the jury was recalled.

Daniel had a correct version of Exhibit 99 to be submitted as Exhibit 106.

Apparently this one wasn't done "European style".

The prosecution had an official Wisconsin Department of Transportation map to be admitted as 107.

Mr. O'Leary called Craig A. Fritz. The gentleman who walked to the stand appeared to be in his 40's; his short, dark hair was devoid of any obvious gray. His beige sport coat, light green shirt and dark hair looked quite professional

Mr. Fritz testified he'd been employed as a detective with the Janesville PD for the past 13 years. Since 1978 he had been a police officer.

The detective had been assigned to secure Bill's Ford Taurus and have it towed to the police department on November 24, 2002. That had been accomplished.

The DA had concerns about how the vehicle had been handled. According to the witness, no officer entered or sat down in the vehicle. Fritz had steered it by standing outside the car with the door open. Then the vehicle was placed in secure storage at the Janesville PD until it would be accepted by the state crime lab the next morning. To secure the vehicle he'd locked it and put evidence tape on it.

O'Leary questioned his witness, "Did you have any contact with the defendant, Mr. Mereness, during this process?"

Fritz had. He stated, "When I arrived at his apartment parking lot, I spoke with him briefly."

"...Did the defendant ask you for any items out of the vehicle?"

"Yes, he did. There were several paychecks laying on top of a briefcase or portfolio on the passenger's side of the vehicle. He asked if he could have those. I told him that he could but I wanted to at least photocopy them before we turned them over to him."

Bill had asked to take his briefcase, but the officer did not allow that.

The defendant had also asked for a copy of the search warrant, and the officer provided one for him later in the day.

Daniel's cross-examination was, basically, a criticism of the way the search warrant was executed. Apparently, a person should not have to ask for a copy, it should be automatically provided. The officer should have had a copy with him at the initial encounter with Bill. Also, the search warrant hadn't specifically said the vehicle was to be seized, so the search should have been executed in the parking lot of Bill's apartment.

Fritz responded to the latter criticism, "The vehicle is mobile though, and to better search it should have gone to the crime lab."

Nothing further was needed from the witness.

Perry Folts called Officer Aaron Pynenberg, who explained that he'd been in law enforcement for 11 years. That seemed hard for me to believe, because the witness looked so young in his police uniform. He had broad shoulders and short, brown hair. He had first been employed at the Combined Locks Police Department and more recently by the Appleton Police. On November 29, 2002, the witness had responded to an automobile crash at 3100 East Enterprise Avenue in Appleton. Pynenberg and his partner understood from dispatch that there was only one person in the vehicle and he was unconscious but breathing.

I was immediately transported back to the scene in my loft on that day when Cathy had gotten the news of Bill's accident. *How many times since then had I wished he'd died that day?*

The police officers had to travel some distance to the scene, so by the time they arrived the fire department was already there as was a Gold Cross ambulance unit. Personnel from the ambulance service were providing first aid to Bill.

Pynenberg then tried to determine what had happened with the vehicle involved in the accident. He spoke to one person at the scene; then when the accident victim was ready to be transported by ambulance to the hospital the officer rode along in the emergency vehicle.

When asked if he could see the injured party in the courtroom, the witness pointed at Bill and said, "He's sitting two to your right with the gray suit on and the maroon and brown tie."

Folts continued to question the officer, "And once at the hospital, did you observe his injuries?"

"Yes."

"And what type of injuries did he have?"

Daniel objected. The question was without foundation.

Werner responded, "Well, as to his observations it's all right."

"I observed an injury to the back of his head. It was bleeding profusely... The paramedics had placed a gauze packaging on it or something to stop the bleeding, but he had a substantial injury to the back of his head and two lacerations to each side of his wrists, on his right and left wrist, which were horizontal across the wrists."

When the ADA asked Pynenberg to explain when he had seen similar injuries, the defense attorney first objected due to irrelevance, and when the question was rephrased, he objected because there was no foundation.

Judge Werner wished to hear a "little bit" about the witness' training and experience.

"I have a two year Associate Degree in Police Science through Fox Valley Technical College and also went through an extensive field training officer program with our department. In conjunction, we did some joint training with the Outagamie County Crisis Unit which handled all deals with suicide attempts and suicidal persons. Based on that training, coupled with my experience on the road, you're trained to detect certain types of injuries such as knife wounds, self-inflicted gunshot wounds, things of that nature, which may tend to show how the person may be trying to commit suicide or hurt themselves intentionally."

Folts inquired, "And have you previously investigated attempted suicides?"

"Yes, many of them."

"And actual suicides?"

"Yes."

"Now based upon your training and experience, the injuries that you observed on the defendant's wrists, what did they indicate to you?"

Daniel interrupted, "Objected to as without foundation, Your Honor."

"Overruled."

"They indicated to me that it was...they showed that the person may have been trying to kill themselves by severing the arteries and veins in the wrists which would cause a person to bleed out and eventually expire."

"And in your experience as an officer and your training, have you ever known such a person to use Saran wrap?"

Again, Daniel interrupted, "Objected to as irrelevant, Your Honor."

"Overruled."

"Yes."

"How would they use that?"

"It could be used in several ways. One of the ways they may use it is to cover the wound after they inflicted it themselves to prevent air from reaching the wound which would cause the wound to bleed more. In other words, sometimes a person will cut their wrists, or something of that nature, and submerge themselves in water to prevent air from reaching the wound also to allow the wound to continue to bleed so they will bleed out and expire. A person can use Saran wrap. I have investigated an incident where a person has used Saran…"

Yet another objection from the defense, "I object to the specific instances, etcetera."

"I will sustain that objection."

The prosecutor moved on. "Now, after you observed his injuries at the hospital did you initially make a decision to place him on a 72 hour mental hold?"

"Yes."

"Why was that?"

"That was done based on, as I said before, the type of injuries that he had, the two slashes on his wrists, and other evidence that was based on the scene. In other words, the actual physical scene itself, the car running itself into the brick wall, indicated to me that he may have…been trying to kill himself, along with his wounds."

Officer Pynenberg went on to describe that the scene of the accident had been in an industrial park, where businesses were closed on that day. Exhibit 112 was a photograph of the car imbedded into a brick retaining wall.

Folts went back to the topic of the 72-hour mental hold. Even it would have been for the defendant's safety, the witness had not put him on hold at first. The ADA wanted to know why.

"He was in ICU at that time, was nonresponsive. The ICU nurse staff had told me that they weren't sure what exactly was going on with him physically, being that he wasn't responsive. They had told me that there might be a mix of drugs or something in his system so they were going to keep him intubated. In other words, with a tube down his mouth that was breathing for him and everything, for some time, so it would be impossible for him to leave of his own will at that point. I conferred with my captain who was on duty at that time, let him know what was taking place and the decision I made at the time, and he concurred at the time that was the appropriate action to take."

Or maybe he was playing 'possum?

"So, initially then, you waited to place him on a hold until he was medically cleared."

"Yes. I should say all the paperwork was completed and placed on the nurse's chart so when he was responsive and out of his coma that they induced that then the hold would be effective."

Mr. Folts thanked the witness.

On cross-examination Daniel wanted to clarify if the 72-hour hold had ever been filed.

The witness did not believe it had been.

During a brief recess, we all agreed Pynenberg's testimony had been effective in suggesting how mentally unstable Bill had been.

Then prosecution called Lieutenant Dan Davis.

Davis, a sharp-featured, good-looking man with dark hair and penetrating eyes, first explained his duties with the Janesville Police Department, "Among other things, coordinating investigations, assigning cases."

The lieutenant had worked on the investigation of Jennifer's homicide and in the early morning of November 23rd, had made a decision to try to locate her estranged husband. He'd contacted the Oneida County Sheriff's Department and asked them to check an address on Pier Lake Road to see if Bill's vehicle was there. After the local authorities had done that Davis requested that they stand by until he'd decided the best course of action.

Folts inquired as to what Davis had intended the Oneida officers do after they located the defendant.

"We wanted to, first of all, notify him of the findings at the house on Sandstone, that Jennifer was deceased then also to talk to him about his activities and movements during that time."

Lt. Danny Davis led the investigation into Jennifer's murder *(Courtesy of The Janesville Gazette)*

The witness continued to explain that about 5:00 on the morning of the 23rd, he and Sergeant Kay Nikolaus left to travel to Oneida County.

The two Janesville officers arrived in Rhinelander about 8:30 a.m. and before meeting with the defendant met with Detective Glenn Schaepe for about a half-hour. Their meeting with Bill had been videotaped and, since he was not in custody, he had not been read his Miranda rights. Davis had advised Bill that he was not under arrest and that he was free to leave.

As per his training, Davis began the interview by asking Bill what he had been doing the day before the murder, November 21st. The lieutenant recounted, "He said that he spent the majority of the day at the Sam's Club in Appleton because there was some type of union initiative taking place that required his presence there for the entire day. And if I remember correctly, he... arrived there at approximately 10:00 a.m., left at 7:00 p.m. and drove straight home to Janesville. And upon his arrival in Janesville, he gassed up his car and went home and went to bed."

After a few objections from Daniel, Folts was finally able to have the witness answer another question, "Did he tell you he had telephone contact with anybody on November 21st?"

"Yes, he did."

"Who did he have telephone contact with?"

"He told me that he left some voice mail messages for Jennifer at her home, on her cell phone, and on her voice mail at Craig High School."

Bill had told Davis that the messages he'd left were about property that had been lost in the move from Columbus Circle and about a birthday card for her from his parents.

The interview with Bill proceeded to his activities on the 22nd of November. The witness recalled, "He got up early in the morning and his son who—when he had gotten home on the 21st, he had found out that his son, Christopher, was having a friend sleep over--and during the early morning hours or approximately sevenish, maybe a little bit before, on the morning of the 22nd, he suspected that Christopher and his friend had intentions of skipping school; so, but unbeknownst to them he had work to do around the house, so he had a conversation with Christopher about whether or not Christopher was going to have a ride to school, and in the initial questioning Christopher said, yeah, he did. A little more time passed. He asked again..."

The defense's objection due to hearsay was sustained.

Folts had the witness pick up the story. Bill told Davis he had eventually taken Christopher and his friend to school at about 7:15 a.m. then returned to his apartment to do some general cleaning while he was waiting for a 9:15 conference call with his boss.

After numerous questions and objections Davis was eventually able to tell the court that the conference call had not taken place because Bill's boss had called him on that morning and rescheduled it.

Lieutenant Davis continued his recollection of the interview. After Bill had found out the conference call was off, he'd decided to get an early start on his travels. He'd left the apartment for Minocqua at about 10:00 a.m. and made one five or ten minute stop at a wayside near Westfield. He'd then proceeded to the Wal-Mart store in Minocqua.

Folts asked, "Did he tell you why he was going to that Wal-Mart store?"

"Yes. He said that it was a combination business and personal trip to the store."

"What was the business reason that he told you?"

"He told me that the Wal-Mart Corporation was considering inserting an optical department in this particular Wal-Mart and, should that happen, that the store would then become part of his territory and he would be responsible for it."

Gee, that's not what Bill's boss said in her testimony.

"And what did he tell you was the personal reason for the visit?"

"That the store manager was a friend of his and had recently been promoted and he wanted to stop and congratulate his friend on his recent promotion."

But Cass Wisco testified that his relationship with Bill was barely civil.

"Did he do anything else while he was at the store?"

"He said that he bought a candy bar for his nephew who he was going to meet at the cabin."

Bill then informed the officer that after he left Wal-Mart he'd gone to his cabin on Pier Lake Road, met Jim and Ryan, had dinner, did some laundry and went to bed.

"Did he ever tell you if he left to make a phone call?"

"Yes, he did. He said that he and Jim and Ryan went into Minocqua to make a phone call because he needed to find out if his son, Christopher, needed a ride to work on Saturday, and the reason they needed to go to Minocqua was because the cell phone that he has doesn't have coverage in that particular area in close proximity to the cabin."

But Christopher testified he never received a call from Bill that night at all. Lies, lies, no wonder the police were suspicious, even if there hadn't been the earlier incident with the furnace pipe. Hopefully, the jury can see why they acted as they did.

According to the witness Bill then told Davis of his plans for the next day. He had some work appointments in Duluth and then he intended to return to Janesville to take Christopher to work, but he hadn't said what time his son had to be at work.

And Jim had testified that Bill told him very early on that Sunday morning he intended to leave directly for Janesville to take Christopher to work. He'd not mentioned anything about Duluth.

Bill also told the lieutenant that his divorce was proceeding amicably. He'd also talked about Jennifer and her debts.

"What did he tell you?"

"He said that she had a lot of debt and that she was, generally, very foolish as far as spending money."

The defendant had given a specific example.

"One instance that he offered was that one time she came home with a $2,000 hot tub before she had discussed making a purchase of that size with him."

"What else did he tell you about that hot tub then?"

"He said that they had a conversation about how she intended to have them pay for it, and she told him not to worry about it, that they could pay for it, and she wanted the hot tub so they could have more quality time together."

"Did he tell you anything else about the hot tub?"

"Well, much later in the conversation he revised the hot tub issue and then he explained to me that Jennifer had made an agreement with the person she got the hot tub from that instead of paying for it she was going to trade labor for the cost of the hot tub."

So had she bought it for $2,000 or bartered for it?

The line of questioning moved to the house closings. Bill told the witness that they had collected $38,000 in equity from the sale. He'd kept $22,000 and Jennifer had gotten between $8,000 and $9,000. Davis recalled that "the math wasn't quite exact".

Jennifer had used her amount as a down payment for the home on Sandstone. It hadn't been enough so she'd gotten additional money from her parents.

The ADA wanted to know if Bill had told the witness whether he'd had any plans for that $22,000.

He had. According to Davis, "He said that he had set the money aside and if things worked out between he and Jennifer that he intended on putting that money back into the—basically into the relationship."

Odd, considering he was the one who wanted the divorce at the time of the house closings.

Bill had also told the lieutenant about Jennifer's dogs. Davis testified, "That they were very friendly dogs, that they're very open to approaching even strange people, they're quiet, they don't bark very much even when people come to the door. And he also told me that he knows that while Jennifer is away that typically the dogs would be caged."

Yes, but what were their bowel habits?

The defendant had also informed the officer that the drive from Janesville to Minocqua took four and a half to five hours.

The two had also talked about Bill's work schedule. The testimony continued, "He told me that he is required to fax his itinerary for the week to his supervisor, and that other than the unexpected change in the conference call scheduled for Friday morning that he had no recent or unexpected changes in his work schedule for that entire week."

What about Duluth and West Allis?

When Lieutenant Davis had asked Bill meeting his brother at the cabin, Bill brought up a doctor's appointment he'd had on Friday.

The prosecution's attempt to find out about that appointment created quite a ruckus.

"Okay. What did he tell you about this doctor's appointment?"

"That he had made some notifications and had cancelled his Friday appointments because he had a doctor's appointment, and that is why he had to satisfy those appointments on Saturday."

"Is that consistent with what he told you earlier?"

The defense attorney objected. The question called for a conclusion.

The objection was sustained.

Folts rephrased, "Had he mentioned the doctor's appointment before this point in time?"

"No, he had not."

"Did he say whether or not he had contacted his supervisor about that doctor's appointment?"

"Yes, he told me...."

Daniel cut in, "It's leading, Your Honor."

Werner spoke, "Sustained, I will strike the answer."

The prosecutor tried again, "What else, if anything, did he tell you about the doctor's appointment?"

"He told me that he had also informed his supervisor of that change."

The defense interjected, "Judge, I would ask that answer be stricken as tainted by the leading question from the District Attorney."

The judge addressed Daniel, "I'm sorry. I couldn't quite hear you."

"I would ask it be stricken, Your Honor. That's the leading response."

"He backed up and asked a question that wasn't leading. Overruled."

Officer Davis indicated that that portion of the interview with Bill concluded about 11:00 a.m. He and Sergeant Nikolaus then went into the parking lot and searched Bill's vehicle; an action consented to by the defendant.

In the gray Ford Taurus the two police officers found nothing of evidentiary value, so the two returned to the sheriff's department and Davis called Detective Goth back in Janesville. Goth had some news.

Davis remembered, "In my conversation with Detective Goth, he had explained to me that one of the construction workers that was next door had seen someone walk away from the Sandstone address and had driven by him a couple of times, so we decided it would be worth a try as a ruse to tell Bill one of the construction workers identified him, that he saw him walking away from the property."

"So you decided to lie to him."

"Correct."

"And that's an accepted police procedure."

"Yes, it is."

"What happened?"

"He denied that that was possible." The defendant also told the lieutenant that the only way someone could drive from Janesville to Minocqua in less than five hours was if they drove 100 or 120 miles an hour.

And what had the traffic data from the DOT shown?

The witness then related that he, Sergeant Nikolaus, a deputy from Oneida County and Bill all traveled to the cabin around noon and arrived at about 12:30 p.m.

That certainly corroborates what Jim said about Bill's return.

Sergeant Nikolaus searched the cabin on Pier Lake Road, but nothing was seized. While the search was conducted, Davis had talked with Jim.

Following that, Davis and Nikolaus left Bill at the cabin and returned to Janesville.

Mr. Folts thanked his witness.

35

The cross-examination of Lieutenant Danny L. Davis was contentious and lengthy.

Daniel purported that while Davis had been informed of Jennifer's death around 7:30 p.m. on Friday, Bill had already been identified as a suspect as early as 6:30 a.m. on Saturday. The witness did not disagree.

If only the jury could be allowed to know about Jennifer's furnace incident and of Bill's first wife's accusation they would see why that was the case! Hopefully, since one of the officers already said he'd been familiar with the residence they will put two and two together. Plus, if they watch any programs dealing with the law, they'll know that close relations are always suspected first in such crimes.

Davis verified that he had told Bill he was under suspicion, and that he'd had the right to refuse the officers' search of his car. Bill had been cooperative with the authorities. Davis related, "He told us that as far as he was concerned we could look anywhere we chose."

The defense attorney asked the witness questions about the search. It was agreed that there had been a "snowbound kit" in the trunk.

Daniel pressed the witness, "And that contained a blanket. Did it contain a jacket?"

"No."

"Did you look?"

"Yes."

"Okay. Why did you look?"

"Because there were several blankets in there, and we took the top off and looked in between every one just to make sure there was nothing being concealed in between any of them."

"What were you looking for?"

"Anything that could possibly have been evidence of the crime."

Where is this going? He must have a purpose in this line of questioning.

"Okay. At this stage of the investigation, how would that determination have been made?"

"Well, we had some basic information on things that could have possibly been found."

"Things listed in the search warrants that were applied for on that day and the two subsequent days?"

"I wouldn't know that because I wasn't part of drafting any of the search warrants."

"Have you seen them?"

"No. I wouldn't even say that I read them."

"I understood your testimony of your duties at the Janesville Police Department are to supervise and assign detectives, right?"

"Right."

"All of the search warrants that I have seen in the record were applied for by Janesville detectives."

"Correct."

"You didn't sign off on those. You don't review those."

"No, I do not."

Had he been caught being inefficient or had he simply trusted his team with their delegated duties?

The defense attorney went back to the search of Bill's car. He reemphasized that the search warrants were issued very early on in the investigation and that the officers had found nothing of evidentiary value, including blood.

The next topic was the seizure of Bill's briefcase. Nothing of evidentiary value had been found in or on it either.

There was a brief skirmish over Daniel's use of the word interrogation when referring to the interview at the sheriff's department in Rhinelander. Judge Werner agreed with the prosecution that the word questioning would be better.

In that interview, Daniel again purported, Bill had been cooperative. The witness agreed.

The defense attorney's tone seemed accusatory, "Then you lied to him, right?"

"Yes, we did." Davis' tone was even, he had been following acceptable police procedure.

Daniel's body language and tone seemed aggressive, "And he told you that an eyewitness identification would be impossible because he wasn't there, isn't that correct?"

I thought Daniel might slam his hand down on the table for emphasis.

"Yes, he did." His voice held a trace of annoyance. One of Davis' eyebrows was raised.

"Okay. And even after he found out that you lied to him he continued to cooperate, isn't that correct?"

"Define cooperate." After the words were spoken the detective's mouth formed a thin line.

This is getting testy.

"He answered your questions."

"He answered the questions."

"Okay. Tell us how you proceeded to the property in Minocqua, the cabin."

The witness' spoke tersely, "He led, we followed."

"With two squad cars."

"No. Sergeant Nikolaus and myself had an unmarked city vehicle, and…"

Daniel broke in, "It wasn't a squad car?"

"It wasn't a marked squad car, no."

"That's not the question. It was a squad car, right?"

It was Folts' turn to interrupt, "Your Honor, I object. It's argumentative."

Wow, no kidding!

Werner responded, "It is argumentative. I will sustain the objection."

The defense attorney withdrew the question, but continued with the theme, "Did you and Deputy Nikolaus go to Rhinelander in a squad car, which I would define as a car owned by the Janesville Police Department and used in police work?"

Oooh!

"Yes."

"All right. The Oneida County deputy was also in a squad car, isn't that correct?"

"That is correct."

"And who led?"

Oh for God's sake he's already answered that question! Will he ever get to the point or is the point to annoy us beyond reason?

"Mr. Mereness."

"All right. And when you got to the property, you didn't have a warrant, correct?"

Asked and answered several times!

"Correct."

"Warrants had been issued by that time."

Mercifully, Folts objected stating, "Asked and answered".

It was sustained.

Daniel argued, "Well, judge, it's setting the scene, but okay."

Really, he is taking some license to argue with the judge about his ruling! When does contempt come in?

"It has been asked and answered," Judge Werner said firmly.

Daniel persisted, this time with the witness, "The answer to that is yes, correct?"

Folts spoke up, a hint of annoyance in his tone, "The objection was it was asked and answered. I don't think Mr. Daniel needs to repeat it for testimony."

Bill's attorney argued with Folts, "Just so I know where to go."

Werner clarified, "The answer was yes."

Gad, can't somebody stop this? People were shifting around in their seats, annoyance setting in.

The cross continued, "And he then gave you and the deputy and—again, I'm sorry, she's a lieutenant now."

"Sergeant."

"Sergeant Nikolaus access to the property, isn't that correct?"

"That's correct."

"And you had free access to the property, correct?"

"What do you mean by free access?"

"You weren't restricted to any rooms. You weren't restricted to not looking in drawers."

"Correct."

"There was no restriction on the amount of time that you had to search that property, is that correct?"

Oh for heaven's sake. This has already been established. Move on!

"That's correct," the witness responded with far more civility than I probably could have.

"And you did garbage, you did the rooms, correct?"

For the love of God, he already said he was outside talking to Jim, the other officers searched!

"I didn't do any of it."

"The other two officers did."

"What the specific mechanics of their search was I don't know."

"You're the head of the detective department in the Police Department of Janesville."

Already established! Isn't there something the DA can do to stop this harassment?

"Correct."

"That's asked and answered, but just to reiterate, correct?"
To reiterate for the 4th time!
"Correct."
"You're responsible for this investigation, is that correct?"
We heard that before too.
You were directing this investigation at this time, correct?"
For crying out loud, how many times is he going to ask the same question?
"Yes, that's correct."
"You were at the scene with two officers, subordinate—one subordinate to you and one basically on loan from Oneida County."
"Correct."
"You don't know what they did in that building, that's what you're telling these people."
"Yes."
"Thank you. That's all I have."
So the whole point was to prove that Davis did not micromanage his investigation. Or was it to suggest that the other officers flushed towels and latex gloves down the toilet to frame his client?

Perry Folts handled the redirect. He first had the witness reestablish that the reason he hadn't participated or supervised the search was that he had been outside talking to Jim.
Hallelujah!
"And did you see whether they brought anything out of the building?"
"Yes, I saw that they did not."
"Now, Mr. Daniel made a production, if you will, out of his definition..."
Touché.
Daniel took issue, "Excuse me Your Honor. I would object to that."
Sustained.
Folts rephrased, "Does your definition of a squad car fit that of defense counsel?"
The defense objected again, "It was defined in that manner."
Werner reacted, "It was defined in that manner. We'll let the officer make his response to this question."
"I would agree that it was a city owned vehicle that's used for police purposes."
"And how would you normally define a squad car?"
"A marked car that has a vis bar on the top and markings on the side so the public would know it's a squad car."

"The vehicle you were operating had none of these markings?"

"Correct."

So no one would know that Bill was accompanied by the cops in that regard, no chance for humiliation or a display that he was a suspect.

"Why did you decide to lie to the defendant?"

"Well, based on the information that had been learned while we were away, that being that some people had seen someone walking away from the house on Sandstone and had driven by him in close proximity twice, our thought process was that that person would know that that happened and that it was quite likely that that was a possibility, and so we decided it was worth a try."

Like he'd said before, it was a ruse.

Folts cleaned up the details about various search warrants, then moved on to why the officer in charge had considered Bill a suspect so early in the investigation.

"For a variety of reasons actually. Generally, it's typical police practice to start with, in this type of an incident anyway, to start looking at people nearest and dearest to the victim and working outward."

Good work!

"And in addition to that, there was a prior incident that our police department had investigated..."

The defense attorney interrupted, "Excuse me, Your Honor."

Folts countered, "Your Honor, Mr. Daniel opened the door to this question."

Werner decided to be heard on the matter and excused the jury. Once they were out of the room he began, "The jury is outside the presence of the court. This is going to be this incident with the furnace pipe."

Daniel responded first, "Correct. My point would be that—I guess I will obviously stand with the record, but I don't recall asking him why he was considered a suspect and we can check the record on that. Second of all, that would be getting in Witty evidence. And third of all, if we get there, that investigation was closed. Fingerprints were taken from the pipe. Mr. Mereness was eliminated."

The ADA had his turn. "Your Honor, with all due respect, he's characterized that incident many times as Mr. Mereness was eliminated. He was never eliminated. The fact that there were no fingerprints didn't eliminate him as being a suspect in that particular incident. He continues to be a suspect in that particular incident. Much like this particular situation, his fingerprints didn't show up on the pipe. So what. It didn't exclude him as a suspect. As far as this incident is concerned, I don't necessarily want to get into the details, but I think that because defense counsel asked when

Jennifer's Justice

the defendant was first considered to be a suspect, since he asked for this officer's—this witness' opinion as to his being a suspect-- he's entitled to give the basis for his opinion why he did consider this particular individual to be a suspect at 6:30 a.m. on November 23rd of 2002, and that's what he's doing. He can simply testify to the fact that there was a prior investigation, a prior incident that was reported to the Janesville Police Department he considered in making his determination."

"Judge, again I would defer to the record. I don't believe I asked him why. I asked him was it a fact Mr. Mereness was considered a suspect, and that was the end of it."

Folts countered, "I think the detective, or the lieutenant is entitled to explain why he was considered a suspect at that time."

"Judge, those questions were only asked in relationship to the necessity of consent, etcetera, etcetera, etcetera, in the cooperation aspect of the investigation we talked about. The State was invited on numerous occasions to disclose Witty evidence if they chose to do that, and we would have had an opportunity to deal with this in a Witty hearing prior to trial.

Werner wanted a quick Offer of Proof so the record would be clear.

The prosecutor began, "Again, why in addition to the procedure of looking closest then working out, why else did you consider the defendant a suspect at that point?"

"Because our police department had investigated a previous incident where Jennifer had said or told one of our patrol officers that she was afraid that Bill was trying to kill her."

"Was there any other reason then at 6:30 a.m. on November 23rd of 2002, that you considered the defendant to be a suspect?"

"Yes."

"What?"

"I had a telephone conversation with his ex-wife, Lyann Beatty, and she also told me that she was very intimidated and very afraid of Bill Mereness."

Oh how I wish I'd have pushed Jennifer into finding out more about Bill's first marriage. I'd had the opportunity at Nicole's party, but I didn't want to butt in.

"Were there any other bases for your opinion that he was a suspect at 6:30 a.m. on November 23, 2002?"

"Yes."

"What?"

"I had a telephone conversation with a co-worker, a Sloan Miller, who had told me that Jennifer had told her that she had been subjected to some very threatening behavior by Mr. Mereness."

Daniel again argued that the State had had a chance to have a hearing on this Witty evidence and they hadn't.

ADA Folts tried again, "We didn't bring this up. Mr. Daniel did. He's arguing coercion by the police department. He, in his opening statement, he said they were engaged in psychological warfare. Frankly, I think they're entitled to explain why they did what they did, particularly when defense counsel opened the door."

Yes, the defense brought it up; it's reasonable that Davis have a chance to explain why.

Unfortunately, Judge Werner did not agree with Mr. Folts or me. He would not allow the jury to hear the testimony, primarily, because the whole thing should have been settled in a preliminary hearing. He also considered it to be unfairly prejudicial to the defendant. The jury was to be brought back in.

Damn. That would have explained the authorities' suspicions and been very damaging to Bill.

On recross, Daniel was able to establish that when Bill had returned to Janesville from Minocqua he had been kept under police surveillance. Two officers had been assigned to that task.

That could add to the supposition that Bill had been a victim of police harassment.

We were granted a 20-minute recess.

As we convened in the hall we discussed Werner's ruling. Everyone was deeply disappointed. The testimony would have really let the jurors know some background on the problems in the relationship. The one saving point was that Davis had partially answered the question before the objection, so they would know that something had occurred. Hopefully, they would conclude that it was some technicality in the law that kept them from hearing the details.

We also realized that it was better for the judge to be conservative, so as not to allow opportunity for appeal, if Bill was convicted. It was a tight rope to walk. It was unfortunate that the prosecution hadn't brought up the testimony in a pretrial hearing, but it might not have occurred to them that Tod would harp on the fact that Bill had been a suspect so early in the investigation, to the exclusion of the real killer. After all, they were not in possession of a crystal ball.

Upon resumption, there ensued a 45-minute argument over possible upcoming testimony from the next witness, Detective Erik Goth. The outcome was that Goth would be allowed to testify regarding a conversation he had with Bill's mother in person, but would not be allowed to speak of a telephone conversation he had with her. Werner argued that with a phone

Jennifer's Justice

call there could be a potential problem with guarantees of trustworthiness because this was hearsay evidence.

Disappointing, because Goth will not be able to relay how LaBelle told him of Bill's admission of guilt and suicide attempt. But there will still be chances to get the information in with future witnesses.

Detective Erik Goth, tall, dark and ruggedly handsome, walked to the stand, took his oath and was seated.

Goth indicated that he'd been a police officer for ten years and a detective for five. He had been assigned to work on Jennifer's case.

Folts had Goth mark, on a large map, the locations of both Jennifer's home and Bill's apartment.

Detective Eric Goth maps Jennifer's route for the jury *(Courtesy of The Janesille Gazette)*

Then the prosecutor had Goth move on to a search of Bill's apartment on November 23rd. The detective had completed the search with a colleague, Detective Altstadt.

Folts addressed his witness, "And what, if anything, of evidentiary value did you find?"

"We collected a Columbia jacket, black and green, a pair of white socks, some indicia of occupancy and I think a couple of portfolio satchels."

Goth later told the court they'd also found a pair of gray sweatpants, he'd forgotten them earlier.

On the 25th of November the witness had executed a search warrant at 5555 East Pier Lake Road in Minocqua, the cabin. In that search he had seized another pair of gray sweatpants, a red rag from the shower, a blue portfolio, a marital settlement agreement, the vacuum canister from the central vac unit, a bag from an upright vacuum, and a pair of tan leather work gloves. He'd also swabbed a spot on the shower floor. The portfolio had contained Jennifer's credit card statements, bank statements and billing statements through August of 2002.

Was that the portfolio the construction workers saw Bill carrying? It had to be; otherwise, why would he have Jennifer's financial papers when they were separated?

Folts inquired, "Did you also prepare a search warrant for the defendant's body at some point?"

"Yes, I did."

"Where did you execute that search warrant?"

"In Appleton."

"And can you explain the circumstances that surrounded the execution of that search warrant?"

"I was at the Devonshire address which is Bill's parents' address. We weren't exactly sure where Bill was at the moment that I went up to Appleton, but while I was there talking with LaBelle, James, Sr., and Sallie, Bill returned home or returned to his parents' address."

"Now, you had a conversation with LaBelle while you were at that residence then, correct?"

"Correct."

"And specifically, did you ask her about whether or not there had been an argument between the defendant and Jim earlier in the week?"

"Yes."

"And what did she tell you?"

"She said they hadn't had an argument."

"And was she corrected at some point by Sallie and then changed her mind?"

"Yes."

"What did she tell you then?"

"Well, she characterized Jim, Jr. as being nervous and not really angry. She said that he had raised his voice and was using foul language toward Bill."

The detective then told the court that during the execution of a search warrant on Bill's car a pair of tennis shoes, a light gray pair of sweatpants and a baseball cap were seized."

The questioning returned to the search warrant for Bill's body on the 27th. They had taken Bill to the Appleton Medical Center. The witness verified that after the procedures had been completed, Bill had gone home with his brother Jim.

Next the prosecutor held up a black coat that was Exhibit 65. Goth identified it as an item that had been found by Officer Lemery in the lost and found at Craig High School.

The ADA returned again to the scene at the Appleton Medical Center. "Now, at the time that you executed that search warrant on November 27th of 2002, did you also speak with the defendant?"

"Yes, I did."

"And what did you tell him before you spoke with him?"

"I told him he was free to go and that his brother was waiting to give him a ride home and he was under no obligation to answer any questions."

"What was the first thing that you talked to him about?"

"I told him that I wanted to ask him about the morning of Friday, the 22nd of November."

"Did he want to talk to you about that?"

"He said no."

"Okay. What did you talk to him about next?"

"I asked him if he bought a coat over the weekend."

Detective Goth then explained that Bill had answered affirmatively. He'd purchased the coat late Sunday afternoon with a combination of check and cash. Bill told Goth he'd bought it to use as emergency road wear in case he had trouble during the winter. Then the police officer had asked the defendant if he'd returned to Scheels after he'd bought the coat. He had.

Folts asked the witness, "What did he tell you?"

"He told me he couldn't remember."

"What was his demeanor at that particular point?"

"Unusual."

"In what way?"

"When I asked him the question if he had gone back to Scheels at all since he bought the coat, he paused for an extraordinary amount of time."

"How long would you say?"

"A minute."

"And then what did he do?"

"He said he was drawing a blank."

Then Bill had told Goth he bought all his Columbia jackets at Scheels and that Jennifer had had a similar coat. He thought he'd returned the coat to Jennifer in November.

Next the witness related that Bill had told him that on Saturday night at the cabin he'd done some laundry, had dinner and gone to bed early.

Goth testified, "I asked if anybody had come to the cabin that night, if he heard a knock on the door."

"Why was that? Why did you ask him that?"

"Because Saturday evening I had requested a deputy from the Oneida County Sheriff's Department to stop by and see if they could get a mileage reading from his odometer; so, I knew, a deputy had stopped by."

Bill then told Goth that on Sunday, his brother had said that he'd heard a knock on the door during the night. Then later in the conversation Bill said Jim had told him about the knocking immediately after it had occurred.

The Janesville detective testified that he had asked Bill one more question, and that was why he didn't want to talk about Friday morning.

Daniel vociferously objected to the "witness commenting on Mr. Mereness exercising his constitutional right not to talk about these subjects with the police."

The objection was sustained.

Folts continued anyway. Daniel repeated his objection, it was again sustained. The ADA wished to be heard, so the jury was excused.

The Offer of Proof included information about Bill's activities on the Friday of the murder. The police officer and the suspect talked about travel time and cell phone records, with Goth challenging Bill's voracity and Bill sticking to his story.

Goth asked one last question, "I asked him if he killed Jennifer."

"What did he say?"

"He said no, and he told me he needed to do his homework, he needed to get his ducks in a row, and we needed to end the conversation."

A protracted argument ensued about Miranda rights.

Daniel purported over and over that once the defendant had said he didn't want to talk any more, the officer was no longer allowed to ask questions. He also threw in a motion for a mistrial.

Folts argued at each juncture that it was a non-custodial interrogation so Miranda warnings did not apply.

Finally, Judge Werner made a ruling. "I think that's the distinction... This is non-custodial. He said no, but then he chose to talk again later. So I'm going to allow it.

Hurrah!

Daniel then asked if court could be adjourned for the day and that they be allowed to argue "this" in the morning. He wanted to argue with research.

Folts, of course, wished to proceed.

The judge said that he'd made his ruling so they would continue.

Bill's attorney perseverated, "What about the issue of him then saying that he exercised his right. That's not admissible. He can't go into I asked him this question and he told me I'm done talking, my ducks, blah, blah, blah. The exercise of the right is not to get to the jury."

Werner sustained that part of the objection.

That's odd. He talked about the ducks and homework then said he didn't want to talk about it any more. Seems like he's being cut off just before the important part.

The jury returned.

The defense attorney wanted the judge to verify that his motion for a mistrial was on the record.

Woah! Can he do that in front of the jury?

Judge Werner told him they'd "talk about that later".

The prosecutor went through the testimony with Goth about travel times and cell phones.

The next area for exploration was regarding Bill's "pretty wrecked" rental car, a Ford Escort.

Goth had executed a search warrant on that and seized a brown leather jacket and a knife.

There were intermittent skirmishes about what could be said about the knife and a conversation the witness had with the Appleton Police regarding the car crash. After each ruling Folts continued, but he was left with little of value.

"Did you have a conversation with them about the crash of the vehicle?"

"Yes."

"You examined the knife."

"Yes."

"What did you see on it?"

"A substance that looked like blood."

Folts next brought up an encounter Goth had with Bill on the 3rd of December. Daniel objected and wanted to be heard. The jury was excused again.

The defense attorney argued that at that time Bill was "shackled to the bed".

Folts interrupted, "Your Honor, if you would let me go—or if defense counsel would have allowed me to continue..."

The judge suggested an Offer of Proof.

"What did you do before you spoke with the defendant on December 3?"

"I talked with his family."

"And who accompanied you when you spoke with the defendant on December 3rd?"

"Detective Craig Fritz and Captain Peter Helein from the Appleton Police Department."

"Did you place him under arrest?"

"Yes."

"Did anybody read him his Miranda warnings?"

"Yes."

"Who?"

"Craig Fritz."

"And did he agree to answer questions after that?"

"Yes."

At that point, the ADA was finished with his Offer of Proof and Werner overruled the defense's objection.

But before the jury was recalled, O'Leary spoke, "Hold it, Your Honor, can we address one more thing? When the jury came in previously, Mr. Daniel spoke up and wanted to make sure his motion for mistrial was on the record, thereby indicating to the jury the State is doing something inappropriate. I think counsel should be admonished about engaging in that type of showmanship in front of the jury after losing an argument to the judge and should not do that when the jury..."

It was Werner's turn to interrupt. "That's not appropriate, Mr. Daniel, and we will take up those matters and those things outside the presence of the jury."

Hah!

The prosecutor began, repeating what had been said in his Offer of Proof.

Then the defense attorney wanted to be heard further on the issue. The jury was excused again. They'd been in the courtroom for one minute.

For about 25 minutes, the two sides argued back and forth during the Offer of Proof. At issue was the conversation Bill had with Goth in the hospital. Bill had wanted to have a meeting with his family, he'd said that he "didn't know why" he had told his mother he'd killed Jennifer. They'd reviewed times and cell phone records again, and talked about the possibility of his confessing, the trial process and prison. Unfortunately,

Goth had told Bill he would only arrange the meeting with his parents if Bill were truthful with him. Judge Werner ruled that Bill's statements were not voluntary because of the "bargain" the detective had made with the defendant. Therefore, they were inadmissible.

This is a dark moment. The judge certainly feels that Goth hadn't played by the rules. Now all of the information he'd gathered was lost to the jury.

Before the jury was called back in it was agreed that the prosecution would finish its direct examination of the witness and then the court would recess for the day. Cross and redirect would occur in the morning.

Once the jury was seated Folts began. "Detective Goth, did you prepare another search warrant on April 17th of this year?

He had. It had been for the septic on the cabin on Pier Lake Road in Minocqua. The officer told the court that nothing of evidentiary value was found in the septic tank at that time.

The ADA had no further questions for the witness. He was to step down, the jury was dismissed and court was in recess for the day.

36

In what seemed like the blink of any eye, we were back on the record at 8:30 a.m. Saturday, August 16, 2003. The courtroom was crowded with media and spectators. There were cameras and reporters from two television stations on the scene as well as the familiar journalists from *The Janesville Gazette* and the *Wisconsin State Journal*. Jennifer's family was even better represented than it had been during the week. Mavis, Michael, Tom, Jr., Bobby, Cathy, Pat, Patti, Marsha, Stephanie and I were there along with newcomers Erin, Jeannie and Jeannie's fiancé, Alex. We took up a full three rows in the gallery.

Judge Werner announced that we were back on the record for the sixth day of the trial. Before the case could proceed, Daniel had a concern, "When do we plan on doing instructions and stuff? Do we know?"

Werner responded, "I didn't think we would do that today."

"That's not why I'm asking."

"Unless we have a lot of extra time today. Next week I would guess. All right. We ready to bring in the jury?"

Daniel piped up again, "Judge, I guess just an observation and a concern or whatever. We have witnesses sequestered. And they're out in the hall reading the *Gazette*."

The judge declared, "Well, I'll ask that they not read the newspaper, any newspaper account concerning this matter. We will bring in the jury and then we'll call Detective Goth back."

The panel members took their rightful places; Goth reviewed his oath and was seated.

Daniel began his cross-examination. The first ten minutes involved clarifying information on various maps. Scales, color, distances to various streets and between houses were all referred to. I did not see any point to the whole line of questioning.

It was next established that although Detective Goth worked on the case a lot, he was never given the title of Lead Investigator. He had been assigned to the case by Detective Martin. He had executed the bulk of search warrants, made trips to Minocqua and Appleton.

The defense attorney then had the witness review all of the search warrants as well as the consent searches and items seized in the searches. It went on and on.

I could only guess that the purpose was to somehow trip up the witness and make him contradict what he had said under direct.

Of particular interest was the exchange about the leather gloves that were seized from the Minocqua property.

Daniel asked, "In terms of where on the scale of tan were they, how would you describe them?"

"Light. Light colored. Cream maybe."

"Cream?"

"On the scale of tan."

The defense attorney gestured with his hands, "So white's here and brown is here. Where is tan?"

"25%."

"And you could describe them as cream, another way to describe them?"

"Yes."

There is no love lost between these two men. I could feel the tension building. No one had said anything the least bit controversial, but it seemed as if we were building to a nasty climax of some sort.

The defense went back to a litany of seized items and whether they had gone to the state crime lab or not.

We arrived at a manila folder. Daniel queried, "You were asked a question, and I'm going to paraphrase it, as to what that manila folder contained, isn't that correct?"

"Correct."

"And your answer from beginning to end was some credit card receipts of Jennifer Mereness', isn't that correct?"

"Yes."

"Okay. And that was the complete answer you gave to this jury to that question, isn't that correct?"

The witness sounded a bit annoyed, "Yes."

Well I'm sure annoyed. He's back to asking questions in duplicate and these questions seem designed to reveal this detective is a liar.

"Would you open the thing? It's a series of dividers, I believe by month. Correct me if I'm wrong."

"Correct."

"All right. Behind the first divider would you catalog to the jury what is contained in there?"

Goth seemed puzzled, "Do you want me to read through all of this?"

"Just what's in that? Are those Jennifer's credit card receipts?"

"Um, there are credit card receipts in here."

"I understand that."

"This is a Bank of America, Visa. Got some dollar amounts on it. Dell Financial Services."

"Who is that stuff addressed to?"

"Jennifer Mereness."

"All right."

"This is Jennifer Mereness WEA Trust looks like maybe life insurance."

"From when?"

"January 23, 2002. This is under January."

"That's when they were living together, isn't it?"

Ahh, I get it. He's trying to prove that Bill wouldn't have taken those documents from Jennifer's because it was from a time they'd lived together and he just had them yet.

Daniel went along in this vein for a long time. Some of the documents were for Jennifer, some for Bill and others for both. We heard about January, February, and were beginning March when Folts, thankfully, interrupted.

"Your Honor, I will stipulate all of them are a mix of Jennifer and the defendant's bills, credit card statements, checking accounts, whatever they might be. I don't think we need to go through every one of them."

Thank you, neither do we, nor does the jury, I suspect.

The defense attorney sounded piqued, "Judge, I will put my case in."

Werner's voice held a trace of surprise, "Do you want to join in that stipulation?"

"No, Your Honor."

Oh dear God, no.

We went along through the documents: check carbons, heating and cooling company invoices, Charter Communications bills, etc. etc.

Then Bill's lawyer was going to try to have the witness summarize, "That goes all the way through to the end of the records in that file, isn't that correct?"

"I don't know if it that's correct. I would make that assumption."

Good.

"Well, let's look then. Let's pick July."

Nooooo!

We went through more of the same. At one point Daniel asked the defendant if two signatures appeared to be the same.

The prosecution objected, it would call for speculation.

Sustained.

The litany painfully continued until the defense attorney asked if he could approach the bench. He had Exhibit 118, which consisted of two of the checks from the file from the month of July.

Neither judge nor prosecutor had a problem with the items being published to the jury.

Wow! All that to prove that the file had contained items for both Jennifer and Bill? It sure seems that we could have gotten to that point a long time ago. Hopefully, the jury is really ticked off and will hold it against Daniel and his client.

The next line of questioning concerned search warrants; what they were for, which residence they were for, how were they executed, if copies had been prominently displayed and so on.

Again, I wasn't sure where the defense was going. Detective Goth showed remarkable patience, although he did appear to be a bit piqued.

Daniel finally seemed to have a point, "So, in other words, if you search someone's place you don't—you're not required to leave an inventory with the owner of that property with what you took?"

"That's not required, correct."

"After, I guess, the aftermath of a search warrant often looks like the aftermath of a burglary, is that a fair statement?"

I get it. It's the harassment angle.

"No." The witness was clearly put off.

This witness will not help the defendant in these claims of abuse of authority by the police. Daniel may as well forget it.

The subsequent questions had to do with the search warrant for "Mr. Mereness' person". But there was a brief "bird walk" to a conversation that had occurred prior to the execution of the warrant.

"Yesterday, you on Direct Examination testified with reference to a conversation with LaBelle Mereness, James, Jr., James, Sr., etcetera?"

"No."

"We didn't cover that in direct yesterday?"

"We covered a conversation. I think you're incorrect in all the participants of that conversation. Jim, Jr. was not there."

Good catch. Goth is really focusing on every word so he doesn't get trapped.

"Okay. Who was there?

"Sallie, LaBelle, and Jim, Sr."

"And that's the conversation she described the conflict between Jim and Bill the confrontation?"

"Right."

So before his body was violated, his brother had sworn at him at told him to leave his parents and the rest of his family alone.

Then they did the "body search" where they took fingerprints. The defense attorney went into tremendous detail as to how that was accomplished; the rolling of the fingers in ink, the redoing of a print if it smudged. They also took blood and hair for DNA and comparison purposes.

Bill's shoes were taken, as were his sunglasses, wristwatch, eyeglasses and necklace.

So they took parts of his body as well as his most intimate possessions. Daniel's got to be hoping the jury's grasped that Bill must have been feeling terribly violated and dehumanized.

We took a brief detour to find out about the phone conversation LaBelle had had with Jennifer on the morning of her death. LaBelle had been concerned that the two women remain friends after the divorce. Bill's mother also had said that Jennifer had sounded fine during that conversation.

So she masked her emotions from her fragile mother-in-law or something happened after that phone call to cause her to be upset.

The defense attorney returned to search warrants, executions and items seized; a knife, day planners, documents, clothing.

When Daniel inquired about a copy of an interrogatory Bill had started to fill out, the witness needed a moment to find it in his report.

The defense attorney asked the witness, "Want my glasses?"

Goth declined.

That was a strange thing to do. Was it an attempt at levity? If so, it failed miserably. The witness looks pretty ticked off. His facial muscles indicate he's grinding his teeth together. Not that I blame him.

The next topic was the search of the septic system. We heard about how the process worked, that the worker had gotten down into the tank with a biohazard suit. But despite all the effort, nothing had been seized.

In his final area of concern, Bill's lawyer had the witness explain that, for all of their looking, no Harbor linen had been found at either the house in Minocqua, or the Sandstone house.

The cross-examination took well over an hour. It had been so detailed and the tension so high that I felt drained for having concentrated on it for such a long time. I could only imagine how Detective Goth felt.

On redirect, Folts covered a lot of territory. Much seemed to be a rehash of previous testimony, but he did have the witness re-emphasize that a blue and black Columbia coat had never been found.

And where would that coat be if it hadn't been dumped to get rid of evidence?

Also, on the 24th of November, Bill had told Goth the reason he'd returned to his cabin after having left for Appleton. He had wanted to get his glasses for driving, some sweatpants and something else. The "something else" had never been divulged.

The ADA also reviewed what Goth had discussed with Bill's mother on two different occasions. On the one occasion she had said that Jennifer had been the one to tell her that she and Bill were getting a divorce.

I was sure that had been gone over so the jury could understand that Jennifer could have understandably been emotional after having had such a conversation.

Folts also had the witness take a long time to explain and highlight on maps the two routes he had taken to Minocqua. It was obvious that Bill had taken the more circuitous route.

But then he'd needed to establish an alibi by stopping at the Wal-Mart.

Finally, the prosecutor asked Detective Goth to review the location of Jennifer's residence on the cellular map.

Folts might have done that in the event that the cell phone evidence is challenged when Daniel presents his case.

On recross, Daniel asked, "You're not a cartographer, correct?" Then he asked the witness to review the scale on two of the maps and confirm that they were "to the exact scale".

That was a bit sarcastic. Unless you were a cartographer you couldn't be relied upon to give testimony about locations on maps?

Judge Werner directed Detective Goth to step down, but he didn't excuse him. The judge then called for a 15-minute recess.

Folts caught the omission, "Is this witness excused, Your Honor?"

Werner spoke to Daniel, "Is he released from his subpoena?"

"No, Your Honor."

There was a brief skirmish about Goth's status. Even though Daniel had not subpoenaed the officer, Daniel was requesting that he "remain". Judge Werner agreed to the request.

During the break we talked little. Just standing near one another in the hallway seemed to be enough support at that time. The experience was clearly having a deep impact upon us all.

The jury returned to the courtroom at 10:40 a.m. Mr. Folts called Peter John Helein as his next witness.

Mr. Helein told the court that he had been a police officer for 20 and one half years. He was an employee of the Appleton Police Department where he held the rank of captain. Helein was the head of the department's investigative services, which was also known as the detective bureau.

Captain Helein testified that on November 29th of 2002, he had been called to the Appleton Medical Center because there had been a collision between a vehicle and a concrete, block, retaining wall on East Enterprise Drive.

The witness' purpose in going to the medical center was to supervise the investigation into the collision. The police intended to determine who had been involved, why the collision had occurred and what events had led up to it.

Captain Helein pointed to Bill as the individual he had seen in the hospital on that day.

While at the hospital, the officer spoke with James, Sr., LaBelle, Sallie and James, Jr. The witness explained the familial relationship each had to Bill.

In his discussion with LaBelle, Helein told her he was trying to find out additional information that would help him better understand why Bill would have intentionally driven his car into a concrete wall.

Mr. Folts addressed the captain, "And what was your purpose in gathering information from LaBelle and the other family members?"

"I wanted to determine if it was necessary or appropriate to conduct a detention on William, mental health hold, because he was a suicide risk."

"Did you speak to LaBelle regarding the defendant's activities on November 27th of 2002?"

"Yes, I did."

"And what did she tell you as far as where he had been on that day?"

Daniel interjected, "Judge, object on the grounds of hearsay, Your Honor."

"Overruled."

The defense attorney was not satisfied, "I would ask my objection be a continuing objection."

"It's continuing," rejoined Judge Werner.

The witness answered the question, "LaBelle told me that William had arrived back in Appleton at her residence at approximately 5:00 p.m. on November 27th."

Helein then said that Bill's mother had described his condition at that time, "LaBelle told me that William was extremely depressed and distraught because he was a suspect in Jennifer's death."

According to Captain Helein, in subsequent conversation LaBelle related that Bill had told her he didn't want to go to prison for 70 years for killing Jennifer.

LaBelle also told the officer that on Thanksgiving Day, Bill had just "laid around the house and slept".

As for Bill's activities on the 29th, the captain recalled, "LaBelle told me that at approximately 8:30 that morning William entered the kitchen at that residence, removed a carving knife kitchen knife and he removed a box containing Saran wrap."

The witness continued, "LaBelle told me that William then walked from the kitchen into the bathroom at the residence."

His mother followed him into the bathroom and watched as he climbed into the tub and assumed a prone position on his back while maintaining possession of the knife and plastic wrap. The knife was described as having a six-inch blade and a wooden handle. It had typically been used to carve turkey.

LaBelle asked the defendant what he was doing.

Bill told his mother that he wanted to die.

LaBelle had then asked Bill, "Did you kill Jennifer?"

Folts queried, "How did she say that the defendant responded to that question?"

"LaBelle told me that William responded to her question by saying, 'Yes, I'm really sorry.'"

"Did she tell you what happened after that?"

"Yes."

"What did she tell you?"

"LaBelle told me that after William confessed to killing Jennifer she walked out of the bathroom and walked away."

A short time later the defendant left the bathroom, gathered up his possessions and departed from his parents' residence at about 9:30 a.m.

Helein testified that the automobile collision was reported at approximately 2:10 p.m. on that same day.

Mr. Folts had no further questions for the witness.

On cross-examination Daniel requested Captain Helein refer to the reports he had filed in the matter. He did.

Daniel began, "Officer, had you ever met any of the persons involved in this discussion: James Mereness, Sr., LaBelle Mereness, Sallie Drier or James Mereness, Jr., prior to November 29, 2002?"

"No."

"So, during this conference, then, you had no background at all on the circumstances of any of these people, is that correct?"

"That's correct."

"You were not aware during the conference, that LaBelle had been for a significant period of time diagnosed as having a manic depressive or bi-polar disorder?"

Oh, now we're going to discredit Bill's dead mother by implying she was mentally incompetent. Is there no end to the lengths these men will go?

"I am not aware of LaBelle's medical history."

"You were not aware of her medical history of hospitalizations for manic episodes, is that correct?"

"Correct."

"You were not aware that she had had a recent hospitalization in September of 2002, is that correct?"

Obviously not, since he already answered that he was unaware of any hospitalizations.

"Correct."

"You were subsequently made aware of the medications that LaBelle Mereness was on at the time you took her interview, correct?"

"That's correct."

Sallie had supplied Captain Helein with a list of the medications her mother had been taking at that time. They were: Navane, Risperdal, Cogentin, Dylantine, Lanoxin, Warfarin and Doxycycline.

Well, certainly, the last two, a blood thinner and an antibiotic, could hardly have affected her mental abilities.

Sallie had told the officer that Navane and Risperdal were antidepressants, Cogentin was for her eyes, and Dylantine and Lanoxin were heart medications.

Well, if she were on medication for depression, I'd say she would be a more reliable witness than if she had been untreated. I hope the DA points that out on redirect. The other meds are insignificant to this line of defense.

Helein also indicated that LaBelle was "hooked to a bottle of oxygen". He had not inquired as to why.

Again, if she were being supplied with an appropriate amount of oxygen, it would actually make her mind sharper. She was a sick woman who found out her son murdered his wife. Now she's dead, so her words can only be heard through other witnesses. I'm grateful that she died. If she had lived until this day the cross-examination would have been devastating.

Daniel's voice brought me back to the present, "Also, during this conversation with her the other people, James, Sr., Sallie and James, Jr., participated in this conference, correct?"

"It wasn't a conference. I interviewed LaBelle asking her specific questions and I interviewed James, Sr. asking him specific questions, as well as James, Jr. and Sallie."

Good job in setting the record straight!

"There were occasions when they would inject theirselves in one of the other person's answer, isn't that correct?"

"That happened on a couple of occasions in the form of encouragement to respond to my question."

"In other words when you were asking LaBelle questions, Sallie Drier would become involved for want of a better word, correct?"

"No, that's not true as I recall."

This witness is not giving the defense attorney anything.

"She would prompt her mother?"

"She, when I asked her father a question, she responded by saying, 'It's okay dad, tell them what you heard.' That's the only thing that she interjected."

"She did not interject when LaBelle was answering questions is that your testimony today?"

Oh, so he said something else before and now he's lying? If so, why doesn't Daniel bring in the document from that previous occasion?

"Yes," replied the witness rather testily.

Helein must have interpreted the question as I had, that he was slyly being accused of perjury.

Things became a bit heated between the defense attorney and the witness. Daniel badgered, Helein stood firm.

"Did she indicate whether or not there were witnesses to the 29th, excuse me, the 27th comment?"

"She told me that William had told her directly."

"I don't think you understand the question."

"I do."

"Were there any witnesses other than LaBelle and William."

"There were two comments that she relayed to me from the 27th; so, I can't answer yes to both. I know that James, Sr. also shared the concern about being extremely depressed and upset, but it was LaBelle."

"Okay. There is really not a question." Daniel's tone suggested annoyance.

Helein was unruffled, "Okay."

"My notes indicate in response to the questions on direct examination you were asked about comments made by, allegedly made by, William on November 27th and you related one incident, is that correct?"

"Correct."

"Now you're saying there was more than one?"

"Well, there were two comments. The first being that LaBelle's observation that William was extremely depressed and upset. And then..."

The defense attorney interrupted, "All right."

Is he trying to shut the witness up?

The officer continued, "Then the other complaint that LaBelle made to me and she said that William made this comment directly to her, 'I don't want to go to prison for 70 years for killing Jennifer.' I don't know if James, Sr. or anyone else was present when William made that second, made that comment to LaBelle."

Oops! It's unlikely the defense wanted the jury to hear that incriminating statement again. This cross-examination doesn't seem to be going too well.

It appeared Daniel was going for damage control, "Okay, I guess where I'm confused, you're calling that a second comment. What's the other comment? You said there were two things that Mrs. Mereness made observations that William was depressed and then there is the comment. Why is this?"

"The first being an observation."

"All right. Not a comment by William?"

"Right."

"One comment by William alleged?"

"Correct."

Oh, dear God, does it really matter if it was an observation or a comment? Will that be the difference between a guilty or not-guilty verdict?

Daniel lurched along, "With reference to the 29th did she say who else was present if anyone?"

"Yes, she did."

"Who?"

"LaBelle told me that William, excuse me, that James, Sr., was also present in the bathroom when William made the comments."

Oh gawd, don't say comments! There was only one comment. Here we go again!

Fortunately, the defense attorney either didn't hear Helein use the plural or he'd had enough of that game. He moved on, "Appleton's interest in Mr. Mereness was under Chapter 51 and 50. 51.15, correct?"

"That's correct."

"And a Chapter 51.15 proceeding which is a mental commitment was never commenced, is that correct?"

"Correct."

"Mr. Mereness was unconscious, correct?"

"On November 29th, yes."

Good clarification. This witness is really on the ball.

"And he remained unconscious for a number of days, is that correct?"

"That's correct."

Then, during a long question and answer session, it was determined that on December 2nd at approximately 12:15 p.m. Ginny Schuettpelz, an employee of the Outagamie Crisis Intervention, conducted an assessment of Bill's mental condition. Captain Helein had been present on that occasion.

Daniel purported, "Mr. Mereness indicated that he had no memory of the events of November 29th?"

Folts immediately objected on the basis of hearsay.

Daniel cited case law.

Werner excused the jury.

The argument was quite lengthy and contentious, with the key lying in State Statute 908.01 (4) (b) (4). That reference indicated that a statement was not hearsay if it was offered against a party. That was not the case here.

At one point Folts suggested that Daniel ask the health care provider to testify. Daniel responded tersely, "I don't need to have to ask the health care provider."

Folts shot back, "This witness certainly isn't the health care provider."

The defense attorney argued, "Excuse me, Your Honor, I don't want to engage in this, but this is a witness to the statement. It doesn't matter whether he is the health care provider. He's already testified."

The judge took a minute to study the statute, then spoke, "I will sustain the objection. Bring in the jury. You have exception, Mr. Daniel."

Bailiff Bliss went to the jury room and opened the door to recall the panel.

Daniel persisted, "Excuse me, Your Honor."

The bailiff followed Werner's command, "Close the door!"

Another long argument ensued about hearsay and the potential testimony of a health care provider.

Folts seemed agitated, "Again, Your Honor, it's the defendant's own comment. Whether or not it's made for medical diagnosis, that's not an issue in this particular case. And whether or not he committed this particular homicide is. I know where this is going. It's one more denial by the defendant without him taking the stand. If he wants to testify he can choose to testify, but he doesn't get to testify through hearsay."

The defense attorney interjected, "I will not dignify that with a response, Your Honor."

Folts took the bait, "I appreciate that."

This is getting pretty ugly. I hope Werner can get things under control soon, it's turning into a real scrum.

He did. The judge took a deep breath and said they'd take the situations one at a time.

Each attorney had one more kick at the cat. Daniel insisted the statement was an exception to hearsay, no matter who offered it to the Court. Folts claimed that the comment wasn't even relevant.

Werner gave his ruling, "I think it is relevant and I think it is an exception. I don't think it comes through Captain Helein, but it will probably come in through her. But I will sustain the objection as to it relates to this gentleman's testimony. We will bring in the jury."

This time the jury made it into the courtroom.

Werner pronounced, "All right. The objection is sustained. Next question, Mr. Daniel."

"That's all I have, Your Honor."

But the jury already heard the answer through Daniel's question. Why were lawyers allowed to ask questions of that type? They all but circumvent objections entirely.

On redirect, Folts attempted to find out if Bill had had any drugs in his system while he was hospitalized, but it was disallowed.

Damn. If the defense can assert that LaBelle's words weren't reliable due to her medications, it makes sense that the prosecution argue the same about Bill. But according to our legal system, it could not be brought up in this way. Is there another path the ADA can take?

The prosecutor was able to guide Helein masterfully in regard to the reliability of LaBelle's statements. It was made clear that despite her physical and mental problems, she had no difficulty hearing or understanding and was oriented as to time and place.

Well done.

38

I was almost afraid to see the next witness. Bill's father had looked so old and frail at the preliminary hearing, I could only guess what another half a year had done to his constitution. He'd been through so much with Bill's confession, attempted suicide, arrest, incarceration, his wife's death, his own testimony in open court against his son. I'd included him often in my daily devotions.

If his body was any indication, James Mereness, Sr. had suffered mightily. He looked like the incarnation of Father Time, walking with difficulty, his gait unsteady. Even Judge Werner showed concern for his well being in saying, "Step forward, please, sir. Watch your step coming up the ramp."

Bill's father was extremely thin. His back was stooped, as if his burdens were indeed pressing him down. His pale skin contrasted sharply with the tans of most other witnesses. His white hair was thin and wispy.

As the elderly Mereness stated and spelled his name for the clerk, his voice was feeble and shaky. His head and arms trembled slightly. *Is that from anxiety or illness?* His was a highly pitiable visage.

DA David O'Leary began his direct examination, "Mr. Mereness, were you married to LaBelle Mereness?"

"Yes."

"How long were you married to LaBelle Mereness?"

"Fifty-one years."

The quiet in the courtroom was palpable.

"And it's my understanding that she passed away on January 2nd of 2003, is that correct?"

His eyes clouded, "Yes."

Damn you Bill Mereness.

"Did you have children with LaBelle?"

"Pardon?" *He's having trouble hearing the gentle tone the DA is using.*

A bit firmer, "Did you have children? Did you and LaBelle have children?"

"Yes."

"How many children did you have?"

"Three."

"And what are their names?"

"William, James and Sallie."

"Is William in court here today?"

"Yes."

"Where is he sitting and what is he wearing?"

The senior Mereness' gaze went to the defense table and he nodded toward it, "He's sitting right there and he's wearing a suit."

This is a very difficult moment. His identification would fit any of the three men at that table.

Judge Werner interceded, "He's right in front of you, sir?"

"Yes."

Werner was in charge, "All right. The record should reflect the witness has identified the defendant."

That shows a tremendous amount of compassion on the part of Judge Werner. What a kind gesture.

The slow, gentle, deliberate questions continued, "And William was born on July 2nd, 1953, is that right?"

Is the DA trying to help the poor man relax? Or is he trying to demonstrate that Bill's father is in possession of his faculties, should Daniel suggest otherwise?

"Yes."

"Does your son wear glasses?"

"Yes."

"How long has he worn glasses?"

"Twenty years."

"What color is you son William's hair?"

"Brown."

"Was your son William married to Jennifer Judge?"

"Yes."

"How long had you known Jennifer Judge?"

"Four years."

"Were you aware that William and Jennifer were going through a divorce?"

"No."

"Your son William never told you that?"

"No."

"And you yourself never spoke to Jennifer about that?"
"That's right."
"Now, at some point, sir, you were made aware of the fact that Jennifer had been killed in her home on November 22nd in 2002?"
"Yes."
"When did you find out about that?"
"It was a Sunday around 11:00, my son Jim called and said Jennifer was dead."
"That would have been the Sunday immediately following her death?"
"Yes."
"After you found out that Jennifer had been killed, when is the next time that you had contact with your son, William?"
"It was about an hour later."
"And what type of contact was that, in person or on the phone?"
"He come to the house."
"Did he tell you why he came up to Appleton?"
"He come to pick up his mail."
"And did you speak with him that day about Jennifer?"
"Yes."
"What did you talk to him about?"
"I, I told him that we knew Jennifer was dead."
"He didn't tell you that?"
"He said that's why he come up, to tell us that."
Sure, right after he picked up his mail.
"Did you discuss any of the circumstances of her death with your son William at that point?"
"No, I did not."
"Did William stay at your house on that Sunday or was this just he stopped by and left?"
"He just picked up his mail and left."
"When is the next time after that Sunday that you had contact either by phone or in person with your son, William?"
"I think he come back Monday."
"And when he came back on Monday did he tell you what his purpose was for coming back?"
"Yes, he said that the Janesville police were harassing him, and he wanted some safe haven to go to."
"So he was coming to stay there with you for a while?"
"Yes."
"How long did he stay with you?"

"Well, it wasn't, it was off and on. He probably slept there two nights and then he would come and go and he didn't stay steady at any time."

"Starting on that Monday when he came there, did you talk about Jennifer or her death at all?"

"No."

"And he came and went. Do you know where he went to when he left your place?"

"Minocqua."

"His cabin up there?"

"Yes."

"And then he would come back to your place?"

"A day later sometimes or the same night at different times."

"I'm going to draw your attention to the morning, Friday morning, of that week. Did you have contact with William that morning?"

"Friday morning?"

"Yes."

"After Thanksgiving?"

"Yes, sir."

"Yes."

Poor poor man. He's trying to be as precise as he can. This has to be unimaginably dreadful.

"He was staying at your house?"

"Yes, he had spent the night there the night before. Thursday night."

"All right. So Friday morning, when is the first time you had contact with William?"

"Well, he, he got up in the morning."

"Do you know what time that was?"

"It was probably 8:00."

"What did he do?"

"Well, he come out and, a little, I don't remember exactly what he done then. But a little later he thought about leaving and taking his car back to Janesville, his rental car back to Janesville."

What's going on here? He can't be going to perjure himself at this point! He must just be confused about the day.

"At some point did you see the defendant in the kitchen retrieving certain items?"

"Yes."

"What did he get from the kitchen?"

"He took what you'd call a butcher knife."

"Backing up a minute. Is there some point you saw your son in the bathroom, you and your wife?"

"That was Thursday morning."

"Okay. Thursday morning?"

"No, it was, wait a minute." *He is confused, poor thing.*

I had an overwhelming desire to jump up and scream at Bill, "See what you've done!"

The senior James Mereness continued, "It was, wasn't that Wednesday morning?"

O'Leary took a gentle approach, "Have you testified, you had to testify about this a while ago, didn't you?"

"Yes."

"Under oath?"

"Yes."

"Sir, I'm going to show you what's been marked as Exhibit 126 and this is a deposition transcript of your previous testimony. And I'm going to ask you to review pages 23 and 24, sir. Can you read and write?"

The witness looked at the document and straightened a bit in his chair, as if he was trying to prove he was still vital enough to accomplish those tasks, "Yes. Okay. It was Friday morning then."

"You had a chance to look at those questions and answers?"

"Yes."

Well done. O'Leary allowed the old fellow to preserve his dignity.

"So, that Friday morning can you tell me what happened when you saw your son that morning?"

"Yes. Friday morning we got up and turned the bathroom light on, and William was sitting in the bathtub with a knife and Saran wrap."

"Was there any water in the tub?"

"No water."

"Was he wearing any clothes?"

"He had sweatpants and a sort of T-shirt on."

It must be so painful to relive that scene.

"Who was in the room when you found your son there?"

"My wife and myself and William."

"Did you ask him what he was doing?"

James Mereness, Sr. checks his previous testimony while testifying against his son for the final time *(Courtesy of The Janesville Gazette)*

"My wife did."
"What did he say?"
"No reply."
"Can you describe the knife that he had?"
"It was a steak knife approximately six to seven inches."
"And you said he had Saran wrap, is that right?"
"Yes."
"Did you ask him what he was doing with the knife and Saran wrap?"

Daniel interrupted, "Objected to as asked and answered. Indicated he did not."

Werner spoke, "I don't think that that's the case. Overruled. You may answer, sir."

"I did not."
"Did your wife?"
"Yes."
"What did the defendant say?"

Daniel wished for the witness' last response to be stricken as hearsay.

The judge ordered it so.

The DA countered, "Your Honor, this is what we were going through before in our motion in limine."

Werner excused the jury.

O'Leary gave his Offer of Proof and Daniel, surprisingly, had no questions or objections.

Judge Werner commandingly made his ruling, "All right, we've gone through this exercise with the second question which was the question Mr. Mereness testified to about you did it or whatever. And I found various reasons to admit it. Found guarantees of, particularized guarantees of trustworthiness for that particular question. Without reiterating the same I'll adopt those findings as it relates to this particular question. I will receive that and I'll overrule the objection and you will have exception and we'll call the jury back in at this time.

The judge advised the jury that the objection had been overruled.

The prosecutor reestablished the scene with Bill in the bathtub and non-responsive to his father's question as to what he was doing. Then the DA asked, "What happened next?"

"Then my wife asked him the question, 'Did you do it?'"
"And what did William say?"
"He replied, 'Yeah, I did it. I done it. Yeah, I done it.'"
"And what happened next?"

"Then we, I told him, well, let's go in the kitchen and talk about it."
"And did you do that?"
"Pardon?"
O'Leary raised his voice a notch but maintained his gentle tone, "Did you do that, go into the kitchen and talk with him?"
"Yes."
"Did he still have the knife and the Saran wrap?"
"No."
"Who had that?"
"My wife took the knife and Saran wrap."
"And you went into the kitchen and talked about it?"
"Yes."
"What did you talk about?"
"We talked about his three options that he had. He stated he didn't want to go to prison. And…"
The DA interrupted then apologized, "I'm sorry, sir. Go ahead."
"They were to go to trial or confess or take your life."
"And you stated he stated he didn't want to go to jail?"
"Jail and or prison, yes."
"Was that when you discussed about going to trial or when you, I'm sorry, when you discussed about confessing?"
"Yes. He had mentioned that."
"Did you talk about anything else?"
"No."
"What did William do after this discussion?"
"He went back to his room."
"How long was he in his room?"
"Probably an hour."
"And what happened? Did he come out of his room eventually?"
"Yes."
"And what happened when he came out of his room?"
"Then he was thinking about leaving, taking his car back to Janesville."
"Did you talk to him?"
"But before he left he, he said he wanted a knife for protection."
"Can you describe the knife you observed him take?"
"I'd call it a butcher knife, probably 12 to 14 inches."
"Sir, I'm going to show you what's been previously marked as Exhibit 115 and ask if you recognize that?"
"Yes."
"Is that the knife?"

"That is it."

"When is the next time you saw your son, William?"

"After he left?"

He's trying so hard to be careful and accurate. Bless his heart.

"Yes, sir."

"It was in the hospital."

"And would that have been the same day?"

"Yes."

"That afternoon?"

"Yes."

"Do you know why he was in the hospital?"

"Yes, he was in an accident."

"I'm sorry sir. Backing up a minute, when he left your house that morning with that knife that you have identified, did he say why he needed the knife?"

"He wanted it for protection."

"Did he say protection from who?"

"No. We asked him that. And he just said protection. We wanted him to give it up; but he didn't want to, so after we talked to him a short time he still took it along."

District Attorney O'Leary had no further questions for Bill's father.

Daniel wasted no time with niceties on cross-examination. "Mr. Mereness, your wife had a history of some mental health issues, is that correct?"

Werner overruled the DA's objection.

The witness never answered the question, because the defense attorney had already posed another, "And do you know what the diagnosis or what the condition was called?"

"Well, it was bi-polar schizophrenic."

"So she had a dual diagnosis. She had both bi-polar disorder and she was schizophrenic, is that correct?"

Schizophrenic? That's the first time I've heard that diagnosis.

"Yes."

"And what would be the symptoms of those conditions?"

The elderly gentleman was getting rattled. "What would be the symptoms?"

"Correct. How, you know, how would they manifest themselves in her conduct?

Oh, the way Daniel phrased that question ought to put the poor fellow at ease.

"It took a period of time to get to where she was and then when she had to go to the hospital. I can't answer the question any better than that."

Doesn't sound like he had a good grasp of her illness, it just sort of "happened".

"When was she first hospitalized for this condition?"

"Back in the 50's."

Dear God, the woman must have suffered mightily.

"All right. And when was she last hospitalized for the mental condition?"

"It was 11 days before Labor Day a year ago."

He sure remembered that specifically. It must have been a real trauma.

"A month and a half before Jennifer's death, correct?"

"I don't know."

"Approximately?"

Judge Werner interceded, "Did you say Labor Day, sir, September?"

"Yes, it was Labor Day that she was discharged."

There was some confusion about dates, but it was finally established that LaBelle had been discharged from the hospital about three months prior to Jennifer's death.

Then Daniel got into medications and treatments. LaBelle had received no medications early on but she regularly saw counselors and doctors. Sometimes the medication seemed to work for a long time; then other times it didn't work, that's when she'd been hospitalized.

The defense attorney asked, "You know the medication she was on in November of last year?"

"She was on Navane and Risperdal."

"Those are antipsychotics, correct?"

"Antidepressants."

He was sure sharp about that difference. Good.

It was next established that over the years LaBelle had been hospitalized about seven times for her mental health issues.

Is this supposed to make the jury think she's unstable? A person who seeks and receives treatment is, generally, in far better shape than someone who denies he or she has a problem! Hopefully, the prosecution will have a mental health professional speak to that.

Daniel finally moved on, "You learned of Jennifer's death from James, Jr., is that correct?"

"Yes."

"Through a telephone call, correct?"

"Yes."

"Sunday afternoon?"
"Yes. Sunday morning."
"Sunday morning?"
"Yeah."
"But he didn't call and say that there might be police around and things. He called and said Jennifer is dead, correct?"
"Yes."

It looks like he's trying to prove that Jim, Jr. lied when he said he hadn't told his parents of Jennifer's death. But with the time of day confusion it's not too clear.

Daniel moved on to Bill's arrival at his parents' home on Monday the 25th, "And he indicated that he came because the Janesville police were harassing him, is that correct?"
"Yes."
"Did he explain to you what he was considered, what he was considering to be harassment?"
"He said that the police followed him to the grocery store and there was a lot of media outside of his apartment and things like that."

Next occurred a brief skirmish over why Bill had gone to his parents' house. O'Leary claimed the question had been asked and answered. Daniel purported he was expanding on the prosecution's questions.

The defense attorney prevailed, "Mr. Mereness, I'll ask the question. Did he tell you why he came home?"

The witness showed a bit of fire was still in the old house, "I just stated that he said the Janesville police were harassing him."

Daniel moved along. "...Your daughter followed this situation by reading *The Janesville Gazette* on the Internet, correct?"

O'Leary objected due to speculation.

The defense attorney tacked on, "If you know?" which apparently made things kosher.

"I don't know."
"She talked about the case, didn't she?"
Another objection.
Another "If you know?" added on.
"I don't know."

He's not helping the defense out one iota.

"You were present when Detective Goth from the police department came on the 27th, isn't that correct?"
"I don't know."

I'm detecting a pattern here.

"There were arguments between James, Jr. and William, isn't that correct?"

"I wasn't present."

"Did you tell that to the detective, either Captain Helein or..."

The witness cut across the attorney, "No, I did not."

"You didn't tell that to Detective Goth?"

"No."

Is this what they refer to as "badgering the witness"?

"The fact is that there were arguments between Jim, Jr., and William, during William's stay, isn't that correct?"

Finally, O'Leary spoke up, "Objection, Your Honor, asked and answered." Werner ruled, "Sustained. No, he said he didn't know. Sustained."

Daniel continued anyway, "Are you saying there weren't or are you saying you don't recall?"

"Can you repeat the question?"

"Sure. You understand the underlying question that I'm asking you whether there were arguments..."

"Your Honor?" O'Leary objected again.

The judge spoke, "Well, it has been asked and answered. Rephrase your question."

Most of the jurors were wearing frowns or scowls.

It doesn't seem like a wise tactic to appear to be picking on this fragile old man.

Daniel plunged ahead, "Are you saying that there weren't conflicts or are you saying that you don't remember whether or not there were?"

"I wasn't aware that there was conflict."

Daniel picked up a document and showed it to the witness. It was a transcript of Bill's father's previous testimony.

The defense attorney quoted, "'At that point again when he came to live with you, thereafter, did you discuss Jennifer's death at all with your son, William?' You answered 'No.' Next question was: 'Did you hear William make any comments at all about Jennifer's death?' and your answer was 'No.' Do you recall those answers to Mr. O'Leary's questions?"

"That's my testimony, yes."

Daniel moved on to page 27, line 19. It was about the scene in the bathroom. The defense attorney asked, "You were an observer to this alleged conversation, correct? You didn't participate in it?"

"I did not ask the question."

He's plenty sharp right now.

"And when Bill started his answer, you interjected that you didn't want to hear about this and you left, isn't that correct?"

"Yes."

Just because he was leaving the room doesn't mean he didn't hear the answer!

Next the defense attorney referenced the transcript from the preliminary hearing. He was trying to prove that Bill's father had, indeed, obtained information about Jennifer's murder from *The Janesville Gazette*.

The DA wished to be heard so the jury was excused.

The opposing counsel cited various references in the transcript. The prosecution purported that if the defense "starts tap dancing down here", they could ask a whole line of questions about the pipe incident and other information from the newspaper. Daniel insisted he was only concerned directly on the issue of whether Bill's father was or was not receiving information.

Judge Werner cautioned the defense, "I understand you're trying to impeach his credibility, but I think it opens up that whole line of questioning."

"Withdraw the question. We'll get on to something else."

Hurrah!

Daniel gave it one last try. He referred to page 72 line 9. "Mr. O'Leary is asking you these questions. Question: 'Did your son discuss with you anything about his concerns about going to prison?' Answer: 'He mentioned that he didn't want to go to prison, yes.' Question: 'Didn't want to go to prison why?' Answer: 'He didn't discuss why. Strike that answer. We didn't discuss why, but...'Question: 'Well, let me ask. You discussed he didn't want to go to prison. Was it for killing Jennifer?' Answer: 'No, he never said any of those words, no.' Do you recall those questions and those answers being given?"

"Yes."

"That's all I have. Mr. Mereness. Thank you very much."

On redirect, O'Leary was able to clean a few things up.

First, it was established that while LaBelle had a history of mental health issues, she had been on her medication at the time of Jennifer's death, and she had been functioning well.

Second, O'Leary reviewed the bathroom scene one more time. "You heard her ask the question and you heard Bill's answer in that bathroom, correct?"

"Yes."

"How old are you, sir?"

"Seventy-nine."

Oh, dear God, he's younger than my dad! He looks 90, poor thing.

"And despite your age, do you have any major health problems?"

"No."

"When your son stated in the bathroom that he did it, to your wife, Mr. Daniel asked you if you turned around and walked out of the room, is that correct?"

"Well, I interrupted at that point and said I didn't want to hear any more."

"Why?"

"Because I didn't want to have to testify against him."

"I have nothing further in this matter, Your Honor."

On recross, Daniel tried to regain the advantage over the bathroom scene by insisting the elder Mereness had not heard Bill's answer because he'd left the room. The witness stood by his testimony. He was not to be shaken from it.

The defendant's father was released. He walked haltingly out of the courtroom.

Court was in lunch recess.

At 1:36 p.m. we were back in session. There were a number of exhibits to be received by the judge, then the jury was seated.

Mr. O'Leary addressed the court, "Your Honor…the State would be resting at this time."

That's it. Our case has been presented. Please let it be strong enough to withstand anything that might come up in the defense!

39

There was no break, no time for us to discuss, as the Court plunged ahead with the business at hand.

Werner announced that there was "something" to be taken up without the jury; they were excused.

Daniel immediately renewed his motion for a mistrial.

Really? I can't even remember why he'd made the second mistrial motion.

The defense attorney continued, "And I would move for dismissal of the information on the grounds that the State has failed to establish by evidence the basis upon which a rational jury could find Mr. Mereness guilty beyond a reasonable doubt."

Honestly? When his own father related his confession? Is this standard procedure in these cases or is he serious?

Naturally, the DA was opposed to both requests. O'Leary was sure there was more than enough evidence for the State to have met their threshold burden.

Judge Werner was decisive and thorough. It was almost comedic that none of the principals could recall what the mistrial motion had been about. At any rate, the judge generalized, "It does not appear that there's an appropriate basis for mistrial to be granted for anything that's occurred in this particular trial up to this point."

As for the request for dismissal, Werner nicely summarized the prosecution's case and pronounced the evidence sufficient. He moved the proceedings along, "So the motion is denied. Of course you have exception. Are we ready to proceed with witnesses for you, then, Mr. Daniel?"

"Yes, Your Honor."

As the jury returned the first witness for the defense was called. Beth Goodenbour, blond, bespectacled and middle-aged, was sworn in and seated.

Ms. Goodenbour was employed by the Oneida County Planning and Zoning Office as a secretary.

Daniel guided the witness through the history of the septic system of the Minocqua home. A permit had been granted in December of 1998, the installation had been completed and, on May 6,1999, the system had been approved for use.

The defense attorney inquired, "Is there an ordinance in Oneida County that requires a periodic pumping of a septic?"

"There is."

The records showed that the Minoqua septic was pumped on September 10, 2001. There were no other records of maintenance, renovation or pumping of that septic system.

The direct examination was over.

Was this supposed to show that the pumping of the system in the winter of 2003 was routine and had been done to satisfy a county ordinance? That would be a very tight ordinance, just a year and a half between pumpings. Our ordinance requires the procedure to be done every three years. Besides, I don't know anyone who would have such routine work be done in the winter.

O'Leary had caught on. He asked Ms. Goodenbour what the Oneida County ordinance required in terms of septic pumping.

"Every three years."

"And you said it was pumped on September 10th of '01?"

"Yes."

"So it would be due to be pumped by September 10th of '04?"

"Yes."

Hmm, nice try.

The next witness for the defense was Candy Arts. Ms. Arts was an attractive woman. She was tall and she wore her frosted blond hair in an upswept style. The witness appeared to be in her late 30's and was sharply dressed in a white, square- necked top and long, dark skirt.

It was established that Ms. Arts and her husband were the owners of A-1 Septic Service and Insulation. They serviced the Minoqua area. Ms. Arts testified that she had received a call from the defendant in April. She did not recall exactly what Mr. Mereness' request had been as it had been an extremely busy time in their office.

Daniel had the witness refer to the transcript of the deposition she had given on June 30th. From page 12, line 20, Daniel read his original question, "And what do you recall about that contact?"

Ms. Arts' response had been, "Just a person calling and saying that they were having problems with their septic."

The defense attorney was done with the transcript. He addressed the witness, "Was the nature of the problem indicated by Mr. Mereness?"

"The nature of the problem was he wasn't sure what was happening but something was wrong with his septic."

"And that's all he told you, correct?"

"Correct."

"Were a lot of people having trouble with their septics in your service area at that time?"

"Yes, they were."

"And for what reason, do you know?"

"Because of a lack of snow cover there was not adequate insulation and the septic drain fields were freezing so peoples' houses were being treated as holding tanks. They had no way of getting it from their house to the field."

"And what are the symptoms, I guess, of that problem?"

"The fixtures in the bathroom, you are unable to flush your toilets. There was some septic backing up into the home through floor drains in the basement. It was not able to leave the house."

"Did you provide service to Mr. Mereness?"

"Yes, we did."

In a long question and answer session it was determined that one of the A-1 septic trucks had been dispatched to pump Bill's septic. The truck already had two loads of effluent on it when the driver arrived at the Minocqua cabin. After pumping Bill's tank, the effluent was spread on one of the fields that the company owned.

Okay, so it's possible his septic was frozen. Nevertheless, the police found latex gloves and towels in the field, items highly unlikely to be flushed down a toilet under normal circumstances.

The defense attorney continued, "Later were you contacted by anyone else concerning that same septic?"

"I believe I did get some phone calls regarding it, but I can't really recall."

"From the Oneida County Sheriff's Department or Janesville?"

Is he leading the witness?

"Yes, I think they did call."

Daniel had no further questions for this witness; Folts declined to cross-examine Ms. Arts.

The defense called Thomas H. Arts.

Mr. Arts, who looked about 40 years old, had dark hair and a moustache. He wore a navy blue polo shirt.

Mr. Arts, as I suspected, was the co-owner of A-1 Septic. With an obvious pride of proprietorship, he told the Court that in his business they installed, serviced, maintained and pumped septic systems.

The witness confirmed that one of his employees had pumped a septic on East Pier Lake Road.

For goodness sake, we know that already. Is this now the "Septic Defense"? We've had the "Random Burglar", "Looking for Mr. Goodbar" and "Dog Poop" defenses, now this. Thank goodness Judge Werner explained what "reasonable" doubt is.

Mr. Arts went on to explain how certain septic fields were chosen for use and how Bill's effluent ended up at field 4-B. "There is really no particular area that it services. It's how it fits into a route. You might pick up a tank in Eagle River and be going to Tomahawk and go by B-4 and drop the effluent there. So there is really no particular area you would go."

The businessman then told the court that he'd owned A-1 for three and a half years and had used 4-B as a discharge field that entire time. Arts also estimated that 4-B had been used about four or five years prior to his ownership.

Mr. Daniel wondered, "Is there any way to estimate how many loads of how many...?"

"How many gallons?"

"...Pump-outs have been pumped on to that plot?"

"Not really how many tanks, but I could give you an idea of how many gallons. By code would you like me..."

"Please."

"By code we are able to put 39,000 gallons per acre per year. Last year we didn't use the entire field. It averaged out approximately 35,000 gallons per acre for the last year."

That's a lot of, umm, effluent. I don't think I'd want to live near one of those fields. And yet, they found only two latex gloves and a couple of towels. Interesting.

Mr. Arts then testified that he had been contacted by the Oneida County Sheriff or the Janesville Police Department toward the end of April. He'd examined the septic tank as required by a search warrant.

"What was your understanding of that purpose?"

"Basically, what I was told was to enter this tank with life support and look for basically anything that was in the tank. I really wasn't given particulars on what I might find, but that's basically what I did is we broke the ice, pumped the tank, put on life support, went in and searched it."

"Had lighting?"

"I used a flashlight, yes, big flashlight."

"And when you, explain that, the pumping out operation. You took the hose down in there and you got the corners and crevices with the hose, correct?"

The witness was very detailed. "Yes. First thing you do when you pump it over we had the truck there. And we had to take the cover off. Take it off, break the ice. There was a lot of ice in that tank. Pump out all the clear effluent with the pump truck where it goes through a four-inch hose into a truck. Once all the liquid is pumped out or the majority of the liquid is pumped out then what I had to do was break up the remainder of the ice, put a ladder in. Like I say, life support, flashlight, go in and search the tank, yes."

"Life support is necessary because..."

"Because of the hazardous fumes."

Ah, must have been lovely for those standing around without life support.

"And how long were you in that tank looking for whatever?"

"I would approximate between 20 minutes and a half-hour."

"How big is a tank?"

"Thousand gallon, approximately."

Mr. Arts explained that the tank was cylindrical in shape and about ten feet long, six feet wide and four and a half to five feet high.

The defense attorney was astounded, "You got in that?"

"Yes."

So this witness was a hero? Or were the police fools for requesting such a search?

Virginia Schuettpelz, who was a clinical therapist on a crisis team in Outagamie County, was the next defense witness. She had worked in that capacity since 1991. Ms. Schuettpelz appeared to be in her 50's and had a somewhat matronly figure. Her brown hair was short, and she wore a brown print jacket over a beige top and black pants.

Ms. Schuettpelz had impressive credentials, having worked in the mental health field since 1966 and holding a Master's degree from St. Louis University.

Folts agreed that the witness was an expert as to evaluating on a crisis team and providing psychotherapy, "but nothing beyond that".

Daniel began, "Do you know William Mereness?"

"Yes, I do."

"And how is it that you came to know him?"

"I was on call the day that we received a call from the Appleton Police Department and I was summonsed to Appleton Medical Center to evaluate his status."

Ms. Schuettpelz had been called on the 29th of November, 2002.

"Would you tell the jury your observations?"

"I was able to view him. However, I was not able to speak with him because he was in a coma-like state."

"And what, could you describe what that is?"

"He was unresponsive, unable to speak."

"Was he able to take direction?"

"No, no."

Or was he playing 'possum?

"Was he attached to various medical apparatus?"

"At that time he was."

"When is the next time, if ever, you saw him?"

"On the 2nd of December, 2002."

"And why that particular day?"

"At that time it was felt that he may be clear enough that I could talk to him and assess his status."

"And what was the process for making that assessment?"

"The process is because of the head injury I was concerned whether he was still not stable, and I asked him to subtract in digits of 7 and I also gave him three words to remember and he was to repeat them to me at a later time in our conversation."

Whoa. I hope I never have to take that test, I'd probably flunk for sure!

"Was he able to subtract in digits of 7?"

"No."

"What is that?"

"That will test if your memory is good or, you know, and your concentration. If you can't subtract your concentration is poor."

Or you're bad at mental subtraction.

"And then what was the giving the three words designed to do?"

"Again, that tests memory and the recall."

The witness indicated that on that day Bill had not seemed oriented as to time, place and event. However, he did seem to understand why he was in the hospital and why Ms. Schuettpelz was there. Since Bill was not a "good reporter" at that time, the witness did nothing further.

The crisis worker saw Bill again the next day. She described her experience, "On December 3, I thought he was doing better. He had more affect, or in lay terms, he was able to respond appropriately to what we were talking about. He had talked about wanting cookies from his mother. And we were able to talk about whether he was suicidal, depressed, at that time."

"Did you draw any conclusion?"

"At the time that I spoke with him he was not suicidal. He had plans of taking the children on a trip which indicates he has a future direction."

"Did you attempt to discuss with him the circumstances that brought him to the hospital?"

"We just discussed that he was in an accident. He had informed me that his wife had died. And so the accident was what brought him in."

"Did you ask him about whether he had a memory of the accident or immediately preceding events."

"He did not have a lot of memory regarding the accident. Prior events I did not ask."

"Do you advise the Appleton Police Department on the filing of what we call 51.15 petitions and, apparently, you call them 72 hour somethings?"

"Yes, we do advise them. They are the ones that have the ultimate decision in actually implementing that detention."

The witness explained that the police had not implemented the detention on December 3rd. Her advice to them had been that Bill was not suicidal and that he was in a safe setting.

Daniel probed further, "As I understand the 51.15 test, it's a threat to yourself or others?"

"That's correct."

"So, did you address that issue?"

"That's correct. And when that incident happened of the accident, he was also possibly under the influence of drugs and alcohol. Therefore, that makes it difficult to assess if it's a mental problem or not."

Wow, she just helped out the prosecution. They'd tried to get in information about drugs or alcohol with Captain Helein's testimony and couldn't. How ironic!

"No, I'm talking about you determined that he was not, strike that. 51.15 requires evidence of some mental disturbance plus being a threat to yourself or to others, correct?"

"Correct."

"You indicated you did not believe because of the setting and the other factors we discussed that he was not a danger to himself, correct?"

"Correct."

"What about the other prong of that test. Whether he was a danger to others?"

"At that time he was not. He was in a somewhat secured environment."

"He was under guard, right?"

"Right."

What is all of this supposed to mean? It doesn't seem to even address that Bill hadn't committed the murder. The fact that he was under guard indicated police harassment? I don't get it.

Daniel spoke, "Thank you. That's all I have, ma'am."

Ms. Schuettpelz stood up as if to leave.

Werner intervened, "Ma'am, you can just have a seat. I'll let you know."

The witness blushed scarlet and sat down, eyes lowered.

Folts handled the cross-examination.

The crisis team member had spoken with the police officers that had brought Bill to the hospital.

"You spoke with Officer Pynenberg?"

"Yes."

"And you were also aware that there had been an indication that he had been drinking?"

"Yes."

The door to this line of questioning had been opened by the defense, I don't think he can stop it now.

"There was also an indication that he had induced other drugs, correct?"

"Correct."

"And were you aware of what those drugs might be?"

"No, I was not because that was already confiscated by the police officers."

"You were aware that he had rammed his automobile into a steel building in the Northside industrial park?"

"Yes, I was."

"Were you aware that he had injuries to his wrists?"

"I believe I was aware of that some time during the course of the three times I met him."

"Now on the second time that you met him, December 2nd of 2002, during that assessment he stated that he never had any psychological problems, didn't he?"

"Yes, he did."

"And he also stated that he had not been depressed nor was he depressed that day, correct?"

"Correct."

"And it's at that time that he reported that he was planning on taking his children to Cancun, correct?"

"Yes."

"And he stated he had been depressed because of a divorce, correct?"

"Yes."

Wait, I thought he'd just told Schuettpelz he hadn't been depressed?

"He never stated that he was depressed because he was being surveilled by the police, did he?"

"No, he did not."

"And then when you spoke to him on December 3rd of 2002, you explained to him that you could provide ongoing therapy, correct?"

"Correct."

"And he stated that he didn't need ongoing therapy at that point?"

"That's correct."

"And you assessed that he was not suffering from a mental, major mental illness at that time, correct?"

"Correct."

"But you felt that he may become a further suicide risk due to the hearings regarding his wife's death, correct?"

"Correct."

Under redirect Ms. Schuettpelz told the court that Bill had told her that his brother had been "rather threatening" to him and that he was concerned about that. She also testified that Bill had indicated that if the need for therapeutic services arose he would seek them.

Werner made it clear the witness was free to go.

This witness offered nothing to exonerate Bill, good.

At that point, Pat Judge, who had been sitting on my right at the end of the row on the aisle, whispered to me that she had to take a break. I took that to mean she would be back shortly.

Next up for the defense was Richard Astin. He was well-dressed in a green shirt and pants. His hair as well as his moustache was mainly brown, with some invading gray.

Mr. Astin was a property appraiser for the City of Janesville's assessor's office. As such he was often out in the city as he had been on Friday, November 22, 2002.

That day, Astin was in the vicinity of Sandstone and Wuthering Hills, covering new construction on Windmill Drive. He observed a car backed into the dead end on Windmill Drive, which was a couple of blocks north of Sandstone Drive. Behind the car, a male walked into the brush with a hard case such as a bow case or gun case.

The witness reported his observations to the police because it seemed "out of place" for the man to be wearing sweatpants and just walk into the brush around 1:00 in the afternoon. Astin did not recall the color of the man's sweatpants.

So here was our random burglar! And the police had been notified of him on that very day! The implication was obvious; the JPD mishandled the case to the detriment of Bill.

Under cross-examination Folts had Mr. Astin mark on the map where the car had been and where the individual had walked. The appraiser explained that the area the man had walked into had an old windmill and brushy fields.

Folts inquired, "So it's a field, vacant? You didn't see him heading in a southerly direction towards Sandstone?"

"No sir."

"And they were carrying what you would describe as bow case or gun case?"

"Yes, hard exterior case.

"Didn't see a hatchet?"

"No.

"Didn't see a maul?"

"No, sir."

"Are there occasionally deer in that area?"

"Yes, sir."

"This would have been around the deer hunting season, in fact, probably the last day of bow season before gun season started, correct?"

"It would have been hunting season. I am not sure when the season ends."

Since there were no further questions, the witness was directed to step down.

Just then a man I had known since childhood, and who worked for the DA's office, hustled down the aisle and sat heavily down in Pat's vacated seat.

I turned to him and said as politely as I could, "Oh, I'm sorry, I'm saving that seat for a member of the victim's family."

He turned to me, face flushed, eyes narrowed and hissed, "I don't give a shit who's sitting here, my daughter's testifying."

I was blown away. Of all the ways he could have responded to me, he'd chosen to be angry and defiant. *Why? Was I the enemy here?*

The defense called Elizabeth Carpenter. Libby had been a student of mine and I had known she was a neighbor of Jennifer's on Columbus Circle. The curvaceous, brown-haired girl approached the stand.

It was established that Libby had, indeed, been a neighbor of Jennifer's, and Jennifer had also been her teacher.

The witness had also met Bill and was familiar with Christopher.

On a Saturday in late September of 2002, Libby had helped Jennifer move.

"And who else was there during the moving process?"

"Jenny Podgorski and Nick Holder."

"And was Mr. Mereness there?"

"No."

"Was Chris there?"

"No."

"Weren't they filling up a U-Haul Truck?"

"They filled up the U-Haul; but the day that we unloaded the truck, they were not there."

"You were there for both ends of that, right?"

"Yes."

"So you helped load up at Columbus Circle?"

"Yes."

"Going to talk about when you loaded up."

"Okay."

"All right. Did there, was some discussion about an axe you had, right?"

I almost laughed out loud. *It's a good thing Josh isn't here, he probably would have.* Daniel had asked the question in the same way the Star Wars character Yoda talked. It was a running family joke whenever someone misspoke in that way.

It's so strange the way these things pop into my head at such a serious moment. Therapist Schuettpelz would probably have a field day with me.

"Yes."

"Could you describe what that axe was?"

"It was large, very big."

"Like three feet?"

"Right."

"So it wasn't a hatchet?"

"No."

O'Leary interjected, "Your Honor, I would object to the leading form of the question."

Werner sustained the objection. *About time.*

The defense attorney continued, "I'm going to show you what's been marked as Exhibit 40 for purposes of this trial. Did you see that?"

"No."

"Maul at all?"

"No."

"During the loading process?"

"No."

"Did you ever see Chris Mereness handle that maul during the loading process?"

"No."

"To your knowledge have you ever seen that maul before in your life?"

"No."

"Going to show you what's been marked as Exhibit 39. This is not the axe you were referring to, right?"

"No."

"All right. And what would distinguish this from the axe that was at the Columbus property?"

"It's smaller. That is way smaller." She pointed to the exhibit before her.

"This could be described as a..."

The witness interrupted, "Hatchet."

"And at any time during the loading process on Columbus, excuse me, did you see the hatchet that is Exhibit 39?"

"No."

"At any time did you see Chris Mereness or Bill Mereness handle that hatchet or anything similar to that hatchet?"

"No."

How did Daniel find out about Libby helping Jennifer move? Surely, she wouldn't have come forward to offer her services for the defense of Jennifer's murderer?

DA O'Leary began the cross-examination, "As I understand it, you loaded all the items on the truck on one day?"

"Yes."

It was re-established that Bill, Chris, Jennifer, Nick, Jenny and the witness had all been loading items onto the truck. Then Libby admitted that she, herself, had not handled all the items that had been put on the truck. Nor had she observed everything that the others had handled.

The prosecutor wanted to know if Jennifer had any tools.

She had.

"Was she handy with tools?"

"No, she..."

O'Leary interrupted, "She used them?"

Libby looked tearful. Her voice had a catch, "She never knew when she would need them, she said."

Jennifer had been dispensing advice, that teacher in her coming out.

Jennifer's Justice

The witness was not aware if Jennifer had owned a toolbox; she'd never seen one.

The unloading of the truck at Jennifer's had occurred after school. The three students had helped move items, including dressers and other large items. Most of her belongings had been placed in the garage, but the kids had gone into the house with some possessions. They'd been in the living room, kitchen and bedrooms. They'd opened and shut doors in their movements throughout the house.

I know where this is going.

"Were you wearing gloves?"

"No."

"Were Nick or Jenny wearing gloves?"

'No.'

Aha, more sources for identifiable but unidentified fingerprints! And the defense had served them up.

On re-direct, Daniel seemed to be going for damage control.

"Were there, you indicated that there was some joking around about the axe?"

"Yes."

"And who was joking around about it?"

"All four of us. Jenny, Nick, me and Jennifer."

"What was the joke of it?"

"'Cuz since it was going we figured it was just going to be her living there. She told us the situation. And I said something like, 'What do you need an axe for?' And she said, 'You never know when a girl is going to need an axe.'"

How ironic in a very sad way. Most of the family members looked down into their laps.

Libby was excused. Her father departed abruptly.

Daniel next called Jenny Podgorski, another one of the students who had helped Jennifer move. She, too, had known Jennifer as a neighbor and as a teacher.

The young lady's testimony was mostly a repetition of Libby's. The only notable difference was that Jenny did not recall any joking about the axe.

So his other witness had been lying?

Jenny was excused.

Daniel requested a break, which was granted for 15 minutes.

Gathered in the hallway, we discussed the lack of real value any of the defense witnesses had been thus far. It seemed that Daniel had made better points in some of his cross-examinations of the prosecution's witnesses.

Either the bailiff or Shelly came over to tell Cathy she would be the next witness for the defense.

Everyone stroked Cathy's arms or patted her back, preparing her for her walk into the lion's den. We were all still completely befuddled as to why she was being called by the defense. Cathy was visibly nervous. Her face was pale; her lips were tight. I imagined her mouth was about as dry as if someone had stuffed it full of cotton balls.

Poor woman. Why should she have to endure this? The anxiety has had to be building ever since she received her subpoena. The murder of one's sister wasn't enough? I cursed Bill one more time, but this time I added a curse for his attorney.

Everyone returned to the courtroom in wretched anticipation.

My beautiful and elegant, but oh so sad, sister-in-law walked to the stand.

Daniel began, "Where do you live?"

"619 Sunset Drive in Janesville."

She's very poised. I hope she holds up if he gets nasty.

"You're Jennifer Judge's sister, correct?"

"Yes, I am."

"And following her death did the police ask you to go over to the house?"

"What house?"

She's on her game! There'll be no fooling her.

"The house on Sandstone."

"They called me on an evening to come over to the house, yes."

"And what did they ask you to do?"

"Just walk through the home to see if I noticed anything was missing."

"And you noticed a number of things missing, isn't that correct?"

"Yes."

"Would you tell the jury what was missing?"

"There was a China cabinet in the dining room and there were two Lladro statues that were missing off that cabinet."

Daniel made a move to ask another question, Cathy paused. The defense attorney must have thought better of it because he said, "I'm sorry. Finish."

"I also searched for some expensive pieces of jewelry that I knew Jennifer had and I could not find them."

"Anything else missing to your observation?"

"No."

It's pretty doubtful that a random burglar would know the value of statues made in Spain and yet miss taking a purse sitting in plain view.

"You also went up to the Minocqua property, is that correct?"

"That's correct."

"And, again, they kind of asked you to check the place, see if there was anything unusual?"

"We did that as part of the estate to secure the house."

Well said.

"You're the personal, you are a co-personal representative with your brother of the estate, is that correct?"

"That's correct."

"And when you were up in Minocqua you found a pair of Mr. Mereness' glasses, is that correct?"

"That's correct."

"And they were found in the drawer next to the bed in the master bedroom, is that correct?"

"That's right."

"And you gave those to the Janesville Police Department?"

"Yes."

"Do you recall when you did that?"

My sister-in-law looked thoughtful. "I believe it was, we were out there on December 31st. It was probably January 2nd or 3rd."

"Also, in your role as personal representative you are aware of the prenuptial agreement of the marital property agreement, isn't that correct?"

"Yes."

"Has the estate taken a position, or have you as personal representative, on whether or not that agreement is valid or not valid?"

Folts objected due to relevance. He was overruled.

"No."

Well they certainly had an opinion, but they hadn't taken any legal position as yet, thank goodness.

Daniel was finished with my brother's wife. He had been remarkably gentlemanly in his treatment of her.

In his cross-examination Folts asked, "You don't know when the two Lladros that you observed missing were removed from that China cabinet, do you?"

"No, I do not."

"Prior to November 22nd of last year, when was the last time you were in your sister's home?"

"Probably late October. We helped move some furniture down to the basement."

More fingerprints!

"So at least three weeks?"

"Yes."

Cathy was allowed to rejoin her family. Everyone surreptitiously congratulated her on a job well done. We were careful so as not to arouse the ire of the bailiff. We hadn't had any scoldings of late and wanted to keep it that way.

Daniel got the judge's attention, "Judge, I think we need…"

Werner finished the defense attorney's statement, "Need to be heard outside the presence of the jury?"

"Yes."

The panel was excused.

First, we had some tidying up of the status of various exhibits.

Second, Judge Werner addressed the defendant directly, "All right, Mr. Mereness, I'm going to ask you certain questions at this point in time that relate to your right to testify or your right not to testify. If you have any trouble understanding me or hearing me, please interrupt me, all right? You'll do that?"

Bill's voice was well controlled, "Yes, I will."

Werner began, "Have you had an opportunity to talk to Mr. Daniel about your right to testify or your right not to testify?"

"Yes, I have."

"And you understand you do have a right to testify?"

"Yes, I do."

"Do you understand you also have an absolute right not to testify?"

"Yes, I do."

"And have you had enough time to talk to Mr. Daniel about your choice either to testify or not to testify?"

"Yes, I have."

"And he's explained to you what those options entail?"

"Yes."

I realized I was sitting on the edge of my seat, shoulders hunched in anticipation.

"And what they might mean or not mean for your case?"

"Yes."

"Do you feel you've had enough time to talk to Mr. Daniel about that decision?"

"Yes, I do."

"And has anyone promised you so that you would give up your right to testify?"

"No, they have not."

"And you're doing that freely and voluntarily?"

"Yes, I am."

"Has anybody forced you or threatened you so that you will not testify?"

"No, they have not."

"And do you, it is your right, then, not to testify?"

"Yes, it is."

"And, again, you've had enough time to talk to Mr. Daniel about that decision?"

"Yes, I have."

"And do you understand that if you are convicted, and there is an appeal filed, that your waiver of your right to testify most likely will not be an appeal issue?"

"Yes, I do."

Judge Werner then asked the same questions of Bill's counsel, with the same resulting answers.

Werner proclaimed, "All right. I will find that Mr. Mereness is waiving his right to testify freely and voluntarily, knowingly and intelligently. That he understands that he does have the right to testify. He understands he has an absolute right not to testify and that he has had sufficient time to confer with counsel about that particular decision. So with that, the defense has rested. Then we can bring in the jury and I can excuse them until Monday, counsel?"

Opposing attorneys agreed.

The panel was brought back in at 3:50 p.m.

The judge addressed them, "All right. Ladies and gentlemen, the defense has rested at this point in time. And with that I think it's an appropriate time to take a break, and we will reconvene on Monday at 8:30.

"Try to get some rest. Please don't talk about this matter amongst yourselves or with anyone else. And with that then court is in recess for today. Thank you. That will be the last time I get you up and down today."

Out went the jury.

Werner explained for the record that counsel had indicated a willingness to have an informal discussion about instructions yet that afternoon. Then, Monday they could proceed quickly as the judge and attorneys would have their formal conference regarding jury instructions.

We left the courtroom. All were a bit shocked at the lack of a solid defense put forth. Not that we believed Bill was innocent, nor did we have any ideas or inclination as to how he could be made to look so. It was fine with us.

40

Sunday was more of a day of reflection and work than of rest. But it was very welcome.

I had a lot to catch up on around the house: laundry, cleaning, mowing. There were groceries to buy and friends to call. I also needed to visit my mom at the nursing home.

My dad agreed to join Josh and me for dinner at our house. We planned for him to come out around 5:00. We'd have an easy meal of burgers and potatoes on the grill.

While I went about my tasks, I thought a great deal about the trial. It had been a whirlwind six days.

The case against Bill seemed strong, but I was still filled with anxiety about what the jury would decide. Since I had so much more information than they had, it was difficult to know how things looked from the perspective of what they'd been allowed to see and hear in court. Ever since the O.J. Simpson trial, I'd felt no case was open and shut.

It seemed to me that Bill had done an exceptional job in leaving nothing to tie him to the scene; no hair, fingerprints or anything that might have yielded DNA. He'd worn a hood so as to hide his identity from eyewitnesses. Likewise, he'd cleaned himself up thoroughly and gotten rid of anything that might have had Jennifer's blood on it. Given the amount of blood there must have been at the scene, that could not have been an easy task. He had planned well and carried out that plan effectively.

It appeared though, that he had not factored in the way that traffic and cell phone use could be tracked.

The microscopic shards of glass represented the teeniest of slip-ups, but would not have been irrefutable evidence on their own.

But the biggest reason Bill was on trial was he, himself. He'd fallen apart, briefly. The aloof, cool, composed veneer had cracked. *That must be plaguing him mightily.* Could he accept the fact that he'd caused his own downfall? I didn't think so.

In order to keep his sanity he'd have to have worked up a way to fool himself into thinking someone else was to blame. Perhaps he blamed his parents for revealing his confession.

He might have blamed his brother for refusing to be his patsy and his alibi. No doubt he blamed Christopher and Sallie, as well, for refusing to stand by him, thus causing him to melt down. Certainly, the police had been out to blame and possibly even frame him from the beginning. They'd harassed him and pushed him to attempt suicide.

I marveled at how all the evidence had been ferreted out by the police and sheriffs who investigated the case. They'd done a remarkable job.

I thought, too, about the way the case was presented. The District Attorney's office had done an excellent job of laying down the pieces of the circumstantial puzzle, from the clerk at Scheels where Bill had bought the coat to his boss and her explanation of his varied work week, it all added up.

Ironically, Jennifer's relatives had opened and closed the testimony. My brother had been the first witness for the State and Jennifer's sister had been the last witness for the defense.

While I thought the various authorities involved had done a fantastic job, it seemed natural for me to wonder if there seemed to be any ways the case could have been stronger. Clearly, had LaBelle's testimony been captured on videotape before she died, that would have had a huge impact on the jury. Had the police thought to check the septic system at the Minocqua house before Bill had it pumped in April, it would have made the gloves and towels irrefutably his. It seemed clear that Bill must have dumped all the clothes he'd been wearing when he committed the crime. If those could somehow have been found, it would have been extremely damning. I wondered if the police had checked the dumpsters at the way station near Westfield where Bill alleged he had stopped. I'd never heard about that. More likely he'd hidden the clothes in his "box of laundry" and then dumped them somewhere in the northwoods in the middle of the night the Saturday after the murder. In that case they would have been nearly impossible to find.

Visiting my mom was difficult. She cried and begged me to get her out of there. She was angry and frightened. All I could do was try to soothe her by saying that her stay could be short if she worked hard on her therapy and regained enough strength to be able to function safely at home. Though I felt I was probably building up false hope. My heart was heavy when I left her.

After I got home I had a little time before my dad arrived for dinner. While there were still tasks I hadn't accomplished, I decided to give them over for a quick ride on my horse, Rose. I needed to do something completely enjoyable. I decided to ride her bareback; it would be faster, cooler for her and I'd feel more connected with her. I put on her halter and lead rope and as politely as I could, hoisted myself onto her back. We rode leisurely around the pasture, following the fence lines. At the far end of the pasture I stopped to let her eat grass. While her head was down I laid my chest down on her withers, my face in her mane. I extended my arms and hugged her about the shoulders.

Josh, Dad and I had a pleasant enough meal, though much of the discussion was about Mom and the trial. I filled my dad in on Jeff's activities out West, and Josh amused us with tales from his summer job doing outdoor maintenance for the school district.

After dinner I called some friends to catch them up on the trial. Everyone expressed concern for the family's welfare and wished us good fortune in the upcoming verdict.

I spent a good deal of time on the phone with Jeff. He brought me up to speed on his reunion week activities. His voice sounded happy as he related stories of old friends and old times. I was so glad he'd gone. Though I had missed him terribly, he shouldn't have had to forgo such a wonderful opportunity because of Bill's heinous act.

Jeff filled me in on his plan for returning home. He'd leave Cheyenne in the morning and drive as far as our friends' house in Sibley, Iowa. That should allow him to be home about mid-day on Tuesday. I told him I was hopeful we would have a verdict by then.

My husband commiserated with me on trial happenings and understood how I was full of hopeful anticipation and dread at the same time. Monday was looming large.

41

On what we hoped would be our final day of the trial the courtroom had a different appearance. There were two podiums directly in front of us that faced toward the jury. Beyond the podiums was a long table filled with the evidence that had been presented in the case: photographs, clothing, the screen, shoes, the weapons. Several easels held the various large maps that had been referred to in the case.

Judge Werner opened the proceedings, "This is the matter of the State of Wisconsin versus William Mereness, 02CF3911. The record should reflect appearance of counsel and the defendant. I think before we talk about instructions you had one last matter that you wanted to tie up, Mr. O'Leary?"

"Correct, Your Honor. Julie Esteil is present from the City of Janesville planning department. She's an assistant planner. The parties have had a chance to talk with her and look at Exhibits 124 and 125. There was an issue of the scale of the exhibits. Parties are stipulating that the scale on Exhibit 124 is correct as indicated. It's one inch equals 20 feet. The scale on 125 is incorrect in there. It is supposed to be one inch equals 80 feet. We are going to stipulate that's the correct scale of Exhibit 125."

"Want to put that stipulation in front of the jury?"

"Yes."

"Do we want to have our instruction conference, then have the jury come out, have that stipulation and I'll start instructing?"

Opposing counsel both agreed with the plan.

"We'll start to clarify what we talked about informally. I assume we want to have a little break between arguments so the jury doesn't have any difficulties focusing on arguments. So, between initial close and Mr. Daniel's we will have a short break. Between Mr. Daniel's and rebuttal we will have a short break."

The defense attorney interjected, "Emphasis on..."

Werner finished the defense attorney's statement, "Short".

The judge suggested they adjourn to the conference room. They remained within until 9:05 a.m.

The jury was seated and Judge Werner addressed them, "Good morning, ladies and gentlemen. At this time, counsel, it's my understanding you have a stipulation you wanted to present to the Court and the jury?"

O'Leary presented his information about the map scales and it was accepted with no argument from the defense.

Judge Werner faced the jury, "All right. Thank you. Members of the jury, the court will now instruct you upon the principles of law which you are to follow in considering the evidence and in reaching your verdict. It is your duty to follow all of these instructions. Regardless of any opinion you may have about what the law is or ought to be, you must base your verdict on the law I give you in these instructions. Apply that law to the facts in the case which have been properly proven by the evidence. Consider only the evidence received during this trial and the law as given to you by these instructions and from these alone, guided by your sound reason and best judgment, reach your verdict. If any member of the jury has an impression of my opinion as to whether the defendant is guilty or not guilty, disregard that impression entirely and decide the issues on facts solely as you view the evidence. You, the jury, are the sole judges of the facts and the Court is the judge of the law only.

"First degree intentional homicide as defined in Section 940.01 of the criminal code of Wisconsin is committed by one who causes the death of another human being with the intent to kill that person or another. Before you may find the defendant guilty of first degree intentional homicide the State must prove by evidence which satisfies you beyond a reasonable doubt that the following two elements were present. One, the defendant caused the death of Jennifer L. Mereness. Cause means the defendant's act was a substantial factor in producing the death. Two, the defendant acted with the intent to kill Jennifer L. Mereness. Intent to kill means that the defendant had the mental purpose to take the life of another human being or was aware that his conduct was practically certain to cause the death of another human being. While the law requires that the defendant acted with intent to kill, it does not require that the intent exist for any particular length of time before the act is committed. The act need not be brooded over, considered, or reflected upon for a week, a day, an hour or even for a minute. There need not be any appreciable time between the formation of the intent and the act. The intent to kill may be formed at any time before the act, including the instant before the act, and must continue to exist at the time of the act. You cannot look into a person's mind to find intent. Intent to kill must be found, if found at all, from the defendant's acts, words and statement, if any, and from all the facts and circumstances in this case bearing upon intent. Intent should not be confused with motive. While proof of intent is necessary to a conviction, proof of motive is not. Motive refers to a person's reason for doing something. While motive may be shown as a circumstance to aid in establishing the guilt of the defendant, the State is not required to prove motive on the part of the defendant in order to convict. Evidence of motive does not by itself establish guilt. You should give it the weight you believe it deserves under all of the circumstances. If you are satisfied beyond a reasonable doubt that the defendant caused the death of Jennifer L. Mereness with the intent to kill, you should find the defendant guilty of first-degree intentional homicide. If you are not so satisfied, you must find the defendant not guilty.

"In reaching your verdict, examine the evidence with care and caution. Act with judgment, reason and prudence. Defendants are not required to prove their innocence. The law presumes every person charged with the commission of an offense to be innocent. This presumption requires a finding of not guilty unless in your deliberations you find it is overcome by evidence which satisfies you beyond a reasonable doubt that the defendant is guilty. The burden of establishing every fact necessary to constitute guilt is upon the State. Before you can return a verdict of guilty, the evidence must satisfy you beyond a reasonable doubt that the defendant is guilty. If you can reconcile the evidence upon any reasonable hypothesis consistent with the defendant's innocence, you should do so, and return a verdict of not guilty. The term reasonable doubt means a doubt based upon reason and common sense. It is a doubt for which a reason can be given arising from a fair and rational consideration of the evidence or lack of evidence. It means such a doubt as would cause a person of ordinary prudence to pause or hesitate when called upon to act in the most important affairs of life. A reasonable doubt is not a doubt which is based on mere guesswork or speculation. A doubt which arises merely from sympathy or from fear to return a verdict of guilt is not a reasonable doubt. A reasonable doubt is not a doubt such as may be used to escape the responsibility of a decision. While it is your duty to give the defendant the benefit of every reasonable doubt, you are not to search for doubt. You are to search for the truth."

Boy, that was excellent, his explanation of doubt would rule out just about anything that Daniel had put forth in his cross-examinations and his defense.

"There is evidence in this case that at the time of the commission of the offense charged the defendant was at a place other than that where the crime occurred. It is not necessary for the defendant to establish that he was not present at the scene of the crime or that he was at some other place.

The burden is upon the State to convince you beyond a reasonable doubt that the defendant committed the offense as charged.

"An indictment is nothing more than a written, formal accusation against a defendant charging the commission of one or more criminal acts. You are not to consider it as evidence against the defendant in any way. It does not raise any inference of guilt.

"Evidence is, first, the sworn testimony of witnesses both on direct and cross- examination regardless of who called the witness. Second, the exhibits the court has received whether or not an exhibit goes to the jury room. Third, any facts to which the lawyers have agreed or stipulated or which the Court has directed you to find. Anything you may have seen or heard outside the courtroom is not evidence. You are to decide the case solely on the evidence offered and received at trial.

"The Court has taken judicial notice of certain facts and you are directed to accept the following as true. That all the search warrants and the returns of search warrants in this case are kept in the files of the Clerk of Court for Rock County. That Exhibit 106 is from the US Naval Observatory Astronomical Applications Department and contains accurate sun and moon dates for Rhinelander, Wisconsin, for November 22, 2002. That Exhibit 107 is the official highway map of the State of Wisconsin. That Rock County Clerk of Court file 02FA901 contains all of the court documents filed in the action entitled William J. Mereness versus Jennifer Lynn Judge. That Yahoo maps list approximate driving time from 2818 Morningside Drive in Janesville, Wisconsin, to Wal-Mart in Minocqua, Wisconsin, to be four hours and 17 minutes and the distance to be 240.9 miles.

"It is not necessary that every fact be proved directly by a witness or an exhibit. A fact may be proved indirectly by circumstantial evidence. Circumstantial evidence is evidence from which a jury may logically find other facts according to common knowledge and experience. Circumstantial evidence is not necessarily better or worse than direct evidence. Either type of evidence can prove a fact. Whether evidence is direct or circumstantial, it must satisfy you beyond a reasonable doubt that the defendant committed the offense before you may find the defendant guilty.

"The State has introduced evidence of statements which it claims were made by the defendant. It is for you to determine how much weight, if any, to give each statement. In evaluating each statement, you must determine three things: Whether the statement was actually made by the defendant. Only so much of a statement as was actually made by a person may be considered as evidence. Whether the statement was accurately restated here at trial. Whether the statement or any part of it ought to be believed...

You should consider the facts and circumstances surrounding the making of each statement along with all of the other evidence in determining how much weight, if any, the statement deserves. When the mental condition of a defendant at the time of the making of any statement against interest is drawn into question, the burden is upon the prosecution to prove beyond a reasonable doubt that such statement was understandingly made and... that the defendant's mental condition was rational and normal so that he understood the substance and import of such statement. If, at the time the defendant made any such statement against interest, his mental or physical condition was such as to deprive him of his normal mental faculties to the extent he did not understandingly make such statement, or understand the substance and import of it, then it is your duty to disregard such statement.

"In weighing the evidence, you may take into account matters of your common knowledge and observations and experiences in the affairs of life.

"Remarks of the attorneys are not evidence. If the remarks suggested certain facts not in evidence, disregard the suggestion. Consider carefully the closing arguments of the attorneys, but their arguments and conclusions and opinions are not evidence. Draw your own conclusions from the evidence and decide upon your verdict according to the evidence under the instructions given you by the Court.

"An exhibit becomes evidence only when received by the Court. An exhibit marked for identification and not received is not evidence. An exhibit received is evidence, whether or not it goes to the jury room.

"Attorneys for each side have the right and the duty to object to what they consider are improper questions asked of witnesses and to the admission of other evidence which they believe is not properly admissible. You should not draw any conclusions from the fact an objection was made. By allowing testimony or other evidence to be received over the objection of counsel, the Court is not indicating any opinion about the evidence. You, the jurors, are the judges of the credibility of the witnesses and the weight of the evidence.

"Disregard entirely any question that the Court did not allow to be answered. Do not guess at what the witness' answer might have been. If the question itself suggested that certain information might be true, ignore the suggestion and do not consider it as evidence. During the trial the Court has ordered certain testimony to be stricken. Disregard all stricken testimony...The weight of evidence does not depend on the number of witnesses on each side. You may find that the testimony of one witness is entitled to greater weight than that of another witness or even of several other witnesses. It is the duty of the jury to scrutinize and to weigh the testimony of witnesses and to determine the effect of the evidence as a whole. You are the sole judges of the credibility, that is the believability, of the witnesses and of the weight to be given to their testimony. In determining the credibility of each witness, and the weight you give to the testimony of each witness, consider these factors: whether the witness has an interest or lack of interest in the result of this trial; the witness' conduct, appearance and demeanor on the witness stand; the clearness or lack of clearness of the witness' recollections; the opportunity the witness had for observing and knowing the matters the witness testified about; the reasonableness of the witness' testimony; the apparent intelligence of the witness; bias or prejudice if any has been shown; possible motive for falsifying testimony; and all other facts and circumstances during the trial which tend either to support or to discredit the testimony. Then give to the testimony of each witness the weight you believe it should receive. There is no magic way for you to evaluate the testimony. Instead, you should use your common sense and experience. In everyday life you determine for yourselves the reliability of things said to you. You should do the same thing here.

"Ordinarily, a witness may testify only about facts. However, a witness with expertise in a particular field may give an opinion in that field. You should consider the qualifications and credibility of the expert, the facts upon which the opinion is based and the reasons given for the opinion. Opinion evidence was received to help you reach a conclusion. However, you are not bound by any expert's opinion.

"Evidence has been received that one of the witnesses in this trial, James Mereness, Jr., has been convicted of crimes. This evidence was received solely because it bears upon the credibility of the witness. It must not be used for any other purpose.

"A defendant in a criminal case has the absolute constitutional right not to testify. The defendant's decision not to testify must not be considered by you in any way and must not influence your verdict in any manner.

"At this time, ladies and gentlemen, we will proceed with closing arguments, and the State will have the opportunity to make the first closing argument. Then Mr. Daniel will have his opportunity. And then, because the State has the burden, the State has an opportunity to make a rebuttal argument. With that, then, Mr. Folts."

42

Assistant District Attorney Perry Folts began, "Thank you. Morning, ladies and gentlemen. First, on behalf of Mr. O'Leary, myself and the people of the State of Wisconsin, I want to thank you for the time that you spent listening to the evidence in this particular case. It's been a long week. You've been in and out of here a lot of times. But we really do appreciate the time that you've spent and the attention that you've paid to the evidence that's been presented. You've heard from many witnesses during this trial. But one voice hasn't been heard. That's the voice of Jennifer Mereness or Jennifer Judge. She wasn't able to be here during this trial because back on November 22nd of last year her life was brutally taken by this defendant." The ADA looked at Bill and, arm outstretched, pointed at Bill with his hand open, palm upward.

A lump formed in my throat. My eyes stung.

"She proceeded home from her job at Craig High School where she was a teacher. She had a family; she had parents, brothers and sisters, nieces and nephews, friends, co-workers that all loved her. She wasn't feeling well that morning, so she left school sometime after 11:00 on the morning of November 22 of 2002. She enjoyed her life, her students. She was looking forward to adopting a child in the fall or winter of 2002. She never got that chance. Her life was brutally taken by this man, here."

Folts again gestured toward Bill. He again shifted his gaze from the jury to the defendant. The panel's gazes shifted with him. It was an effective tactic.

"She decided to proceed with her life after the divorce had been filed. She was moving on. The defendant announced his decision to get a divorce while they were closing on one house and were supposed to buy another house. He took some of that money--gave her a little bit. She didn't even have enough left for the down payment on the new house. If her mother hadn't come and helped her that day she wouldn't have had a place to stay when they left. Does that sound like that's the way that you start an amicable or friendly divorce? I don't think so.

"After moving into her new house in mid-September she was moving on with her life. She had contacted a lawyer. She was moving forward with the divorce. They were challenging the prenuptial agreement. There were clearly some ongoing disagreements between the parties. Even her lawyer advised her on at least two occasions to file for a harassment injunction. Again, does that sound like that's a friendly divorce to you? Jennifer never got the chance to start her new life.

"Remember back on November 21st of 2002 she got the angry phone call from the defendant? Her co-worker overheard that. Then just the very next day her life was taken."

Folts moved to the exhibit table. He picked up the weapons, one in each hand, and held them aloft.

"Ladies and gentlemen, around 11:30, thereabouts, on November 22nd of 2002, Jennifer was struck by this maul and this hatchet six times. Six times. And this hatchet struck her in the back of the head in a criss-cross fashion and severed her brain and she died."

There was not a sound in the courtroom. A pin dropping would have sounded like a mortar explosion. The lump in my throat grew larger.

"It's interesting to note that when you look at the photographs from that particular day, you've seen these, the hatchet and the hammer are laid neatly and meticulously at her head. Who was the neat and meticulous one?

"Again, we know that Jennifer left school some time after 11:00. She left a voice mail for her friend, John Furgason, around 11:20 telling him that she was going home sick. It takes about ten minutes to get home so she would have arrived about 11:30. Maybe a little bit after that. And it's within minutes that Jeff Jones hears a woman screaming, yelling, call it what you will, within minutes of that. He then proceeds up and talks to Nick Demrow who didn't hear the scream. Hadn't had his attention called to the door yet at that particular point. Then they watch the door. They don't see anything. They decide what do you think we should do? And it's at that point within minutes that they see someone leaving, leaving from the west end of that residence."

The assistant district attorney moved to one of the maps on display. He traced the route as he spoke.

"And that person goes out from that Sandstone address, walks behind the houses next door, heads up the street and eventually goes down Sandhill. Nick Demrow decided to follow. Came down the road, passed him here on Wuthering Hills. Went down Sandhill, turned the corner, came around on Windmill, back on Wuthering Hills. When he came back down he was about 100 feet down the road. Saw him from the back. He never really got a good look at him, unfortunately. But he did describe him. And how did he describe him? A male. Thirty-five to 50 years old. Dark hair, white leather-like gloves. Glasses. Gray sweatpants. And we've seen at least three pair of gray sweatpants the defendant owned, black and blue Columbia-style coat, Columbia-style jacket, which we know, at least the one that the defendant and Christopher and Jennifer had in the house at some point, no longer exists. Where did it go? And he was carrying two bags. Mr. Demrow followed this particular person. Didn't get a good look at his face.

"Now, what's the next thing that we know? John Furgason arrives home about 6:45 p.m. He finds Jennifer. Finds her in this state. Blood has soaked into the carpeting, is dried. Her body is cold and stiff. She's been there for quite some time. This didn't happened later in the afternoon. It didn't happened during that evening. It happened between 11:30 and 12:00 on the morning of November 22nd of 2002. Again, those weapons were neatly and meticulously placed by her head. Jennifer's dogs were still in the cage. She would have let them out if she could have had time. But immediately upon arriving home she was confronted by this defendant."

Folts gestured toward Bill for the third time. The jury turned to look at him once more.

"She tried to escape. She tried to get out that front door. She screamed. That's what Jones heard and relayed to Demrow. But she didn't make it. The door got opened. She was struck. She was dragged back in and brutally beaten by this defendant with those two tools."

The prosecutor extended his arm and this time pointed to the weapons on the exhibit table. The jurors followed his movement.

The thought I'd had over and over since Jennifer's death sprang into my mind again. *Dear God. How close she had been to freedom. Just a few extra steps and she would have made it beyond his grasp.* I wondered again why that had made it even harder for me to accept her fate.

Folts continued, "Now, how do we know that this defendant killed her? First, the physical evidence. You'll recall that that basement window was broken. Glass was collected from the scene. The crime lab analyzed that glass. They collected it. They have it here. What did they compare it to? Well, you remember that when they vacuumed his car they found a couple tiny shards of glass. Those glass fragments or trace evidence were found in the defendant's car just two days after Jennifer's homicide. The examiner looked at the glass, compared it for color, density and refractive index. The pieces were too small to compare for density, but he found that both the color and the refractive index matched the window from Jennifer's basement. Again, he couldn't check for density because the pieces were too small. This wasn't glass from a drinking glass. This wasn't automobile window glass. This was glass from a window just like that window that was broken in Jennifer's basement. He said that it was likely that that glass came from that window.

"What else did we get from the scene? Footwear impressions. And there has been a lot of talk about what those impressions show. And if you want to see this you ask to see it, you can look at this yourselves. Look at the impressions that are on here. Look at the distinct patterns that you can see from those shoes and the heel and toe. Then take a look yourselves at the pattern of the old shoes where the wear pattern didn't match. But it was the same general tread design. Same horseshoe type patterns. The same circles around the heel. Would a newer pair just like this, a newer pair of these shoes have caused those impressions? Those shoes just like Chris described that his father had which are now nowhere to be found? Would they have caused those impressions? I submit that they would.

"There's been some talk about fingerprints. People with gloves don't leave fingerprints. In fact, if you recall that the fingerprint examiner didn't even find Jennifer's prints on the doorknob to her master bedroom, the front door or the garage service door. She lived there for a month and a half. Her fingerprints weren't there. Why would we expect the defendant's to be, especially when we know that the person seen leaving the scene was wearing gloves, making it highly unlikely not only would they not leave fingerprints, they wouldn't leave any DNA, ladies and gentlemen. Those are non-issues, ladies and gentlemen. Don't get confused by something that's not important. Fingerprints aren't all that's cracked up to be. This isn't television. We don't get to write a script, don't get to make it all interesting. Oh, we don't find fingerprints and that's a murderer. The experts said they don't always find fingerprints at the scene of the crime. In this case they didn't. He was wearing gloves. The glass and the footwear impressions are similar. That is not coincidence, ladies and gentlemen.

"What else do we know? The blue and black Columbia coat. Chris saw a blue and black Columbia coat in the closet at he and his father's apartment within a week before the homicide occurred. It has not been found. It's been replaced. I wonder why? Chris was wearing a liner from that coat. It was left at school. It's been retrieved. We have it here. It's a black liner. Matches the black sleeves on the Columbia jacket that it came from."

Folts picked up the coat in evidence, the one purchased at Scheels with a combination of cash and check. The one that Bill went to extraordinary lengths to leave no trace that he had purchased.

"This was the new coat purchased by the defendant. Similar but it has a dark gray sleeve and a gray liner that matches the sleeves. That's the way they make their coats. That's why this liner came from the blue coat with a black sleeve just like was described seen leaving the scene but has not been found following the homicide. That coat, the missing coat, hasn't been found in the cabin. Wasn't found in the car. Wasn't found in the apartment. Wasn't found at Sandstone. It is nowhere to be found. Why is that? It was evidence that the defendant destroyed. And we're going to come back at some point. We're going to talk a little bit more about that coat when we talk about what the defendant had to say about it.

"What's the next thing we know? Let's talk about the defendant's conversations with the police. First person he talked to was Detective Sergeant Schaepe from Oneida County. He says that the conference call that he had scheduled that morning with his supervisor Caroline Hetrick was cancelled by her that morning. What did she tell? It was cancelled a day or two earlier. Hmm? He says that because that conference call got cancelled that he decided to get an early start on his travels to Minocqua. He left at 10:00 a.m. on November 22nd of 2002. Those are his words to Detective Sergeant Schaepe. He says that he arrived in Minocqua at the Wal-Mart at about 3:00 p.m. The security tape there actually shows him arriving at about 3:26 and that receipt that we had presented to us, I think, actually shows a purchase time on that candy bar that was so important to him of 3:34:42, so we know he was in the store in Minocqua right around 3:30 p.m. that afternoon. That candy bar he told Detective Schaepe he bought for his nephew; but yet, he insisted that he needed the receipt to turn in on his expense account. Again, Caroline Hetrick, his supervisor said, that's just not true. He didn't need that receipt. But why did he volunteer that to Detective Sergeant Schaepe when he talked to him on the morning of November 23rd of 2002? Why at that point did the defendant think that receipt was so important?

"He also said that he stopped at that Wal-Mart that afternoon to congratulate his friend, Cass Wisco. Cass Wisco said that's not true. 'I'm not his friend. He's not my friend. We don't get along all that well. We have not since he trained me in Iowa several years ago. He sort of abandoned me during training. I didn't have much to do with him. He didn't have much to do with me.' This defendant was looking for an alibi. He certainly didn't get it in Cass Wisco.

"Also, keep in mind that the defendant submitted an itinerary for the week that included November 22nd. And on that itinerary, particularly for Friday, he was supposed to be in West Allis, Wisconsin. And you recall that his supervisor, Caroline Hetrick, said that he had never notified her of any change. Yet, he shows up in Minocqua. The next police officer he talked to was Lieutenant Davis. He told Lieutenant Davis that he took his son to school the morning of November 22nd about 7:15 a.m. He then went home to deal with that conference call which again he tells Lieutenant Davis was cancelled that morning by his supervisor. Not true. He then decided again to get an early start on his travels. He told Lieutenant Davis, 'I left at 10:00 a.m. on the morning of November 22nd of 2002 to travel to Minocqua.' He said that he would have to travel 100 to 120 miles per hour to make it any quicker than that. He said that he stopped at a wayside for maybe five or ten minutes. Nothing unusual. Detective Altstadt, he drove that route, same route, during about the same hours, couple days later. Traffic may have been a little bit heavier on Friday than it was on Sunday as far as volume was concerned. But if you recall, from Mr. Stein's testimony, the average speeds were fairly similar. In fact, actually, the average speeds on Friday, typically, the further north that you got were significantly faster than the average speeds on Sunday because it was some type of an accident or obstruction of the highway at some point on Sunday that slowed traffic down to about 65 miles per hour or so. Where on Friday afternoon as you got further north it was going almost 80 miles per hour. Now, the defendant claimed you would have to go 120 miles per hour. Well, at 71 to 72 miles per hour it would take three hours and 20 minutes to drive 240 miles and that's the distance that we're talking about. You can do the math yourselves. If it were to take the defendant four and a half to five hours, you would have to drive at an average speed of 48 to 53 miles per hour. Have you ever driven at 48 to 53 miles per hour on an interstate, particularly on deer hunting weekend? You probably wouldn't be here today. You would be killed by the traffic as it ran over you, as you were practically standing still compared to the other people on the highway.

"The defendant told Lieutenant Davis that he had gone to that Wal-Mart store in Minocqua, which, by the way, if you are on the Oneida County map going from Janesville north, Minocqua is out of the way. Okay. He went north beyond where he needed to go. Came back down and around instead of coming across Highway 8 and heading up directly to the cabin from the south. He was looking for that alibi and it just didn't pay off.

"He got to the cabin about 4:00 or 4:30. He says he had dinner. He did laundry and he eventually went to bed. Told Lieutenant Davis there was no cell coverage at the cabin. Where was the defendant around midnight that evening when Christopher got a hold of him on the cell phone? Cell phone doesn't work at the cabin.

"Let's see. Blue coat, the shoes, the other evidence could be anywhere in the north woods if you're out there at that time of night. He told Lieutenant

Davis that on November 23rd he got up and he was going to go to Duluth for business. And then later he tells him, 'Well, no, I was going home to take my son to work.'"

Once again the prosecutor pointed to a map on an easel.

"Look at the state map, ladies and gentlemen. Duluth. You're not going to get much further than that from Janesville. It's going to be difficult to get from here to here, get your son to work in the afternoon. Where was he going? He doesn't even know. He couldn't keep his story straight at that point.

"The next officer he talked to was Detective Goth. They had a conversation on November 27th of 2002, after the defendant had been taken to the hospital in Appleton and certain items were taken from his body. He told Detective Goth that he had purchased this coat that we've talked about. This new blue and gray Columbia-style jacket that you've seen before, he says he purchased that on Sunday at Scheels Sporting Goods. Ms. Dexter from Scheels was here and told you that he received a receipt the first time he was in when he paid $125 in cash and the balance with a check. A check with identifying information on it. And she told you that he then came back to the store, I believe it was twice, to get additional receipts. Well, once to come in and give them cash for the check. And then he called and wanted another receipt which he then came and retrieved and all of those receipts are here. Now why did he want to get rid of that check? Because it had identifying information on it. He didn't want anybody to know that he had purchased a new coat."

Strangely, the defense attorney interrupted the ADA during his closing argument, "Do you have the exhibit number, Perry?"

What's this about? It sure seems pretty inappropriate.

Folts tossed the information out, then continued with his closing.

"Ninety-six. Detective Goth asked him why he wanted that coat. He said, 'Well, I need it for emergency. I keep it in the back of my car.' Well, you know he already had a black and green Columbia jacket at home that he could have used for that. Wears his leather jacket, apparently. But more interestingly, what did he tell his brother Jim about why he wanted to buy that coat? He was going to buy it for Christopher. For Christopher. Christopher doesn't even like that coat. Doesn't even like that style of coat. All he would wear was the liner from the black and blue one. Christopher was surprised that his dad would even think of buying a coat like that for him; but yet, that's what the defendant told his brother Jim. Told him why he wanted the money from Jim so he could buy that coat. Again, that coat's never been found even though this defendant told Detective Goth that it had been returned to Jennifer's house. It wasn't there. The defendant wore it that morning, November 22nd of 2002, and later destroyed it.

"Detective Goth spoke further with the defendant. Talked to him about the morning of November 24th of 2002. That was the Sunday after the murder. If you recall, recall that the defendant got up, left Jim at the cabin. Jim felt sort of stranded there because he wasn't quite sure how he was going to get out. Only had the quarter tank of gas. Was a little worried about him and his son running out of gas because he didn't know the directions out of there. His brother didn't care. He left. Then he came back. And what did he come back for? When he first told Detective Goth was he came back to get his glasses, sweatpants and something else. Now we never learned what the something else was, but it doesn't really matter. Then after some consideration, Detective Goth said what did you come back for? And the defendant said sweatpants and something else. And when confronted about the glasses he said, 'No, that's not true. I never said that.' The glasses. What's important about coming back for those glasses? Do you remember brother Jim said that on the evening of November 22nd, when the defendant arrived, he was cooking? And the whole time he was running those glasses under the water. What happens to any evidence when you wash it? It goes away. It's destroyed. He washed them multiple times. Don't be fooled. It wasn't by the grease. There was a lid on there. What did he do? He changed glasses. Put on a new pair, and continued cooking. But he wasn't scrubbing those under the water. It was that first pair that he had worn up to the cabin, that he wore when he killed Jennifer.

"Detective Goth finally talked to the defendant about his activities on November 22nd of 2002. And, specifically, Detective Goth asked the defendant where he was between 11:30 and 12. The defendant told Detective Goth that he was somewhere between Stevens Point and Portage at about that time."

The prosecutor referred to the map of Wisconsin once more. "Well, here's Stevens Point, ladies and gentlemen. That is a long, long way from Edgerton, ladies and gentlemen. What's important about that is that we know that at 12:10 p.m. on November 22nd, there are cell phone records that show that the defendant was within miles of Edgerton, Wisconsin. Let's take a look at those cell phone records real quick. You will recall we had a list of these phone calls that were read by Mr. Boyd from US cellular. And the first call that morning was at 6:46 a.m. and that was on the East Milwaukee tower off of the X antenna."

Mr. Folts walked over to and pointed to different locations on one of the vivid cell maps, "That would be out here, ladies and gentlemen. This is the

X antenna of the East Milwaukee tower. The defendant's apartment is over here. Jennifer's residence was here. The X antenna on East Milwaukee tower encompasses the general area of Jennifer's residence. What was he doing at 6:46 a.m. out in this area? There is no physical way he could have been anywhere near his apartment when he made that call. Just not possible. Call number two was 7:34 a.m. It was made from the East Milwaukee Z antenna.

"That would be this antenna here facing the pink area. Is that possible he was at his apartment at that point? Sure. Because there is some crossover between these areas. He's back maybe at that point. 7:43 a.m., that call is off the Janesville Mall tower. The X antenna. This antenna that covers the gray area. Up here. Where is he now and why? 8:11. The call is off the East Milwaukee X tower. Again over here. Not by his apartment. Out here. 9:17 a.m. This was an interesting call on the Janesville Craig X tower. This area here. Now, could that have been his residence here? Sure. Could have been Janesville Craig. 9:45. Janesville Craig X tower, same thing. Number eight. At 10:03 a.m. East Milwaukee X tower. Again, out here. Apparently this blue area. Ninth call. 10:50 a.m. Let's see. I left for Minocqua at 10:00. 10:50 a.m. about the time it would take you to get to Madison if you had actually done that. There's a cell phone call off the East Milwaukee Street X antenna. Again, right here. What's included in there? Jennifer's residence. Call number 10. 12:10 p.m. that afternoon. The Edgerton Y antenna. The Edgerton Y antenna. The yellow area from the top of this map. Somewhere in that vicinity. In fact, next call shortly thereafter within minutes is in the Madison territory which is north of here. He has now, ladies and gentlemen, begun his travels north at roughly noon on November 22nd of 2002. And he has traveled from that Sandstone address where he killed Jennifer, out Highway 14, and up the interstate; and we can now track him on up that interstate through Madison territory, through Stevens Point territory, through the Wausau territory and to Rhinelander. And you can look at the state map and find each of those locations. And you, yourselves, can conclude where he was at the time this homicide was committed and shortly thereafter.

"Frankly, ladies and gentlemen, the defendant's explanation of his whereabouts, his alibi, is just physically impossible. Physically impossible. He was here. He did it. It's just what he told his mom and dad. 'I done it.'

"Let's talk about the defendant's family. Brother Jim says the defendant's neat, meticulous. Had nerves of steel. Those same nerves of steel he demonstrated while he walked calmly from the evidence, being followed by Nick Demrow. The same nerves of steel he demonstrated while he talked to various police officers. You know, it's interesting that while he was in Appleton on November 21st, the day before Jim was supposed to go hunting at the cabin, he didn't leave the key. Didn't leave the key although that was the original plan. But, you know, when he figured he was killing Jennifer the next day, he figured he would need that alibi. Jim will be the good one. I will have him buy groceries at a certain time, pay cash, get a receipt. I will be able to use that. Won't be any identifying information from that. It will be from Tomahawk. That will work. Tells him to call the next morning between 8:00 and 10:00. Why is that? Well, I don't know. At any rate, Jim didn't do it, and he got mad at him because he didn't do it. He wasn't following his directions. Trying to set up that alibi. It didn't work. Remember when the defendant arrived at the cabin Jim said they began unloading things? The one thing he said that the defendant wouldn't let him touch when they were unloading things was the laundry. And then he went down into the basement with that laundry and was there for about a half-hour to do a single load. At least the only load that Jim saw. But he wouldn't let Jim and Ryan come down in the basement. He got mad at them when they tried to do so. Wonder what that was all about? More importantly, how did Jim say that the defendant looked when he arrived? He looked tough, stressed out, like he had the world upon his shoulders. If I had killed somebody, I would have the world upon my shoulders. He would be stressed out. Even more importantly, there were a couple scratches on his forehead. Think back. Although we didn't get a whole lot of information from the crime lab analyst that checked for DNA, he did say he found a cap in the defendant's car that had two spots of blood, that matched the defendant, on the forehead area of the cap. Now, how would you cut yourself in the forehead? Coming through a broken window? Possible. Being scratched by the victim, Jennifer? Possible. The defendant's brother, Jim also saw scratches on his arms. Wouldn't be unreasonable to get scratches like that if you had been in a struggle as you were killing Jennifer. Washed his glasses repeatedly. Trying to get rid of the blood that had been smeared on those glasses. He changed his glasses. He put those in the drawer. And then he later came back for them on Sunday. But, yet, he told Detective Goth, 'I really don't remember. I didn't come back for those, no, no, no, no way'.

"Seems to me that several occasions at least prior to him receiving the head injury and the suicide attempt that he had difficulty with his memory. You know, he couldn't even remember when he talked to Detective Goth that he had gone back to Scheels on two other occasions. Why was he hiding that? Jim said on November 23rd on Saturday, that the defendant got up and said he was going to Janesville. Never mentioned Duluth. He was going to Janesville to take his son to work. Well, tells others he was going to Duluth. Can't have it both ways. He can't keep his stories straight now. Jim told you that on November 24th on Sunday that his brother, the defendant, left but then came back, and when he came back he picked up a pair of gray sweat pants and some shoes. Now, we've seen another pair of shoes that Jim says those kind of look like them, but where do they come from? There is no chain of custody on those. There is no evidence where they came from. They could have been purchased after this incident for all we know. We know where the shoes we have came from. Those came out of the defendant's vehicle. We know Christopher said he had another pair just like those. Christopher lived with him. He saw them all the time. He knows what kind of shoes his dad had. Jim, he's not quite sure. Said they might have been the pair. At any rate, those were never found before the ones that have matching tread impressions were. But where's the newer pair? He also told Jim that he had to buy that new coat for Chris. And he told the police he needed it for an emergency. Again he's now having so much trouble with the stories he's telling, that he can't keep them straight. On November 25th, Monday, Jim and his brother have some words at their parents' house. Jim's concerned. He wants the defendant to leave. Jim's been dragged into this. Jim's then six-year-old son has been dragged into this. I don't blame him for wanting him to leave. Just get away from us. Leave us alone. Look what you're putting us all through. And at that point what's even more interesting is the defendant asks him about those receipts from Scheels. Did you tell the police about the coat or the receipt? Why would that be important to the defendant? Don't tell them about that. I don't want them to know. There were some claims that the defendant was afraid of Jim because of this discussion. But yet, you know, on November 27th, after the body search, after the defendant's been to the hospital to give body fluids and so on, the hair samples etcetera, who's there to give him a ride? Jim. Is he reluctant to ride home with him? He was so afraid of him. Gets in the car alone. Goes home. They go home. Have hamburger together that mom makes. Doesn't sound to me like he was too afraid of his brother, Jim.

"Who's the next family member we heard from? LaBelle. The defendant's mother. Now deceased. She's in the hospital coming to see the defendant, her son, who has attempted to commit suicide. Runs his car into a brick wall, slashed his wrists. She has a discussion with Captain Helein. Captain Helein says that LaBelle tells him that she hears the defendant on November 27th say, quote, 'I want to die. I don't want to go to prison for 70 years for killing Jennifer.' At this point those nerves of steel are beginning to crack. Friday, November 29th, 8:30 a.m. LaBelle sees the defendant go into the kitchen, retrieve a knife, Saran wrap. He then goes and gets into the bathtub. The defendant says, 'I want to die.' At that point both LaBelle and the defendant's father are present. And LaBelle says, quote, 'Did you kill Jennifer?' unquote and the defendant responded, 'Yes. I'm really sorry.'

"Ladies and gentlemen, those nerves of steel finally crack, and for the first time since the defendant killed Jennifer, he told the truth. He told the truth. Because he cracked. That weight that was on his shoulders, when Jim saw him on Friday night after the murder, got so heavy that he just couldn't take it any more and he cracked. And he told the truth.

"Finally, ladies and gentlemen, there's James, Sr., the defendant's father. Seventy-nine years old. You saw him. He didn't want to have to be here testifying against his...son, but he did what he had to do. He told you about that morning on November 29th, the day after Thanksgiving when he and LaBelle found the defendant in the bathtub wearing his sweatpants and a T-shirt with the knife with the Saran wrap. And he said LaBelle said, 'What are you doing?' And the defendant didn't reply. And LaBelle then asked him, 'Did you do it?' And the defendant said, 'Yeah, I done it.' Then what happened after that? The defendant gets out of the bathtub. LaBelle takes away the knife and the Saran wrap. They have a conversation in the kitchen. Dad says, you know, son, I think you have three options. You can confess, and they talked about confessing. You can go to trial or you can commit suicide. The defendant goes to his room for a while. Then decides he's going to leave to take his...rental car back to Janesville. Retrieves a knife for protection. The same knife that was later found in his car with what appeared to be blood on it from slashing his wrists in an effort to commit suicide. And the car that was crashed into that brick wall in Appleton. The defendant chose option three. His dad next sees him, the defendant, in the hospital after that suicide attempt. His dad didn't want to be here. His dad didn't want to have to testify against him. But he did. Ladies and gentlemen, he told you what the defendant said, 'Yeah. I done it.'

"Ladies and gentlemen, this evidence taken as a whole, proves beyond a reasonable doubt that this defendant intentionally caused the death of Jennifer Mereness. When you consider carefully all that evidence, you will find this defendant, William Mereness, guilty of first degree intentional homicide. Thank you."

Judge Werner thanked Mr. Folts and then announced a ten-minute recess before we'd hear from Mr. Daniel.

43

The defense attorney began his summation. Had I known he was going to talk for an hour and a half, I would have taken a bathroom break after Folts' closing argument.

Daniel began by thanking the jury for their "attention and seriousness". He noted that the stakes were high for Bill, Jennifer's family and the greater community. He compared what we'd done for the past week was "kind of the opposite of a baseball game". I didn't get the analogy.

Bill's attorney appreciated that they didn't have "anybody go to sleep on us". He was grateful for the jurors' intensity and curiosity.

The defense attorney continued, "And we're now getting to the part where you take over and it becomes your responsibility to determine what this evidence or from our view what this lack of evidence demonstrates. And, we trust, when we get done with this and you look at this basically lack of evidence, that you will conclude as we would urge you to conclude, that the State has not proved beyond a reasonable doubt that William Mereness is responsible for Jennifer's death."

The jury was advised that it was necessary to talk about "what the case is not". It was a given that Jennifer's death was a tragedy to her, to her family and for the students at Craig, but those things were not to be considered.

Whoever "did this" deserved to be punished because they "did something terrible". But, Daniel contended, the consequences of an erroneous verdict were serious for Jennifer's family and society as well.

Bill's lawyer then apologized for a whistle he was making when he talked. He had a "chunk out of a tooth" that was bothering him.

That's a strange thing to bring up to the jury. Is he hoping to elicit sympathy?

Continued warnings about a wrongful conviction of Bill meant that the police would close the book, the identifiable but unidentified prints would go in the file, the identifiable but unidentified DNA would go into the file and the person who "did this" would go free.

The next area of concern was that of the judge's instructions, which would be provided for them in written form. The jury should not speculate about what the judge told them or, "boy, get in an argument about what reasonable doubt means or something like that". They were to be concerned with what the burden of proof meant and what quantity of evidence there was.

Bill's lawyer told the jurors that while the State didn't have to prove motive, motive was not evidence of guilt.

So is he conceding that Bill had a motive to kill Jennifer, but he hadn't acted on it?

As for Bill's alibi, if he was in Edgerton, "obviously he didn't do it." Daniel continued, "But if he was in Janesville along with 65,000 other people." The sentence was left without an end.

Next, the jury was given advice on credibility, "Who's telling you? Why are they telling you? Were they in a position to see what they're telling you about and do they have any reason to fudge what they are telling you?"

Does that refer to his father in the bathroom scene? His brother who was jealous of Bill's more successful life, the police?

Daniel then talked of Bill's refusal to testify, "...in a criminal case, silence is a denial and it's a denial of each and every allegation that they are making against you. And it's a denial that shouts as loud as anyone testifying from the witness stand or any other piece of evidence in a case."

The defense attorney explained that he had to do "a couple things at once", like rebutting Mr. Folts' closing argument and giving his own argument while anticipating that Mr. O'Leary would have the chance to "finish up".

Besides the whistling tooth, Daniel had another apology, "And as you probably caught on, I start with my papers neatly organized. By the time my mouth gets going somehow my papers move around. I've never understood that, but that happens to me. So, I'm going to ask you to bear with me if I get scattered a little bit. That's my excuse. Whether that's a good reason or not, I don't know, but that's the excuse I've got."

Well, you're a professional attorney. You hold peoples' fates in your hands. Get some assistance and learn to deal with the problem, stop making excuses!

The panel was advised that unless all the evidence pointed to the only thing that could have happened they were obligated to return a verdict of not guilty.

A summary was begun, "And listening to the State's argument as I heard it and wrote it down, Mr. Mereness is a bad guy. He was in a bad situation with his divorce, with nerves of steel and after being under police scrutiny in which he was followed, searched; he or his stuff was searched eight times, five times over the period of that week. Was told that there were eyewitnesses. That physical evidence was taken, right, his blood and stuff. And before any results of any of that stuff came back, right, he was put upon and under all that pressure, the hell with it. And he had that moment where he just gave up, and their case stops. Their case stops. There is not one shred, and we'll get to shards in a minute, of physical evidence that links Mr. Mereness to this scene of this horrible, horrible, horrible homicide."

Well, I agree that Bill did do an excellent job of planning and "executing" the killing so as not to leave direct physical evidence. And as for the defense attorney's warning about a scattered delivery, he wasn't kidding.

Daniel reiterated the falsehood from his opening statement, that Nick Demrow said he'd never seen that man before in his life.

That wasn't what he said!

It was purported that the prosecution's case was full of "could-haves" and "would-haves". All of those exonerated the defendant.

The defense attorney got back to the summary he'd started, "...Mr. Mereness wasn't truthful with the police and because he wasn't truthful with the police, whatever that means, he should be found guilty of first degree homicide? With the potential of the person who did this going free? Wasn't truthful with the police? The police weren't truthful with him."

He should be found guilty because the lies he told the police didn't match reality, in the form of other witnesses' testimony.

After that, Daniel's delivery became even more and more disjointed. He talked about the Marital Settlement Agreement and how it was "consistent". There was a restraining order and a harassment order that, "some lawyer" testified about. But, Bill's attorney explained, "Nothing was filed."

The weapons were the next topic. They had not been connected to his client except for when Christopher, almost ten months after the murder, took one look at and identified the hatchet. "Those are the stretches that are being made here in an attempt to implicate William Mereness."

As for Nick Demrow's description of the man he'd seen leaving Jennifer's house, "...matches probably 25 percent of the people in this room".

Regarding the timing of the murder, Daniel purported that the prosecution in its closing arguments slid the time frame a bit. The upshot was that the jury was to accept evidence in the light most favorable to the defendant. Specifically, "So if it's 10 to or whatever, so? All this other stuff about driving and all these other things, what's the point? It's been established, right, where he was, in the direction he was travelling....He's in Minocqua at 3:34 or whatever it is...So, if she didn't get home until 11:40, and Mr. Mereness was in Edgerton at noon, a lot of stuff had to happen in 20 minutes."

So now who's sliding the times around? Mr. Boyd of US Cellular testified that the call from the Edgerton sector was at 12:10 p.m., not noon.

Bill's lawyer's opinion was that the shards of glass that "could not be seen by the human eye" and were not physical evidence "from which anyone can conclude beyond a reasonable doubt someone was there." He explained that because the state crime lab expert said the glass was consistent with the glass in Jennifer's window, it was simply a part of the "could-have, would-have, would-have, could-have, should-have case".

They are one piece in the circumstantial puzzle.

Footwear was the next topic for criticism, "This is who the State relies on for their investigations. This is who the State relies on for their testimony in solving crimes. He came here and said the shoes that were recovered from Mr. Mereness' car, I guess, maybe they were recovered from the apartment, all right, he looked at them. He looked at the pictures. And he said they're like them but they are excluded. That's like saying, yes, we have a picture of a Chevy Impala and that Chevy Impala looks like 5 million Chevy Impalas that they make. Yeah, they look the same. But that one is not the one we're looking at because it is distinguished. There is something about it that's different. And that, as the examiner indicated, ends the story."

Except that the expert said the shoes were excluded for wear, not for style.

Then it seemed as if the defense attorney was helping the prosecution, but I guessed he was suggesting that Bill's son and brother were liars. "And then, well, Christopher the guy who told you about the hatchet, right, is the guy that tells that your dad's got another pair of shoes, right, leaves at the cabin, uses these to cut the lawn. He has his other pair of shoes at the cabin. Jim Mereness says, yeah, those are the shoes that he took back out of the cabin." Then Daniel claimed, "Those shoes were a knock-off."

A "knock-off"? Is he trying to say they were planted or didn't exist?

On to another topic, "There are no prints from William Mereness in that house. And their explanation is, again, don't be confused by what's not there. And their explanation that his prints aren't there is that he could have worn gloves. And if he wore gloves he wouldn't have left prints...That doesn't explain the unexplained fingerprints, does it? We have identifiable but unidentified fingerprints, follow where they are trying to get into the garage door. Then we have them on the screen at what the State is saying is the entry point, right? Then we have them on the master bedroom door. So there are fingerprints."

Yes, and a plethora of witnesses have testified that there were people in that house: installing windows, helping Jennifer move in, relocating furniture.

Bill's lawyer continued, "The other problem with there are no Mr. Mereness' fingerprints in there is because he was wearing gloves well, unfortunately, you've seen these pictures. All right? You've seen the damage that was done. And if this person had the white—I guess the police officer wanted to make them beige-- gloves having left that scene, they're not white or beige any more, are they? That doesn't wash. Don't be confused what's not there. Don't be confused if there is not any evidence; basically, I guess, because we don't have any."

Sarcasm is not a very good defense.

Daniel next talked about the Columbia coat, but I didn't really understand what he was saying except that the coat had been split with Christopher wearing part. The defense attorney again referred to Christopher as "the same guy that identified and tried to place the hatchet".

He's taking every opportunity to impugn Chris' character.

More sarcasm was used regarding the receipt from Wal-Mart, "But keeping the receipt for the candy bar was a sinister plot to establish alibi."

In reference, then, to the Columbia coat receipt from Scheels Daniel argued the prosecution couldn't have it "both ways".

Well, why not? If one receipt was kept to establish an alibi and the other needed to be destroyed because it would prove a replacement coat had been purchased, it actually was both ways!

The defense had a concern about the blood found on Bill's hat. "... Somehow the State considers to be evidence of him having a struggle with blood all over everything. So, now, let's just think about this one a couple of ways. If the blood got on the headband during this death struggle, there would be blood of Jennifer's. There would be blood all over it. You know, you get a little pimple or something on your forehead get a lot of blood, microscopic dot of his own blood is evidence of this homicide."

The prosecution had not suggested that the hat had been worn during the commission of the crime. They suggested, possibly, he'd put the hat on after his forehead was scratched by broken window glass or by Jennifer.

The only consistent thread in the case, Daniel insisted, was Bill's protestations of innocence.

So why did Bill crack? According to his attorney, "Did they start confusing him when they stopped him in the pitch black, and there is an exhibit that tells us, I believe, sunrise was around 7:00 that morning he was stopped at 6-ish in a back woods road up north."

Ah, yes, the astronomical, "Doing it European Style" defense.

Daniel took advantage of the prosecution's inability to refer to the pipe-stuffing incident and Bill's first wife's claim of attempted murder, "And the police department without a shred of evidence say the, quote, estranged husband with knowing nothing about the divorce, nothing about Jennifer Mereness, nothing about Bill Mereness, write down the suspect and we're off to the races."

The subsequent stretch of Tod's summation was even more difficult to follow; it seemed to be a stream-of-consciousness monologue. I was able to extract that the police had lied to Bill and that the divorce had not been contentious.

The defense attorney got back on track a little, "And from then on in, the eye was on the prize. There was not one bit of investigation that went anywhere other than an attempt to make a case that doesn't exist. And if you listen to Officer Schaepe's testimony, Lieutenant Davis' testimony, consistently we have an eyewitness. You can't have an eyewitness. He wasn't there. I wasn't there." I took that last bit to mean Bill claimed he wasn't at Jennifer's.

Daniel insisted that Bill had been "detained", because Schaepe said he was not to get out of Oneida County. He elaborated, "He's then brought in police escort. Schaepe squad car, Bill, squad car. This is all voluntary and I'm cooperating because they told me that I wasn't under arrest. I'm a suspect but I'm not under arrest. And he's shaken and he's concerned about driving. But I can't let anybody drive because of company rules. I would have thought maybe we could make an exception there, but that's not his train of thought at that point. If he couldn't drive he would stop. So we get to Oneida. Got another two-hour conference. Detective Schaepe, two hours it was taken. When all these inconsistencies were supposed to have happened. He didn't show the video. It's their burden of proof. When the presentation of evidence raises issues, questions, credibility, benefit of the doubt goes to Mr. Mereness."

Is he suggesting that the prosecution would have used the tape of Bill's interrogation if it really proved he kept changing his story? That with the police officers' testimony they could "fudge" the truth? Maybe the DA should have played the audio tape and shown the videotape. But because they were both lengthy they probably would have put everyone to sleep. By using direct testimony, the district attorneys were able to get to the salient points. But that also allows the defense to cast the authorities as evil-doers.

During another long treatise, Daniel referred to the testimony of Detective Erik Goth regarding the portfolio of receipts he'd recovered during one of the searches. He concluded, "Does it mislead? Is it trying to direct you to a false conclusion? Absolutely. Absolutely." Then the defense attorney was even more accusatory, "So when you...listen to the State tell you what you should believe, believe Detective Goth about what was said in those statements, I submit to you you're hearing what Erik Goth thinks is going to convict Bill Mereness. And that's the beginning and the end of what you're going to hear from Mr. Goth. And the proof is in the pudding. You all saw it."

Wow! That's a pretty strong statement to make about a police officer.

Next, the defense attorney went through the actual crime sequence. He put forth that given the time line, autopsy results, body position, blood spatter, earring location and proximity of Nick Demrow's car to Jennifer's front door, the murder could not have happened at 11:40 a.m. He emphasized, "It's just physically impossible to have occurred that way."

To bolster his supposition, Daniel referred to lights that were on when Furgason arrived at the house, the front door being unlocked, and the dog cages that were still clean when the police arrived.

The defense attorney put forth his theory of the crime, "It has all the earmarks of a burglary. We have identifiable but unidentified... fingerprints at a place where someone would attempt entry to the house, right? Garage service door...That didn't work. It was closed, so they broke through, whoever this was, broke through the screens. All right. Left the fingerprints all over those screens. All right. Walked across that concrete. Fresh concrete floor. At least concrete and dust. Went upstairs. Left prints in the master bedroom door. Excuse me. Rifled the master bedroom. Took the expensive jewelry and a couple statues. That's an explanation that is supported by the facts and the evidence as to how that window got blown."

Bill's lawyer needed a moment to check his notes before he could move on.

Daniel then talked about circumstances, his own behavior in college, Bill's alibi, the phone call about property from the Columbus Circle house, the divorce and exchange of financial information. Finally, a point was made, "But when you take that thought together with the fact that this is a chance meeting, all right, it's a chance meeting. Well, how do you set up an alibi two weeks before a chance meeting? Now, I don't know how you do that. Again depending on how you do the testimony, Jim Mereness said they had been talking about this for what, a month or so?"

Well, they'd been talking about Jim hunting at the cabin for a month. Bill wasn't going to be there, so as he planned his crime he realized he would be able to use Jim's trip as an alibi.

The defense attorney continued to tilt at the prosecution's case. "The next, I guess, stretch that we're somehow to draw conclusions from is that Mr. Mereness was going around doing some errands and we are supposed to conclude…he was stalking her house or something. Well, and using the phone, the last phone call he made was 10:50. He made the next one was 12:10 in Edgerton. And this was the extent we got facts jimmied to make a case. Ignoring beyond a reasonable doubt. Ignoring simple physical facts." Daniel gestured to the cell maps, "Ignoring that if we were truly interested in figuring out whether the Sandstone property is blue, I'm pointing at all colors, whatever blue or orange or whatever, how do they want you to determine that which doesn't really make a lot of difference anyway? Want you to determine it by looking at an unscaled map."

Next, following a rant about "the cell guy", which cell tower picks up calls, a map that was merely a representation, Detective Goth's cartography skills, and map colors, the defense attorney summarized, "That's the kind of evidence they're asking you to find somebody guilty of first degree murder on.

"A person that was seen leaving the house at 10:40, excuse me, 11, whatever. Talked about this, didn't happen then, but the person that they saw leave left and walked at a normal pace. Nick Demrow drove past him twice on a city street. Person was walking normally, acting normal, carrying a couple things. Did not have a hat. Did not have a hood…There is no car in the vicinity that matches. 10:40. No one gets into a car. It's all residential. The closest place that you would have, you know, hide a car in a parking lot or something is the subdivision or the shopping mall with Home Depot and all the rest of the stuff. So, this person who has now committed a brutal murder, a bloody, brutal murder, walks all this distance, right, doesn't have any discernible blood, right. Mr. Demrow didn't see any blood. We still have white gloves with no blood on them. Didn't have blood on them on his jacket. That's the big mystery. Didn't have any blood on the sweatpants. Didn't see any blood. This person just committed this crime. Got himself undressed. In the midst of this residential construction. Somehow disposed of all this stuff...Cleaned himself up. Changed into civilian clothes and was clear in Edgerton at noon."

His argument does make me curious as to how Bill had been able to change out of his bloody clothes. Maybe he'd taken off his coat and then had a disposable cover-all on and stuffed it into one of the bags he was carrying. But, Bill's lawyer makes himself look disorganized and unprepared or even shifty when he keeps referring to the wrong times on that day.

Daniel moved on to the evidence from Paul Stein of the Wisconsin DOT. The defense attorney asserted that Stein had not said he knew a particular vehicle had traveled at a certain speed. He'd only given data as to average speeds at collection sites.

That is true, but Stein also said a slow-moving vehicle would have caused a real problem at those times.

A very scattered tale followed. In it, Daniel talked again about the glass shards, the identifiable but unidentified fingerprints, the fact that someone vomited in the toilet, the missing statues and jewelry, DNA, the shoes and Christopher's lie about the hatchet. It held no new information or theory. The defense attorney did say that he found it "bordering on outrageous" for the State to ask the jury to use an excluded shoe pattern to "convict a guy of murder 1".

Next, Daniel reviewed the search warrants and the items seized. He emphasized that evidence did not exist so, "Could-have doesn't make it, would-have doesn't make it, possible doesn't make it."

The defense attorney cautioned the jury to be sure to consider evidence as per the judge's instructions.

While Daniel expressed that it was unfortunate that Bill's mother had passed away, he insisted that during the bathroom scene there had to have been more conversation than what had been reported to the jury. He also reminded the jury of LaBelle's mental and physical problems.

Her memory really needed to be maligned one more time.

As far as Bill's confession to his parents was concerned, the jury needed to put themselves in Bill's position for that week. His wife was murdered, he was a suspect, police went through his "whatever" with a fine tooth comb, tried to trip him up and followed him. He went to Appleton where his brother and sister wanted nothing to do with him. He was aware that just recently 13 death row inmates in Illinois were exonerated by new evidence. His father told him one of his options was to kill himself. He was in "despair" and drove his "stupid car into that wall". To sum it up, Daniel said, "...He had a momentary lapse and before that he has consistently maintained that he wasn't involved."

After acknowledging that he had spoken for "way, way too long," Daniel reminded the jurors that this was one of the most serious things that would happen in their lifetimes.

The defense attorney finally finished, "And we have every confidence you are going to give it your best, you are going to follow your instructions, and we're not going to convict on would-have, could-have, believe what's not here, etcetera, etcetera, and we are going to return a fair and just verdict. It's going to say not guilty. Thank you."

We were allowed a ten-minute break. I noticed others, like me, were letting out enormous sighs of frustration and exhaustion. It would have shocked me to find out the jury felt otherwise.

At 12:04 p.m. court was back on the record. It was O'Leary's turn to rebut Daniel's closing argument.

Oh dear, I hope he doesn't take it point by point.

44

In his rebuttal, O'Leary had good news and bad news for the jury. He told them he was going to be the final attorney "arguing at you today", but they were still going to have to listen a little longer.

The DA first talked about Bill buying a replacement coat. While, he admitted, that in and of itself was not a big deal, it was their job to take all the facts and consider them together. After doing that, he was confident that the only reasonable conclusion they could draw was that the defendant killed Jennifer Judge.

The prosecutor reminded the jurors that Christopher testified that his father had owned shoes of the identical style to the ones that left prints at the scene.

As for fingerprints, O'Leary said Daniel had assisted the State in having the young students who had helped Jennifer move testify. They could certainly have left the unidentified prints behind.

The jury was warned against doing as the defense attorney had suggested by going on "wild goose chases" looking for "what else could there have been?" They needed to focus on what there was.

In terms of the eyewitness testimony, the DA reiterated that Nick Demrow was 100 feet away from the man who left Jennifer's house and he saw the man from the back and the side only. His description of the individual did fit Bill: middle aged, male, dark hair, glasses, Columbia coat, gray sweatpants, carrying two bags.

Next, O'Leary reassured the jury that the police had acted in a legal manner throughout their investigation of the case. From interviews to search warrants, all was carried out lawfully.

The district attorney was passionate about motive, "...I want to understand why Jennifer's not here. I want to understand why a human being would take those weapons and beat her skull in. It's absolutely impossible for me to use my logic and say how any other human being would say this is a good idea. I'm going to take these items and strike her in the head so hard six times as to kill her. We don't have to prove motive."

The jury was reminded of the statements of Bill's mother through his father and Captain Helein. They were cautioned that while Christopher may have misspoken about the hatchet, his testimony should not be discounted. He'd testified about the shoes as well as the coat that Bill replaced just two days after the brutal murder.

O'Leary asked the jury to recall that on Sunday Jim and his son were abandoned at the Minocqua property by Bill, only to see him return to the cabin for tennis shoes and gray sweatpants. Jim also testified that the shoes shown to him in front of the jury looked like the shoes Bill had retrieved from the cabin. That bolstered Christopher's testimony.

The prosecutor brought up Daniel's incorrect references to the time of one of the incriminating phone calls. According to the actual time of the call, Bill would have had adequate time. He said, "Plenty of time to kill her, pick up his bags, back out that side door, head to the back of the house, get to his vehicle, drive up the interstate…because he's heading north away from the scene."

Phone records showed that in the morning of the murder Bill was in the sector where the victim lived, he was around her home if "not in it".

As for the supposition that the murder couldn't have taken place when the prosecution said he had because Nick Demrow would have seen it, O'Leary explained that Demrow's attention had not been on the door until Jeff Jones alerted him. The prosecutor pointed to the floor plan of Jennifer's house, "Was that door open at some point? Absolutely." That explained how the blood got out there. "She screamed for her life. She tried to flee out that door. He caught her and smacked her in the head, drags her back inside, throws her down and she died in her front foyer there as he's smashing her skull with an axe. Absolutely true."

Oh God. I hadn't planned on reliving that during the closing arguments. My stomach poured out acid, my throat tightened.

The panel was asked to recall the testimony of Penny Patterson, how she'd overheard the angry phone message Bill had left Jennifer at school. Also, they'd heard that Jennifer had had an 18-minute phone call with Bill's parents on the day she was killed. She'd had to tell them about the divorce. She was upset after that and went home.

O'Leary traced Jennifer's movements on the floor plan and brought her personality into the courtroom when he talked about the dogs, "Came in through the garage, comes over here and she's murdered there. Doesn't even have time to let the dogs out of their cage. Dog lover that she is, she would let her dogs out…How else do we know that? She still had her keys in her hand when the attack took place." The prosecutor referred to the house plan again, "These are the basement stairs on Exhibit 74. He comes up from the basement stairs where we knew he broke in from the windows...She drops her keys. Her keys are right there on the steps...She tries to scream and get out of the house...That murder occurred as soon as she got home. That's what Mr. Jones heard. The scream so eerie to him, that he stopped listening to the radio, turned it off to try to hear some more. Got out of his car. Was so concerned he went up to his fellow carpenter in the car in front of him and said, 'Did you hear that lady screaming?'"

Yes, it must have been a truly primal scream.

O'Leary moved on to discuss the defendant's mother. He put forth that LaBelle had been stable at that time, she'd been out of the hospital for months and was on her medication. Besides, Bill's father had also heard what LaBelle had heard.

The prosecutor cautioned the jury that they should think about the entire circumstances when considering why Bill tried to kill himself after he confessed to his parents. They were reminded that the first option James, Sr. suggested to his son was that Bill tell the truth. Then Bill had said he didn't want to go to prison for 70 years for killing Jennifer. After that he attempted to kill himself. "As James, Sr. said, the defendant had three options."

The DA summarized, "From my point of view when you consider all of the evidence that we've submitted to you, all of the information that you have and you apply it as a whole you have one option. And that is to find the defendant guilty of first-degree intentional homicide. I want to thank you for your patience and time listening to our case. That's all I have, Your Honor."

He's done a good job of refuting the suggestions Daniel made. We're in pretty good shape, hopefully!

Judge Werner then had the clerk select the names of the alternates from the tumbler. She read, "Kelly Hayden, Mark Chapman, Yvette Pearson."

Werner asked the three alternates to go to the jury room and collect their things. Bailiff Bliss would take care of them so they wouldn't have any contact with the regular jurors.

Gosh, after all this time spent, those three will have no input and can't even say goodbye to their fellows. Seems stringent, but is probably what the law requires.

The three alternates left the courtroom.

Judge Werner noted for the record that the alternates were outside the presence of the court. He then gave the 12 jurors their final instructions, "The time has now come when the great burden of reaching a just, fair and conscientious decision of this case is to be thrown wholly upon you, the jurors selected for this important duty. You will not be swayed by sympathy, prejudice or passion."

The judge explained that the two possible verdicts were guilty or not guilty. Since it was a criminal case, the verdict must be unanimous. They were to select a person to preside over their deliberations. He or she would also sign and date the verdict when they had agreed upon one.

Next, the judge directed the clerk to administer the oath to the bailiff. She read, "Do you solemnly swear that you will to the utmost of your ability keep all jurors sworn on this trial in some private and convenient place subject to the discretion of the Court until they have agreed on their verdict or are discharged by the Court, and that you will not before they render their verdict communicate to any person the state of their deliberations or the verdict they have agreed upon so help you God?"

Mr. Bliss answered solemnly, "I will." I had no doubt of that.

The panel went into the jury room to deliberate at 12:35 p.m.

45

We went to lunch. On the way I called Jeff to let him know the jury was out. I would call him again when there was a decision.

Everyone was extremely nervous about the pending verdict. The two possibilities were discussed. In case the jury found Bill not guilty, all were glad that the DA had the back up of the bail jumping charges. Those two could still net a 10-year sentence which was admittedly too little, but at least something.

We also had a lot of anxiety about how much time it would take for the verdict to be returned. Cathy's brother Michael warned that no matter how convinced individual jurors were of Bill's guilt, they would take ample time to review the evidence and do a thorough job. He was quite sure we were looking at a three-hour minimum.

Since I had known there would be a wait of some time, I had brought along magazines and playing cards. While I knew it would be difficult to focus on anything at all, light reading or a simple card game might help to pass the time.

As we drove back to the courthouse, we saw two of the jury alternates standing on the corner outside a café with another man. Passing them by, I saw the three turn and start walking up courthouse hill. I assumed they were going to retrieve their cars from the courthouse parking lot and go home.

After we'd all gathered in the hallway outside the courtroom, I was surprised to see the two alternates and the third party come through security. I approached them and introduced myself. The person I didn't know turned out to be the husband of one of the jurors. I told the two alternates that everyone in the family appreciated their efforts in the case. I also explained that I had been sorry when their names had been pulled as alternates. They had also been saddened by that turn of events. They both had wanted to be a part of bringing in the verdict. Both vehemently stated that they would have found Bill guilty. But, since they had not been able to speak of the case with the other jurors, they really had no way of knowing how those left on the panel would vote. They were so invested in the outcome of the trial that they were also going to stay until the verdict came in. I was really impressed with them and their dedication to justice.

The time passed slowly, everyone milling around to talk with other family members, police officers, the district attorneys, Shelly and members of the media.

The hallway of the Rock County Courthouse where we awaited the verdict

A group of us entertained the idea of, should the verdict be guilty, naming the cabin for Jennifer. When Jennifer's nephew James suggested "Jennifer's Justice" everyone immediately approved. It would be a perfect name.

At that moment I secretly decided I would make a sign for the family to erect at the cabin. It would be my gift to Jennifer's family after the sentencing.

I got impatient and induced Josh, Nicole and her brother Michael to play a game of Euchre. It was hard to concentrate, but we did have a bit of fun considering the circumstances. I passed my magazines around to anyone who was interested in thumbing through one.

The minutes ticked by. Around 4:00 p.m. we started wondering what we would do about supper. We were afraid to leave in case the jury came in, but in an hour or so we would be getting hungry. Some ideas were tossed out; we could order pizza, someone could do a run for subs or other sandwiches. We decided to think on it for awhile.

Fortunately, we did not have to make a decision because at about 4:15 p.m., we were advised that a verdict had been reached. I took a deep breath and sent up a final plea. Family members grasped one another's hands to bolster courage. We filed into the courtroom for the last time in this trial that had so consumed our lives.

Judge Werner began, "...We're back on the record in the matter of the State of Wisconsin versus William Mereness, 02CF3911. It is my understanding from the bailiff we have a verdict so I assume we can bring in the jury."

The jury entered the courtroom at 4:17 p.m.

Werner addressed the panel, "Miss Hahn, it looks like you're the foreperson. Am I correct?"

Juror Hahn rejoined, "Yes, I am."

"You folks have reached a verdict?"

"Yes we have."

The paper with the verdict was handed from Miss Hahn to Bailiff Bliss who delivered it to the judge. It seemed as if the bailiff was walking in slow motion.

I realized I'd been holding my breath. I tried to concentrate on inhaling and exhaling.

Judge Werner spoke, "...I have received a verdict and it does read the Honorable Richard T. Werner presiding. We, the jury, duly impaneled and sworn to try the issues in the above-entitled action, find the defendant, William J. Mereness, guilty of first degree..."

A roar went up behind us. I turned around to see Jim and Christopher yelling, "Yes! Yes!" and pumping their fists in the air.

Judge Werner snapped to attention and commanded, "You'll be removed if you continue that!"

Everyone in Jennifer's family tried to stifle their tearful expressions of joy and relief by burying our faces in our hands. Then, in a compulsion to share those feelings family member turned to embrace family member.

I was deliriously happy.

Werner continued, "Guilty of first degree intentional homicide as charged in the information. It is dated today's date signed by Ms. Hahn as foreperson. Folks, I'm going to ask you individually and I'll start with you, Mr. Scott. Mr. Scott, was this and is this your verdict?"

Juror Scott replied, "Yes, sir."

The judge did likewise with the other panelists: Miss Morrison, Miss Wulf-Rice, Mr. Hager, Miss Henthorn, Miss Yoemans, Miss Funk, Miss Carlson, Miss Trail, Mr. Wallace, Ms. Hahn and Mr. Whipple. Each one, in turn responded in the affirmative.

I wanted to jump up, shout for joy and run out of the courtroom. I was sure everyone did. But we needed to stay until the last word was spoken.

Judge Werner thanked the jury and told them that their service in the case was complete. He informed them that they did not have to answer questions about the case from anyone other than the Court, but there was no requirement that they maintain secrecy about what had occurred in the jury room. They were excused.

Next, the judge revoked Bill's bond.

This time it's forever!

The sentencing was scheduled for November 7, 2003, at 9:30 a.m.

Judge Werner remanded the defendant into the custody of the sheriff, then pronounced, ""These matters are in recess."

Bobby, Cathy and Nicole comfort one another after the guilty verdict *(Courtesy of The Janesville Gazette)*

We nearly bounded out of the courtroom. Hugs and handshakes were exchanged all around. Faces were frozen in smiles; eyes glistened.

Bobby and Cathy went around inviting everyone to their house for a celebration.

Josh and his cousin Michael planned to stop for beer. Nicole rode with me because she wanted to witness me going into a liquor store and purchasing champagne, which I had every intention of drinking and, of course, sharing with others.

I called Jeff, and he, too, was thrilled with the news.

At my brother's house we celebrated for several hours: family, prosecutors and police, many who had brought spouses along. It was a wonderful time, this team united in justice, Jennifer's Justice. We felt truly happy for the first time since our Jennifer had been forced to leave this earth.

46

I had been so focused, we all had, on August 11 and then the verdict. I guess it was naive of me to think that after that it would be "over". While we were pleased that justice had been served, there were still emotions and situations to be dealt with.

The day after the verdict, Bobby, Cathy and Nicole went up to the cabin in Minocqua. I fiddled the day away catching up on some chores outside and in the barn. I was happy to be outside after so many days cooped up in the courtroom. Jeff was due home in the afternoon, so I was eagerly anticipating his return. I wasn't nearly as completely exhausted as I had thought I would be.

Just as I finished mowing the lawn, Jeff drove in the driveway. As he got closer, my eyes began to tear up. By the time he pulled up I was bawling uncontrollably. He had rolled down the window and I leaned in and put my head down. I just sobbed. He stroked my head. Finally, I composed myself enough to speak. "I'm so glad you're home. I didn't want you to go, but I couldn't ask you to stay. It's the hardest thing I've ever done." I began crying anew.

After I helped Jeff unload the Avalanche, I was feeling better. We had a normal evening, sharing our experiences, having dinner and doing nightly chores.

After Jeff went back to work on Wednesday, I had the burning desire to get away from it all. I called the Grand Hotel on Mackinaw Island, Michigan. They had a few vacancies for Saturday night only. I had a pony ride booking for late Friday afternoon, but could run up to the island Saturday. I'd have to find other accommodations for Sunday, then come home Monday. With school starting on Tuesday, I had little flexibility, but I was going to give it a try.

Since I knew Erin was working, and didn't want to complicate things for Cathy, I called Nicole. I asked if there was a chance that she, Erin and her mom would be able to go on a quick get away. She explained that Erin was moving home from Madison on Saturday. I knew that all of the family members pitched in together when one moved, so I was out of luck. I thought about going by myself or asking another friend to go. I didn't really want to be alone and it seemed all of my friends were busy with back to school duties.

I called Jeff at work and told him my dilemma. "I'll go with you," he said.

"But you just got home."

"That's okay. I've got some money left over, we'll just take off."

I was tempted. But I knew I had to find out Josh's schedule to see if the horses and dogs could be managed. "I'll check with Josh on his schedule and call you back, okay?"

"Sure, I'll be right here."

Unfortunately, Josh had a very tightly packed weekend with work and a Brewer's game he'd planned for since June. I could try to cobble together care for our animals by friends and neighbors, but I didn't really feel up to that. I called Jeff.

"Josh is booked. I guess I'll just stay home."

"It's okay with me if you go alone, I can take care of everything at home."

"Thanks, honey, but I think it's best to just stay home. Maybe the two of us can go to a movie or something. It is great to have you back."

"If you're sure."

"I am...I think."

So I spent the next few days catching up on tasks put aside during the trial, visiting my mom, and a bit of time lazing in the hammock in the shade. I took some naps and took the dogs on long walks. I tried to get myself to write, but wasn't in the mood.

On Tuesday, I nearly cried again because I had to go to school. I told Jeff, "This has been the summer from hell, and now it's over. How am I going to get up the energy to teach these kids, not to mention supervising my student teacher?"

"You're a pro. You'll get going once you're there. I know it."

"I hope so."

Jeff was right. It felt like I had never been gone. It, actually, felt good to have a distraction. Meeting my student teacher was a delight. Tanya seemed like a real go-getter. She was enthusiastic, but realistic. I was feeling somewhat better, but still longed for a total get away.

One day a colleague stopped by my room during his preparation period. He'd just read the *Gazette*. He wanted to warn me that the notice for the foreclosure on the Sandstone house was in there. I appreciated being forewarned. It was always most difficult when I saw such things without expectation.

On Friday evening, I received a call from Bobby. He asked how the year had started. We exchanged stories. It always amazed me how much we thought alike about our professions. Then he said he wanted to ask a favor of Jeff and I. He said I should feel free to say no. I thought perhaps he was going to ask us to go up to the cabin and cut trees and brush as he had proposed for last February.

Bobby's request stunned me, "We just picked up Jennifer's car from the police. We are going to let it go back to Ford or the dealer or the bank, we don't really know what will happen specifically. Meantime, we have no where to park it. Would you mind if we parked it somewhere at your place?"

This was so personal, Jennifer's very own car at my house. I'd look at it countless times a day. But I could not refuse. If this struck me hard, I could not imagine what it was doing to Bobby and Cathy at this time. I could not make them try to find another place for it. "No, of course we don't mind. You can leave it here as long as you need to." I'd deal with my own feelings later.

"Thanks. It will probably be just a short while, until we deal with the details. Could I bring it out tomorrow morning?"

"Don't worry about a timeline for moving it. Sure, you can bring it out in the morning, but let me sleep in until 7:30, will you?" I knew he was always up by 6:00 a.m., and I was wanting to enjoy a day I could sleep a bit longer.

"That's fine. I'll be there about 8:00."

The next morning, Bobby drove into the driveway with Jennifer's Taurus. Erin followed in their Tracker. I put on my shoes and walked outside while Bobby parked Jennifer's car on the grass across from the garage in front of the hay wagon.

Bobby got out and inquired, "Is this an okay spot?"

"Sure, we'll move it if we need to. Just leave the keys here."

"We only have the one set. You won't lose them will you?"

"Haven't lost a set of keys yet." I tried to reassure him. He sure didn't need the hassle of acquiring a new key. "We'll just hang it on the key ring and it should be perfectly secure."

"Okay." Bobby's response did not reflect full confidence.

"Really, it'll be fine. We may need to move it if the grass needs to be mowed under it and around it."

"Oh, I don't imagine it'll be here that long."

"Well, just in case."

"All right." He sounded just like my dad when he had been cajoled into agreeing to something he didn't want to.

"Then it's settled." I turned to Erin, who had been quietly observing our verbal ping-pong match. "Do you have anything special scheduled for the day?"

She responded, "Not really, just some errands and cleaning my room here for the big move."

Bobby added that they had some errands to run, and that they'd better be going. I showed him where the keys would be hanging. I reminded him of our garage code, in case he should need to access the keys and we were not at home. We said our good-byes.

I did my chores and tried to ignore the car. I felt quite emotional about it being there. The last time Jennifer had been in it she had been moments from her death. This was going to take some time to process.

After an entire week passed I felt I was dealing better with the car. It was all I had had of Jennifer's since I had taken her dogs up to Wisconsin Rapids at the time of the funeral.

I retrieved the key, unlocked and opened the door. It smelled dusty. It had been in impound and now out in the sun for a week. I looked inside. On the passenger's seat was a bean-filled neck pillow. I smiled to myself. A small collection of CD's was neatly stacked by the stick shift. I almost felt like I was violating Jennifer's memory by looking through them, but I couldn't help myself. Aretha Franklin was on top. There was one by Neil Diamond. I'd had enough. I closed the door and locked it with the remote. I walked away. Another day I'd sit in it. I'd feel the steering wheel, look in the rearview mirror. Perhaps I'd check the glove compartment. I wanted to feel her person through her possessions, but couldn't take any more right then. The CD's had been enough.

At 2:30 a.m. on Sunday, September 14, I awakened with my heart pounding. I was sweating. I'd been having an awful nightmare. It took me a few minutes to shake off the immediate effects. I went to the bathroom, then into the kitchen to get a drink of water. I sat down and thumbed

Jennifer's car parked at our farm after the police released it

through a catalog. The contents of the nightmare came back to me. Some of our friends were moving from their farm. They were having an auction of their household belongings. Jeff and I went over to help out. In broad daylight people kept coming into the house to kill Jeff, our friends and me. We had to kill the attackers in self-defense. We hit them with whatever we could grab; I remembered using an umbrella stand. We took knives away from our attackers and stabbed them with their own weapons. There were no guns, but the people kept coming and coming. I was exhausted but we could not stop fighting or they would kill us. Finally, we killed all the attackers and they lay dead all over our friends' house. Their bloodied corpses littering the stairs, living room and kitchen. We collapsed in exhaustion.

And that's exactly how I felt, exhausted. I certainly understood the significance of being attacked, but the other parts of the dream had me puzzled. Why were our friends involved? Why were there so many people attacking us? I wondered if anyone could interpret the nightmare for me. I tried to put the thoughts out of my head. I ate a carton of yogurt and finished looking at the catalog. It was one of my favorites, with many western items in it. I wasn't able to really concentrate on it. I set it aside for another time. I went back to bed and, fortunately, was able to get back to sleep.

In the early morning hours of Tuesday, September 16, I awoke in the same state. I'd had another nightmare. This time it was just me. It was dark and I was outside somewhere on a street. There was a man after me, trying to kill me. My recollection was not completely clear. I didn't know if the man was someone I was acquainted with or not. I did recall events clearly. The man had had a hatchet. He had somehow caught me and I wrestled the hatchet away from him and hit him with it. He was completely bloody, but somehow still alive. He got the hatchet back and was chasing me down the middle of the street. Blood was spewing out in front of him as he ran. The blood reached out for me like fingers. I screamed and ran and ran.

Jeff turned in his sleep. I didn't want to awaken him, but I wanted comfort. I spoke quietly, hoping he was awake, "I just had another horrible nightmare." Jeff grumbled and rolled over. I wouldn't wake him. I'd deal with this myself.

Like two nights before, I got up, went to the bathroom and got a drink of water. I sat on the couch. This had to stop. I was exhausted. I had to teach all day and spend the evening at our Back to School Night. I knew I'd had adrenaline rushing through by body, and that would leave me drained. I hoped I could get home for an hour or two between school and

Back to School Night to take a quick nap. Otherwise, I'd be playing catch up all week. I returned to bed and went through the relaxation technique of contracting and relaxing muscles throughout my body. It must have worked because the next thing I knew, the 6:00 alarm went off.

I got through the day at school and quickly came home for that much-needed nap. Jeff had offered to do the chores after he got home from work. I couldn't get to sleep right away but dozed heavily after that, because when the kitchen timer went off after an hour my left shoulder was numb and I had some deep creases in the skin of my upper arm. I felt a little better, but still tired. After a successful "meet and greet" with our parents I got home about 9:00 p.m. Of course I wasn't able to sleep then, because I had a little adrenaline rush going from being "on stage", so I watched the Brewer game on TV and got to bed about 10:30. I hoped, fervently, I would have no nightmares this night.

Wednesday morning I awakened pleased to have had no bad dreams. School went fairly well and I went home. I sat down to read *The Janesville Gazette*. On the front page was the photo of Bill in his prison orange. The title of the accompanying article read, "Mereness bill tops $40,000". *This whole thing is not going away at all!*

The article stated that we Rock County residents had paid $41,894 for the murder case so far. After reviewing the basics of the case, the article said that Bill still "doesn't qualify for a state-paid public defender because he owns a lakefront home in Minocqua". An affidavit filed on Bill's behalf read he "has no income, no cash and no liquid assets". Judge Richard Werner had found Bill to be indigent.

Werner had then appointed Robert Junig to represent Bill in the bail-jumping charges. The article continued, "Junig will be paid $70 an hour, which is the minimum rate set by the Wisconsin Supreme Court".

According to the Rock County Clerk of Courts and the Rock County Sheriff's Department the costs of Mereness' murder case included: $23,472 for defense attorney Tod Daniel; $9,156 for motel rooms and dinner for jurors; $5,899 to pay overtime for sheriff's deputies to guard the sequestered jury around the clock; $1,788 in witness fees; $850 for bus transportation for the jury; $607 for juror lunches at the courthouse and $122 for transcripts by court reporters.

Next, the article paraphrased Rock County Corporation Counsel Thomas Schroeder. Schroeder was confident the county would recoup the expense of providing a defense attorney for Mereness. The county had put a lien against the Minocqua home.

Finally, Schroeder addressed the wrongful death lawsuit Jennifer's family had filed against Bill. If the family were to win the case, they would recover his half of Jennifer and Bill's estate, which included the Minocqua home. Schroeder said he was confident an agreement could be worked out with Jennifer's family.

What in the world is going on here? While as a Rock County taxpayer I surely did not want to pay for Bill's defense, but her family? That would be immoral. Did the law mean that should Jennifer's family win their civil suit they would be obligated to pay Bill's defense and other trial costs? It couldn't be. But, if that was so, why in the world would the family bother with the suit when they just have to turn over large sums of money to his attorney and to the county? I hoped this wouldn't turn out like Josh's accident had, but I feared the worst because of our experience.

Due to his accident, Josh had medical bills of over $200,000. The individuals who caused the accident had minimal insurance, so Jeff's and my auto insurance and medical insurance paid the lion's share of the bills. Our lawyer at that time who, ironically, was Tod Daniel, advised us that there was nothing to be done. Josh would never receive a personal injury payment. In the state of Wisconsin, should there be a settlement; the insurance company stands in front of the victim to recoup any money they had paid out. Jeff and I were in complete disbelief. We had always thought that because we paid insurance premiums, the company accepted the risk. Not so. I don't believe I'll ever get over my outrage about that. What in the world does an insurance company stand to lose? They receive premiums up front then a payback if there is a settlement. Josh had not only been a victim of another person's poor driving; he was the victim of our legal system. Consequently I had a great deal of skepticism about this. It would not surprise me if Jennifer's family would end up being victimized again.

I knew it was so important for Jennifer's family to have the cabin in Minocqua. I hoped the law would be in their favor, so they would not have to feel the outrage I continued to feel.

The nightmares stopped, thank God. But I was having trouble unwinding at the end of the day and was pretty much going on automatic pilot at school. I was happy my student teacher was very competent. She helped keep me sharp and filled in some enthusiasm that I was uncharacteristically low on.

In mid-September Bobby called one evening. He was wondering if I had ever rented a U-Haul trailer.

"Heck no!" I replied. I told him I'd checked into it once when we were moving and the price had been prohibitive.

My brother agreed, "Wow, I just can't believe how expensive it is. We need to move a lot of Jennifer's belongings into the house in Minocqua. It's costing us a bundle to keep it in the storage shed."

"I can imagine. But you know you can always borrow our horse trailer, although we will need it five weekends in a row beginning the last weekend of September. We've got pony rides lined up both Saturdays and Sundays throughout the fall. That doesn't really give you any opportunity with school in session."

"We're anxious to get this done as soon as possible, to save costs; but I had no idea how much the truck rental would be. It would almost make sense for us to just buy a small horse trailer like your old one. How much did you say those were?"

"Well, you could probably find a new one for about $3,500. We just sold our used one for $2,200."

"Oh, I thought you'd told me a lower figure. Guess we'll go back to the drawing board."

"Don't forget, after Halloween our trailer is available."

"Thanks, I'll keep that in mind; but I really think we need to get going on this."

A few days later Bobby called to say that they'd rented a U-Haul. He wondered if they could park it at our place overnight. He didn't really want to stir up questions in his neighborhood.

"Of course, bring it out whenever you need to. I wish I could go with you guys and help move Jennifer's things."

"That's okay. You know it's really something Cathy and her sister have to do."

I hadn't realized Patti was going to be involved, "Oh, so Patti is going to help?"

"Yes, she and Mike are meeting us up at the cabin. Hopefully, we'll be able to make the weekend manageable."

"I'm glad you are getting together on this. It should make it nicer."

He agreed, "By the way, do you still have your 'pig iron'?"

"Yes, it's in the barn. Do you need to use it?"

"If I can get a chance to move a few rocks up on the property it might help. Could you leave it out for me to pick up when I get the truck?"

"No problem. I'll set it out."

The evening the truck was dropped off, Bobby gestured toward Jennifer's car, "It should only be a few more weeks until the car is gone. We've just about got that straightened out."

"There's no hurry. Jeff moved it yesterday so I could mow under and around it. It started right up."

"That's good."

After Bobby and Cathy left, I had another uncomfortable sensation. It was strange to think of the vehicle containing Jennifer's belongings sitting in my circular driveway. I was glad I didn't have a key, so I couldn't look inside. Between the truck and Jennifer's car I felt her presence more than ever. The cool fall weather reminded me that it was getting close to a year since she'd been taken from us.

Attempting to be positive and productive, I began to work on the sign for the cabin. After school and chores I'd sit down at the computer designing and redesigning, trying to find the perfect font, artwork and color scheme.

Once I'd settled on the design I spent my evenings preparing the wood, transferring the design and hand painting it.

The work was very therapeutic.

When I had the sign finished, Jeff helped me with the design and construction of the post structure that would hold the sign and anchor it in the ground.

I was very pleased with and proud of the final project. I was anxious to give it to Jennifer's family after the sentencing. When I'd told Bobby about the sign, he'd filled me in on the plan the entire Judge family had to go up to the cabin and have an early Thanksgiving before Tom, Sr. and Mavis headed to Arizona for the winter. They were also planning to cut down some trees and other brush that were blocking the view of the lake. Bobby had asked to borrow our chain saw so he could help with the lumberjack work.

I had encouraged my brother to set aside some time over the weekend to install the sign and make the cabin officially, "Jennifer's Justice".

47

November 7, 2003. It was just two weeks shy of the first anniversary of Jennifer's murder. It didn't feel like justice had been swift, but considering all the investigation that went into a case of this nature as well as the time it must have taken the District Attorneys to plan an effective prosecution, it seemed reasonable. I was very relieved this day had finally arrived.

I was glad that Josh was going to attend with me. It had been very comforting to have him present for the two days of the trial. I had taken on the role of supporter for Jennifer's immediate family, but had found that I, too, needed support.

All the packing logistics offered a sense of normality to the morning. I'd finished feeding the horses and dogs, given the dogs some exercise and started packing my vehicle. I'd loaded the chain saw, gas can, post-hole digger and sign when I encountered a problem with the post. I wasn't able to fit it's L-shaped bulk in the back of the Avalanche. I decided to go inside, eat breakfast and think about my dilemma. Josh had a suggestion, "Couldn't we just put everything in the bed of the truck?"

"Do you think that would be a good idea, given that we would be leaving the vehicles in the courthouse parking lot, a place frequented by criminals?"

"I see your point."

We decided to drive separately. He was to take the post, which would hopefully not be seen lying down in the truck bed. I would keep everything else under lock and key in the back of the Avalanche.

Black clothing seemed appropriate for the day. I dressed in my black denim suit jacket and skirt. While my emerald earrings didn't match, I wore them as a silent tribute to the Irish Judges.

We left the house at 8:50 a.m. It was a very cold, clear morning. There was significant frost on the grass and the thermometer in the rearview mirror read 28 degrees. *What a tremendous contrast this is to the sultry 90-degree days of the trial less than two months ago.*

It was obvious to me that my head was a lot clearer on this drive than it had been throughout the trial. I hadn't felt "foggy" at that time, but I must have been to a certain degree. Today I was acutely aware of the scenery as I drove east on Highway 14 then south on Highway 51. When I approached courthouse hill on Parker Drive I noticed there was a statue in the park directly ahead of me. Though it was probably about 50 feet tall, it had never registered in my mind during all my previous trips on this exact route. I studied the statue as I was stopped at the stop sign waiting to cross Court Street and enter the courthouse parking lot. From a distance it appeared to be made of gray granite. Atop the tall stone tower was a human figure that looked like a soldier in a Civil War uniform.

One day I will look at that statue more closely. How ridiculous that I'd lived in this community for nearly 50 years and been involved in this trial, but I've been so ignorant about the immediate surroundings.

Entering the courthouse I met Michael and Pat Judge, Tom, Jr. and Marsha. Interestingly, they also were wearing black. After greeting hugs all around, I commented on our choice of clothing color. Marsha complimented my outfit; she especially liked the contrasting stitching on the skirt. I lifted my hair to show it was also on the jacket. She suggested I wear my hair up to allow the stitching to be seen.

"You know, I thought of that, but didn't feel the occasion warranted an updo."

Pat commented dryly, "I think the occasion warrants our best party wear."

Everyone laughed. The woman at the information booth smiled at us.

I mused aloud, "I wonder what people would think if we'd shown up in sequined ball gowns and tuxedos?"

Again, we had a laugh. Michael nodded as if he thought the idea would have had merit if we'd thought of it sooner.

At that time, Tod Daniel and his intern walked past the group. We fell completely silent. I watched them out of the corner of my eye. They did not look at us.

After the defense attorney was out of earshot, Marsha said she was looking forward to seeing Bill in his orange jumpsuit. We all discussed whether or not the convicted murderer would be allowed to wear regular clothes or not. Michael thought perhaps he would. Tom was sure that since he'd been convicted he would be wearing restraints. Pat mentioned that he might even be wearing a stun belt since there had been a recent incident in Milwaukee County where a prisoner had grabbed a deputy's gun during a sentencing.

Jennifer's Justice

I had read an article about that incident too. *Dear God, that's all we need!*

We proceeded through security, greeting the guards as if they, too, were now part of our greater family. They kindly told us we'd be in Courtroom C on the third floor.

In front of the courtroom we met up with reporters from WCLO. Kyle and Steve told us we couldn't get into the courtroom yet because "Juvie Court" was still in session.

Ah, that would explain why I just saw one of my former students in the stairwell.

The young man had had a plethora of problems during his eighth grade year, and despite the many private talks I'd had with him and my team's efforts to work with him, it looked like he'd not had much success turning his life around. *What another sad situation.*

There was a significant crowd gathering. A television crew, ADA Folt's wife, Officers Goth and Fritz, Bill's first wife, Ann, one of her daughters, Christopher, Jim Mereness as well as Sallie Dryer and her husband were all present. William Mereness, Sr. was noticeably absent. That did not surprise me, given the stress the poor man must be still feeling.

Bobby, Cathy, Patti and Mike Barker arrived. More hugs and kisses were exchanged. Mavis and Tom, Sr. arrived. Tom, Sr. was walking slowly and with the aid of a cane. He and I shared a very long embrace after he greeted me with his usual, "Hi sweetheart".

"You look good, how are you feeling?" I inquired.

"I'm doing okay."

"Well, given the circumstances, that's probably all right." I squeezed his arm.

He sighed. "I guess so."

"Are you going to come and visit us in Arizona this winter?" Mavis queried.

"I'd love to. Will you write a note to my boss that you excuse me from my teaching duties for a couple of weeks?"

She laughed.

Stephanie Judge arrived. We chatted a bit. It was good to see her again. On the way up the stairs I'd told Marsha how much I'd enjoyed getting to know Stephanie better during the trial. "You must be very proud to have such a kind, intelligent daughter."

"We have been very lucky with both our kids, thanks."

"I don't know James as well as Stephanie, but he seems like a wonderful young man. And, I don't think it's just luck. You two did a great job with them."

"Well, thank you, we are very proud."

Suddenly, the official voice of Bailiff Bliss was heard, "Media may enter."

Shelly, the victim-witness liaison, approached the family, "I'll be determining who comes in and where they sit." *Good. We sure don't need to get into a competition for seats on this day of days.*

We followed Shelly.

Courtroom C was a mirror image of courtroom D where the trial had taken place. The judge's bench was on an angle to the front and right. The witness chair was to his right. However, the prosecution table was still on the left as we faced front, so we would still sit on the left side of the courtroom. Now the jury box, which was where the media had set up, was directly ahead of us. I was very glad that this had not been the configuration we'd had for the trial. With this arrangement, the family would not have been able to see the jurors' faces. For me, it had been an important component.

We filed into the pews. In the front row from left to right were Stephanie, Marsha, Tom, Jr., Mavis and Tom, Sr. The second row consisted of Josh, me, Mike Barker, Bobby, Cathy, Patti, Pat and Michael Judge. Behind us were the two police officers.

Bill's family sat across the aisle.

The door to the right of the courtroom opened. Bill walked in. He was wearing the short-sleeved orange jail jumpsuit with an off-white thermal long-sleeved shirt underneath. I could not see if his ankles were shackled or not.

Mr. Bliss made his announcement, "All rise, Branch Six is now in session, the Honorable Judge Richard Werner presiding." I imagined that was the last time I would hear those words. *Today they feel familiar and comforting.*

Judge Werner spoke quietly and with solemnity. This was the case of The State of Wisconsin versus William Mereness. We heard the case number for the last time, 02CF3911. The judge wished the record to reflect the presence of the attorneys for the State and the defense as well as the defendant, William Mereness. He told those present that the sentencing was today and that we'd have a chance to review the presentence investigation.

Werner asked DA David O'Leary if the victim's family was aware of the sentencing today. The DA indicated that they were and informed the judge that Patti Judge, a sister, Cathy Luchsinger, a sister, Pat Judge, a sister-in-law, and Michael Judge, a brother, wished to speak to the court.

Jennifer's Justice

There was a brief skirmish between Daniel and O'Leary as to whether the statutes allowed for a sister-in-law to speak. Judge Werner pronounced that while the sisters and brother could speak, the sister-in-law could not.

Werner indicated the first person could come forward. Patti stood, then hesitated. O'Leary and Folts were motioning to her to come forward. Cathy gave her a little shove in the behind. With her paper in her hand, Jennifer's sister walked to the witness chair.

Patti spelled her first and last name for the record and said, "I am Jennifer's sister." It struck me that she used the present tense. It seemed discordant. I had gotten so used to Jennifer being referred to in the past tense.

Patti told the judge that her family had received hundreds of letters about her sister. Each writer had told of how Jennifer had touched their lives. Patti was going to read from one of those letters. It was from one of Jennifer's former students.

Reading glasses perched on her nose; Patti started to read from the letter. She also began to weep. She put her fingers to the bridge of her nose to try and regain her composure. There were few dry eyes in the courtroom. Kindly, the Bailiff, Mr. Bliss, brought two boxes of Kleenex to Shelly. Stephanie took some, as did Marsha. Marsha distributed them to her mother and father-in-law.

Patti read, "Dear Jennifer's Mom, I have known Jennifer Judge ever since she moved to Janesville to become next door neighbors with my family in Columbus Circle. Jennifer was very friendly and just bubbly. She fit into the neighborhood right away. She would come over to our house to talk or hang out as she pleased. She was always such a warm and welcoming person. It amazed me how she had met more people in our neighborhood in the first two weeks upon arrival than my family had known in our eight years of living in our house. That really proves her outgoing personality.

"Whenever Jennifer would stop by for a quick hello I always felt her cheerfulness. She was one of those people that you could tell everything to and she would care. I really respected her opinions and advice. Even though she had only lived in our circle for two years, it seemed like I had known her forever. When my sister JoEllen was sick in the hospital, she called from Minocqua inquiring if there was anything she could do. She always put other's needs before hers.

"Which brings me to my classroom experiences with her. Mrs. Mereness had a very tough position to fill coming into Craig High School half way through the year and filling a teacher's spot, not to mention a Spanish teacher. I remember how she would call me to see what we had learned and what we were presently studying. She was very concerned about being the best teacher she could be. I really admired that in her. I know she has succeeded at doing that. Jennifer brought so many smiles and laughs to the classroom. She wanted us to do well, and she really cared about each of us on a more personal level. She started the class out with goofy jokes or sayings on the board, which would crack smiles on everyone's face. Jennifer related with all her students, and she could tell when someone was having a bad day. She would cheer them up with candy or just being her fun self. When a student had a headache, she gave them a back rub to ease the stress in their life. The headache went away, too. Even though she could not have a child, she took us all under her wings as her own. No matter how rough of a day she was having, she'd crack a smile and cheer everyone else up. Jennifer made so many goofy faces, and I would crack up seeing her carry, or rather, drag her suitcase/briefcase down the congested hallways calling, 'Beep, beep'. Jennifer was an amazing teacher. She taught me Spanish and most importantly how to enjoy life.

"I'm really going to miss Jennifer, but I know she is in heaven. She has left so many beautiful memories, and she has touched so many people's lives. I will always hold a special place in my heart for her, and I believe her spirit has lived on. She truly was an awesome, caring individual who will be missed by many people. Some people come into your life and fade away, while others stay forever and dance little footprints in your heart.

"I'm deeply sorry for your loss, but she is in a better place. My ten-year-old neighbor said, 'God must have really needed her'."

Most of the family laughed a bit amid their tears. The bailiff held up his hand to us, but only Josh and I noticed. *My God, surely we can show some emotion today? I understand it was important that the jury not see emotion from the gallery, but there is no jury today. Why would the court rules be so insensitive and inhumane?*

After thanking the judge, Patti rejoined the family.

Cathy was next to speak. She told Judge Werner she was going to read from a letter the police had found at Jennifer's house. They had kindly turned it over to her after the trial. It was an open letter Jennifer had written to her friends and family. Cathy, too, peered through her reading glasses.

How far we've come since our halcyon days in college. Now we're wearing reading glasses and bifocals.

My sister in law began, "What can I say? The past six weeks have been filled with all kinds of stuff ranging from excitement and anticipation to surprise and confusion to pain and difficulty.

"The good thing is that I don't anticipate it getting any worse-when you're at the bottom, there's only one direction to go and that's up! Right? Well, that's what I keep telling myself!

"I am writing to thank you all for your support as I weave my way through this mess. Honestly, if it weren't for your cards, phone calls and visits, I'm not sure I'd be able to stand firm. 'Does your voice mail say Jennifer Judge? That's cool!' 'You had better be smiling right now 'cuz I am!' 'Be strong honey.' 'It's about time you listened to someone!' 'Why that #@&*%$#!' 'What can I help you with?'

"Mom spent a week with me and called at least three times a day. She wanted to make sure I was, number one, okay and number two that I didn't change my mind. She unpacked my kitchen and organized it, she lined all my drawers, tiled underneath my sinks and gave free hugs in between.

"Mom and Dad—you have been great, gone above and beyond the call of duty. I'm glad you're my parents.

"Brother Mike—you tell me to hold or fold; I'm following your advice to the letter.

"Cathy—thank you for your strength. Yes, my lawyer has good teeth.

"Patti and Tommy—thanks for giving me something to smile about.

"Ken—you bit your tongue and didn't say, 'I told you so'. You came so close, but didn't—thank you.

"John, yes—it's Judge and it's gonna stay that way!

"Amy—these boots were made for walking and that's just what they'll do...

"So—what do you do when life gives you lemons? Make lemonade and lots of it! How am I making lemonade? Well, I'm participating in a program to get licensed as a foster parent I will be done in December and then will begin to take in kids. I figure that I am able to make connections with kids in the classroom—maybe I'll be able to do it in a home setting. I'm also working at Kohl's Department Store as a cashier. It's something to get me out of the house, gives me a little giggle money and a nice discount to shop with. But you know me—cashier today, store manager tomorrow! I'm trying to decide on what steps I'm going to take professionally. I'm either getting a master's in educational leadership or getting certified to teach another language—probably French, Japanese or Russian.

"I'm still working on unpacking. I'm amazed at how much crapola one can accumulate.

"I think I'm working at the ECHO dinner for Thanksgiving and going to Arizona for Christmas. I hope to spend spring break someplace warm and next to the water. I do have special criteria for where I go though—no sight seeing! I'm going to plant myself in the sand, read some good books and eat to my little heart's content. Okay—a margarita or five or six might be in order too! One problem though, no one to go with! Any takers? I'll translate for free and promise not to let you get lost in a foreign country!

"Anyways, thanks for all your support. I'm keeping a stiff upper lip and continue to believe that things happen for a reason. Life is 10% what happens to you and 90% what you decide to do about it. I'm finally doing something about it and have a new attitude. Samuel Bennett Mereness will never be—maybe that's a good thing. But Samuel Bennett Judge is something you can count on!

"Thank you, thank you, thank you, your daughter, sister, auntie, pal and future parent, Jennifer Judge."

Wow that was powerful, really her words from beyond the grave. What a spirited woman she was. I hope I would have volunteered to go on spring break with her.

Cathy thanked the Judge and stepped down from the witness stand. When she sat down I noticed Bobby put his arm around her. That was such a supportive gesture, it made me tear up all over again.

It was Michael's turn to speak. He informed the court that he intended to speak about his sister's life.

"Thank you. On behalf of the Judge family, the parents of Jennifer Judge, Thomas and Mavis Judge: Jennifer's siblings, Tommy, Cathy, Patti, and I, Michael; and 11 nieces and nephews, we would like to thank the court staff of Rock County for their professionalism and understanding in providing the expertise in bringing this trial to a conclusion. In particular we wish to thank the District Attorneys, David O'Leary and Perry Folts, who were very patient in explaining the process and the evidence to my family as this case unfolded and for their hard work and expertise in obtaining a just and right guilty verdict against the defendant. And, also, we wish to thank the citizens of Rock County who not only have emotionally supported the Judge Family through this terrible ordeal but also a representative sample of the citizens of Rock County which formed the jury that unanimously found that the defendant, William Mereness, killed my sister, Jennifer Judge.

"The Judge Family also wishes to express their thanks and gratitude to the family of the defendant and in particular the father of the defendant, James Mereness, Sr., who came to this court and told the truth to the jury that his son, the defendant, did admit to him that he killed my sister, Jennifer Judge. And also Jim Mereness, Jr., the defendant's brother, who came into this court and told the truth in stating to the jury the unusual circumstances and activities that the defendant was involved in the day after the murder. And, also, we wish to thank Christopher Mereness, the son of the defendant, who came to this court to tell the truth of the missing Columbia jacket and shoes that were in the closet only the Wednesday before the defendant killed my sister. And, also, the defendant's sister, Sallie, who through this entire ordeal for the past 11 months has been so supportive of the Judge Family and despite the embarrassment, the angst and the great unhappiness that this defendant had brought to his own family, the Mereness Family, came to us to offer their comfort and truth to help convict their son, their brother, their father, of this heinous crime which he caused upon my sister, Jennifer.

"To the Mereness Family, the Judge Family says a heartfelt thank you."

Michael read on, announcing the title to his presentation, "Reflections of Aunt Jenny. My sister, Jennifer, was a very positive, can-do person. When I left for college, she was four years old. I was the big brother – she was the baby sister. She wasn't baby sister for long..."

Michael paused for a moment because everyone in the family laughed again. Mr. Bliss shook his head at us and walked over to stand against the wall next to Stephanie. *That seems completely uncalled for. While I know decorum is important in a courtroom, we are hardly out of control. It's polite laughter for a loved one, now gone. These words provide a second eulogy. What harm can it possibly do? There is no jury to influence. Can the family not be given this one concession?*

Michael continued, "...for she forged ahead in life to grow into the dynamic and loving person we all came to know. As a Spanish teacher in several high schools throughout Wisconsin, Jennifer showed her enthusiasm, her commitment to her students and colleagues in her role as teacher and as a person. She consistently welcomed students with problems to come to her. She willingly helped out colleagues and friends. She volunteered wherever there was a need. She opened the horizons of her students by organizing and chaperoning dozens of trips to Mexico, South America, and Spain. Everyone of every age loved her fun spirit, her compassion, and her extraordinary mastery of relating to children.

"That word 'children' was the most important word in Jenny's vocabulary. When it appeared that she could not have a child of her own, she worked three jobs to exhaust all medical possibilities, no matter how remote or painful to her personally. After many years of trying to adopt, and the defendant doing what he could at the very end to terminate the last attempt for adoption, Jenny still picked herself up and attempted to reconcile herself to the fact that she might never have a child.

"And so, even after that terrible day when the defendant advised my sister at a real estate closing in front of a group of strangers that he not only filed a divorce against her but he had contacted the adoption agency to cancel the adoption, Jennifer in a matter of days picked herself up. Several days thereafter she applied in Rock County to become a foster parent.

"Jenny was the mother every child would choose. She had a significant influence on her 11 nieces and nephews, all of whom were at the trial at various times. Jenny babysat for them all on countless occasions since she was 12 years old. When they were young she always managed to sit at the children's table, and as they grew into teenagers it was they who fought to sit with Aunt Jenny. She was so full of fun and really understood them. The sound of their laughter together is a sweet memory to the Judge Family today.

"She kept her private sorrows to herself. The Judge Family knew none of her difficulties with the defendant until after he filed for divorce against her. She concentrated on giving joy to others and not burdening others.

"Jenny will surely be missed by the Judge Family.

"Lies. If there is one pervasive thing that explains the life of the defendant, William Mereness, is that he is the consummate liar, one who cannot confront or tell the truth.

"A lifetime of lies and masquerading the truth has caused his entire extended family, even his father, siblings and his own son, to come before this court to insist that the truth about the defendant be told. Any investigation of the defendant's statements or excuses turn out to be continued falsehoods and untruths.

"Even at this darkest hour, which will affect the remainder of his life on this earth, the defendant, William Mereness, continues to deny the reality and the truth of what he did to my sister, Jennifer.

"Your Honor, my father and I in the first week of August 2002, at the urging of my sister, Jennifer, took Bill, the defendant, on a fly-in fishing trip into Canada. We invited him to accompany us and seven of our friends. During that week, Your Honor, on numerous occasions when we had a chance to fish together, he told me how much he loved my sister and showed me a picture of the boy, Samuel, that they were going to adopt. There was no indication that there was any marital stress between he and my sister, Jennifer. But only three weeks thereafter, the defendant, William Mereness, commenced a divorce action against my sister with no notice to his family, to the Judge family or even to Jennifer."

Suddenly, Bill, who had remained motionless throughout the past hour, turned and said something to his attorney. Bill then hastily scribbled something on the pad of paper in front of him. It was then that I knew he intended to speak. There was something he was going to say about that fishing trip. I anticipated his speaking with intense dread.

Michael continued, "After their home was sold in the first week of September, 2002, he absconded with the net proceeds of thirty-some thousand dollars, and attended the closing for the purchase of their new home by serving Jennifer with a Summons and Petition for divorce, and announcing that he had called the adoption agency to cancel the adoption. Your Honor, he did this in front of all the personnel at the bank who were closing the transaction. He would not allow Jennifer to use any of the funds realized from the sale of their home to purchase the new home, and my parents had to step up to give Jennifer enough down payment funds to close on the home. This, Your Honor, was so evil. His intent was to hurt and embarrass Jennifer by not only commencing the divorce but by announcing that her opportunity to adopt Samuel was now over.

"Within days, I assisted Jennifer in obtaining competent and aggressive divorce counsel. Our continued advice to Jennifer was that no man that would care for you and love you would hurt you in such a way. With our support and advice, and to her peril, Jennifer hung in there. Although the defendant on many occasions wanted to reconcile, brought flowers, made numerous telephone calls to Jennifer to reconcile, Jennifer continued to tell him, 'No, you have hurt me too much'. The marriage was over. And the defendant, bully that he was, realized that Jennifer was going to stand her ground. And she stood her ground with her life.

"Your Honor, I believe this Court understands what the Judge family has gone through over the past 11 months since Jennifer was killed, and what each of us will reflect on as far as this case is concerned for the rest of our lives. But, Judge, I also want you to know what occurred to the Judge Family on the night when the news began to spread that Jennifer was killed. We're sure that every parent, every family tries to brace itself for news of an accident of a loved one, of one of your children, even a serious sickness; you try to anticipate that, yes it may happen, but you're trying to believe that it won't happen to you or your family. The one thing that you do not anticipate ever occurring to your family is someone to commit an evil act upon one of your loved ones. You don't ever anticipate, dream, or even have a nightmare of one of your loved ones being hatcheted and mauled to death. That is what the defendant did to our daughter, to our sister, our Aunt Jenny.

"Your Honor, to receive that phone call from my sister, Catherine, who after having verified that Jennifer was indeed dead; for her to call me at 2:30 a.m. and in the midst of shock, tears and confusion, I realize that we are in the midst of a nightmare that we cannot understand. Trying to make some sense out of the situation and fighting off shock and confusion and tears, I realized that I had to make telephone calls to my brother, Tommy; to my sister, Patti; and to my parents in Arizona. And I made those calls to my siblings, Your Honor, at 3:00 in the morning, trying to explain to them what happened and to hear their reaction of shock, and fear, and tears, and so many questions that I could not answer. The question I had of my siblings, Your Honor, was how do I call Mom and Dad in Arizona and explain to them that Jennifer has been killed by an intruder? And there is no one in Arizona to comfort my parents, there is no support group, there are no children. My parents are 1,500 miles away. How do I tell them of this terrible event over the phone? Your Honor, I will never forget that phone call to my mother and father telling them that their daughter, Jennifer, is dead – not of an accident, not of an illness, but as a result of being hatcheted to death by an intruder. Your Honor, I will never forget the crying and the wailing that I listened to on the other end of the phone that night as a result of the despicable, heinous act that the defendant caused upon my sister."

Everyone was crying. Quite surprisingly, at that point, Mr. Bliss, the bailiff, took one of the boxes of Kleenex and walked down in front of the pew to offer it to Mavis and Tom, Sr. He then returned his original position on the other side of the room.

He's going to allow us some space for our grief. *Thank goodness.*

"Since that time, Your Honor, the Judge family has steeled itself, has stood together, and we are so thankful that Rock County stood with us in achieving justice for the most evil, heinous act that can be committed under the laws of the State of Wisconsin by the defendant, William Mereness.

"Conclusion. Therefore, Your Honor, the defendant by his heinous, evil act, has removed from this earth a wonderful, joyous person who brought so much good and happiness to so many people. He has removed her from having a relationship or influences with not only her family but also her students and her friends for the remainder of our lives – never to return.

"Your Honor, therefore, we are asking you to sentence the defendant, William Mereness, to prison for the remainder of his life with no chance of parole."

Everyone was crying. Josh asked Stephanie for the Kleenex box. He offered the Kleenex to me, then put his arm around my shoulders and gave me a hug. It was a very comforting gesture. I wiped my eyes and blew my nose as silently as I could. I didn't want Mr. Bliss to come back.

Next, District Attorney David O'Leary spoke. He reviewed that the brutal nature of the crime was a reflection of the defendant's nature. During the presentencing examination by a Mr. Matthew J. Fredricks, the trial and the investigation everyone had been amazed by his cold, unfeeling, unwavering manner. When he'd been confronted with the irrefutable cell phone records, Bill insisted they were wrong. He had lied to the victim about his criminal past, which came out in the adoption proceeding.

He'd lied to Barb Tesch, the lady he'd dated after Jennifer's death. He'd sought her out in the want ads despite his insistence that he hadn't been involved with anyone after Jennifer. When Mr. Fredricks caught Bill in that lie, the only response he showed was to drop his head.

When Bill was convicted of false swearing, a case in which he'd gone to great detail in using a photocopy of a check in court, he said his father must have done it.

In the battery of his son, when he ripped his earring out, he said he didn't do it.

According to Mr. Fredricks there had been lies about Bill's employment history. Bill had said he'd left his other job with Super Value for "bigger and better things". In reality, he'd been terminated for dishonesty.

Bill had said he didn't use drugs. In his medical records, amphetamines and opiates were what most likely caused his "comatose" state after he'd run his car into the wall.

O'Leary insisted that the Court must consider the defendant's nature when sentencing him. He showed an amazing lack of emotion during the victim's families' testimony.

On the day before the trial, Bill violated the terms of his bail. He contacted his father to pressure him into changing his story. Bill still denies that occurred.

Bill talked about the affect his mother's death had on him. There was no empathy; he was solely concerned for himself.

Bill's sister had tried to get Bill to take responsibility for his actions. He insisted he had to consider his own life first.

Mr. Fredricks was impressed with the lack of emotion showed by Bill during his presentencing evaluation. He showed no anger or sadness, except when caught in the lie about his new girlfriend.

There were the statements that Bill's father gave regarding his confession. James, Sr. had advised his son he had three options. After mentioning the first, which was to tell the truth, Bill replied that he did not want to go to prison. The other two options were suicide and go to trial. Bill attempted option number two by taking drugs and running his car into a wall.

Bill had a history of domestic violence. He had kicked his first wife, Ms. Beatty, and broken her ankle as well as a finger. He was arrested for disorderly conduct for pushing her. He denied any involvement, saying she hurt herself. Despite being convicted of domestic violence with his son, he still denied his guilt.

As for the murder, it was a pre-planned event. He had an established alibi in the wings. He relied on his brother to get groceries in Tomahawk and to pay cash and save the receipt.

I looked over at Jim, Jr. His face was red and he was rubbing it. He was obviously upset. *He's probably reliving his brother's attempts to use him to get away with murder, poor man.*

The DA continued. According to Mr. Fredricks, Bill attributed his guilty verdict to individuals who lied in court. When Mr. Fredricks asked Bill why people might do that, Bill said he would have to ask them. By denying his guilt, Bill was spitting in the victim's family's face and the victim's face. He has told nothing but boldfaced lies.

O'Leary urged the judge that he should be sentenced according to State Statute 973.1, sub 1 G, sub A: life in prison with no chance of parole. Bill was a danger to society and needed to be behind bars for the rest of his life.

Defense attorney Daniel spoke. He never stood up. His voice was very quiet and he showed absolutely no enthusiasm for his words. Daniel reminded the court that throughout the proceedings and to this day Bill maintained his innocence. While the Wisconsin Statute did require a sentence of life in prison, the court did have some options. Bill would not be eligible for parole until he was 70 years old. The court should not attempt to look into the future and know what Bill's life would be like in twenty years. He deserved a chance to be reevaluated at that time.

That was it. The defense attorney took less than two minutes to appeal to the judge about his client's sentence. It was shocking to me that Daniel had not only said very little, but that he'd not bothered to get up out of his chair or put any enthusiasm in his voice.

Judge Werner then asked Bill if he wished to speak. He replied, "Yes sir." He spoke in his flat, monotone voice. I could only see the left side of his face, but I could not detect a flicker of emotion. His voice held none. He wished to extend his sympathy to the entire Judge family. He acknowledged the verdict and stood before the court to say that he'd never raised a hand to Jennifer, let alone strike her. He had far too much admiration for the person Jennifer was to ever commit a crime that heinous. It was well beyond his physiological fortitude as witness on the fishing trip when Tom, Sr. had a treble hook caught in his forearm.

So, that was what he'd noted during Michael's speech. How his squeamishness at a fishhook in his father-in-law's flesh was proof that he could not have murdered Jennifer. He's an amazing person. Would a psychiatrist find he had a dissociative disorder? He truly does seem to be in complete denial of his murderous act.

Bill finished his speech by saying that he believed he was found guilty because individuals had given false witness and testimony.

It was time.

Judge Werner was set to speak, then give the sentence to Jennifer's murderer.

Werner began by stating that the presentence evaluation had been prepared at his request. He would consider it and all others when determining the sentence. Judge Werner wished to reiterate that the jury found Bill guilty and in his mind and the eyes of the law he was guilty.

The offense was the most serious in the state of Wisconsin. The jury had heard the evidence and so had he.

Werner said he'd viewed the photos of the victim and the murder was brutal and violent. The hatchet and maul were used with extreme force. There was no way to minimize those facts.

Next, Judge Werner reviewed Bill's character. There was his criminal record. As far back as 1996 there had been disorderly conduct; three misdemeanors for which probation had been assigned. Bill had denied responsibility, he'd blamed his father, his daughter and others. He also took no responsibility for the abuse to his first wife and to his son.

The only positive aspect Judge Werner found in Bill's character that, except for one problem, he'd been employed throughout his life.

The judge found Bill to be manipulative, controlling and less than forthright. He'd shown no remorse in this matter. He'd minimized his actions here and in other cases. He'd blamed others and said they had given false witness.

Werner added that Bill had shown no remorse, sadness or anger over Jennifer's death. The judge had observed him and characterized him as detached, aloof, cold and had showed no emotion in the loss of his wife.

While the judge could find very few positives about Bill, he did know that the public had to be protected.

I realized I was holding my breath, as I had so many times during the trial.

Werner was going to invoke the full extent of the law. If he did not, he explained, it would unduly depreciate the heinousness of the crime. He was sentencing Bill to life in prison in the State of Wisconsin. He would not be eligible for extended supervision.

Bill never flinched. He continued to look straight ahead.

Judge Werner covered all the legalities. Bill had the right to seek post conviction relief. Mr. Daniel was to assist if Bill chose to do so. The appeal must be filed within twenty days. After that, Mr. Daniel had no further responsibility to represent him. If he could not afford an attorney he could have a Public Defender assigned.

Bill Mereness, convicted murderer receives his sentence *(Courtesy of The Janesville Gazette)*

The judge addressed the murderer, "Do you understand?"
"Yes."

Judge Werner announced that the matter was closed and the court was in recess.

Jennifer's family was in tears again. Mavis put her arm around her husband, the father of their murdered daughter, Jennifer. Bill's family was all weeping as well. The DAs turned to us and smiled and nodded. Mr. Bliss approached the bar on the other side of the family. He very carefully positioned his back toward the defense table. His hands were in front of his torso. He gestured both thumbs up. It was a shocking display of emotion by the bailiff! His face was a stoic as ever, but he got his message across. It was incredibly touching. I forgave him for everything that had come before.

Shelly ushered the family into the jury room. Josh and I hung back, but Patti insisted we come along. Tom, Sr. was having trouble getting up from the pew. I offered to help and he turned me down and said he would like Josh to help. It was touching to see my tall, strong son be very gentle with his "Grandpa Judge."

The jury room was surprisingly small. It was filled nearly to the walls with large tables arranged in a square. There were comfortable upholstered chairs and nothing more. However, the room was very bright, having many windows overlooking Atwood Avenue and Courthouse Park. It wouldn't be such a bad place to spend time. I imagined our jury in a similar room going over evidence and coming to the unanimous conclusion that Bill was guilty. *Bless them.*

Once in the jury room David O'Leary told us that Bill might very well appeal on the grounds that something in the trial had been done incorrectly. The DA was confident that there would be no problems in that regard. They had held plenty of motion hearings to be sure the case was airtight. He imagined the many hearings had been annoying to us, but they had been necessary.

No one in the family said anything. Although I'd never heard anyone complain about the hearings, I think all were at the point of exhaustion and simply couldn't muster up the energy to speak. Thankfully, there had been precious little to criticize in the investigation and prosecution.

The prosecutor explained that any appeal of that nature would be handled by the Attorney General.

Additionally, according to the DA, Bill could appeal on the grounds that his defense had been incompetent in some way. Should that happen, O'Leary and Folts would have to defend Tod Daniel. No one in the room thought that would be a pleasant task.

Next, O'Leary told us that the bail-jumping charges were no longer of use. They had served their purpose, keeping Bill behind bars during the trial. The DA was very reluctant to make Bill's father and sister come down to testify if the charges were pressed.

No one in the family indicated they had a problem with that decision. It had been a nice trump card, should Bill have been found not guilty or Judge Werner not sentenced Bill to the maximum. The bail jumping conviction could add years to his sentence, thereby pushing back any possible parole date. Gratefully, it was no longer of consequence.

Finally, O'Leary told the family that they would soon be receiving information about the state's victim program. He urged all to register, as that would give them up to date information on Bill's appeals and incarceration. I was happy to hear that our tax dollars were going to support such a worthwhile program.

The DA wanted to know if family members had questions. Bobby asked the DA to confirm that he was not concerned about the possibility of an appeal being successful. Both Folts and O'Leary were positive that everything had been carried out in the most legal fashion.

Mavis wanted to know where Bill would be imprisoned. O'Leary explained that as soon as they were done with the bail-jumping situation, Bill would be taken to Dodge County for "processing" into the Wisconsin Prison System. After that he would be sent to one of the maximum-security prisons: Waupun, Green Bay or Columbia. He, personally, hoped it would be one of the first two, as they were less modern and comfortable. *I would prefer an island prison, like Alcatraz, but with really cold weather, like Siberia.*

No other questions were forthcoming, so O'Leary advised us to call Shelly if any questions came up in the future. Shelly confirmed she would be ready, willing and able to help.

Finally, David O'Leary thanked all of us for our assistance and co-operation throughout the many months since Jennifer's murder. He wished us well.

The family filed out of the jury room, through the courtroom and out into the hallway. I was a little surprised that all the media people were gone. I imagined they must have gotten all they needed from the statements of Patti, Cathy, Michael, the DA, Daniel, Bill and Judge Werner. There was little else to be said.

Bill's family was waiting. We all hugged one another and wished each other well. I told Jim he was "a good man." He thanked me.

As we left the second floor, the security men called out their good-byes. I told them I hoped they wouldn't mind if we said we never wanted to see them again. They understood.

I helped Tom, Sr. get out to Mavis, who was waiting in front of the courthouse in their white van. I asked Mavis to wait just a minute so I could show them Jennifer's sign. Josh retrieved the post and I got the sign. When we held it up for them in the parking lot they were astonished. They loved it. Mavis patted my forearm and told me she didn't know how to thank me enough. Tom put his hand over his heart and said it was a wonderful thing. I told them I was thrilled that they loved Jeff's and my work and that we were able to do something for the family. Mavis instructed me to be sure to go up and stay at the cabin whenever we wished. I thanked her. They drove off.

Bobby asked Josh and me if we could bring the post, sign and other items to their house so they could load it into their vehicle there, but he was very concerned that they would not be able to fit the post into their Trail Blazer.

En route, I called Jeff to tell him of the sentence. He was pleased. When I told him that Bobby might not be able to take the post up to Minoqua he suggested that we drive up Saturday and install the sign ourselves, then drive home. I thought it was a brilliant idea and told him I'd run it by Bobby and Cathy.

Mike Barker thought the idea was great, "a real family thing to do." Cathy was pleasantly surprised. Bobby couldn't imagine we'd want to do such a thing, but welcomed us if we wished. It was settled. I headed home. Josh went to meet his friend for lunch.

It was sunny, windy and cold. I walked the dogs. I looked up at the bright blue sky and wondered if Jennifer knew. I felt relieved but unbelievably exhausted. It was finally "over". I went into the house, moved one of the couches so that it was in full sunlight, curled up on it with a blanket and took a blessed two-hour nap with my two cats, Skinny and Boots.

Epilogue

Saturday, November 8, 2003, was another sunny, cold day. I thought that the skies should be great for the lunar eclipse that was to occur at about 8:00 p.m.

Jeff and I did the chores. I read *The Janesville Gazette* as I ate breakfast. The photo on the front page was of Tom, Sr. and Mavis. It was of award-winning quality. It showed the anguish and relief of parents who had been through hell in the loss of their daughter and betrayal by their son-in-law.

The unimaginable grief of Tom and Mavis Judge *(Courtesy of The Janesville Gazette)*

Mercifully, justice had been served and their daughter's murderer would spend the rest of his life behind bars. The article was an excellent summary of the sentencing.

We packed up the Avalanche and left at 8:30 a.m. We stopped at the Quick Trip and bought three more *Gazettes* and a *Wisconsin State Journal*.

I knew the family would be anxious to see the local articles, and I wanted every couple to have their own copy of the remarkable photo of Tom and Mavis.

At Cathy's request, I'd also videotaped the Friday night news from Channel 3. We were able to get the 5:00, 6:00 and 10:00 programs. It had been their camera in the courtroom. However, since I'd also seen Joe Mason from Channel 27 at the courthouse, I recorded that channel's news at 10:00 p.m. All four programs were similar. They reported the sentence, had a film clip of Judge Werner speaking and showed some additional clips from the courtroom, including Bill and Jennifer's families. One newscast showed Jennifer's now-familiar real-estate photo. On three of the programs, part of Patti's emotional reading of the student letter was included. It was the part about Jennifer leaving footprints on the hearts of many. The stories were well done and heart-rending.

As Jeff drove north, I worked on the laptop on this book.

I wondered what Bill had been thinking when he took this exact route on his way to Minocqua after he had murdered Jennifer. It was still inconceivable that such a thing could have happened.

Jeff and I had decided that we would not intrude on the gathering of the immediate family. We'd packed an overnight bag in case of emergency but intended to return home after putting up the sign. I'd packed a lunch we could eat in the car so we could decline any request to join in the noon meal.

As we neared Tomahawk, we saw the ground was covered in an inch or two of snow. It looked beautiful. The display on the rearview mirror read 17 degrees. We hoped the ground hadn't frozen too deep or we could have made the trip in vain.

When we arrived at the cabin at 12:30 p.m., we were greeted at the door by Bobby and Cathy's lab, Suzy, and Tom and Mavis' Bichon, Muffin. Muffin was the spitting image of Jennifer's Luna. I felt a twinge in my heart. Perhaps I should have kept BC and Luna after all.

It became obvious that we might not be able to stick to our plan to leave immediately after installing the sign. Everyone was so warm and welcoming. The fire in the fireplace created a cozy atmosphere. The cabin was absolutely lovely. I could completely understand why Jennifer adored spending time there.

Most everyone looked wind burned and exhausted. They'd been cutting trees and stacking the wood all morning and intended to continue after a break for lunch.

Jeff and I were shown around the cabin, though it was truly a log home, being a year-round dwelling of over 2,000 square feet.

The cozy interior of Jennifer's cabin

The living area had a vaulted ceiling and was overlooked by a loft. Two large windows flanked the fireplace, whose stone was identical to that in our home. The windows faced the west and Pier Lake. We could see where the trees had been cut and the stacks of logs as well as a huge pile of brush that had been formed on the slope between the house and the lake.

Cathy told me, "That pile is for the bonfire we're having tonight, and you're staying for it." It was not a request, but a demand. I felt a swell rise in my chest.

"That's so nice of you, but we have no intention of intruding on your family's day." She shook her head.

Upstairs was the small loft with a comfortable sofa. I imagined Jennifer cuddling up there with her dogs and a book or magazine. From that spot she would have had a fine view of the lake.

The serenity of Pier Lake

Also upstairs was the large master bedroom with bath. I tried not to think about Bill washing away Jennifer's blood in that shower stall.

Above the garage was a very long room that had two large dormer windows and had been furnished since Jennifer's murder with five twin beds. It was referred to as "the bunkhouse". It would make for lots of extra sleeping room, especially during ski season.

As we descended to the main floor, we were besieged by requests to join in the luncheon. We declined and said we would head out to put up the sign, if we were told where to locate it. Mavis spoke, "I'd like it right where my pumpkin head is at the end of driveway."

Mavis had stuffed one of those large, plastic "pumpkin bags" with leaves. It was in the perfect spot, on the far side of the driveway under some small birch trees. It made me feel good that she'd spent time thinking about the best location for my work.

Jeff moved the bag and I began to dig. The ground was not frozen in the least. The bag of leaves had probably insulated it sufficiently. The soil was quite loamy, but I quickly encountered many lemon-sized rocks. Jeff and I were both digging when Michael Judge appeared on the scene. He was soon joined by his brother Tom. They announced they were there in a supervisory capacity only. We laughed and apologized for not having brought hard hats for them.

Jeff switched to the post hole digger and progressed rapidly. I relieved him and in a short while, we thought we should check and see how the post looked with the hole at that depth. Our supervisors agreed. It looked spot on.

We began to fill the hole. Jeff and the two brothers thought we could do without the cement if we just used a lot of rocks to fill in the hole along with what dirt we had removed. That was fine with me!

Patti and Mike Barker, Bobby, Cathy and Mavis had arrived on the scene. They explained that Tom, Sr. wished to be with us, but would have difficulty navigating the long gravel driveway.

We understood.

While Mavis took her Muffy for a walk, the rest of us found larger rocks to put into the hole. Soon it was filled. As Jeff bolted on the cross bar, I jogged up to the house to get the sign. I did the honors of hanging the sign on the eye screws.

Everyone thought it was wonderful, beautiful and perfect. I was proud and well satisfied with the location and appearance of the sign.

I got out my digital camera and took pictures of the family members around the sign. Then Mavis insisted Jeff and I have our photo taken with our handiwork. We acquiesced.

On the way back to the house, we were told that we were expected to stay for dinner, the bonfire and then overnight. Again, we declined. Everyone appeared annoyed. Since it was still early, we did offer to stay and help with the afternoon logging operation.

Several dead birches were felled by the guys, while Patti, Cathy and I lugged cut sections and stacked them neatly.

Cathy surveys our work at the cabin

More and more brush was added to the bonfire pile. It was becoming enormous!

It was a happy and productive afternoon. At one point I spotted a bald eagle circling above the house. I excitedly told the rest of the group. We watched the majestic bird soar for a long time without flapping its wings. I thought of the Native American Prayer I was planning to give to the family members on the anniversary of Jennifer's murder. I would work with my computer publishing software to create a frameable background with the poem. I hadn't decided what I was going to use as a background, and now I knew. A soaring eagle would be perfect with the poem, which read:

" I give you this one thought to keep.
I am with you still I do not sleep.
I am a thousand winds that blow,
I am the diamond glints on snow,
I am the sunlight on ripened grain,
I am the gentle autumn rain.
When you awaken in the morning's hush
I am the swift, uplifting rush of quiet birds in circled flight.
I am the soft stars that shine at night.
Do not think of me as gone—
I am with you still,
In each new dawn."

As it began to grow dark, we determined our work for the day was done. We headed into the cabin.

The fire in the fireplace was welcoming. Tom, Sr. thanked Jeff and me for our help and then insisted that we stay for dinner and overnight. Jeff and I remained resolute. We planned to leave after a brief respite.

Abruptly, Tom, Sr. and Mavis announced they were leaving for Mass. They were up and out of the house in minutes. Now we certainly couldn't leave until they returned.

It was growing quite dark. The roasting prime rib was filling the house with its aroma. A debate developed as to when to start the bonfire, before or after dinner. Since it would most likely burn for hours, the final decision was to light it as soon as Tom and Mavis returned, before dinner. After continued pleas for us to remain, we agreed to stay for the bonfire. Then, all insisted, we should eat dinner before heading home. Cathy had tears in her eyes, "Everyone wants you to stay."

"We just don't want to intrude on your family," I reiterated.

"But you *are* our family."

I was very touched, "I'll talk to Jeff."

We relented.

The bonfire was fantastic! The flames leapt high into the night sky. There were great showers of sparkling embers that resembled fireworks. It struck me that the embers were carrying our troubles away and with them our happy thoughts up to the heavens where Jennifer was watching.

We admired the fire, the millions of stars and watched the full moon rise over the house. In a short time the lunar eclipse would begin.

Mavis, Patti and Marcia had created a marvelous repast. After toasting the day we indulged in prime rib, mashed potatoes, a fabulous lettuce and fruit salad and Black Forest cheesecake.

Then everyone crowded into the east-facing rooms to watch the total lunar eclipse. It was amazing. I remembered once hearing an astronomer refer to a total eclipse as "an astonishing cosmic co-incidence". *What a wonder that it has happened on this evening!*

At last the time had come for us to leave. The family urged us to stay one more time. We insisted we had to go. They were worried about our finding our way in the dark or hitting deer on the narrow dark roads. After I told everyone I'd driven up a remote mountain road at night while pulling my horse trailer, they gave up. We promised to be careful.

After hugs and kisses Jeff and I were on our way. As I took one last glance at "Jennifer's Justice" I felt a real sense of accomplishment and closure. I hoped the rest of the family felt the same way.

Perhaps we could begin our lives anew.

Cathy, Michael, Mavis, Tom, Jr. and Patti at Jennifer's Justice

About the Author

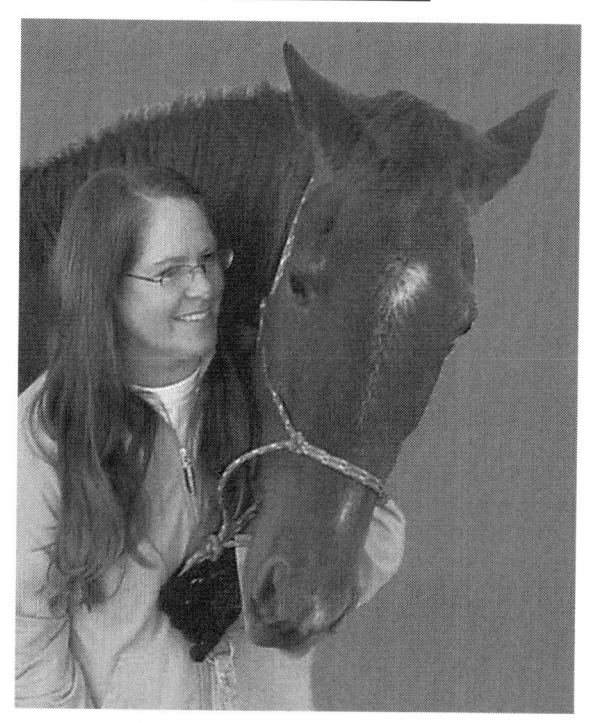

Dierdre Luchsinger-Golberg was born and raised in Janesville, Wisconsin. She earned a BA in Education at the University of Wisconsin-Madison and immediately embarked upon a 27-year career, teaching a myriad of subjects including algebra, art, biology, English, Spanish and U.S. History. Teaching in both parochial and public schools, most of her years were spent working with eighth graders.

The author was very active in her teachers' union, serving on the executive board, numerous bargaining teams and several terms as president.

An accomplished tennis player, Dierdre became a certified official for the United States Tennis Association and earned a place on the officiating teams for NCAA national events, the World University Games and the U.S. Open.

A lifelong animal lover and outdoor enthusiast, Dierdre, her husband and son live on a farm with their horses, goats, dogs and cats, many of whom are rescue cases.

Mrs. Luchsinger-Golberg is a passionate student of natural horsemanship and is currently working toward the creation of an education center based upon the principles of natural horsemanship.